VOLUME 2

LATIN

AMERICAN

URBAN

RESEARCH

Latin American Urban Research

VOLUME 2

REGIONAL AND URBAN
DEVELOPMENT POLICIES:
A LATIN AMERICAN PERSPECTIVE

FRANCINE F. RABINOVITZ
and
FELICITY M. TRUEBLOOD
Series Editors

GUILLERMO GEISSE
and
JORGE E. HARDOY
Volume Editors

S A G E PUBLICATIONS
Beverly Hills / London

For information address:

SAGE PUBLICATIONS, INC.
275 South Beverly Drive
Beverly Hills, California 90212

SAGE PUBLICATIONS LTD
St George's House / 44 Hatton Garden
London E C 1

Printed in the United States of America

International Standard Book Number 0-8039-0166-6

Library of Congress Catalog Card No. 78-103483

FIRST PRINTING

ACKNOWLEDGMENTS

Once again we gratefully acknowledge the contributions of the Center for Latin American Studies of the University of Florida, Gainesville, and its director, William E. Carter, to the publication of this series. The present volume is the product of the efforts of a great many persons including Amy Bushnell, Alexandra Calas, Frederick V. Gifun, Dora López, Leonidas F. Pozo-Ledezma, Charles J. Savio, Roberta W. Solt, Alejandro Vélez Gómez, and Menno Vellinga. It goes without saying that this volume would not have been possible without the collaboration of Guillermo Geisse, director of the Centro Interdisciplinario de Desarrollo Urbano y Regional in Santiago, and Jorge E. Hardoy, Chief Researcher and former director of the Centro de Estudios Urbanos y Regionales in Buenos Aires. We thank them all.

Francine F. Rabinovitz
Felicity M. Trueblood

CONTENTS

7

Preface

REGIONAL AND URBAN DEVELOPMENT POLICIES

FRANCINE F. RABINOVITZ and FELICITY M. TRUEBLOOD

Only rarely is a series of articles commissioned in one language and published in another. We have deliberately chosen to do so in this case because it seemed to us that in the general and continuing discussion of Latin American urbanization, the voice of Latin America itself is often excluded, in part because of the difficulties of language. The choice of the theme of this volume, regional and urban development policy, is indicative of the importance which is accorded today in Latin America to urban and regional programs alongside the better-known effort to develop national or sectoral plans. The aim of the volume is to provide an introductory overview of theoretical bases for and operating experiences with regional and urban development efforts to date in Latin America.

To U.S. social scientists, two aspects of the volume may be surprising. The first is the heavy emphasis on regional policy, including rural as well as urbanized regions, in a series devoted to Latin American *urban* affairs (see the essays by Babarovic, Cárdenas and Pérez Montás). While the tradition of city planning is much older in Latin America than that of regional programming, as Geisse and Hardoy point out in their introduction, modern multisectoral development policy for subnational areas in Latin America is almost wholly associated with regional units. Regional development policy, growing out of programs for river basins, has today come to include urban centers as the focal point for "growth poles" within regions (Friedmann, 1971). But, outside the framework of growth pole theories, there are very few examples of systematic efforts to attack metropolitan or urban problems, other than special programs to provide housing for the poor or to deal with "marginal" groups. Some major existing examples of urban land reform and metropolitan planning efforts are discussed in the volume's case studies, but they in a sense over-, rather than underrepresent the extent of urban-directed policy-making. Hardoy, Basaldúa, and Moreno (1968), in a detailed analysis of the state of urban policy, identify only four countries—Bolivia, Venezuela, Chile, and Ecuador—which have attempted to introduce programs to provide rational urban development policies. Cuba is the only country in Latin America which has, since the mid-1960s, incorporated a spatial dimension into its socioeconomic development plan. A recent survey of sixty major regional programs in Latin America indicates that only five subnational policies have a "major orientation" to metropolitan area development. The most sophisticated efforts are those of the "Executive Group for São Paulo" and of the Technical Office for Planning and Coordination of the Metropolitan Area of San Salvador. For five other big cities—Buenos Aires, Mexico, Bogotá, Lima, and Santiago—studies are under way of the cities and their immediate areas of influence, but these have not gone beyond a preliminary phase (Stöhr, 1969).

Thus, if we approach urban policy from the Latin American perspective, we must inevitably center our attention on the region and examine programs for the city region as a center of areawide economic development. Guillermo Geisse and José Luis Corragio emphasize in their essay the potential pitfalls of growth pole decentralization theories for directing the growth of metropolitan areas, as have others (Rodwin, 1970). They argue that it is difficult to change the direction of population concentration in large metropolitan areas, even given programs to alter the pace and direction of rural to urban migration. They suggest instead a model for integrating metropolitan regions to which growth has and will gravitate, rather than for either centralization or decentralization. (But the diseconomies of concentration are also apparent, as Rubén Utria indicates.)

The second aspect of this volume which may seem unusual to U.S. social scientists is the exclusive focus on policy concerns rather than on the formulation and testing of hypotheses with empirical data. In the United States, while both practical and academic concerns have been pursued within the context of the rapidly growing field of comparative urban studies, many investigations are cast either within a behavioral or sociological framework, or in an institutional mode. In Latin America, serious students of urban affairs more commonly view cities in terms of the problems created by accelerated urbanization or the management of national development and change. While there are data-oriented programs under way within Latin America, they are seldom conducted without explicit reference to policy-making. Viewing urban research from a Latin American perspective thus produces a somewhat different orientation from analysis of the subject through North American eyes.

All the authors of the introductory essays share a concern with the inadequacy of the theories underlying urban analysis to explain the range of problems and issues with which they are dealing. Thus each author self-consciously examines an approach which might be taken to urban theory. Included are analyses of the ramifications of a concept focused on spatial relationships (Melchior), conflicts between a focus on growth pole urbanization rather than on integration of metropolitan areas (Geisse and Corragio), and an effort to underline the perspective produced by emphasizing social rather than economic models (Utria). The case studies also reveal a number of fundamental philosophical differences among the authors, particularly in regard to the treatment of "marginality." There is deep disagreement on whether a central problem created by accelerated urbanization is the integration of migrants and the urban poor in Latin America, or whether urban development in its present form is a symptom of the contradictions arising from the existing economic and social systems, of which marginality is very much a part. All these theoretical fragments are derived from problems of concern to urban policy, which Jorge Hardoy amply outlines. It may be that the scope of theoretical issues raised is narrowed by an underlying interest in things capable of being changed in systems of cities. But, although theoretical understanding of Latin American urban affairs need not necessarily be limited to such a field, relevance to issues of government policy is one appealing criterion for determining where to begin in theory-building (Nelson, 1970).

This is not to suggest that there is not an equally great need for tools to evaluate policy development and outcomes. Babarovic's essay is devoted to developing a method for applying growth pole theory to the problems of rural marginality. Most of the authors of case studies, while bringing to bear whatever rough quantitative approximations and observations are available to bolster their subjective evaluations of existing programs, stress the need for more systematic tools for policy evaluation. To date, however, only the largest regional development efforts, in Northeastern Brazil, the Guayana in Venezuela, the Cauca Valley in Colombia, and Chile, have received intensive evaluation (Robock, 1965; Friedmann, 1969, 1966; Rodwin, 1969).

To us as social scientists in the field of comparative urban studies, a reading of these essays and cases suggests two things. First, analyses of urban and regional development policy focus more heavily on economic, demographic, and physical aspects than on political dimensions. Second, political questions are never far from the surface, particularly in the evaluations made by authors of case studies, although these writers have not been able to go very far in examining them. The various aspects of the question of who holds power are apparent in a number of instances. Stöhr (1969) discusses a number of different manifestations of this question. One is the relationship of the tradition of centralization and concentration and regionalization. A second is the impact of formal municipal autonomy and formal subnational regional dependence, on the emphasis on regionalization. A third is the impact of political competition among different regions (e.g., between the Andean region and the new oil centers around Lake Maracaibo and the national capital of Caracas in Venezuela or in Colombia, between traditional agricultural centers like Cali and Bogotá), which is often reflected in competition between regional institutions, on national integration. A fourth is the use of new development regions as a mechanism for opposing dependence on foreign countries. A fifth involves the role of the specialized institutions created to deal with new urban and regional growth activities versus traditional ministries. A sixth involves relationships between subnational entities and the federal government. (Note that here only Neira, writing about Brazilian development, speaks of the state government as a significant actor in regional development.) The essay by Geisse and Corragio suggests that existing proposals for the decentralization of space have not adequately faced the difficulties of implementing such a dispersion both physically and politically.[1]

Other issues grow out of the changing context of Latin American cities and the accelerated pace of urbanization in Latin American nations (Nelson, 1970). A number of the authors of case studies speak of the need for public participation in community affairs and also of the urban worker's need to improve his economic condition. But in several cases the mechanisms for participation and increases in the standard of living are potentially in opposition (see Neira, Tobar, Robles). As Hardoy points out, much of the experience in dealing with the poor arises from agricultural development strategies in depressed areas, as in the case described by Cárdenas, whose technical and engineering approach does not provide a basis for participatory policies. The political reasons for the absence of urban development policy in most countries in Latin America raises a different kind of developmental issue. Why is it that policies for the fastest growing sectors of Latin American space are more antiquated than those for undeveloped borders and interior areas? Still other questions arise in relation to the differential population growth envisioned by the growth pole plans. How do structures in a city in a depressed area (such as in the Recôncavo da Bahia in Brazil, for which see Neira) accommodate or resist planned changes in its economy? To what extent and why do circulation systems (see Melchior) influence the speed of change? Are there differences in the political processes which result in growth pole cities, from those of the massive traditional centers or areas of natural resource strength?

All these are questions which arise in the context of concerns about national change and policy in this volume. But existing research on political change has given little attention to urban political analysis in this form. Most studies have been oriented toward exploration of the utility of urbanization as a causal variable explaining national economic or political development (Kaufman, 1970; Nelson, 1970; Friedmann, 1971; Rosenthal, 1971). We hope therefore to use the third volume in this series as a mechanism for stimulating and presenting research which brings together these rather different traditions and methodologies, in empirical analyses of the politics of urban and interregional conflict which speak to current problems and definitions of national development policy.

NOTE

1. Recent suggestions for orienting urban research on the United States are remarkably close to this perspective. Oliver Williams (1971: 19), suggesting theoretical bases for uniting the wide variety of research concerns of analysts of the United States, says: "The first objective for contemporary urban political analysis is to identify the control mechanisms which manipulate space and place for the allocation of social access. These are the power structures of urbanism." See also Kaufman (1970) for efforts to apply this point of view to Latin America.

Preface

REFERENCES

(The materials cited below and in the introductions to other sections are heavily derived from U.S. sources, since these statements are meant to provide an orientation for U.S. readers who seek to relate easily accessible materials to the Latin American materials which follow.)

ab

FRIEDMANN, J. (1971) "Urbanization and national development: theory, policy and practice." UCLA School of Architecture and Urban Planning. (mimeo) A revised version will be published in 1972 by Sage Publications (Beverly Hills and London) under the title, *Urbanization, Planning, and National Development.*
–– (1969) Urban and Regional Development in Chile: A Case Study of Innovative Planning. Santiago: Ford Foundation.
–– (1966) Regional Development Policy: A Case Study of Venezuela. Cambridge, Mass.: MIT Press.
HARDOY, J. E. (1970) "Urban land policies and land use control measures in Mexico." Prepared for Ad Hoc Expert Group Meeting on Urban Land Policies and Land Use Control Measures, United Nations, December.
–– R. O. BASALDUA, and O. A. MORENO (1968) "Draft report on urban land policies and urban land control measures in South America." Prepared for Center for Housing, Building, and Planning, United Nations.
KAUFMAN, C. (1970) "Latin American urban inquiry: some substantive and methodological commentary." Urban Affairs Q. 5: 394-411.
MORSE, R. (1971) "A framework for Latin American urban history." Yale University Center for Latin American Studies. (mimeo)
NELSON, J. M. (1970) "Thoughts on next steps for the study of urban politics in Latin America." Prepared for the Comparative Urban Politics Colloquia, Ph.D. Program in Political Science of the City University of New York and Comparative Administrative Group, American Society for Public Administration, March.
ROBOCK, S. H. (1965) Brazil's Developing North-East: A Study of Regional Planning and Foreign Aid. Washington, D.C.: Brookings Institute.
RODWIN, L. (1970) Nations and Cities: A Comparison of Strategies for Urban Growth. Boston: Houghton Mifflin.
––, ed. (1969) Planning Urban Growth and Regional Development: The Experience of the Guayana Program of Venezuela. Cambridge, Mass.: MIT Press.
ROSENTHAL, D. (1971) "Politics and social structure in urban India." Presented at the Association for Asian Studies, Washington, D.C., March.
STOHR, W. (1969) "Materials on regional development in Latin America: experience and prospects." Prepared for the Curso de Planificación Regional del Desarrollo, Seminario sobre Aspectos Sociales del Desarrollo Regional, UN/ECLA (CEPAL), Santiago.
WILLIAMS, O. P. (1971) Metropolitan Political Analysis: A Social Access Approach. New York: Free Press.

PART I

THEORETICAL

APPROACHES

TO URBAN AND

REGIONAL

DEVELOPMENT POLICY

The studies which make up this volume have been grouped in two parts. The first, which follows, consists of theoretical essays providing a multidisciplinary approach to regional and urban development policy thinking in Latin America. In selecting the authors of the essays and the themes treated, we were searching for a theoretical framework as an antecedent to pragmatic policies. Urban and regional development programs are still new in Latin America, and planning systems, adequately integrated spatially or by sectors, still do not exist. In spite of almost two decades of experience with national economic development planning, there has not been much progress in incorporating into these plans either spatial variables or designs for regionalization. The first essay, by Hardoy, outlines the key problems urbanization and urban reform policies must contend with and a model for such efforts in the future.

Without consideration of their political or administrative organization, institutions and plans for regional development existed in some Latin American countries long before the adoption of a national planning system. In Brazil, Colombia, and Mexico, the experiences of the Superintendency of Development of the Northeast (SUDENE), of the Corporation of the Cauca Valley, and of the Río Balsas Commission are almost two decades old and precede the adoption of national plans. In other Latin American countries such as Chile, for example, the gradual adoption of national development plans made evident the need to regionalize the nation. Chile is at a more advanced stage than Argentina and Venezuela, where in 1967 and 1969, respectively, national laws were passed establishing systems of regionalization of national capacity without their really functioning. In Cuba, the experimental and dynamic character of the Revolutionary Government is reflected in adoption of a system adjusting development at the regional level to the changed possibilities and needs of Cuban life. In the Dominican Republic, Haiti, Bolivia, and Paraguay, regional systems do not yet exist.

Given Latin America's vastness, geographical and cultural heterogeneity, and uneven development, many national governments have begun to accept regional organization as a means to coordinate efforts, evaluate programs, and improve their efficiency by decentralizing the implementation of these policies. Ivo Babarovic deals in his essay with one of the key problems in this effort, the use of regional poles to overcome the problem of rural marginality, particularly in Brazil. In addition, Latin America has begun to be interested in the development of international regions minimizing the effects of barriers artificially created by administrative and political lines, which impede better utilization of resources and expansion of markets. Enrique Rubén Melchior here discusses the rationale for both international and national spatial integration in Latin America.

The first efforts to guide the physical development of Latin American cities are much older. The first architect-engineer-urbanists trained in European schools, particularly in France and Germany, go back to the beginning of the century. Their efforts, purely physical and backed by static and restrictive legislation, lack breadth as well as economic and political support. They constitute an interesting step in urban aesthetics rather than a solution to problems of social and economic life. The rapid and unbalanced urban growth of the last decade provided evidence of the need for new efforts. Governments have responded with the view that there are no local solutions to urban problems and that an adequate geographic distribution of productive investment, human resources, and services is fundamental to regional and national development and, therefore, the basis for urbanization policies. During the 1960s there have been significant experiences in spite of the fact that basic financing for urbanization policies still seems very far off. Through these experiences, limited in their objectives, we are searching for ways to prevent deterioration of the physical and social infrastructure; to create, in other words, the preconditions for an integrated solution in the future.

There are current experiences which, in spite of their limitations, no doubt possess audacity or future vision. In contrast, the plans for the great metropolitan areas and principal cities show deficiencies of effort, poverty of analyses, and too little preoccupation with factors relating to implementation. Geisse and Corragio provide a new rationale for metropolitan development which contrasts both with traditional plans and with the decentralization strategies propounded by many regional planners.

All authors included in this volume are native Latin Americans and reside in Latin America or have resided there during the greater part of their lives. We have intentionally searched for researchers or specialists with diverse experience and disciplinary training and for men who have shown great dedication to and concern with the problems of development in the area. The contacts among the majority of the authors are as great as their residence in countries geographically removed from one another permits. Their studies, therefore, can be accepted as the individual position of a group of persons active in the teaching, research in, and conduct of national and international programs of regional and urban development in Latin America.

Chapters 1 and 2 present urban policy approaches to development; chapters 3, 4, and 5 present regional policy viewpoints.

G. G., J.E.H.

Chapter 1

URBANIZATION POLICIES AND URBAN REFORM IN

LATIN AMERICA

JORGE E. HARDOY

The following essay is divided into two main parts. Its first sections are devoted to a description and evaluation of the character of urban society and the process of urbanization in Latin America. The next section discusses changes possible in this process starting from a justification of the need to formulate urbanization policies. Then, the key problems to which urban reform must address itself are identified. Finally, an urban reform model is developed to meet them.

I believe that urban reform is the indispensable instrument with which to achieve an urban society attuned to the aspirations of the population of Latin America's cities. In order to prepare this essay, I consulted an extensive bibliography. Regrettably, there are almost no studies of urban reform in developing countries. This is in contrast to the extensive theoretical bibliography available and that of practical experience in agrarian reform. It will not escape the reader that the influence of agrarian reform studies appears in the organization of this essay and in the urban reform model I propose.

THE PROCESS OF URBANIZATION IN LATIN AMERICA

Certain Essential Statistics

The characteristics of the process of urbanization in Latin America have been the object of numerous studies and publications (Hauser, 1961; Hardoy and

Author's Note: The author wishes to record his gratitude to the Concilium of International Studies and the Center for Latin American Studies of Yale University for the facilities and support they provided during the preparation of this essay. The author is equally indebted to Ralph Gakenheimer and Richard Morse for their comments. English translation by Felicity M. Trueblood.

19

Tobar, 1969; Beyer, 1968; Dorselaer and Gregory, 1962; American Behavioral Scientist, 1969; Centre Nacional de la Recherche Scientifique, 1965; Calderón et al., 1963; Boletín Económico de América Latina, 1968: 76-93). One of urbanization's most notable aspects is its rapid growth in almost all countries in the area and the potential it enjoys to maintain or accelerate the present rate. In 1968, there were fifteen metropolitan areas in Latin America with more than 1,000,000 inhabitants—four in Brazil and three in Mexico—eleven between 500,000 and 1,000,000 inhabitants, twenty-three between 250,000 and 500,000 inhabitants, and seventy-six between 100,000 and 250,000. A total of one hundred fifteen metropolitan areas existed in 1968 with more than 100,000 inhabitants, twenty-seven of which were in Brazil, twenty-six in Mexico, and eleven in Argentina (Rand McNally, 1969).[1] Within ten years, in 1980, it is estimated that twenty-seven cities will have more than 1,000,000 inhabitants (Banco Interamericano de Desarrollo, 1969: 49). Within thirty years, in the year 2000, if present growth tendencies continue, there will be one metropolitan area of more than 20,000,000 inhabitants (São Paulo), two with more than 15,000,000 inhabitants (Mexico City and Buenos Aires), possibly four with more than 10,000,000 inhabitants (Rio de Janeiro, Lima, Bogotá, and Santiago), and a total of between forty and fifty areas having more than 1,000,000 inhabitants.

Two factors are of fundamental importance in the urbanization of Latin America. First is the existence of an elevated and continuous natural growth rate due to the fact that birth rates have remained almost stable for several decades while death rates have been in decline (Population Reference Bureau, 1969). Second is the heavy migration from rural areas, including country towns and cities, to the principal urban centers of each country, especially to national capitals and regional industrial centers. The impact of internal migration on urbanization varies according to country and region, but it is estimated that it represents between thirty and fifty percent of urban growth (Arriaga, 1968).[2] Two other factors are of less importance. International migration between Latin American countries has not to date been significant, but could be in the future. For example, Argentina receives unskilled labor from Bolivia, Chile, and Paraguay, and, in recent years, professionals and technicians from Uruguay; Venezuela attracts unskilled labor from Colombia; Honduras from El Salvador, and various Caribbean countries attract migrants from Jamaica, Trinidad, and other islands. International migration from countries outside the area to Latin America has declined perceptibly in total volume since the years immediately before and after World War II. The exception has been migration to Venezuela.

If present tendencies are maintained, the population of Latin America will double in twenty-four years and the urban population in seventeen. By contrast, the present world population will double in thirty-six years (Population Reference Bureau, 1969). The growth of Latin America's population is quite uneven. It is much more accelerated in the Central American countries, including Mexico, than in the tropical and Andean countries of South America, and higher in the latter than in southern South America and the Caribbean. Disparities by country are also well known: Costa Rica will double its population in eighteen years; Venezuela, Colombia, Ecuador, Mexico, Paraguay, El Salvador, Honduras, and the Dominican Republic will double in twenty-one years; Uruguay, on the other hand, will require fifty-eight years to double its population, and Argentina, forty-seven. In twelve Latin American countries the annual rate of population growth is three percent or higher (Population Reference Bureau, 1969).

In 1970, various Latin American countries will undertake decennial population censuses. It will then be possible to verify projections based upon the censuses of 1960 or earlier. Nevertheless, preliminary data from the Mexican Census of January 1970 permit the deduction that general population growth in that country as a whole and of its urban population maintained the cited trends.

Regarding the population of Latin America as a whole, there are differing projections. In mid-1969, it was estimated at 276,000,000 people by the Population Reference Bureau, and for 1970 was projected at 275,000,000 by the Organization of American States (OAS, Departamento de Asuntos Sociales, 1967)[3] representing a growth in population of between 68,000,000 and 76,000,000 since 1960. The rate of population growth per one thousand inhabitants for 1970, like that for 1960 and estimated for 1980, is the same: twenty-nine per thousand. Of the growth in population of 68,225,000 projected by the OAS between 1960 and 1970, 51,099,000 would be absorbed by urban areas and 17,126,000 by rural. In 1970, 54.4 percent of Latin America's population would be urban as compared to 47.7 percent in 1960. The Population Reference Bureau estimates a total population of between 756 and 638 million for the year 2000, if fertility rates established by the United Nations remain constant or if one accepts a mean projection also calculated by the United Nations. Even if one inclines toward the lesser figure, the United Nations' minimum projections for Latin America in the year 2000 are 510,000,000 urban inhabitants and 130,000,000 rural or a total of 640,000,000 (United Nations, 1969: Tables 29, 36, 37; pp. 56, 71). These figures are very different from other, more widely circulated projections.[4]

Characteristics of the Urbanization Process

No country in Latin America, with the possible exception of Cuba, has attempted to direct in coordinated fashion productive urban investment, the building of regional and urban infrastructure, and the location of human resources using a spatial criterion of national scope. Even if one accepts the difficulties inherent in implementing this process of direction in countries operating under a market economy, it remains significant that only rarely have these criteria been articulated in national development plans. Under such circumstances, urbanization is a spontaneous process carried out without basic coordination between the investments of public and private sectors, investments which thus favor large cities over small and which ignore the needs of rural areas. In spite of this, urbanization in Latin America has positive effects at the same time as it aggravates, because of the way in which it is occurring, various negative aspects of development. Among positive characteristics the following are fundamental.

Urbanization Reduces Pressure upon Rural Areas

Independently of the way in which urbanization is taking place, the physical incorporation of several million rural inhabitants into urban areas signifies that every year spontaneous accommodation to existing structural situations is produced in each Latin American country. The causes of rural migration have received the attention of numerous specialists. In each country, and in each region, the causes of migration may have a different origin, but they are basically related to the need, on the part of a large rural mass, to seek employment, better services, and opportunities in general. The greater economic dynamism of the cities is thus counter-poised against the more accelerated demographic pressure of rural areas. If the localization of productive urban investment and population were made in a more orderly way, greater equilibrium between areas of repulsion and absorption could be obtained. Unfortunately, this is not taking place.

Certain countries like Haiti and Jamaica possess evident rural saturation (Matus, 1969). In others, such as El Salvador, Trinidad, and Costa Rica, rural saturation will occur before the end of the century if present patterns of demographic growth and population location continue. In Peru, Guatemala, Ecuador, Colombia, and in the majority of Latin American countries, areas of rural saturation coexist with uninhabited zones which are rich in natural resources and could be colonized. In many cases, rural saturation is the result of the relationship of the land-tenure and productive system to the natural increase of the population. In others, rural saturation has been a consequence of the change generated by the production system in the ecological conditions of a particular area.

At present, all Latin American countries are dependent on growth in agricultural production in order to sustain continued economic growth. The objective of agrarian reforms attempted in Latin America is that of improving the rural population's standards of living, avoiding monopoly of uncultivated lands, and promoting an increase in agricultural production. This cannot be achieved, however, only by agricultural means and by turning over land to farmers *(agricultores)*. The present crisis in agrarian production is the result of other crises. Agrarian reform cannot be isolated from other structural reforms. Educational, health, and public services programs are as important to the rural population as are technical and credit assistance, creation of new commercial mechanisms, diversification of the rural economy, and an adequate degree of decentralization of the industrialization of agrarian production. Many regions require, in addition, a different scheme of urban settlement which would serve a new rural dynamic.

The principal centers of the present system of urbanization are a legacy of the colonial period. The majority of small and intermediate centers were built and interconnected during the boom period of raw-material exports by Latin American economies. Regional urban systems serve rural areas badly because they are composed of hundreds of small towns—static and of too small a scale to be provided with indispensable services. These systems of urban settlements almost exclusively cover territories explored and colonized during the colonial and neocolonial periods. With the exception of Venezuela and Brazil, they are the same territories which have been exploited for at least fifty years.

By not having expanded the internal frontiers of our countries in a significant way and by not having improved the conditions of rural production, the latter has declined in relation to total population. Thus, in spite of migration to the cities, the pressure on rural areas in the process of exploitation will continue to intensify. In the year 2000, there will be between 130 and 240 million rural inhabitants, that is, between 20 and 130 million more than in 1960. The population must find work in an agrarian economy which to date has not created sufficient employment in terms of number and remuneration. At the same time, available employment will become more technical and influenced by the standards of urban life. Yet, a major part of the success of any program of economic and social development resides in the national capacity of each country and the collective capacity of Latin America to increase and complement agrarian production and develop income redistribution and retention of the rural population. This capacity is the complement of a process of industrialization and urbanization directed at the search for improved regional equilibria.

Urbanization Creates Expectations and Raises Aspirations

Almost all authors who have studied internal migration agree that the majority of migrants who arrive in cities prefer the way of life they encounter there to that of their places of origin. Migration decided, the new urban family assumes, in spite of the limitations it finds, an expectant attitude, if not an altogether optimistic one, in the face of an environment comparatively richer in possibilities and interaction (Peattie, 1969a). If that positive attitude and those expectations were correctly channelled, they could be used to promote political and economic change. Yet not all new inhabitants of a city are prepared to take advantage of the more varied and better coordinated opportunities. Urbanization permits improved labor union organization, though to date this has not been reflected in greater political maturity. Neither has it been reflected in more active political participation by the urban population. The present-day urban model of Latin America, with strong primacy and weak physical integration, coupled with the simple subsistence economy under which a good part of the urban population lives, discourages participation.

If the indispensable freedoms were made available, it would be possible to achieve improved organization and wider participation by taking advantage of the above-mentioned motivations and the new communications media. The desire to change the social structure of its component countries is clearly evident in all Latin America, and the city should be used not only as an economic necessity, but also as an instrument of political and social change.

Urbanization Permits a New Type of Social Structure

Social mobility appears to have been greater in Argentina, Chile, Mexico, Uruguay, and Venezuela, countries which, in general, are those with the highest gross national product per capita, the most literacy and industrialization, and which are, at the same time, the most urbanized. In these countries, worker and student groups and a new entrepreneurial class, occasionally aided by competent groups from the clergy, army, and public administration, participate in the life of the nation with wider vision, seeking to counteract the dilatory action of traditional groups. Nevertheless, participation by these groups suffers frequent interruptions due to changing political situations. Worker participation is additionally limited by the difficulties encountered by workers' children in attaining higher education. It is also only in recent years that the attitude of a part of the clergy and the army, sectors traditionally linked to the most conservative groups of each country, has changed (see, for example, Gall, 1970). Social mobility, even though still very limited, is greater than in Nicaragua, Guatemala, Honduras, and others, whose agricultural production and domestic and foreign commerce are controlled by *latifundistas* and financiers in close alliance with foreign interests. Even in the first group of countries, social mobility is greater in national capitals and industrial centers than in the service centers of rural areas.

Urbanization Stimulates Industrialization

Industrialization is concentrated in limited areas of the most developed Latin American countries. In the less developed and less urbanized countries, industrialization almost does not exist. Until a few years ago, industrialization in Latin America was directed toward import substitution in each of the national markets. The latter coincides with the largest concentration of urban population which constitutes the principal or only consumers' markets for local manufacturing production. Some major industrial plants processed raw material for foreign markets and were located in export ports. Industrialization, in its first stages, was propelled into serving the urban population and foreign markets. In quantitative terms, the employment of labor in urban centers was more important, but in both cases the location of employment stimulated national and international movements toward the cities.

The development of transportation and communications media permitted the expansion of national markets. Certain industries producing consumer goods serve an entire country and are generally concentrated in the principal cities. These cities' rapid growth is due in large part to the location of these industries. On the other hand, industrialization in rural areas is almost nonexistent. Yet, isolated, specialized plants do exist in rural areas, plants devoted to the processing of agricultural products such as sugar, grain, and textile mills, tea-drying concerns, regional refrigeration plants, and tanning factories, and other plants devoted to conversion of expendable natural resources such as refineries or coke producers.

Urbanization Permits Better Services for a Greater Percentage of the Population

The majority of Latin America's rural population lack adequate housing. Only a few rural areas have electricity. Water supply services are precarious. Rural roads are habitually impassable for prolonged periods. The urban housing deficit grows annually in each of the Latin American countries. In none of them are a sufficient number of urban housing units being built to absorb the population growth of the cities. The urban services deficit—sewage rather than running water and paving, telephones and transport rather than home lighting and electricity—is enormous. Only in sanitary and educational services is there, as compared to other services, some (if insufficient) progress. Yet the deficit in these services is equally large, and their quality and the efficiency of the existing infrastructure leave much to be desired. Withal, and in spite of the misguided approaches which may be observed in many cities, an important investment effort has been made in paving and networks of running water and electricity. This is not the case with the housing problem, in which the advantages of population concentration have not been capitalized upon.

One of the reasons for the low level of services and the growth in service deficits is the way in which the process of urbanization takes place. Low densities, social segregation, bad transportation, and a lack of public assistance services are factors contributing to misuse of existing urban services. This is an alarming situation and must be added to the percentage of those without access to education. Urbanization permits provision of better services, and undoubtedly increases annually the number of those receiving services. But the increment, at least in essential services, does not keep pace with the more rapid growth of urban population. Some studies point out that public works constitute a reason for migration, and, therefore, a means by which to direct migratory flows (McGreevey, 1968). Unfortunately, public works have not been used to promote better direction of the urbanization process.

Urbanization Permits Creation of a National Conscience

Latin America contains many regional pockets in which customs, dialects, handicrafts, and productive techniques have undergone almost no change for centuries, and the population scarcely participates in the economic and political life of their country. In terms of percentages, they are especially important in Bolivia, Peru, Ecuador, Paraguay, Guatemala, Mexico, and Haiti. The impotence of such groups in the face of the impact of more evolved societies is well known. Yet, neither do the majority of urban dwellers in Latin American countries participate actively in political and economic life in spite of the predominance among them of representatives of what we might call an urban and industrial society. Their participation has not been encouraged, their capabilities have been doubted by decision makers, and their spontaneous nationalism has been manipulated to avoid their conversion into a dominant force.

It is impossible to develop a country on the basis of inequality and without the participation of its population. If the people do not understand the problems, they do not identify with the solutions offered, and therefore do not support them. Thus, two problems appear important. First, almost all Latin American countries possess great cultural diversity for historical and geographic reasons. The way in which the transportation and communication systems were developed made regional disequilibria more acute. Regional identifications exist which often weigh more heavily than comprehension of national problems. These identifications have been used to disturb political and institutional life and even have been the motive for secessionist attempts. Nevertheless, valorization of and respect for regional customs and identification may be compatible with the development of national identification. A nation's people must also have objectives uniting them in a collective effort to impel development and abolish privilege. As Leopoldo Zea (1965: 9) said in referring to Latin America: "these peoples and their men had made and were making history . . . a part of the history of mankind . . . and with history, a culture, that is, a complex of values and principles, which only lacked their giving it consciousness."

The culture of the Latin American countries is already predominantly urban and the most widely diffused values and principles are those of an urban culture. But *what* urban culture? That of a society divided into a marginal majority and a minority which controls decision-making; divided into the committed and the indifferent, or that of a society which voluntarily accepts the sacrifice of individual positions in the search for common goals? Nation-building is the most urgent need in Latin America at the present time. If it is correct to assume that the cities permit better education, participation, and integration, it is of fundamental importance to recognize that the characteristics of these nations will depend in large part upon the society that is formed in the cities.

The way in which urbanization takes place reflects, in addition, the existence of precarious, dependent economies of limited dynamism and unbalanced and unplanned regional development. Under these circumstances, urbanization in Latin America has well-known negative aspects.

Urbanization Reflects the Fact that in Each Latin American Country There Are Few Alternative Forms of Employment

After World War II, undoubtedly as a consequence of urbanization rather than expansion of the economy, the occupational structure of Latin American countries underwent rapid change. Change was not uniform. Some countries already had, prior to 1945, an occupational structure which reflected advanced urbanization and significant industrialization. Others, even in 1970, continue to be rural in production and in the distribution of labor force.

The best-known changes in the occupational structure of the majority of Latin American countries have been the increase in the number of professionals and unskilled urban workers, expansion of the service sector, and incorporation of women into the labor market. Behind these changes lie two significant facts: (1) the apparent inability of the agricultural sector to increase production and absorb rural unemployment and solve the problem of seasonal employment, at the same time it attempts to improve the general standard of living in rural areas, and (2) the spontaneous channelling of migration from rural areas and rural service centers to the few dynamic centers which exist in each country.

Almost all the comparatively large urban centers of each country grow at a rate superior to that of national population. In other words, the principal urban centers of each country absorb an important part of surplus rural population, surplus in terms of existing means of exploitation. It is the principal industrial cities, seaports, national and a few provincial capitals, and centers created as a result of the new exploitation of expendable natural resources which attract the majority of rural migrants and the small groups of immigrants from outside Latin America. Recent censuses accentuate the historic tendency toward increasingly unbalanced national and regional urbanization. Even in countries with less primacy, like Brazil, Colombia, and Mexico, the concentration of population in São Paulo, Bogotá, and Mexico City has increased in relation to total and to urban population.[5]

The situation is such that in countries having high rates of unemployment, any public works program embarked upon by the national government or by a public agency provokes spontaneous migration of uncommon size to the particular construction areas. Only a portion of the migrants will find employment at their destination. Even so, a larger number of unskilled workers than of white-collar employees will establish new residences there. This transfer of rural unemployment to urban areas—the examples of Brasília and Ciudad Guayana are illustrative, as are Chimbote in Peru and the hydroelectric complex of Chocón-Cerro Colorado near Neuquén in Argentina—reflects the scarcity of alternative sources of employment offered by national economies in Latin America.

Costs of Settling New Urban Population Exceed Investment Capabilities of Each Country

Settling a new urban inhabitant signifies, at the very least, granting him remunerative employment, housing with indispensable services, and community facilities. If present patterns in the creation of sources of employment persist and if development of industry in general and the construction industry in particular continues to be attempted at unreal and almost unattainable technological levels, an increase in unemployment and underemployment and a larger deficit in housing, services, and community facilities may be foreseen. The most visible result in our cities is limited and costly housing in relation to the investment capabilities of each country's population, services rapidly becoming inadequate, and new sources of employment requiring high investment for each new job created.

Housing is one of the most difficult problems faced by Latin America. The crisis is the result of a political and social system which has not known how, or cared, to satisfy the basic expectations of rural and urban populations, and which based upon maldistributed economic earnings the ostensible development dynamic of the nations it controlled. Housing constructed by governments and private interests, frequently financed by international agencies, is very costly.

My criticism is not directed at the level aspired to but rather at the fact that this level is unreal and ends by favoring middle-income groups who have savings and can absorb the cost of housing produced individually and at higher interest rates.

The countries of Latin America do not have a construction industry prepared to initiate massive prefabrication. This is not, in many countries, for lack of technical and administrative ability. Massive industrialization applied to production of housing cannot develop with polarized credit systems, extraordinary fragmentation of urban and suburban land, and lack of coordination among public investments and between public and private investment. The construction industry is itself fragmented into numerous individual and professional contractors who act in response to individual clients. Thus, the housing construction industry is not organized like enterprises producing popular consumer goods on a large scale such as refrigerators or automobiles. In addition, in Latin America, it is even cheaper to build, especially if we consider maintenance costs, an individual dwelling of brick or block with a concrete roof semi-prefabricated on the site than equivalent square-footage using prefabrication techniques in a multistoried building.

In Latin America, there are hundreds of millions of people who live in the shanties of city and country or in the streets. Many are elderly or children; others are sick. Many are recently arrived in the cities, while others live on rural parcels which they do not own or which, because of successive fragmentation, have become unproductive. In 1960, the accumulated housing deficit was estimated at 20.3 million units, of which 6.6 million were urban and 13.7, rural (Utria, 1966: 260). These are the poorest rural and urban groups, living on the edge of indigence, without the training and health to compete for employment. Nevertheless, many of those living in urban shacks have permanent jobs. Family incomes are regular and expand because various members of a family share income; they are adequately dressed and acceptably nourished. They constitute a marginal population from many points of view: spatially, because they live on the city fringe; economically, because their lack of training makes them unproductive; socially, because neither the law nor existing institutions seeks their incorporation into a more dynamic society; politically, because they do not participate in the decisions defining their country's orientation, and, consequently, in their own destinies. They will form the less conformist and more easily organized groups which will demand their rights and roles in society.

In order to provide housing for a population undergoing rapid growth, it has been estimated necessary to build 23.5 million new units between 1960 and 1975, of which 18.7 million should be urban (Utria, 1966: 260). These estimates do not include the units necessary to absorb the existing housing deficit or to replace those which annually should be declared obsolete.

Urbanization Outstrips Industrialization and Creation of
Urban Sources of Employment

Urbanization without industrialization does not provide for the growing urban population's expectations. In the developing countries, this situation is aggravated by lesser demand for the services common in developed economies. While it is not known whether it is possible to prescribe an ideal rate of urbanization in relation to a country's capacity to generate urban and rural employment in integrated fashion, there is consensus that Latin American countries have not industrialized with adequate speed and spatial distribution. The percentage of urban population and the rate of growth of total population in each Latin American country are much higher than those justified by these nations' stages of industrialization (Friedmann and Lackington, 1967; Boletín Económico de América Latina, 1968: 211-229), if one compares these indices and the percentage of employment in the industrial sector with the rates of today's most industrialized and urbanized countries in a similar phase of their development. Perhaps it is an inevitable regional and national asynchronism; perhaps it is even necessary in countries in which structural transformations are produced in a disintegrated and territorially limited way.

This form of development undoubtedly accelerates migrations, as the Brazilian Northeast demonstrates. In this vast and underdeveloped region, public institutions promoted a concentrated industrialization effort in the cities of Salvador and Recife, which absorbed three-fourths of investment in the region. This investment, however, by its very nature, was not sufficient to meet new demands for employment caused by large rural migrations.

In Latin America, urban productive investment was not used to modify existing spatial schemes of urbanization. On the contrary, investment served to accentuate the interior's dependence on one or two national centers, and differences between developed and underdeveloped regions of each country.

Urbanization Has Negative Repercussions on the Productivity of the Tertiary Sector

This is the inevitable corollary of the preceding point. The censuses of each Latin American country reveal a tertiary sector overexpanded in relation to the needs of public administration at different levels and to the services which each country may offer.

It is difficult to describe all groups involved in the tertiary sector of each country, but their number bears no relation to employment possibilities. For this reason, it is customary to attribute to the tertiary sector itself its low productivity and depressed salaries. There are political and social considerations supporting this employment policy, even at the cost of keeping salaries low. But to the tertiary sector's inefficiency and high relative cost is also added its negative influence on increase in national productivity.

Cities Are Not Adequately Prepared To Act as Regional Development Poles and as Centers of Social Integration

The concentration of resources benefits a large number of inhabitants of a particular country, and this concentration is one of the explanations for the national and regional primacy of a few cities in each Latin American country.

But at what point does this concentration reduce the possibilities for expansion of national and regional markets?

In recent years, many authors have cast doubt on the validity of a development model based on expansion and modernization of the industrial sector and on the comparative backwardness of the agricultural sector.[6] Others have questioned the importance of the concentration of investment and human resources in one or two national centers and criticized the negative effects of the latter on regional development. Governments invest in certain cities because they apparently obtain better political and economic dividends in the short term. Yet is this not a way of mortgaging future development?

We know very little about the relation between urbanization and regional development. My impression is that the *way* in which urbanization is taking place, not urbanization itself, may be converted—because of greater costs, because of the previously mentioned limited dissemination of the benefits of urbanization, and because of the privileged competition with rural investment— into a limiting factor for regional development.

It is sometimes claimed that in contemporary cities a society is being born in which rigid social stratification will be reduced, the population is trained to execute the roles appropriate to a modern society, and wide political participation is achieved. The limitations of our urban centers in these respects are enormous. The cause is simple: the power groups controlling the decisions which could modify this situation are not interested in changing it. A society's structural transformations are not obtained by adding new schools, health centers, and jobs. The functional transformations of a city are not achieved by construction of new housing, kilometers of pavement, water pipes, and drains, more electrical energy, telephones, and automobiles. The cities ill serve their populations and nations, not because they are well or badly planned or because they are big or less big, but rather because the society which inhabits the cities, as well as the society the cities serve, has not been committed to political maturity, participation, and political development. In other words, it is true that because of the characteristics urbanization assumes in the Latin American countries, it aggravates major structural problems, which a different kind of urbanization could reduce. Yet is not the very way in which urbanization (with its characteristics) was and is taking place the most accurate reflection of a political and social system which can no longer contribute any basic solution to the area's economic and social problems?

Urbanization Outstrips Creation of New Institutions and Modernization of Existing Ones

Those living and working in urban agglomerations which in one or two decades have doubled or tripled their populations are those who notice institutional lag most, though this process does not pass unperceived by those living in cities with a slower rate of growth. Institution-building is a phenomenon difficult to quantify because institutions constitute the reflection of a system, and it is the system which has demonstrated its limited predisposition to change and to adjust itself to the needs of a society with demands and necessities, customs and norms, but also with means, ways of participation, and a much richer education than a generation ago.

The private sector has profited from urbanization. In Latin America there is not a clear or highly developed awareness of what urbanization signifies as a potential factor of change. Thus the private sector has rarely supported measures, which, in general, have been too moderate anyway to reorient the process of guidance, correction, and control presented by the public powers. The attitude of the public sector in confronting the problems of rapid urbanization is, in turn, inadequate. The first defect resides in the definition of the roles and responsibilities to be fulfilled by those levels of government and institutions involved in the process of urbanization. If roles and responsibilities are not defined, the lack of coordination and the low efficiency of the technical and financial offices concerned should not surprise us. An immediate consequence, aggravated by the scarcity of available investment and human resources, is the lack of programs or of coordination of these institutions' programs and investments. Attempts are made to direct a highly dynamic and little-studied phenomenon, urbanization, with antiquated administration—rigid, badly furnished with technicians, and limited in jurisdiction. It is not even known how much public and private sectors invest annually in the cities and in what programs and activities. The result is that investment responds not to priorities but to group interests or to individualistic programs of different public agencies.

URBAN REFORM IN LATIN AMERICA—WHY IS IT NECESSARY?

Many writers have attempted to define the range of national and regional urbanization policies and of local policies of urban development (Friedmann et al., 1969; Hardoy et al., 1969a). Along general lines, they coincide in that they treat it as a process of distribution of capital and human resources in macro- and micro-regions, which, in turn, must complement each other in a more efficient way than is true at present. Urbanization policies must define the roles of the most important urban agglomerations in the urban-regional system, correlating regional development with the urbanization process. Urban development policies must take into account also the requirements of urban agglomerations. The result would be the determination of the best urban system for each country and for the different regions of each country in terms of the type of development desired and based upon the particular phase of development of the country or regions.

Urban reform is necessary, in the first place, to establish these policies, which still do not exist in the area, but the need for which is increasingly agreed on. Analysis over time of the population distribution of a particular country, investment, and the network of transportation and infrastructure reveals that, in Latin America, national schemes of urbanization persist which correspond to a model formed during the colonial period and consolidated after the nineteenth century, when the export process took hold. The industrialization produced in certain countries in the early twentieth century and in others in recent decades did nothing more than consolidate this model by reaffirming the interior's dependence on the principal city of each country—almost invariably the national capital—or, in the best case, upon one, two, or three additional centers. This excessive centralization appears to have been counterproductive. In the smaller-sized countries, like Haiti, Panama, Honduras, and Guatemala, the principal center is not able to serve the nation efficiently. The centralized functions concentrated therein are not complemented by infrastructure or by a complementary network of centers of different rank and characteristics. In the large countries, like Brazil, Mexico, Argentina, Peru, Colombia, and Bolivia, which are characterized by geographic disparity, bad regional interconnections, and different regional cultural roots, centralization of the most important decision-making powers and administration has limited the initiative of regional groups. This is contrary to the objectives of an urbanization policy, which, as previously mentioned, are to achieve better spatial integration, overcome regional disequilibria, and break with internal political, economic, and cultural colonialism.

In the second place, urban reform is necessary for better integration of urban and rural areas. In Latin America, it is customary to accept a theory of regional development poles which has restricted influence because implicitly it is believed that industrial development per se constitutes a step forward for a particular region. Yet, in general, in the cases attempted, adequate employment has not been generated, existing rigid social structures have not been weakened, and neither distribution of income nor the way in which regional resources are used has been modified. In spite of promotion of the industrial development of these poles, with costly and advanced technologies, their capacity to absorb unemployment is limited, and they attract, on the other hand, a large proportion of the modest capital and foreign exchange available. The impact of a concentration with such characteristics on a rural area in which systems of production have not been simultaneously changed is obvious: the promotion of expectations which are reflected in new migrations to a destination which does not offer solutions either. In addition, since industrialization is an incomplete form of development and has not, in general, been promoted simultaneously with rural development, its benefits have been regionally limited. The creation of regional development poles in Latin America, in the few cases in which these poles have been developed with some effectiveness, has demonstrated that, when they were promoted in inhabited but little-developed regions, they destroyed numerous small labor-intensive regional industries. This, in turn, accelerated movement toward rural cities even more poorly prepared than principal ones to receive this migration. To put it another way, an urbanization policy must promote simultaneously the balanced progress of industrial and urban areas, and rural and more traditional ones.

In the third place, urban reform would limit the influence of pressure groups which, to date, have determined the spatial characteristics of urbanization in each Latin American country. The present power structure has failed. It has not promoted sustained national development, created sources of employment for a rapidly increasing population, or improved the general standard of living of the majority. The development concept of these groups is reflected in an urbanization scheme based on regional disequilibria and underemployment, and on an expensive model of the city, with precarious services, in gradual deterioration.

In the fourth place, urban reform is necessary because the occupational structure has undergone significant changes and will continue changing. The most significant change, already noted, is the transformation of Latin American societies from rural into urban ones. In 1970, more than half the Latin American population was considered urban. In parallel fashion, the percentage of labor employed in agricultural and extractive activities decreased, even though this is not yet reflected in fundamental changes in national economies, which continue to be predominantly export economies with a small range, by country, of raw materials.[7] The way in which urbanization is occurring reflects the concentration in a few centers of a numerous population without adequate training but with great expectations, better informed and organized in the search for opportunities different from those of their parents or the migrants who preceded them.

Urbanization and changes in the occupational structure have worked hand in hand. The incorporation of women into the urban occupational structure, in a more significant degree than that of the rural one, introduced an additional dimension into a limited employment market. Urbanization has also facilitated limited social mobility, as is demonstrated by the large number of professionals or white-collar employees among the children of those who were craftsmen or unskilled laborers a generation ago. Even so, access to university education by children of working-class families continues to be limited. In the face of this social situation, unsatisfactory but of greater fluidity than that of a generation ago, the governments of Latin America are still indecisive as to whether to apply an employment policy justified by the high rate of unemployment, or a policy directed toward increasing production, pressured by the need to incorporate a new technology which would place a growing number of manufactured products on a more competitive level with those produced outside Latin America.

In the fifth place, urban reform is necessary because the level of housing, public services, and community facilities is declining in the cities. Few people are concerned with this decline in an organized way. Unemployment is officially hidden, and underemployment is not even mentioned; the housing shortage is talked of; power failures, lack of water, and the inefficiency, crowding, and dirtiness of public transportation are criticized; the lack of schools, hospitals, parks, and athletic fields is analyzed; and the poor access roads to cities and the scarcity of parking are protested. But the destruction of the natural landscape or the contamination of air and water are hardly noticed. Each theme is discussed in an isolated and disjointed way. No notion exists that it will be increasingly more difficult to find the most elemental well-being in the cities.

In the sixth place, urban reform is necessary because even if governments decided to pursue policies such as those previously mentioned, they would encounter institutional problems. Taxes, especially those applied to consumer goods, have greater effect upon lower- than higher-income groups. In order to obtain credit, a cosigned endorsement is necessary, which is generally outside the reach of low-income groups. The law is not equal for different sectors of the population. In addition, municipal governments maintain inefficient and antiquated technical offices, ill-provided with the most indispensable specialists and even worse financed. Almost no national government in Latin America has attempted to supplement the limited capability for action of municipal governments with credits and technical assistance.

WHAT ARE THE CENTRAL PROBLEMS URBAN REFORMS MUST CONFRONT?

Land

The growth of the main metropolitan areas of Latin America exhibit an accelerated centrifugal character. Mexico City, São Paulo, and Buenos Aires, the three most important metropolitan areas by population, land area, and production, are examples of the fact that physical growth is taking place through expansion of peripheral areas, many of which were devoted to rural uses until a few years ago, and not through increasing population density.

Between 1950 and 1960, the population of the Mexican Federal District grew 59.6 percent. In 1960. the Federal District included the majority of the population of the metropolitan area of Mexico City. Though during those ten years Mexico City absorbed 597,388 of the 1,820,434 new inhabitants of the Federal District, the most accelerated growth occurred in neighboring municipalities: Ixtalalaco, Ixtapalapa, and Madero, in the Northeast, East, and Southeast, where, after 1940, new industries were established, and in the South and Southeast, in Coyoacán and Obregón, which are predominantly residential districts. Of the municipalities of the Federal District, it was precisely Mexico City—that is, the old urban core—which grew least during the period 1950-1960: with only 26.7 percent, its growth was less than half that recorded by the total Federal District. Lower than the rate of the Federal District's growth and scarcely higher than that of the delegation of Mexico City, were growth rates of municipalities which are still predominantly agricultural, like Xochimilco and Milpa Alta (Oldman et al., 1967: 5-11).

The national census of January 1970 confirmed this centrifugal tendency. Between 1960 and 1970, the population of the Federal District increased 43.8 percent, from 4,870,876 to 7,005,855 inhabitants, but the metropolitan area of Mexico City which includes, in addition, various municipalities of the state of

Mexico, reached 8,541,070 inhabitants, reflecting the spectacular growth of this small and almost completely urbanized state which doubled its population—from 1,897,851 persons in June 1960 to 3,797,861 in January 1970—in less than ten years. It was municipalities in the state of Mexico, outside the Federal District, which sustained exceptional growth during the last ten years: Ecatepec, 441.3 percent; San Bartolo Naucalpan, 335.3 percent; and Tlalnepantla, 254.4 percent (Tiempo, 1970).

The cases of São Paulo and Buenos Aires are similar. Between 1940 and 1950, greater São Paulo grew 5.3 percent, but while the municipality of São Paulo, which in 1940 included the immense majority of the population of the metropolitan area, grew 5.2 percent, the suburbs grew 8.8 percent as a whole. Between 1950 and 1960, greater São Paulo grew 6.2 percent. The growth of the municipality of São Paulo was 5.7 percent and that of the other municipalities, 9.8 percent. In 1967, the percentage of population of the municipality of São Paulo, in spite of its growth, had declined to 73.87 percent of an area approaching 7,300,000 inhabitants.[8]

Between 1947 and 1960, greater Buenos Aires grew by 2,065,579 persons. The entire population increase occurred in the municipalities surrounding the federal capital. The city of Buenos Aires maintained an almost stable population during those thirteen years (Vapñarsky, 1969).

These three examples indicate that suburban municipalities and jurisdictions have almost totally absorbed the population growth of recent decades. Analysis by political jurisdiction also shows that the growth of suburban areas has not been equal. Lines of public transportation, highways, industrial locations, the price of land, the availability of public services and community facilities, and topography have all had their influence to lesser or greater degrees. Even districts with the poorest topographical conditions, the dry lake bed of Texcoco on the outskirts of Mexico City, for example, end by being occupied. Certain metropolitan areas, having outrun the possibilities of the natural site on which they were founded, face grave problems of physical expansion in the presence of horizontal urbanization of low density.

Estimates of the deficit in urban housing and of the urban population living in shantytowns vary and there are notable differences among those of the Latin American countries and even among the cities of a single country. A recent study of the population of the *barriadas* or *pueblos jóvenes,* as they are now called, in eleven cities in Peru, which as a whole had 3,336,357 inhabitants in 1967, estimates it at 804,878 persons or 24.1 percent of the total. Seven years before, in 1961, the population of these eleven cities was 2,589,488 persons and that of the barriadas, 667,740, or 25.7 percent of the total. The projection for 1975 is a total population of 4,994,788 persons, 1,217,709 or 24.3 percent of which will live in barriadas. In 1968, 20.9 percent of the population of Lima, 40.0 percent of Arequipa, 64.7 percent of Iquitos, and 70.2 percent of Chimbote lived in barriadas (Oficina Nacional, 1970). This study of the population of the Peruvian barriadas is important because the Peruvian Government has recently admitted it is unable to reduce the national housing deficit or even build needed new urban housing, since public investment must be directed toward national development objectives (Sistema Nacional, 1970: 6). The situation is grave in all Latin American countries (Hardoy et al., 1969a). This establishes the need for a strategy different from that of letting the market remain free to find its own solutions.

Services

Finally, a word regarding the state of urban services (OAS, Departamento de Asuntos Sociales, 1967).[9] In all Latin American countries, with the exception of Paraguay, Haiti, Guatemala, and Brazil, the percentage of population supplied with drinking water increased during the past decade. As a whole, in Latin America, the percentage so served rose from 68 to 70 percent. In certain countries, like Venezuela (60 to 88 percent), Uruguay (70 to 82 percent), Panama (82 to 100 percent), Honduras (49 to 97 percent), El Salvador (65 to 99 percent), Argentina (65 to 75 percent), and Nicaragua (37 to 51 percent), for example, the increase in numbers of persons receiving running water reportedly has been significant. Conversely, in many Latin American countries, with the exception of Venezuela, Panama, Nicaragua, Honduras, El Salvador, and Costa Rica, the percentage of urban population served with sewage has decreased, and in some, like Mexico (70 to 52 percent), Bolivia (40 to 16 percent), Brazil (54 to 20 percent), Paraguay (23 to 13 percent), Chile (40 to 34 percent), and Argentina (42 to 34 percent), the percentage decrease was quite large. As a whole, in Latin America, the percentage so serviced decreased from 52 to 37 percent.

Comparable tendencies regarding provision of other indispensable services like electricity and transportation, and unemployment and underemployment are not identifiable. Nevertheless, these three brief analyses of demographic growth, housing, and urban services reveal a critical situation which governments are facing with scarce resources, lack of priorities, and unclear conceptions of the action they should take.

A PROGRAM OF URBAN REFORM

Almost all investment by public and private sectors has direct or indirect repercussions upon urban systems. One of the objectives of national and regional urbanization policy is to define the roles and functions of centers making up urban-regional systems within a national economy and their interrelation with each other and with other countries. The first objective is to restructure urban-regional systems and the cities.

This policy must accept in the short and medium term that only with great difficulty can the Latin American countries create, individually, adequate regional equilibria and that under these circumstances certain disequilibria are inevitable. It must also take into account that promotion of international nodal regions (urban-rural), combining intense agricultural and natural resource exploitation with industrialization directed toward regional and extraregional markets, may be the beginning of a new type of economies of scale for wider transfer of business and technical knowledge and for alternatives to migration. What I am suggesting is promotion of new spatial systems which, on breaking with the colonial and neocolonial models, can extract the advantages of gradual national and Latin American integration.

If the historical model is broken and present tendencies modified, a new series of centers will arise, to which a good part of economic investment and new urban population should be channelled. By new centers, I do not mean new cities which should be founded. It is possible that founding new cities may be necessary, especially in uninhabited territories or in those already inhabited in which new natural resources are being exploited. Nevertheless, existing cities will continue to have the advantage. It is because of their new population, three or four times greater than at present, and their new functions, more diversified than at present, that they will fit the definition of new cities (United Nations, 1967: 39-45). Large metropolitan areas will continue to play roles as international centers, but it is possible that their contacts with non-Latin American countries will diminish on a percentage basis, because of more decentralized contact with foreign countries as a consequence of more balanced distribution of economic activity and population. In this sense, in a continent in which population will triple or quadruple during the remaining thirty years of this century, almost all cities will be new cities.

New urban population, many times greater than at present, and new economic activities, more diversified than at present, will be located on the periphery of existing cities or form conurbations composed of urban centers of different size, better interconnected among themselves, and having new functions.[10] They will be located on the periphery, because remodelling central and highest-density districts of existing metropolitan areas is much more costly, even if urban and suburban lands are completely government-controlled. In addition, remodelling central districts implies expropriation which presents enormous political and financial difficulties and rests on the value of properties in the hands of private interests, which to date have rejected or limited any progressive attempt.

One of the preconditions of urban reform is redefinition of problems truly those of urban centers, and of problems which, although they affect urban centers, may be attacked by other types of organizations. For example, unemployment and underemployment are the most serious problems afflicting the Latin American countries. Their persistence has repercussions on the levels of housing and services offered to the urban population. But, although unemployment and underemployment are spatially localized in metropolitan areas and cities, their solution cannot be sought locally, but rather regionally and nationally. Predefinitions are basic to attaining what Myrdal (1966) has called "urban life with quality" or to permitting the population "opportunity to participate fully in the political and economic life" of their respective countries (Fitch, 1970). Urban reform cannot be achieved under the existing system of interests, the present tenure system of land and real property, the tax system in force, the present economic orientation, and the uses to which institutions and laws are put.

Urban reform should be started by the creation of legal, institutional, and financial conditions permitting public control of the urban and suburban land necessary for expansion of existing cities and those to be built. Without public control of land, there is no solution to the present situation, much less to that of the future. Urbanization takes place in extremely limited areas of the national territory, and land, in fact or potentially urban and suburban, is subject to continuous and unnecessary subdivision in order to increase its sale or rental value to private speculators who seek rapid gains from the added value created by urbanization.

With the exception of central commercial and residential districts, high- and middle-class suburban residential neighborhoods, close to main access routes to the city and lines of transportation and mobility, and special locations, land does not, at present, generally enjoy a very high price. On the other hand, its increase in value is constant. In order to continue attracting low-income groups, speculators promote new subdivisions, more and more distant and poorly serviced, which are only partially occupied. Because of the relatively low cost of suburban land, it is possible to control its rise in price, its subdivision, and its misuse by controlling the land market.

For example, in Santo Domingo, in suburbs not too distant from sources of employment, land has a value of about $4 to $5 U.S. per square meter in lots of 200 meters square with some infrastructure sold on installment plans running many years.[11] In 1967, in the lakebed of Texcoco, near Mexico City, lots of 160 square meters were selling for $8 U.S. a square meter in installments over a seven-and-one-half-year period (Oldman et al., 1967: 179 ff.). Also in 1967, lots being developed in El Alto, on the outskirts of La Paz, had a value of $0.50 U.S. per square meter (Hardoy et al., 1969a: 19). Undeveloped land may be obtained in zones of future development in the immediate vicinity of almost all large metropolitan areas of Latin America at prices which oscillate between $1 and $2 U.S. per square meter or even less. State intervention in the land market may cause prices to fall, as may be seen by the experience of Chile through the action of its Civic Improvement Corporation (Corporación de Mejoramiento Urbano— CORMU). Prices are considerably lower in smaller cities. Obviously, in cities with special topographical limitations, like Caracas, Rio de Janeiro, and Quito, prices are comparatively higher. In central and prestige residential districts of large cities, increases in the cost of land have also been proportionately large.

In addition, in some cities like Buenos Aires, Rosario, Montevideo, and others, governments own important and strategically located land which they do not use. These areas are dedicated to uses which have lost fashion or which governments are permitting to fall into disrepair in order to favor minority political and economic groups. Nationalization of the railroads in Argentina put at the disposal of the Argentine Government significant land in the central districts of Buenos Aires, Rosario, Córdoba, and, in general, in the principal cities of Argentina. Employed only partially for operations or for railroad-car parking, their use is uneconomic in relation to the development tendencies and needs of these cities.

In many of the central cities in Latin America, the Army maintains considerable amounts of land for barracks, warehouses, and even exercise fields. They constitute islets incongruous with the residential and even commercial uses which surround them. In Peru, the new invasion districts of the cities of the arid coast are the deserts on their North and South, which are public lands. These are all examples of the fact that, in many cases, there are potential bases for a land policy of wide range. In other cases, governments divest themselves of important urban or suburban areas in order to favor partisans of groups in power. In Santo Domingo, for example, as a consequence of appropriation of Trujillo's property, the government found itself owner of important urban and suburban areas. By ceding these areas without cost to supporters of the existing government or permitting their invasion by middle- or high-income individuals, it lost a unique chance to direct urban development. In Port-au-Prince, suburban lots have frequently been given to backers of the official régime. Cases of municipalities divesting themselves of lands which they possess in order to balance their budgets are not infrequent.

Investment in urban and suburban lands is a practice attempted by almost all private sectors of the urban population. It is the way in which, depending upon their capacity to save, these sectors attempt to counteract the effects of inflation and monetary devaluation. Urban developers and speculators are careful to see that the market offers opportunities for all. Urban speculation is thus only the result of the limited investment alternatives available to small and medium savers. The heavy saver obtains different interest rates for his capital, but he, too, has found in urban and suburban lands the incentive of sure gain at little risk. This situation has no solution within the existing systems of interests which supports such speculation.

In developing economies, the cost of the most indispensable urban services cannot be absorbed if extremely low suburban densities and mixed and incompatible land uses persist. Overextended and costly public services absorb limited investment resources, leaving entire districts without such services. In addition, the price of land has been the fundamental factor in separating the different socioeconomic classes living in a city.

The first stage of urban reform must be, then, government intervention in the urban and suburban land market to the extent possible: in the short run, determining the bases permitting its effective control; in the medium and long run, establishing price levels compatible with future needs. In parallel fashion, measures must be taken to discourage speculation and "disinflate" the cost of land. These measures should be: a progressive tax upon owners of more than one unimproved urban lot or tenure unit—that is, a tax on unused land; each family unit may have its own lot and dwelling, but a progressive tax will be applied to owners of more than one house or dwelling unit. Action should be most intense in areas of future expansion. For this purpose, the limits of urban areas should be defined very broadly, with a view to their inevitable expansion. The urban reform I am suggesting respects property, but its fundamental objective is to eradicate speculation and exaggerated profit.

Seed money is necessary in order for the government to intervene in the land market. The necessary sums are not out of the reach of a majority of the Latin American countries. This capital could come from funds voted annually by Congress or the Executive, from mortgaging publicly owned urban lands, from an extraordinary tax, from bond issues, or from bank loans. What is basic is that the government control the private market. Lands acquired by the government could be rented or given in usufruct to nonprofit organizations, industries, or individuals. They should not be ceded, but their users should have assured tenure for preestablished periods and in accordance with stipulated conditions. Without public control of urban and suburban land and without control of speculation in prices and rents of dwellings, the effects of other measures for urban reform will be diluted. What would be the objectives and effects, for example, of centralization of construction credit, or coordination of public investment if the urban land in question has previously been fragmented?

The complement of the above measure is coordination of public investment. All Latin American countries have numerous programs for building dwellings and providing urban services and community facilities. Each administration imposes its own programs. National, provincial, and municipal governments all have such programs, as does the private sector. Nevertheless, no Latin American country is approaching its objective in housing, urban services, transportation, education, or health. Few governments explain clearly why goals are not achieved and why social programs are delayed and priority is given to other activities. Tacitly, it is recognized that explanations of this kind are political suicide for the administration making them. They constitute public acknowledgment of an unjust situation which operates against the interests of the majority of the population. Only in those cases, certainly extremely limited in number in the history of Latin America, in which the majority of a nation's population voluntarily accept integrated national direction is it possible to count on individual sacrifice and collective effort (Peattie, 1969b).[12]

All Latin American countries are facing the problems of urbanization with inadequate investment resources. Nonetheless, public investment may be oriented so as to obtain the greater benefits of a national and regional scheme of urbanization. This signifies that economic development plans must have physical expression and a social dimension. It also signifies acceptance of the fact that we are proceeding toward a model of the city different from what we have known to date, a city whose functioning will depend upon the way in which these investment resources, in spite of their inadequacy, are used.

When funds are not abundant, and in Latin America this situation is chronic, housing plans are postponed. If budget cuts are imposed, the simple solution is to reduce or eliminate programs having an apparently minor reproductive effect: social plans, for example. Only recently has the economic value of investment in education been recognized. It is now accepted that, without education, without a population having the necessary scientific and technical preparation, a nation cannot evolve. Health and the way in which the population lives also influence a nation's productivity. Even accepting that resources for urbanization are insufficient, their use in complementing public control of urban and suburban land is basic to improving the city as a center of living and production.

Public credit is scarce and has favored those who already have acquisitive power and property. It is commonly directed, through private banks, to financing luxury articles or used for speculation. Public credit for financing low-cost housing is customarily solicited individually, and its payment is an individual responsibility. Private credit rarely participates in financing low-cost housing. Private banks and insurance companies have participated in the financing and sale of housing units for medium- and high-income groups by means of credit granted to individuals. Occasionally, public credit supports the action of cooperatives, labor unions, and other nonprofit organizations. The above-mentioned credit policies have only encouraged individual and isolated housing built by contractors at the request of the person soliciting it.

This focus not only increases construction costs considerably, but also those of drafting and overseeing the work and of administering credit granted. The discrepancies in levels and criteria for housing for members of the same socioeconomic group which still survive in public credit agencies are well known. Adequate use of public credit through cooperatives and nonprofit organizations is undoubtedly a way of avoiding its misuse and polarization, and of promoting construction of housing, urban services, and community facilities in those neighborhoods of the cities whose advancement is given priority. It would be an adequate way of complementing in massive form, and not individually, industrial and agricultural development programs being carried out at the regional level.

Two additional aspects appear important to me. Public credit must be channelled to projects in integrated urban and suburban neighborhoods and not exclusively to construction of housing. In the second place, a substantial percentage of the profits or interest earned by capital of banks and private insurance companies should be earmarked for construction of integrated neighborhood projects for low-income groups.

Technical assistance to regional and municipal organisms in charge of implementing national and regional urbanization policies and of local policies of urban development is the complement of measures previously discussed. Thus, a first step is to define the responsibilities of existing organisms or those to be created, which, at the different political-administrative levels of a particular country, will assume the tasks of analysis, planning, or execution relating to the process of urbanization. Only Cuba in Latin America has a National Urban Reform Council (Consejo Nacional de Reforma Urbana) with its different provincial councils (Sánchez Roca, 1960: art. 7), but even in Cuba regional development policies are imprecise and badly integrated with the national development plan, in spite of the interdependence sought in investments made in a particular zone (Junta Central de Planificación de Cuba, 1968: 135; United Nations, 1968). In other Latin American countries, there have been to date only partial efforts of limited action and effect regarding urbanization schemes and the cities themselves (Hardoy et al., 1969b).

It falls to the national government to define national and regional urbanization policies, but regional and local groups must participate actively in their elaboration, adjustment, and implementation. Due to the centralism which has characterized governmental decisions in Latin America, provincial and local governments lack the personnel and institutions to carry out these responsibilities. Of fundamental importance are special credits for organizing agencies for analysis and planning, credit and technical assistance for reorganizing governmental administration, expansion of rural and urban cadastral surveys, and preparation of offices and assistance to complement technical groups.

Control of the land, and coordination of investment, credit, and technical assistance will permit implementation of a new spatial distribution of economic investment and human resources—and consequently of land use—at regional and local levels. These are preconditions for avoiding continued development of the negative aspects of urbanization and for guaranteeing that the future model of the city will better serve Latin American societies.

NOTES

1. These data have been derived from information included in the table for metropolitan areas and the table of inhabitants of cities and towns (I-12 to I-23). Information concerning cities having more than one million inhabitants is from 1968; this is not the case with figures for smaller metropolitan areas, which are drawn from various years, although in every case post-1960.

2. Of the combined growth of cities having 20,000 inhabitants or more, 58.0 percent in Mexico, 66.4 percent in Venezuela (without considering external migration), and 70.2 percent in Chile were due to natural increase (Arriaga, 1968). It is possible that in still predominantly rural countries having a high rate of natural increase internal migrations contribute a larger proportion of urban growth than in already urbanized countries with a low rate of natural increase.

3. In 1960, the total population of Latin America was 206,766,000 persons. That projected for 1970 was 274,991,000 persons (OAS, Departamento de Asuntos Sociales, 1967).

4. During the early years of the 1960s, the most frequent projection for the year 2000 was 600 million persons: 360 million urban and 240 million rural.

5. The Mexican Federal District included 13.9 percent of the Mexican population in 1960, and 14.4 percent in 1970. But it represents 17.6 percent of the national population in 1970 if we include the population of the municipalities of the state of Mexico which make up a single urban area with the Federal District.

6. Stavenhagen, Chonchol, and Ahumada, among others.

7. The percentage of population employed in the primary sector of the economy in 1960 was 50 percent; the extremes were Argentina with 22 percent and Haiti with 85 percent (OAS, Departamento de Asuntos Sociales, 1967).

8. Data extracted from a lecture by Eugenio Gramusso before the Asociación de Planificadores Paulistas, São Paulo, November 11, 1969.

9. In the housing section, general data and data by country are included concerning the percentage of urban population receiving drinking water and sewage service.

10. This tendency is already evident in many examples: the São Paulo-Santos, Rio de Janeiro-Niteroi concentration, 500 kilometres in length, which includes a population at the moment already in excess of fifteen million inhabitants; the Buenos Aires-La Plata, Rosario-San Lorenzo conurbation, 400 kilometers in total area, with a population of more than twelve million; the Bogotá-Medellín-Cali triangle, which, covering an area of 35,000 square kilometers, also includes the cities of Manizales, Pereira, Ibagué, Armenia, and Palmira, or eight of the twelve principal cities of Colombia and a total of more than seven million inhabitants.

11. Data obtained by the author during a study visit to Santo Domingo in March 1970.

12. "We learned that the Revolution, for Cubans, is not an event; it is a process, an undertaking; it is a commitment" (Peattie, 1969b: 659).

REFERENCES

American Behavioral Scientist (1969) "Social science and urban development in Latin America." (May-June).

ARRIAGA, E. (1968) "Components of city growth in selected Latin-American countries." Milbank Memorial Fund Q. 46, 2: 237-252.

Banco Interamericano de Desarrollo (1969) El desarrollo urbano en América Latina. Washington, D.C.

BEYER, G., ed. (1968) The Urban Explosion in Latin America. Ithaca, N.Y.: Cornell Univ. Press.

Boletín Económico de América Latina (1968) "The urbanization of society in Latin America." Volume 13, 2.

CALDERON, L. et al. (1963) Problemas de urbanización en América Latina. Brussels: PERES.

Centre National de la Recherche Scientifique (1965) Le problème des capitales en Amérique Latine. Paris.

DORSELAER, J. and A. GREGORY (1962) La urbanización en América Latina. Fribourg.

FITCH, L. (1970) "Eight goals for an urbanizing America," pp. 51-74 in M. Meyerson, ed., The Conscience of the City. New York: Braziller.

FRIEDMANN, J. and T. LACKINGTON (1967) "Hyperurbanization and national development in Chile: some hypotheses." Urban Affairs Q. 2, 4: 3-29.

FRIEDMANN, J. et al. (1969) Chile: La década del '70, contribuciones a las políticas urbana, regional y habitacional. Santiago.

GALL, N. (1970) "Latin America: The Church militant." Commentary 49, 4: 25-37.

HARDOY, J., R. O. BASALDUA, and O. MORENO (1969a) Política de la tierra urbana y mecanismos para su regulación en América del Sur. Buenos Aires: Editorial del Instituto Torcuato di Tella.

—— (1969b) "La tierra urbana: políticas y mecanismos para su regulación y tenencia." Desarrollo Económico 9, 34.

HARDOY, J. and C. TOBAR, eds. (1969) La urbanización en América Latina. Buenos Aires: Editorial del Instituto Torcuato di Tella.

HAUSER, P., ed. (1961) Urbanization in Latin America. Paris: UNESCO.

Junta Central de Planificación de Cuba (1968) La planificación económica en Cuba. Habana.

McGREEVEY, W. (1968) "Causas de la migración interna en Colombia," in Empleo y desempleo en Colombia. Bogotá: Centro de Estudios sobre Desarrollo Económico, Universidad de los Andes.

MATUS, C. (1969) "El espacio físico en la política de desarrollo." Revista de la Sociedad Interamericana de Planificación (December).

MORCILLO, P. (1970) "Del deterioro de Cali a una política urbana." Monograph 20 presented to the United Nations' World Seminar on Shantytowns and Uncontrolled Settlements. Medellín, Colombia, February.

MYRDAL, G. (1966) "National planning for healthy cities: two challenges to affluence," pp. 3-22 in S. Warner, ed., Planning for a Nation of Cities. Cambridge, Mass.: MIT Press.

Oficina National de Desarrollo de Pueblos Jóvenes, Presidencia de la República del Perú (1970) Incidencia de la urbanización acelerada en ciudades con poblaciones de 25,000 y más habitantes. Lima.

OLDMAN, O. et al. (1967) Financing Urban Development in Mexico. Cambridge, Mass.: Harvard Univ. Press.

Organization of American States (OAS), Departamento de Asuntos Sociales (1967) Datos básicos de población en América Latina, 1970. Washington, D.C.

PEATTIE, L. R. (1969a) "Social issues in housing," in B. Frieden and W. Nash, eds., Shaping an Urban Future. Cambridge, Mass.: MIT Press.

–– (1969b) "Cuban notes." Massachusetts Rev. (Autumn): 652-674.

Population Reference Bureau (1969) Cifras de población mundial, 1969. Bogotá: Oficina en América Latina del Population Reference Bureau.

Rand McNally (1969) The International Atlas. Chicago.

SANCHEZ ROCA, M. (1960) Estudio y orientaciones sobre la ley Constitucional de Reforma Urbana. Texto íntegro y sumario alfabético. La Habana: Editorial Lex.

Sistema Nacional de Planificación, Presidencia de la República del Perú (1970) "Sector vivienda–Documento interno." Lima.

Sociedad Colombiana de Planificación (1969) Proyecto de Ley de Reforma Urbana 1, 2. Bogotá.

Tiempo (1970) Volume 56, 1452 (March 2). Mexico, D.F.

United Nations (1969) Growth of the World's Urban and Rural Population, 1920-2000. New York: Department of Economic and Social Affairs.

–– (1968) Aspectos administrativos de la planificación. New York.

–– (1967) Planning of metropolitan areas and new towns. New York.

UTRIA, R. (1966) "Los factores estructurales del desarrollo y el problema de la vivienda en América Latina." Boletín Económico de América Latina 11, 2 (October).

VAPNARSKY, C. (1969) La población urbana argentina. Buenos Aires: Editorial del Instituto Torcuato di Tella.

ZEA, L. (1965) América Latina y el mundo. Buenos Aires: EUDEBA.

Chapter 2

URBAN POLICY
METROPOLITAN AREAS AND NATIONAL
DEVELOPMENT

GUILLERMO GEISSE and JOSE LUIS CORAGGIO

The Metropolitan Area in the Development Process

The metropolitan areas (MA) of Latin America are the objects of an as yet unresolved dilemma in the development planning of their respective countries. They are considered obstacles to development because they absorb resources from the "interior" in their growth, elevate social costs of urbanization, and are the integrating center of the national subsystems of the international capitalist system, thereby accentuating dependency relationships. On the other hand, they are justified as a means of reaching the levels of economic efficiency exhibited by the "developed" countries. Our judgment is that this is a dilemma based on assumptions that will lose their validity in the future. The first such assumption is that geographic concentration is an exclusive attribute of the economies of the capitalist market and thus constitutes an obstacle to socialization of the economic surplus. The second is that the conflict between efficiency and equity objectives necessarily carries a conflict between central and peripheral regions within a country. These assumptions have given rise to an ideology of planning paradoxically shared in its regional spatial dimension by two antagonistic political philosophies. The expression of this consensus, regional decentralization, is supported both by Marxist postulates and the criteria of priority of U.S. technical assistance programs.

However, events demonstrate that the forces promoting national development operate in a manner contrary to decentralization. This is made obvious by the underutilization of many planning efforts. The central metropolitan areas continue to grow at the highest rates, achieving absolute populations of such magnitude that their primacy will be maintained in the future by mere endogenous natural growth, independent of the migrations that originated their expansion.

Despite this fact, the attention paid by planners to the development of metropolitan regions (MR) of Latin America has been of importance only in the past three years. Systematization and diffusion of knowledge resulting from initial case studies have yet to be accomplished. Nevertheless, there are certain observations which, for the present, we can put forth in the form of hypotheses establishing the necessity of overall revision of the prevailing concepts and orientation of regional planning in Latin America. These hypotheses are the following:

(1) differences in social welfare between individuals within the metropolis are as great as differences between regions which have led to the proposal of regional decentralization policies;
(2) members of lower socioeconomic strata of metropolitan regions tend to outnumber their counterparts in peripheral regions; and,
(3) lower strata of metropolitan regions more clearly perceive inequalities between social strata than do their counterparts in the rest of the country.

Ignorance of these facts can lead planning from underutilization to misuse of policy instruments, causing deterioration in income distribution between strata of the population as a result of policies supposedly designed to improve income distribution between regions.

A second-order observation is that the methods of analysis and planning utilized most frequently in Latin America have arisen from the experiences of backward regions and are not applicable in regions in which all known levels of development coexist in the same space. Without pretending to arrive at generalizations for all of Latin America, we hope, in this essay, to initiate discussion of these ideas and their implications.

The Historical Tendency toward Metropolitan Expansion

The historical explanation of the accelerated expansion of metropolitan areas in Latin America lies in the functioning of its national economies closely tied to world centers of power, the local industrialization process having been an accelerating agent of the economic and social forces leading to concentration and internal colonization. The "dependent" condition of the Latin American economies is directly associated with the international division of labor imposed on the basis of an external evaluation of the comparative advantages of each country or region. Originally, the capital metropolitan areas of Latin America were enclaves of drainage to the imperial metropolis (their generally coastal location and the design of the transport infrastructure attest to this). In a second period, their endogenous growth, accelerated by their international connections, gave impulse to a cumulative process reinforcing the capital metropolitan area while setting up subsystems of internal enclaves directly linked to it. This was the stage of import substitution. At present, a third period seems to be evolving:

a reopening of the national economies for the purpose of incorporating them into the international capitalist market. This is the stage of efficiency and diversification of foreign trade which promises to accentuate the centralization process of Latin American economies. In fact, the capital metropolitan areas provide the best conditions for productive efficiency, capacity for "modernization," and the existence of a power structure permitting "dialogue" with world centers or competition with other centers of a similar level of underdevelopment.

Confronting this process, a group of factors is joined favoring an apparent internal decentralization. Thus, sensitivity[1] to inequalities in welfare and "community development," considerations of military strategy, and the necessity of maintaining population enclaves in the "interior" cause the power structure to introduce criteria for the selection of public works projects that do not necessarily correspond to effective demand. However, such actions are not aimed at integrating the regions with each other so much as improving the conditions for fulfilling their roles as directly dependent on the capital MA and indirectly on world capitalist centers. In the face of evidence that this process only accentuates the enclave condition of interior points, there are those who argue for creation of true development poles based on dynamic industries surrounded by a diversified complex of activities in order to avoid the drainage effects to which the MA subjects them. One of the expected effects of such actions would be the strengthening of local decision-making forces, thus alleviating the scarcity of "entrepreneurial capability" and making possible greater decentralization of power in the national context.

Options for Future Development

The fact that the international division of labor and territorial specialization at the international level worked to the detriment of the economic condition of the Latin American countries does not signify that, at the national level, interregional territorial specialization would necessarily lead to the deterioration of certain regions or the country in general. On the contrary, interregional specialization is a necessary, though not sufficient, condition for national development, providing that allocation of activities is a product of autonomous national decisions and mobility of the factors of production is guaranteed by growing socialization of the economy's surpluses.

Although in the following sections we refer extensively to spatial tendencies implicit in the present structures of the Latin American countries (which assumes the permanence of their relations with the capitalist system), it is evident that at least three options are open in this context. Latin American countries could (1) continue within the current situation of dependency, procuring improvements in some quantitative indices of growth which are generally accepted as indicators of "development" within the system; (2) attempt to overcome the conditions of underdevelopment through greater national autonomy in the handling of key variables of development, gradual internal socialization of the means of production, and greater economic efficiency through expansion of national markets; or (3) move to break the dependency relationships and adopt methods of production and values peculiar to the specific country and distinct from those utilized as yardsticks for measuring levels of underdevelopment in the capitalist world. This is the case of Cuba.[2] The authors do not have sufficient information concerning the effects of the Cuban revolution on the spatial organization of the Cuban economy. For the present, they will limit themselves to observations regarding countries in the second option mentioned above and, in particular, regarding the case of Chile, whose future tendencies appear more clearly marked.

Regional Specialization and Social Equity: "The Country as a Large Region"

Foreseeable tendencies in the location of activities in Chile follow the direction of growing territorial specialization. Concurrently with the increase in the degree of population concentration around the capital metropolitan area, at present one of the highest in Latin America (with 33 percent of total Chilean population), there are indications of relative deconcentration of industrial production as measured by the differential rates of growth of the center with respect to the rest of the country. While the capital metropolitan area offers the best prospect for the population and for the production of goods and services oriented toward internal consumption, the "interior" regions have the resource potential for exportation whose exploitation demands the increasingly more intensive use of machines.

This is nothing else but a tendency toward spatial dissociation of future industrial increment (industrialization) from population increment (urbanization).[3] This tendency will continue if the emphasis on industrial export diversification based on national raw materials is also continued. The extent and efficiency of such specialized regional patterns will depend on the capacity of the national economy to satisfy the needs of physical integration by means of interregional transport and communication at relatively low cost. Transport and communication networks should improve notably, not only between each industrial region and the national service center (Santiago), but also among the regions themselves. On the other hand, the sociopolitical feasibility of the described regional pattern will depend on the degree to which the national government succeeds, first, in "the appropriation of the utilities of the big national and foreign investments," and, second, on the distribution of social benefits among the various strata of the national population.

Spatial growth tendencies in the form indicated have already begun to press on planning. In effect, national economic and social policies such as nationalization of the regions' basic export industries have paralleled investment increase in the social infrastructure of the Santiago metropolitan area,[4] and effective improvement in the national transportation and communications network.[5] Our hypothesis is that geographic population transfers from the regions to the Santiago metropolitan area have been stimulated by such government policies, while policies producing effective transfers of social benefits among the population have been lacking or disregarded. Welfare differences among sectors of the metropolitan area are as great as differences between it and the rest of the country. Regional average indicators of social welfare often utilized as justification for regional decentralization policies are poor indicators and bypass the crucial problem of the great internal differences within the central metropolitan region itself.[6] If the above-stated hypothesis is correct, it would lead to recognition of social differences within the Santiago MA as the focus of the national planning process. Rather than continuing to fail in its regional decentralization policies, national planning should concentrate on gaining control of the production system leading to concentration and of the mechanisms for distribution of the social benefits derived, which is a matter of persons rather than regions.

Regional Planning and MA

Although it is generally agreed that differences among the various types of regions call for different planning methods and techniques, principal advances in the theory and practice of regional development have been derived from experiences or attempts at development in relatively backward regions. In this way, the main body of regional planning doctrine has subtly been imbued with a series of assumptions with respect to the specific conditions of backward regions. Growth poles have become the most fashionable planning device all over the underdeveloped world.

The growing sense of failure arising from unsuccessful attempts to promote substantial development in the regions on national peripheries, the conviction that the problem lies not so much in the backward regions as in their coexistence with the most developed ones in the same national space, and the search for world markets through the centers most able to compete, have begun to shift part of the analytical and regional planning effort toward the capital metropolitan areas (Rofman et al., n.d.; CIDU, n.d.; CONADE, n.d.; ONDU, 1967).[7]

Characteristics of Metropolitan Regions

Generally, in the bounding of planning regions in the national territory, criteria are adopted—not always identifiable—which include components of homogeneity and nodality with different weights for each region. In the specific case of metropolitan regions, the nodal component predominates. Given the high level of activity in the capital and its intense interaction with its immediate areas or centers, the adoption of boundaries that go beyond community limits or even limits indicated by residential density becomes necessary. Thus, the MR would include not only the MA's urban core, but also small- and medium-sized centers located within an imaginary line drawn by levels of interaction (current or potential) as well as areas of primary exploitation and empty areas. In the Chilean case, the Santiago metropolitan region covers four provinces occupying

5.2 percent of the nation within which are located the Santiago MA with 3.2 million people, and the Valparaíso MA with 600,000 people, as well as eight cities of 20,000 to 100,000 and thirty of 2,000 to 20,000. The region encloses an area whose limits are within a two-hour automobile trip from the center of Santiago. Fifty percent of the total population, sixty percent of the urban population, seventy percent of the industrial labor force, and thirty percent of the agricultural production of the nation are concentrated in this area.

The specific conditions of MR in less developed countries make necessary rearrangement or total reconstruction of the usual regional planning schemes. Some of the relevant characteristics are their great importance within the national context; their accelerated pace of change, well above that of the rest of the country, and, in some cases, comparable to that of the large cities of "developed" countries. In addition, the high level of internal interaction relative to other regions is important, as is the relative accessibility among the component subareas of the MA, and the method of spatial extension of activity within the region starting from the MA.

The great importance of the MRs within the national context forces a restructuring of the procedures for establishing the objectives of the region. In confronting the planning of the MR, development objectives cannot be formulated on a reclamation basis relative to the rest of the country (a method generally used in "interior" regions with respect to the MR). Furthermore, because of the great importance of the MR in the national context, it is unacceptable that there would be conflicts between the region's and the nation's goals, since in such a case achievement of regional goals would lead to strong impairment of the nation.[8] However, determination of the objectives of a metropolitan region should be undertaken with special care, since there is not a direct transfer from the national order to the regional. The statement of objectives can be made at different levels of generality. The more general and objective—e.g., increasing the welfare of the population—the more feasible will be direct adoption for the region. To the degree that general objectives are stated in vectors of more specific objectives, that much more should be the contribution of analysts of the region for transforming them into a regional image efficiently leading to achievement of national objectives. An example of these difficulties arises from the national objective of more equal redistribution of the benefits of development which, under circumstances of immobility of human and natural resources, may have as one of its facets the subobjective of decentralization in favor of lagging regions. If one attempts to apply directly the objective of decentralization to the internal districts of a region (metropolitan or not) one may worsen national inequalities among strata of the population.[9] Since lower-income strata tend increasingly to move toward metropolitan centers, it is necessary to return to the immediately superior objective—more equal distribution—and see what specific form it should take in the region.

On the other hand, national global planning requires parallel national spatial planning. Although we do not yet possess a clear knowledge of the relationship between spatial structures and performance of the social system, we have begun to advance in the sense that a national plan "assigns" functions to distinct regions or nodes of its space. In this case, we are not dealing with "redistribution" but rather with considerations of national efficiency. In either case, the MR receives, on the one hand, an assignment of "basic" functions which it should fulfill with respect to the rest of the country or foreign nations, and, on the other hand, the indication to establish a vector of objectives leading to achievement of national goals. It can be tentatively postulated that the general objectives for the MA[10] are expressed as to: fulfill efficiently the basic functions assigned in the national order, and advance toward the goal of distribution of the benefits of development within a determined rate of growth. However, it is possible that in some Latin American countries the objective of improving distribution among the population may be attained more efficiently through redistribution among regions than through an intrametropolitan one.[11]

The accelerated pace of change in MA emphasizes the necessity of basing the planning of a metropolitan region on long-run projections, given the irreversibility of spatial structures. The existence of a "history of change" and the importance of the endogenous component also make achievement of extended projects more feasible in these regions. At least a "vision" of the region twenty or thirty years in the future should be projected, including basic characteristics of the future structure. Thus, the analysis would not be centered so much on a "potential" as on a known socioeconomic base.

The relatively high level of interaction between internal spatial elements of the MR, in comparison with those of peripheral regions, suggests that the strategy of internal integration, usually proposed for the latter, should be more an integration of strata of the socioeconomic system in the case of the MR than of spatial subareas of the region.

The degree of accessibility—in terms of time, physical, or economic distance—between distinct subareas of the MR and its center is generally superior to that existing within peripheral regions. This means that the friction of space does not act as a protective barrier for the less developed subareas within the region. Therefore relatively autonomous development poles cannot be established within the territory of immediate influence of the metropolitan center. The characteristic pattern of the spatial growth of human activity within an MR is one contiguous extension from the center in a process of suburbanization of the population and productive activities. This process, which may have a discontinuous stage, especially for industrial activities, assures predominance of the MA within its region. The theory and practice of regional planning have been directed, explicitly or implicitly, to large spaces where the friction of space plays an important role. To apply the instruments and categories thus developed to the MR as if the reduction of the diameter of the region were merely a quantitative problem could lead to serious error and underutilization of policy instruments.

The differences between an MR and any other region in a national system are of a quantitative type. This requires the introduction of new categories of analysis and instruments of planning. It seems relevant to visualize the MR as a "great city."[12] This is not to say that each MR is today a great city or that one should necessarily adopt the objective of converting it into one. At present, elements of a structure of the "miniature large space" with friction (relatively isolated zones, almost completely immobile social sectors, lack of integration, subsystems without relevant interaction, and so on) coexist with elements of the great-city structure (high rate of weekly, sometimes daily, mobility of skilled strata of the population, relatively little distance-time friction in the transportation of goods, suburbanization processes for some industrial establishments, growing spatial dissociation of the different stages of economic activity, and the like).[13] What is proposed here is that there is a tendency at work aimed at the growing conversion of the former structure into the latter. If this is indeed so and is duly recognized in time, one begins with a great advantage in interpreting present reality and in proposing strategies of change.

Tendencies Toward Change in the MR: The MR as a Great City

A twenty- or thirty-year projection of the development of an MR cannot be accomplished without simultaneously projecting salient features of the national and international context. In the case of adopting either policy option 2 or 3, the strategies of change should be applied to the existing structure which has implicit tendencies whose knowledge is essential (above all in the case of option 2). Therefore, the following refers to this "basic" situation which we define as the growth at an accelerating pace of Latin American MR within the capitalist system. Our purpose is to suggest that the most probable course of evolution of the MR in this context is that which tends toward the configuration of a great city,[14] basically a process of suburbanization at the regional level starting from the current capital MA. This is not an obstacle to the coetaneous occurrence of a partial process of deconcentration,[15] oriented toward other regions of the country. However, we assume that the probabilities of regional suburbanization are superior to those of interregional deconcentration for whatever activities decide to abandon the metropolitan area,[16] except for those primarily oriented toward a natural resource complex located in a peripheral region. A proposition of this sort should incorporate not only the tendencies implicit in the present structure but also structural changes in process. Among others, probable changes should be considered in technology, in the behavior of decentralized agents of production and of the government itself, in the distribution of income, in the patterns of demand, and in resource endowments.

The suburbanization process of the MA will have at least two sequential stages. The first is one of contiguous suburbanization characterized by net population loss in the central core, location of industries on the borders of the MA (later enclosed by advancing residential use of land), and the appearance of service and commercial centers as alternatives to the core center. Processes producing these changes include the mechanism whereby the use of land is allocated among competing activities to the most profitable (in favor of service activities with a higher threshold size requiring a central location); growing external diseconomies generated by productive activities and the population itself which are borne by the population and businesses located in the central core (such as congestion and smog); and technological and economic changes modifying locational factors for large- and medium-sized industries, causing them to choose peripheral locations. These processes in turn generate a series of effective demands for infrastructure favorable to suburbanization, which the government generally satisfies, concentrating investment efforts in the peripheral areas of the MA to the detriment of the central core. This spatial extension is usually oriented along transportation axes radiating from the MA. Interradial segments also fill up, though with a certain delay.

The second stage is one of discontinuous suburbanization. On reaching a certain point in the described process, six phenomena appear with growing intensity. These are strong demands for green spaces and cultivable lands; and problems of accessibility to the central core which gives high weight to the cost of a journey within the dense urban areas. Then location in one of the extremes of the urban star can no longer be properly considered a central location within the region, although it is within the municipal limits of the MA. There is also a growing delay between settlement along the axes and provision of infrastructure services due to the high costs involved and the growing inefficiency of the public sector in managing a city of such size.[17] A decrease in economic distance relative to other, smaller centers occurs which, located along transport routes, offer locations which do not create problems in the functioning of the productive process and signify only a relatively small increase in distribution costs. Technological changes make possible the independence of a growing number of large enterprises from urbanization and localization economies, facilitating their location in peripheral centers of the MR. Thus the process of suburbanization leapfrogs in space to smaller centers located on the region's periphery, leaving green spaces and agricultural land between.[18] On the other hand, the necessity of generating their own localization economies may influence businesses in the same branch of production to agglomerate, giving rise to the appearance of specialized centers or areas within the MA.[19]

The process described may not be carried out exactly in each and every Latin American metropolitan region. Factors such as the historical spatial development or topography can produce distinct spatial specifications in the process for each case. Nevertheless, socioeconomic processes exist which are common to all of them[20] to greater or lesser degrees, and sooner or later will begin to occur as long as the capital MA are maintained within the current system.

Probable changes in the determinants of localization patterns support the prospect of growing regional suburbanization and partial interregional decentralization.[21] Growth rates of population and income within the MA have important economic consequences such as the introduction of standardized production processes for mass consumption goods; growing problems of supplying the urban complex with perishable products of prime necessity; an increasing interest in the internal market on the part of foreign capital; changes in the structure of urban demand, with a strong increase in the use of services; and conditions increasingly closer to saturation of immovable resources (land, air, water, infrastructure, and so on) with the consequent growing costs. In turn, these changes modify the patterns of localization of diverse activities, making possible the location outside the MA of large plants, self-sufficient with respect to maintenance services, and permitting introduction of industrialization and packaging techniques near the sources of raw materials. They also introduce commercialization and distribution mechanisms which act as incentives for standardization of production and facilitate the suburbanization of the population through location of integrated commercial centers on the fringes of the capital MA. As a result of appropriation of existing firms and installation of new firms oriented toward the local market by foreign capital, efficiency criteria of location are introduced which in many cases point to the periphery of the capital MA or even farther away, breaking through the inertia of national businessmen. Internal demand is created for services such as tourism generally oriented to resources outside the capital MA. The threshold population size for economic provision of services is reduced, which makes their dispersion possible throughout the MR. Vertical growth in certain areas of the MA is also difficult, inducing spatial extension of urban settlement.

Industrial technological changes, which occur at an increasingly accelerated pace insofar as the process of "modernization" proceeds in the MA, also have direct and indirect effects such as an increase in the average size of the productive plant and growing participation of foreign capital in the ownership of industries through the technology-capital symbiosis. This leads to a change in the legal-administrative structures of business toward more efficient corporate forms; a growing automation of production processes; general acceleration of the pace of obsolescence of productive equipment; and, finally, increasing concentration of power in integrated enterprises. These changes favor geographic separation of the processes of each economic activity, basically the processes of production with respect to those of management and administration, and increase the probabilities of relocation of existing plants as an optimization instrument.

Technological changes in the transportation sector have two fundamental aspects: introduction of more efficient and more rapid modes of transport between urban centers at a faster rate than the parallel improvement in intraurban transport; and the growing availability of the automobile as a means of individual transportation. The principal effects are to increase the relative importance of the intraurban component of transport costs within the MR, accentuating the attraction of peripheral locations for industry, and to facilitate the suburbanization of the population with a clear social bias in favor of high-income groups.

Within the "modernization" process being experienced by the MR, one can expect also the introduction of specialized new modes of communication, as well as diffusion of traditional means such as the telephone, and the substitution of messages for physical movement. As a consequence of these changes, tendencies toward suburban regionalization are accentuated by permitting the dispersion of central services with a high threshold (e.g., banking services), and by facilitating the geographic dissociation of the processes of a single economic activity.

As a result of growing problems and social tensions in the MA, political change will develop. First, there will be increasing "politization" of certain sectors of the population such as university students, and increasing attempts to control the activities of large enterprises, directly by the government or indirectly by unions (by demanding compliance with social welfare laws, and the like).[22] Growing "sensitivity"[23] to existing external diseconomies will develop, with the consequent attempt to stop them or to attribute them to those who cause them; growing "sensitivity" on the part of the government will develop in view of the evident inequality within the MA. These phenomena also have an effect in favor of suburbanization or decentralization through the drive of large enterprises to minimize public control over their employment policies or production techniques; the housing plans of the government (oriented toward large land areas of lower cost in the periphery); the plans for construction of a system of service centers—of primary education, health, and the like—which improve living conditions in peripheral areas; and the plans for dispersion of university centers (and eventually of industrial centers) to prevent intensification of social conflicts.

A New Focus

What would be the effects on regional planning of adoption of the image of the MR as a great city instead of as a "miniature large space?" The regional planner, trained in the theory and practice of the development of backward regions, now finds himself facing the MA and its immediate satellite subsystem of urban centers and areas and must propose a plan for this creature called an MR. The metropolis ceases to be a distant monster whose tentacles absorb regional resources and becomes instead the center of the region under study. If the planner fails to change his mental state, he may commit errors in analysis and in the proposal of policies for such a subsystem of centers and areas.

In the first place, basic supporting theories and their corresponding strategies change. In the case of the adoption of the concept of the region as a "miniature large space," the theory of growth poles appears to be a good starting point. This, in turn, determines a large part of the main divisions of investigation or research. The concepts of economies of location and, above all, urbanization are emphasized, together with the degree of diversification of the distinct centers of the subsystem and their possibilities for endogenous growth. An attempt is made to calculate multipliers and their effects and a greater degree of closure for regional centers on the MA's borders appears implicitly desirable. These attempts made within the actual framework of entirely open economic systems having a small total diameter produce logical problems. The search for an "opposing" growth pole within the MR becomes fruitless if the region's boundaries are correctly defined. Second, the basic concept of mobility (and accessibility) here is a spatial one. This leads to studies in depth of the conditions of physical and economic accessibility by means of a description of transport infrastructure and its possible changes. On the other hand, emphasis is placed on infrastructure decisions which need to be made in order to achieve greater spatial accessibility. This is found to be relatively simple and, at best, one begins to speak of sequences, costs, and the like or to propose alternatives such as impeding accessibility in order to favor autonomous growth of peripheral centers within the MR. Third, institutional analysis gives great relevance to the possibilities of spatial decentralization of power and administration, with the implicit or explicit vision of strong local governments. Once again, in the actual context of a great city, this task becomes almost impossible since the margin for decentralization and its social utility are severely limited by the system's small diameter.

What would happen instead if we were to adopt the view of the MR as a great city? In the first place, efforts to identify or promote one or more integrated polarized centers opposing the gravitational forces of the metropolitan nucleus would lose relevance. In effect, it is unlikely that good urban planning would lead to making each district a diversified unity with industrial, service, commercial, and other activities. It makes more sense to think of zones having a degree of specialization in accordance with their acquired locational advantage and foreseeable tendencies in the market system. Thus, for example, in the case of the central region of Chile, over the long term, it would no longer be important for Valparaíso to incorporate dynamic new industries. It could be allowed to remain an area providing transport, commercial, and tourist services to the rest of the central region, without preventing employment of Valparaíso residents in industries located in other centers or subregions, or preventing the location of industry in Valparaíso because of its natural advantages. The explanation for this change of focus is, again, that in a system with a high degree of accessibility and mobility the population can take advantage of the benefits of industrialization or service-sector growth without having to live in the place where these activities are located. Patterns in the spatial division of labor which may be unacceptable at the international or even interregional level are perfectly acceptable within a city. On the other hand, a large portion of external economies are transportable at low cost so that dispersion of centers generating urbanization economies loses much of its importance. This occurs equally with regard to the direct or indirect impact of each new enterprise, although this is not to say that knowledge of the impact on the region as a whole is unimportant. Other factors of location, however, typically intraregional, appear as important, including easy access to transportation channels, the degree of air pollution and its possible control, the existence and degree of pollution of water for industrial use, cost and availability of sites, and the topography (Stevens et al., 1967).

The instrumental elements of spatial planning in this case approach more the ordering of the use of land (zoning, appropriation of increased value, and so on) than the creation of growth poles.[24] The general consensus is that geographic dissociation of functions ceases being a problem and becomes an instrument for the efficient ordering of space. The idea of a great city leads to concentration on efforts to achieve efficient spatial ordering of activities and to increase the mobility of the population, giving it access to the benefits of development, before trying to orient dynamic activities toward the areas whose situation we wish to improve. Using industrial location as the principal instrument of redistribution can be highly inefficient in this context. With respect to spatial mobility, it has become evident that its principal determinants are not the physical frictions of space but rather the social and occupational mobility of the population.[25] Thus, for example, study of income distribution and the location of different population strata would receive priority, as would complementary studies of the levels of technical-professional formation, human resource training programs, and all mechanisms permitting increase of spatial mobility through redistribution of income. Finally, with regard to institutional aspects, attention would be concentrated on the central use of the most efficient instruments permitting the desired socioeconomic ordering of space, as well as an analysis of private or mixed organisms making decisions throughout the entire region. In parallel fashion, in studies of the relevant power structure, greater weight would be given to analysis of the national structure than to that of local groups.

In the same way that development and underdevelopment coexist and the progressive great city coexists with backward regions, two alternative theses coexist with respect to the spatial structuring of all Latin American nations: centralization and decentralization. Although formulation of dichotomous categories is useful in some cases, we believe that in the case of decentralization—increasingly converted into a theoretical concept due to unavoidable changes in socioeconomic reality—it is not applicable to many Latin American countries today and may possibly be extended to all Latin American nations. Decentralization of power and deconcentration of activities in space were originally raised under the banners of redistribution, but the rigidity of the capitalist dynamic blocked their advance. Decentralization proponents then managed to sustain their position with arguments of efficiency in the long run without being able to demonstrate the existence of a relatively clear relationship between spatial structure and economic development.[26] It is becoming increasingly evident that within the capitalist system the energies spent in the decentralization battle only bear fruit when strong economic reasons exist supporting the movement to the periphery. Not even the existence in regions of Latin America of human groups of low mobility living under subsistence conditions has been able to cause drastic change in this situation. On the other hand, internal rural-urban migration has been exhausted in some countries, while in others it continues to draw most of the political attention inspired by interior regions. Thus, in many countries today, decentralization means more a redistribution among MA within the country (and beyond that, a redistribution among certain groups in those areas) than a drastic restructuring of economic space. Paradoxically, foreseeable tendencies in terms of locational factors in the ruling national and international context seem to indicate probable generation of a level of interregional deconcentration and a high level of regional suburbanization principally induced by foreign enterprises motivated by economic interests.

In other terms, the centralization-decentralization dichotomy tends to distract attention from the really important problem in Latin America. This is the necessity of permitting vigorous social restructuring and participation of all members of society in the benefits of economic growth, controlled and propelled by endogenous forces. With respect to the particular problem which concerns us here, and given agreement on directing the process of national development by evolutionary or revolutionary means, we attempt, then, to recognize that both the great city, as well as the theoretical decentralized system, may be instrumental in men's search for well-being. Even though the process of centralization has been an instrument and an effect of the process of exploitation of the national hinterland by the national metropolis and of the latter by the international metropolis, it is possible that in the future certain forms of deconcentration could be more efficient instruments of internal and external exploitation of men by men as demonstrated by current tendencies of the present structure. And, just as it is admitted that the development of productive forces achieved by capitalism has been an improvement over previous forms of organization and should be exploited as a starting point for even better systems, so, too, can the great city be understood as a superior form of habitat required by man for his development.

Without a doubt, drastic or gradual change in the structure and objectives of society can modify specific internal forms of the great city, but will not alter its decisions or its preponderance as an efficient spatial organization in the service of social development.

NOTES

1. This "sensitivity" arises principally from the flaring up of conflicts caused by inequalities.

2. A country is "underdeveloped" in relation to another which is perceived as "developed" and to which we attach the goals of the former. By this token, Cuba would not be an underdeveloped country (in spite of its low per capita income), at least with regard to world centers of the capitalist system, which are not within its frame of reference, and is surely perceived as "developed" by many sectors of the world which share its value system and goals.

3. This thesis is based on the accepted fact that development of the country will depend in large part on diversification of industrial exports of raw materials in which the country has a comparative advantage, whose deposits are found dispersed over the length of the national territory from the extreme North to the extreme South, with a scale of production permitting them to pay for their own social infrastructure, whose technologies are capital-intensive and whose production is oriented more to the international market than to the local market concentrated in Santiago. See Geisse (1965).

4. In the first place, we can point to the large investments for the extraction and industrialization of copper in northern and central Chile, the development of the pulp and cellulose industry, and the establishment of petrochemical industrial plants in the central and southern parts of the country. Second is initiation of a rapid transit system in Santiago with

an estimated ultimate investment of $700 million. Third, is the fact that seventy percent of public housing (representing seventy percent of total housing built during the past ten years) has been built in the Santiago metropolitan region. In the private sector, participation in the metropolitan region is even higher.

5. During the past decade, the North-South longitudinal freeway network was completed, electrification of the railroad network was begun, and a national television network was put into operation—all making even smoother the flow of goods, population, and information from the core center to peripheral regions.

6. Improvement in income distribution between regions can bring deterioration in such distribution among population strata (intranational). See Coraggio (1969).

7. See also the publications of the Executive Group of Greater São Paulo (GEGRAN) and of the Ministry of the Treasury of the state of Guanabara, Rio de Janeiro, regarding development plans for the São Paulo and Rio de Janeiro regions, respectively.

8. It is unlikely that this would occur, but for two distinct reasons: we are dealing with a case in which the national power structure is almost totally identified with that of the MA, and thus the objectives of the governing group will be translated as much into national objectives as into those of the MR.

9. This is different from the situation in which excessive decentralization can produce a negative effect on other objectives (e.g., growth of gross national product) which worsens the national welfare.

10. This expression of objectives is independent of which of the "options for future development" is adopted. Of course, their achievement would vary from one case to another, and new objectives could appear.

11. A general approach to the problem would be to begin from some minimum standard and proceed to raise it gradually while all the regional population surpasses it. It is possible that in the first instance the substandard groups would be located beyond the metropolitan area, but upon reaching a certain level both the metropolitan and interior groups would start to appear as subgroups, with the proviso that the latter would be quantitatively more important in those countries with a high degree of urbanization. In any case, regional averages do not reflect this situation.

12. This vision does not refer to the "urban scene," but rather to the functional characteristics of the subsystem.

13. The relative importance of each component structure varies for each Latin American country.

14. This term has implications similar to "megalopolis" coined by Jean Gottman (1961) for the principal urban complex of the capitalist system. We have preferred not to use this term for the purpose of reserving it for extreme cases, such as the Rosario-Buenos Aires-La Plata urban complex could become in the next decades. In each case, polycentrism is a relevant characteristic for distinguishing them from conventional cities.

15. The term "deconcentration" should be understood as the tendency for productive activities to locate outside the center or region under discussion. The term "decentralization" refers additionally to decision-making and administrative activities, both public and private.

16. It can be argued that a model of spatial development by "diffusion" from a single point is not the only possible one. One can think of models of growth starting from various preestablished points or even of models of growth by random chance. However, the fact that the MA have become true centers of accumulation through exploitation of their hinterlands makes one believe that diffusion impulses will be derived from these centers. This scheme is easily applicable in the case of countries with more than one first-order MA. In order to simplify our exposition, we have assumed that only a single relevant MA exists.

17. In most Latin American areas, there have been no changes in municipal organization based on independent local governments, even though the problems generated by urban expansion demand an approach on a metropolitan-regional scale.

18. In turn, the latter growth starting from these centers and from the MA may begin to induce axial urban extensions along highways and waterways, compartmentalizing green or agricultural areas.

19. Within the pampa region of Argentina there are numerous examples of highly specialized centers of less than 10,000 inhabitants located only a few kilometers from MA. See Coraggio et al. (1970). In the case of Chile's central region an example is Casablanca.

20. The exception is Cuba.

21. A work partially referring to these factors is Alonso (1968). See also Karper and Gokhman (1968).

22. Both are apparent in Argentina.

23. This "sensitivity" refers not so much to a change in the basic values of the capitalist system as to the preoccupation with dysfunctional situations and the idea that effects can be alleviated without attacking structural causes.

24. As for mechanisms which can be extended to the regional level, see Hardoy et al. (1969).

25. Although the authors lack statistical information, there is evidence that spatial mobility has increased notably in Cuba in recent years.

26. Decentralization is often criticized as a restriction to economic development as measured in total growth rates and accepted as an alternative "a posteriori" upon accumulation of the surplus of distribution. In fact, decentralization is sometimes used not only as an instrument of distribution but in terms of efficiency with a broader horizon. However, this statement has not been proved nor is it convincing to justify centralization as a product of market behavior, which as a truth criterion is highly questionable.

REFERENCES

ALONSO W. (1968) "The location of industry in developing countries." Presented at Inter-Regional Seminar on Industrial Location and Regional Development, Minsk, August. (mimeo)

CIDU (Centro Interdisciplinario de Desarrollo Urbano y Regional) (n.d.) Proyecto macrozona central de Chile." 1a. y 2a. etapas y documentos de trabajo 1 al 20. Santiago: CIDU. (mimeo)

CONADE (Corporación Nacional de Desarrollo) (n.d.) Organización del espacio de la región metropolitana de Buenos Aires: Esquema director año 2000. Buenos Aires.

CORAGGIO, J. L. (1969) "Elementos para una discusión sobre eficiencia, equidad y conflicto entre regiones." Working paper 1, Centro de Estudios Urbanos y Regionales, Instituto Torcuato di Tella.

— — et al. (1970) "Caracterización funcional de las ciudades de la región pampeana." Buenos Aires: Facultad de Ciencias Económicas, Universidad Nacional de Buenos Aires. (mimeo)

GEISSE, G. (1965) "Información básica para una política urbana regional." Cuadernos de Economía (Universidad Católica) (Santiago) 6 (May-August).

GOTTMAN, J. (1961) Megalopolis. Cambridge, Mass.: MIT Press.

HARDOY, J. E., R. BASALDUA, and O. MORENO (1969) "La tierra urbana, políticas y mecanismos para su regulación y tenencia." Desarrollo Económico 9, 34.

KARPER, L. N. and V. M. GOKHMAN (1968) "Peculiarities of modern urbanization and industrialization of production." Presented at the Inter-Regional Seminar on Industrial Location and Regional Development, Minsk, August. (mimeo)

ONDU (Oficina Nacional de Planeamiento y Urbanismo) (1967) Plan de desarrollo metropolitano Lima-Callao: Esquema director 1967-1980. 2 vols. Lima.

ROFMAN, A. et al. (n.d.) Prediagnóstico de la estructura productiva del Gran Rosario. Buenos Aires: Centro de Estudios Urbanos y Regionales, Instituto Torcuato di Tella.

STEVENS, B. et al. (1967) "An investigation of location factors influencing the economy of the Philadelphia region." RSRI discussion paper 12, March.

Chapter 3

REGIONAL POLICY
THE SOCIAL VARIABLES OF REGIONAL
DEVELOPMENT IN LATIN AMERICA

RUBEN D. UTRIA

To judge by recent indicators, reduction in adverse disequilibria in the internal spatial structure of development and in the settlement and rational management of land—the essence of the discipline known as regional development—will constitute a strategic element of Latin America's development policies in the 1970s. Like import substitution and industrialization in the fifties, and national planning and economic integration in the sixties, regional development appears destined to become one of the principal concerns of planners and strategists of Latin American development.

This supposition is not founded only on recognition that in each recent decade the policy of Latin American development has been a kind of panacea. There are also other considerations of great weight. One is the feeling that recent industrialization policies in each country brought with them reinforcement and sharpening of internal regional disequilibria. This has been accompanied by serious social and economic disadjustments, such as accelerated urbanization and social marginalization, and it has become a new and powerful obstacle to accelerated development. Another consideration is that pressures from passed-over regions and localities are being increasingly felt.

A further consideration is the growing recognition by Latin American planners of the need to incorporate social and territorial variables into existing models for interpretation and manipulation of the development *process.* Developmental strategists and planners are also increasingly sensitive to and interested in what might be called *"the drive to the interior."* This generates an

Author's Note: Although the author is an adviser to the United Nations in the social aspects of regional-development policy and planning, the ideas and opinions expressed herein are his exclusive responsibility. English translation by Alejandro Vélez Gómez.

approach which pays due attention to internal development and systematic expansion of the economic and social space of each individual country without overlooking the external variables which have captured political strategy in the past two decades (Matus, 1969).

Given this approach, regional development is identified with the search for a spatial structure for national development which achieves the following objectives: (a) an increasing level of efficiency based on organic incorporation of all natural and human resources and strategic management of social and economic space; (b) adequate territorial distribution of the efforts and benefits of development, in an attempt to eliminate adverse regional contrasts; (c) organic and just interregional relationships; (d) realistic conditions for self-sustained and growing internal development; (e) occupation and methodical preparation of national territory to orient and facilitate development of human settlements and community life; and (f) systematic incorporation of popular and local initiative and participation (ECLA, 1969a).

Decreases in regional disequilibria—and national displacement of industry, systematic expansion of economic space, orientation of human settlements and broadening of internal markets, and the objectives they implicitly contain—are purposes embodying complex social processes. Decisions as well as methodological and operative instruments necessary for strategic management of regional development and regionalization of policies constitute political and institutional processes. Above all, man and society are both the *subject* and the *end point* of such development efforts. These circumstances give high social content to the different regional-development policies.

In the context of the underdeveloped countries, regional development seems more complex and significant than simple location of extraregional resources, or efficient exploitation of a basic resource, generally of the extractive type. Regional development involves promotion mechanisms which generally are frustrated by lack of adequate social conditions permitting transfer of resources to localize, take root, and be consolidated and multiplied systematically (Ziolkowski, 1969; Utria, 1969a). Resource exploitation involves simply installation of industrial enclaves which—by the generally extraregional and extranational destination of their production—do have not the capacity to generate authentic development at the local level. In Latin America, it is easy to find examples of these approaches to regional policy.

The process of stimulating the population consists in large measure of freeing and putting into operation individual and collective human potential, awakening a local conscience regarding the dynamic role which the region must and can play in national life, as well as the search for achievement of regional aspirations through acceleration of development. This all seems to indicate that the phenomenon involves two different types of processes: one endogenous, by which human potential and natural, economic, and institutional resources are freed, combined, and developed through an accelerated process of social change; and another, exogenous, by which links are created with the rest of national life and the economy. The former appears a basically local responsibility and is close to the joint values, motivations, and attitudes of the population, as well as to the availability of local resources. The latter process is related to the capability for action and organization of the central controlling power, and, therefore, constitutes a basically national or supraregional responsibility.

Through this process of simultaneous development of the population and its natural resources, social institutions are perfected and strengthened, and the economy expands beyond the requirements of internal consumption. The production system acquires export capacity and, at the same time, raw materials and capital, from abroad. Through this continuous growth of exports and imports and the accompanying favorable balance in the internal economy, and the spread of human and institutional resources that induced these processes, the region may acquire the dynamism necessary for self-sustained development.

This broad concept of regional development is operating in limited fashion, though on firm ground in Latin America. If we analyze carefully the motivations of recent regional-development policies in certain countries, we can observe a basic enlargement of concepts. It appears that a current with new ideological content is orienting Latin American thought in this field. In practice, the past currents revolved around the stimulation of depressed areas, such as in the case of Brazil's Superintendência de Desenvolvimento do Nordeste (SUDENE); reconstruction of the economy in zones devastated by earthquakes and other accidents such as in Valdivia Province in Chile; exploitation of hydraulic resources, as in the Corporación del Valle del Cauca (CVC) in Colombia, or the Balsas, Lerma, and Papaloapan river commissions in Mexico; and exploitation of basic natural resources, such as the Corporación de la Guayana Venezolana (CGV).[1]

Looking backward, the construction of Brasília did not simply mean the building of a new national capital. The intention of the planners of this new city was to produce significant alterations in the spatial structure of Brazilian development. Although at present no serious evaluation has been made of this experience and doubt has been expressed about its validity, the few years this new city has been in operation appear to be stimulating a gradual shift of the center of gravity of Brazilian national development. According to some, these economic and social changes will be perceptible in wide zones of Goiás and Minas Gerais and in the modifications of the flows of activities and social and economic interchange in the traditional poles of São Paulo, Rio de Janeiro, and Belo Horizonte.

The new scheme of regionalization recently established in Chile does not constitute simply a new political-administrative arrangement; it also is a strategy for regionalizing and decentralizing Chilean development.[2] The long-term national-development strategy promulgated by the Peruvian government in November 1968 clearly established as an objective of development policy obtaining improved population distribution over Peruvian economic space, and preventing the traditional concentration in metropolitan areas and coastal zones.[3]

The Venezuelan government has also put into operation a new regional-development policy, and has introduced regional zones in the nation to serve as the basis of the new strategy.[4] The Argentine government, too, is reorienting development policy in this direction through the new "national system for planning and action." Law 16964 of September 30, 1966, and its respective regulations divide the nation into eight "development regions" and establish operating conditions for decentralization of development policy at the level of each region.[5]

In Colombia, the Administrative Department of Planning has just concluded studies relating to the nation's regional structure and to formulation of a regional-development policy (Departamento Nacional de Planeación, 1969). At present, the government is preparing to present the appropriate draft bill to the Colombian Congress.

The political and ideological components, as well as the social repercussions of these new regional-development concepts and practices, transcend conventional ranges and tools. This process of reformulation is barely in its initial phase, and it is still difficult to detail its true content. It might only be a way of expressing the frustrations experienced by Latin American countries over more than a decade of exercises revolving around formulation of development policies and plans at the national level. It is also possible that they may only be a reply to the growing pressure and clamor of leaders of peripheral regions and localities. Whatever their motivation, what is certain is that this process is under way and could become a focal element of development policy in the next decade. In any case, what should not be overlooked is that such reformulations imply significant modifications in the traditional tendencies of Latin American development, and, therefore, alterations in the accompanying social structures. In this context, it is imperative to bear in mind the dynamics of the principal social sectors of regional development.

SOCIAL ASPECTS OF REGIONAL DEVELOPMENT

The principal social problems of development affecting internal regions of Latin American countries do not constitute isolated phenomena, nor do they appear to be exclusively generated on a regional and local plane. Neither do they appear to originate only in processes exclusively "social" in nature. In analyzing their origins, nature, and future, one has the feeling that they constitute the results of a complex combination of factors—historical, political, ecnomic, social, and physical-geographic. These social aspects can be analyzed through a double, although interrelated, approach: the social repercussions of tendencies of the development process followed by different countries; and conflicts deriving from the social nature of processes of development.

Social Repercussions of the Development Model

The spatial structure of Latin American development is in marked disequilibrium, giving rise to strong regional contrasts and dichotomies. Such disequilibrium appears both in continental terms and in the internal contrasts of each of the different countries. Even today, systematic studies of the structure supporting this reality do not exist. Therefore, these remarks must be taken for the moment with the appropriate dose of caution.

In the first place, the culture, economy, and other expression of development appear principally localized along the coast or nearby (see Stöhr, 1969; ILPES, 1968). The continent's interior has been preserved and continues to be less developed, as in Argentina, Brazil, Ecuador, Peru, and Venezuela.

In the second place, the spatial structure is characterized by strong and increasing regional disequilibria. At one extreme, one or a few poles and their respective areas of influence concentrate the greater part of investment resources, services, productive activity, and, in many cases, population; at the other, an extensive periphery exists relatively stagnant, or simply marginal in relation to the general development process accomplished in the rest of the particular nation. Extensive territories in Brazil, Colombia, Ecuador, Bolivia, Mexico, Peru, and Venezuela are examples.

Regional Dichotomies

This picture of disequilibria manifests itself in several countries through a host of marked regional contrasts.[6] One is the contrast between *dynamic* and *depressed* regions. In the former, production grows at rates similar to those of industrialized countries, while the population increases considerably. In the latter regions, the economy declines or remains stationary at the same time as the population tends to migrate to dynamic regions in search of employment opportunities and better services. This need not necessarily be negative if dynamic regions are able to absorb these migrants and satisfy their expectations. A second contrast is the existence of *rich* and *poor* regions. Rich regions have relatively high per capita income levels and measure high on other socioeconomic and sociocultural indicators, while in poor regions such indicators are low and precarious. Third, there is a contrast between *modern* and *traditional* regions. The former are characterized by the innovative and modernizing vigor present in both their economies and the rest of their social institutions. The latter remain bound instead to the most traditional forms of production and social organization. A fourth contrast is that between *metropolitan* and *rural* regions. Metropolitan regions contain a share of the nation's population exceeding the maximum scale of adequate size for the functioning of human services, while in rural regions the population is dispersed without a hierarchy of urban nuclei. Finally, there is the contrast between *relatively autonomous* regions [7] and *dependent* regions. The former have relatively self-sustained development and are capable of operating on the basis of their own internal markets—and even of subsidizing other markets—while the dependent regions need constant transfers of resources from the national government or from more dynamic regions in order to survive. This situation could have positive results within the framework of a global strategy for regional development aimed at counteracting these disequilibria. This solution, however, has adverse consequences when dependence prevails and there is no authentic economic integration. Furthermore, under these conditions, a state of economic and political dependence arises.

Such contrasts may be easily seen in the concentration of people, production, and income in the principal regions of each country and their respective urban centers. By 1960, one-third of the Latin American population lived in cities over 20,000 inhabitants and nearly one-fourth in cities of over 100,000 inhabitants. Ten cities with more than one million then contained about 13 percent of total population; in 15 of the 21 Latin American countries, half or more than half of the urban population lived in a single city. Other countries also revealed equally high indices of concentration: 47 percent in Chile's capital; 70 and 40 percent in the two largest cities of Ecuador and Brazil, respectively; and 40 percent in Mexico's metropolitan area. On the other hand, very low population densities were found in certain rural areas. In over 40 percent of the Latin American territory, population density did not reach one inhabitant per square kilometer and over two-thirds of Latin America's land area did not contain five persons (ECLA, 1969b: part 1, ch. 2).

In addition to these demographic disequilibria, greater ones exist in economic activity. Recently, it was estimated that more than one-third of the value of Latin America's industrial production came from the Buenos Aires, São Paulo, and Mexico City metropolitan areas, and that in several countries the two or three most important industrial centers together account for a highly significant proportion of total national production. In Argentina, two-thirds came from greater Buenos Aires and Rosario; in Brazil, 80 percent from the São Paulo-Guanabara-Belo Horizonte triangle; in Chile, 66 percent from the cities of Santiago and Valparaíso; in Mexico, 45 percent originated in the Federal District and Monterrey; in Peru, 56 percent came from Lima-Callao; and in Uruguay, three-fourths from Montevideo (ECLA, 1969b).

Added to regional disequilibria in economic activity are disequilibria in regional distribution of income. For example, it is estimated that, in Brazil, average per capita income indices as compared to the national average were 51 for the Northeast, 60 for the North and Central-West zones, 96 for the East, and 144 for the South. In Mexico, average rural family income was little more than 40 percent of average urban income, and as compared to average per capita income in the Federal District, average regional income indices were 35 for the Pacific, South, and Central zones, 54 for the North and Gulf of Mexico, and 93 for the Northern Pacific. At the same time, income is concentrated in metropolitan areas where the greater part of modern industry is located. It is estimated, for example, that in the case of Argentina, Chile, Mexico, and Peru, 45 percent of gross domestic product is generated in greater Buenos Aires, 43 percent in Santiago Province, 35 percent in Mexico's Federal District, and 40 percent in the city of Lima. In contrast to this high concentration of income in metropolitan areas, there are large human agglomerations with extremely low levels of productivity and income, such as in Southern Mexico and the Brazilian Northeast. In the latter, which has been described as the vastest zone of misery in the Western Hemisphere, some 25 million persons live on an annual per capita income of under one hundred dollars.

Examining in detail the nature and origins of such disequilibiria, one has the feeling that they are tied to the implicit or explicit strategies traditionally pursued[8] by the Latin American countries. There are those who affirm that these disequilibria are consubstantial with such strategies and tend to be consolidated to the extent these strategies take hold (Stavenhagen, 1969).

In effect, the most representative characteristic of Latin American development strategy from the beginning of the Republican era to recent years is the concentration of efforts in those cities and areas in which there is already an accumulation of services, population, and, therefore, of potential markets. This accumulation was operative under the Spanish and Portuguese domination. Spatial localization responded exclusively to the interests and functional ties of a colonial economy. In fulfillment of these objectives, the focal points of Latin American colonial development in each country were those ports best connecting areas of raw material production and the Spanish or Portuguese mother country (Furtado, 1969). The economic space utilized was limited to areas of direct influence in the dependent economy. In this way, the coastal spatial structure oriented abroad, which today also characterizes Latin American development, was defined and consolidated.

This structure was not altered significantly after colonial times when centers of world economic power shifted to other countries. This structure was not altered later during the crisis in the international system of centers of economic power during the Great Depression and World War II, or during the recent era of "import-substitution." On the contrary, there is evidence that this structure was consolidated even further through concentration of new infrastructure, installation of social services, expansion of bureaucratic services, and installation of new industries.[9]

It might be thought that these characteristics and influence on regional disequilibria are exclusively of an economic nature and that they do not necessarily have social repercussions. In the Latin American case, such an estimate does not seem warranted. These characteristics all contain social and political motivations and processes, complex historical influences, and socio-cultural values. Without adequate consideration of these forces, it would not be legitimate to attempt an interpretation of, much less a solution to, regional-development problems.

Social Effects of the Concentration of Development in Coastal Regions

Aside from the positive economic effects flowing from the concentration of development in coastal zones in many Latin American countries, the isolation of extensive interior regions brought with it the marginality of important natural resources and sectors of the population. This forces the latter to emigrate constantly and increasingly in search of job opportunities and services. At the same time, the lack of interior communications and interconnection contributes to orienting migratory and colonization flows to the coast, with corresponding saturation of narrow coastal bands linked to large seaports. This explains in part the great human agglomerations in Argentina around Buenos Aires and the mouth of the Plata; in Brazil, surrounding Rio de Janeiro, Santos, São Paulo, and their area of interior production, Belo Horizonte. This is also the case with the extensive Northeast belt surrounding Salvador, Recife, Fortaleza, Natal, and others; in Venezuela, around La Guaira-Caracas; in Peru, through the Lima-Callao metropolitan complex; and, in Ecuador, surrounding Guayaquil. Mexico and Colombia, for reasons due more to national topography and historical factors other than the pattern of development, present a different physiognomy. The same may also be said of Bolivia and Paraguay because of their land-locked nature. Such concentration would have a different connotation from a social point of view if coastal lands were adequate to ensure important agricultural development and if industry were capable of productively employing all the population.

The Incidence of Polarization

Polarization of development, which has made possible reliance on industrial markets and economies of scale in production and resource exploitation, has also contributed to strengthening regional disequilibria. In the first place, concentration of investments, services, and power has encouraged concentration of population in one or many metropolitan areas whose rates of demographic growth exceed the economy's ability to provide sufficient employment and services. This has been reflected in emergence of increasingly marginal population groups which make more dramatic the deficits in services, distort the unskilled labor market, and move to the cities the burden of social conflicts generated in the rural environment by generations of stagnation, impoverishment, and unsatisfied expectations. Second, such "metropolitanization" has discouraged formation and consolidation of secondary poles and medium-sized cities, which were in the past nuclei for development of many interior regions and which could serve at present as the vanguard of a regional-development strategy. Third, this polarization of population makes more difficult and costly supply and management of social and urban services because they exceed all appropriate scales of organization and financing. Fourth, and as a result of the polarization of opportunities, the best-trained individuals and groups progressively abandon rural areas and medium- and small-sized cities for the large poles. This means that the former areas lose systematically their potential human resources for progress and are increasingly left at the mercy of groups that are most traditional and least apt to struggle for local change. This explains in part why in many countries social change in rural areas is slower and even contrary, leading to greater impoverishment and new forms of dependency. This contrasts with the case of urban centers which are modernizing rapidly. Fifth, polarization also leads to a concentration of modernization, creating so-called "islands of modernity" which are in vivid contrast to the underdeveloped patterns. Such islands do not have the ability to radiate their influence positively and transform the nonmodern sector. Instead, what occurs is that they exercise a negative influence through their drain of human resources and the economic and political dependency they impose. This does not mean that all polarization is incapable of benefiting the periphery. The situation would be different within the framework of a new regional-development strategy.

The Effects of Dependence

The characteristics of dependence of the Latin American economy have caused many social problems relative to regional disequilibria. On the one hand, its raw material, monocultural export nature caused historically privileged and priority development of the respective regions of production at the expense of remaining regions not engaged in the export process. Such is the case of coffee regions of Brazil and Colombia; sugar regions of Central America and Peru; banana plantations in Ecuador and Caribbean countries; petroleum fields in Venezuela; the nitrate industry initially and later copper in Chile; and, finally, the tin mines of Bolivia. It should be kept in mind, however, that such "development" has generally been limited to the infrastructure indispensable for processing and transportation; has benefited only management, intermediaries, and merchants, and, to a lesser degree, the workers most closely linked to production. Net benefits are systematically exported to the national capital or to international centers without producing multiplying effects within the regions.[10] In what measure does this shifting of benefits affect the population of these regions? Is this transfer necessary for the capitalization required by national development? And, if it is necessary, for how long?

In the second place, as a result of the progressive self-sufficiency achieved by the industrialized countries, international trade, and the dynamism in recent decades of Latin America's urban-centered, import-substitution industrial development, agriculture and small-scale mining have been losing priority. The lack of systematic expansion of domestic markets has not permitted replacements for the traditional demand of international markets. This has contributed to growth in the urban economy, accompanied by decrease in the rural, with corresponding adverse impact on the population of peripheral areas.

In the third place, the indiscriminate importation of capital goods and technology from industrialized countries permitting modernization of certain sectors of production brings certain interrelated social problems connected with regional development. On the one hand, such capital goods and technologies can only be operated efficiently with ample scales of production. This prompts location of industrial complexes in the large urban centers and leaves rural areas and peripheral regions on the margin of industrialization. How does this affect the population living outside industrial centers? In order to give attention to these social factors, should industry move to where the population is or vice versa? Or does an intermediate solution exist? On the other hand, equipment and technology have been conceived and designed to produce goods and services, which, even though they may be destined for mass consumption in industrialized countries, can only be purchased by higher-income sectors in Latin America. In this way, the process of import-substitution aimed basically at the production of automobiles, electrical and electronic appliances, cosmetics, and other consumer goods has been directed toward creating and satisfying the demand of higher-income groups (ECLA, 1969c). This has meant ignoring the demand of broad popular sectors, particularly the population of peripheral regions. The lack of manual tools and equipment, raw materials, and mass consumption goods has weakened the economy of peripheral areas. Which technology and which structure of goods and services could best contribute to decreasing regional disequilibria and incorporating rural sectors? Does the problem not lie solely in technological dependence, but rather in the lack of an adequate regional-development strategy which takes these social implications into account?

In the fourth place, due to the high relative cost of goods and services produced by this type of industrialization, the market's expansion can only operate in a vertical sense. That is, in this system, the same group of consumers buys more different types of goods or the same goods more frequently. Through concentration of income and market, traditional poles have been able to secure their position as exclusive beneficiaries of development, with consequent exclusion of the population of peripheral regions. To what extent does this "verticalization" of markets contribute to accentuating existing regional disequilibria? How could an internal or "horizontal" market expansion be achieved within the technological patterns currently in vogue in Latin American industry (Matus, 1969)?

The Social Effects of Lack of National Integration

Another of the characteristics of the patterns of development in most Latin American countries is lack of adequate integration. The different regions and territories of each country are not linked in an organic way, permitting incorporation of all available human and economic resources and sharing in the fruits of national development by the population of all regions. This does not mean that all areas of national territory should receive equal treatment and similar benefits. This would be equivalent in some cases to wasting resources on areas having little to offer and in others to ignoring potential resources and favorable opportunities. It would signify renunciation of the possibilities of strategic manipulation of development policy according to time and priority. What is involved here is, rather, achieving an adequate degree of *integration* of different territorial areas and population into the national economy and life.

As a result of this lack of integration and, indeed, the prevalence of an integration pattern based on dependence, most Latin American countries present a picture of a dynamic, industrialized, super-region concentrating economic and political power as well as culture, surrounded by regions of little or no dynamism. This situation, and the economic, political, and cultural relationships operative in such regions, determine the social behavior of the total population and its representative sectors. Such behavior has importance in consolidation of and increase in regional inequalities. Naturally, it must also play an important role as an obstacle to any strategy to overcome such disequilibria.

Super-regions tend to treat other regions in colonial fashion. The former play the part of producers of manufactured goods, and the latter, that of suppliers of raw materials and consumers of manufactured goods, a consequence of which is the unfavorable transfer of benefits and resources to super-regions. When super-regions have access to sufficient markets of their own, other regions' markets are underestimated, and subsidies are transferred in their favor. As previously mentioned, certain super-regions in Latin America are arriving at a phase of development permitting them to maintain or continue to grow without regard for population in remaining regions.

In regions of limited dynamism and those which are stagnant, the attitudes of dominant groups and the population in general are quite different. It is believed here that the region does not have either the resources or the capability for action necessary to accelerate its development. Little can be done without the tutelage of the central power. This attitude, which is in many cases the result of unfavorable treatment received by the region over long periods, reaches such extreme lengths that the action of local leadership is sometimes limited to obtaining and exploiting paternalistic subsidies. Another variant is the systematic struggle for privileges and prerogatives of a customs, tariff, or financial nature. Under the pretext of stimuli to local development, these become a permanent system of subsidies to the exclusive benefit of certain groups. Still another variant is the permanent confrontation of two or more regions in attempts to control local governments or their benefits.

In the absence of a strategy of national integration and the social behavior it spawns, development efforts are frustrated. For example, stimuli and subsidies, whether systematic or accidental, may produce adverse effects. It is well known that in many cases the greater part of extraregional aid, domestic and foreign, which these regions receive, ends in the hands of dominant local groups who export it anew, generally in increased form as a result of large profits and certain types of manipulations, to the nation's capital or abroad. Dependent regions in this way come to disburse greater resources than they receive. This explains in part the failure policies of national integration have traditionally had in most of Latin America. Is this lack of integration due exclusively to political and economic centralization, or are there other contributory social factors rooted in peripheral regions? Could a strategy of a purely economic nature facilitate integration?

SOCIAL ASPECTS DERIVING FROM THE SOCIAL NATURE OF DEVELOPMENT

Social Aspects Inherent in the Population's Role

No consensus exists among development planners and scholars concerning the most accurate way of defining the development process. However, as understanding deepens and the development problem is faced, its eminently social character becomes more evident. Changes in the structure of production, consumption, and savings; incorporation of technological progress; capability to administer and multiply reproductive resources; and modernization of institutions are linked in large measure to the conduct and effort of man and society. Economic resources are absolutely necessary but insufficient alone to spark development of a given country or region. There are those who maintain that, for this to succeed, population armed with vitality and aptitudes is necessary, as is an institutional framework sufficiently flexible to withstand the social changes such a process involves.

Such conditions are not available in the majority of peripheral regions. The socioeconomic, cultural, and psychological composition of wide sectors of the population is deficient. Representative groups are not capable of playing a dynamic role. Thus, investment dries up or flows to more prosperous regions; opportunities for employment become scarce. At the same time, income becomes concentrated, social mobility is halted, and the middle sectors gradually become poorer. All of this coincides with weakening of the region's traditional economic base. A vicious circle is produced, in which depression, dependence, or marginality affect the population adversely and also then limit the possibilities of accelerating development. This explains the persistence and consolidation of regional disequilibria. It also constitutes, therefore, an important factor in any regional-development policy and strategy. Keeping in mind the above-mentioned considerations, the following social areas merit detailed consideration: (a) conditions for community development; (b) characteristics of demographic structures; (c) settlement pattern; and (d) human attitudes regarding geographic and climatic barriers.

(a) Conditions for Community Development

According to the United Nations, community organization and development are related principally to the population's capacity to respond to development stimuli and commitments.[11] One of the most important aspects of this capacity involves the *images, attitudes,* and *motivations* of the population vis-à-vis development. These attitudes determine the population's response in undertaking and accelerating the processes of transformation and modernization involved in development and in acquiring the appropriate degree of motivation to produce more and better, and to progress socially, culturally, and politically. A region whose inhabitants have positive images of development and its benefits, who are ready to strive both individually and collectively to achieve this goal, and who have faith in their own capability is fertile soil for application of regional-development policies. What the population then needs are stimuli and instruments so that it may itself unleash its own development.

Another variable is the degree of *community and functional organization* required to perform an active role. Population constitutes a resource when it is grouped and integrated to a degree sufficient to acquire a reasonable level of consensus and unity of action; i.e., when a series of values, sociocultural patterns, and interests assure the population some cohesion and permit its members to feel, act, and project themselves with relative unity. This implies existence of internal bonds, and a community of aspirations and organization. With this approach, everything should be translated into a series of functional organs—associations, labor unions, pressure groups, political parties—and a leadership which catalyzes and guides the population. If the population is organized, and to the degree that such organization becomes more efficient and the leadership more authentic, the population is in better condition to participate in the tasks of development. Conversely, a region lacks a basic requirement for development when its population is culturally, socially, and politically dispersed, or when action and public opinion organisms do not exist in it to channel popular energies and aspirations, or when it has no reasonably authentic leaders.

This is the case with many lagging regions. The population has lost the necessary degree of cohesion. Its most dynamic members systematically migrate. Leadership is in the hands of small groups of local politicians lacking vision or capability, and in particular in the hands of family groups interested in perpetuating the conditions of exploitation and social injustice favoring their economic and political interests. Under these conditions, it becomes extremely difficult for collective attitudes and motivations for development to emerge. Therefore, the population cannot be counted on as a basic resource to accelerate development.[12]

If the aforementioned propositions—officially supported by many governments and specialists in various continents—are valid and applicable to Latin American reality, it would be fitting to answer such questions as: Which are the most adequate means for rapid transformation of popular images and motivations? How can the effects of the inertia produced by long periods of stagnation and marginality be counteracted? How can the images, attitudes, and motivations of different sectors of the population be conciliated? How should this population be organized, at the regional, local, or small-group-with-specific-interests level? How should values facilitating cohesion of the population be identified and consolidated? Would organization of the popular classes not contribute to increasing conflicts of interest among different social strata? Or are such organizations necessary to counteract and overcome the power of groups benefiting from regional and local stagnation?

(b) Demographic Characteristics and Tendencies

Population characteristics will continue to play an important role in defining conditions of development of numerous regions. The size of the population clustered around some cities and their surroundings during a long historical process was a determining factor in the location of new investment in the past three decades. Conversely, smallness or dispersal of population has in other regions influenced industry and commerce against locating in these areas. At the same time—and particularly in the case of regions without abundant resources—relative excess population has caused precarious social conditions which have not represented a sufficient attraction for investment. In turn, population growth rates have contributed to accelerating impoverishment of vast sectors of the population, especially in those regions in which production has grown at modest rates or basic productive resources—particularly arable land—are not abundant or have been withdrawn partially or totally through unproductive *latifundismo*. This appears to be the case in many mountainous regions of Bolivia, Colombia, Ecuador, Mexico, and Peru. Surplus population has to migrate constantly to lower and coastal regions in search of land and employment. The age profile of the population also exercises influence over conditions for development. Those regions having an adequate proportion of young people and children have potentially the labor force required by rapid industrialization and, in addition, the dynamic elements necessary to ensure the population's more active and deliberate participation. The absence of such resources has resulted, in many regions, in the loss of opportunities offered by colonization and regional development projects.

(c) The Pattern of Settlement

Energizing development becomes more difficult in the case of regions in which population is more dispersed and in which a hierarchy of urban centers does not exist. The existence of regional development poles and production and service nuclei of subregional character seem indispensable as basic structure for the organization and operation of productive processes at the regional level (Friedmann, 1969).

It is lamentable that in recent decades many medium-sized cities in peripheral regions stagnated and declined. Regional-development policy will have to be aimed at creation and strengthening of such regional poles. According to some specialists, opportunity and priority should now be given to emerging cities which show some dynamism (Neira Alva, 1969). Setting such strategy in motion involves complex social processes and important decisions reorienting investment and decentralizing power. What effects could a reorientation of this type have on the functioning of the national economy? To what extent could the supposedly irreversible character of concentrated urbanization become an obstacle?

(d) Attitudes Regarding Geographic and Climatic Barriers

There is evidence that adverse geographic and climatic barriers have shaped attitudes and social behaviors opposed to regional development which persist even though a majority of the Latin American countries now have the necessary resources and required technology for development at their disposal. The social character of such attitudes is manifested in cases in which, thanks to highly motivated regional communities with adequate leadership, such barriers have been overcome. Introduction of air transport in Colombia more than fifty years ago permitted development of several regions geographically isolated by the three *cordilleras* which cross the country from North to South, before highways could be constructed. This same type of reasoning is also valid with respect to health barriers inherent in geography which affect development of many regions, particularly in tropical and subtropical zones. Malaria continues to decimate the population of numerous regions of Central America, Colombia, Ecuador, Peru, Bolivia, and Paraguay. Fear of this disease hindered arrival of peoples from neighboring areas—particularly the Altiplano and the slopes of the Andes. This barrier slowed the displacement of peoples from the Altiplano and Andes slopes who descend in search of lands to colonize. Fear of this disease—which Venezuela eradicated in a short time—contributed to directing migrations to the great urban centers.

These geographic barriers also give rise to myths which affect migratory flows to the detriment of some regions. The movement of population through various thermal stages is hindered by psychological obstacles. The Altiplano's population is said to be unable to adapt to lowlands and vice versa. This is important in countries like Peru, Ecuador, Colombia, and Venezuela, which have all thermal stages and great geographic contrasts. Adequate studies of this matter are lacking, and some persons sustain the validity of such myths. Nevertheless, the experience of developed countries suggests that psychology plays an important role in this case. Whatever the degree of truth in the myths, there is no doubt that planners must give attention to this phenomenon.

Social Aspects of Strategic and Political Management of Regional Development

Regional development may be identified with the search for decrease in adverse regional disequilibria through a spatial structure of national development assuring efficiency based on organic incorporation of all natural and human resources and strategic management of economic and social space; adequate territorial distribution of benefits of development; just interregional relationships; and conditions for self-sustained domestic development. Regional development is both an *end,* to the extent that it seeks the benefit of the different regions, and a *means* of national-development strategy. Regional-development policy and planning embody strategic management and definition of alternatives, whatever their range and intensity. From this are derived numerous social implications which must be managed. Some of these implications are related to the conflicting character of decisions inherent in the objectives, means, and dynamics of regional development. Others refer to the confrontation with *localismo.* Still others pertain to the extraregional character of strategic objectives of regional development.

The conflicting character of the major portion of these decisions has diverse origins. The central objective of a regional-development policy cannot be equal distribution of resources, stimuli, and benefits. If the present injustices characteristic of the Latin American spatial structure are taken into account, this would be equivalent to perpetuating the above conditions. What is instead involved is strategic distribution of resources, stimuli, and benefits as a function of the aid needed by each region to integrate itself into the nation; the national interest in incorporating unexploited resources in various regions; the satisfaction of certain tactical objectives of a supraregional nature (expansion of economic and social space, border integration of commercial and industrial activity, and the like); and alterations induced in the spatial structure of development (the Brasília project, for example). Other objectives are inherent in the need to achieve these goals through a sequence using successive stages and an order of priority assigned to these goals for political and social reasons. This whole process of formulating policies and planning implies conflicts of interest and vertical imposition of functions and commitments. This is aggravated in Latin America because there is inadequate popular participation in decision-making processes. Regional development, thus understood, embodies alteration in local inertia, correction of deformities in the development process, and modification of the power equilibrium as much at the national level as at the local. On the other hand, it also involves a confrontation with *localismo*. Definition of options and assignment of priorities constitute exercises which in practice become awards of privileges to some and injure and frustrate others. How can regional and national interests be conciliated in coherent policies and strategies? How can the centralist mentality of planners accustomed to acting at the national level, disregarding regional opinions, be transformed? And how can regional and local leaders be made to accept the need to put aside their interests and aspirations in favor of the goals of global development policy? Confrontation of all these problems creates a powerful explosion of social conflicts.

Social Problems Deriving from Relationships Between Regional Institutions and the National Government

Studies do not exist to permit extracting theories concerning the dynamics of these relationships. Common sense would indicate that, at the very least, two issues should be confronted by planners. The first is the need for an adequate dose of administrative decentralization as a condition for regional development. The second is related to the adequate dose of solidarity that regional entities must profess to the national state and to the nation's general interests. There is both a need for a national conscience concerning the problems of regional development and for institutional infrastructure; but there is also a need for regional solidarity.

National conscience refers to the degree of consensus which must be held by representative sectors of the nation concerning the need to undertake efforts to diminish pronounced regional disequilibria. Such conscience should be based principally on the twin consideration that these disequilibria constitute obstacles to national development and involve unjust treatment of population affected. In addition, such disequilibria—and worse still is the concentration of development in Latin America—are not produced at random. They are the result of a political and economic force which operates through a development concept and strategy, a type of exercise power, a manipulation of the economy and corresponding location of industries and markets, a degree of foreign dependence, and many other factors. As both cause and effect of such manipulations, values, and activities, a series of interests have been generated and strengthened favorable to such disequilibria. Obeying impulses of self-preservation, these interests conspire against attempts to modify existing conditions. One is thus faced with the presence of a series of shoals of a political, social, and cultural nature which make regional development difficult.

Planners should be prepared to confront reaction from beneficiaries of the status quo, reaction usually bearing direct relationship to the strength of regional disequilibria. In order to counteract this, it is necessary to create a new national conscience around the need to diminish regional disequilibria and enlarge economic and social space to incorporate new resources and markets. Without this new conscience, translated into political programs with popular backing and backed by private investors who believe decentralization of development can represent real benefits, regional-development efforts may be frustrated.

If these considerations are valid, *the institutional infrastructure necessary* for regional development to operate should encompass endogenous as well as exogenous factors. Reforms of the institutional administrative system should be introduced permitting a degree of delegation of power to regional governments and organisms. This is necessary not only in the public sector but also in the private. There is a tendency to see centralism only in the public sector while ignoring or justifying the impact of private sector administrative centralization. The truth is that the latter is as harmful as the former, particularly in a context like the Latin American, in which economic activity is basically in private hands. Such reforms should include regulations and laws facilitating effective administrative decentralization. For such administrative decentralization to function, it would also be necessary to have mechanisms at the regional level capable of setting regional development into motion at the operative level. The eventual vacuum left by the national government and national and international administration of private enterprises must be filled by local organisms with the capacity and initiative to plan and operate. An autonomous regional corporation or any other type of similar organism can assume at the local level the role played by the national government. A new concept of management of regional branches by private firms could constitute an alternative to the institutional infrastructure required by regional development. Adequate supply of human resources is also important. Without such resources, it is not possible to unleash the social dynamism required for development of a region. Until the local community can generate human resources itself in sufficient quantities to assume delegation of powers, it will be necessary to "decentralize" the market for professionals. This should not be understood as an isolated measure. It should form part of a system of change in the values, attitudes, and motivations of the educational process and in the professional formation of new generations. To what point do these innovations on the local level involve substantial changes in the power structure and in the whole traditional system of public and private administration? In what sense would this new institutional infrastructure operate as a simple delegation of central power?

Another variable is *regional solidarity.* As compensation for administrative decentralization, regional institutions must give their loyalty to national interests and the central government. This loyalty centers on fulfillment of national goals and identification with the values and symbols representative of the nation which assure national cohesion and solidarity. This framework also includes a spirit of solidarity with other regions of the nation, translated into a regime of fraternal coexistence and loyal rivalry. Lack of adequate treatment of this competitive aspect may easily lead to negative situations such as those in which one or more regions conspire to monopolize the resources and benefits granted by the nation, or an irresponsible competition is unleashed to award greater tax breaks and incentives in the search for investors.[13] There are still other aspects to elucidate: for example, does there exist in Latin American countries a feeling of national solidarity? Are national symbols powerful enough to assure the degree of solidarity which decreasing regional disequilibria requires? What interests and what social groups embody such symbols?

Social Aspects Deriving from Functions and Status of the Region

Rational integration of different socioeconomic spaces designed to achieve incorporation of a nation's resources, and systematic treatment of regional disequilibria which overcome marginality and stagnation of large areas must be translated in practice—if policies are actually set in motion—into a new framework of regional status and function. Concepts of status and function go farther than typologies based on general characteristics of different regions (urban, industrial, rural, uninhabited, and so on). Within the framework of such policies, assignment of status and function should have a functional base from which each region is considered an "organic unit" of national development, and, therefore, a "specialized unit" within the national life and economy. In principle, such an assignment would be based on the resources and talents of each region, as well as the objectives and requirements of national development strategy.

This assignment and the corresponding performance of status and function bring with them diverse social factors, among which are the status assigned to each region; specialization; the new relationships flowing from integration into the rest of the national life and economy; and the operational capability each region must demonstrate.

Assignment of status to each region may give rise to social conflicts and to positive psychological stimuli. Conflicts could arise from changes in the balance of power which any modification is status implicitly involves. In many cases, such changes embody concessions of privilege to some sectors at the expense of others, leading to serious conflicts of interest which may gravely affect regional development policy. But positive motivations—or positive regionalism—may also be generated in a region when the state and public opinion assign to it a contribution of importance and significant benefit to the rest of the nation, or when its leaders, its products, or examples of its culture attain public recognition at the national or international level.

Specialization may also give rise to social problems. When specialization coincides with the region's tradition and talent, problems are reduced to strengthening these factors and setting in motion a modernization process permitting greater productivity. Planners and strategists could find themselves confronted by conservative tendencies and attitudes, which it would be necessary to treat on the educational and psychological level. When new specialization is introduced into regions without existing talents, the problem is more complex. A process of adaptation is involved here.

National integration is both an objective and a means of regional development. As an objective, integration of a region into the rest of the nation seeks its economic, physical, political, and psychological incorporation. On a theoretical plane, the first goal—economic integration—seems possible through progressively tighter functional relations between regional and national production and markets. Such relationships acquire their own dynamism when positive circumstances are combined. One such would occur when both levels—regional and national—achieve advantages from this interchange. Another occurs when the regional economy produces surpluses and their benefits are reinvested in the region. This presupposes local dynamism and an organizational and internal operational capability in the region. Still another occurs when this process of production and commercialization takes place without onerous privileges, leaving the national economy, as well as other regions, at a disadvantage. These embody social and political processes which escape the restricted framework of narrowly defined productive and commercial activities.

Physical integration is related to communication and access the region should enjoy vis-à-vis the rest of national territory and external centers of immediate importance to its economy. Due to the great mobility characterizing human beings—particularly during the process of urbanization and accelerated social change facing a majority of the Latin American countries—indiscriminate intensification of access and communication may cause unfavorable effects in some regions. These may facilitate a provincial exodus to metropolitan areas without contributing to interconnecting different localities and centers of production.

Political integration refers to the system of ties which assures the population and its representative sectors participation in national power and the process of decision-making, as well as in all advantages emanating from the nation. The range of this topic transcends the restricted meaning of "administrative integration," in which it is sufficient that the national government merely authorizes powers, and that regions appoint a few delegates to public representative bodies. The problem also encompasses local and regional access to decision-making on politics, social and economic programs, and the whole complex of problems implied in regionalization and detailing of such policies and plans (Friedmann, 1969). The regional community should by its participation come to experience a feeling of "forming part of" or "being integrated into" the nation. This sensation—which is psychological—constitutes one of the most powerful ingredients in impelling regional development.

The regional operational capacity required by development also gives rise to social problems. Accelerating development embodies self-generation of resources, energies, and self-help. What is involved is not only effort but a *challenge* directed at the entire regional community, its symbols and values, and to all that constellation of factors which might be called the *regional feeling.*

Linked to this is another no less decisive requirement: the region's operational capacity to set in motion the appropriate processes. Policies and objectives proposed to this point presuppose a capacity for initiative at the local and regional level. Provincial and local governmental institutions and social-service agencies do not generally function efficiently in Latin America, whether administrative dependencies of the national government or locally elected bodies. Their weakness is in part a result of administrative concepts which do not correspond to local social and economic reality, of anachronistic legislation which negates the initiative of local officials, bureaucratic centralization, lack of coordination among national organisms responsible for social and economic activities at the local level, and lack of technical assistance to provincial and local authorities in the administration and planning. These deficiencies are not insurmountable. A majority of Latin American countries are attempting to overcome them. They appear, however, to be deeply rooted. In many countries, the formulae for distribution of responsibilities have been tried and repeatedly changed in the course of the traditional struggle between federalism and centralism without strengthening the local government. Municipalities have persisted in all Latin American countries since the colonial period as basic units of local government, but, instead of gaining experience and vitality, they have lost functions due to their incapability to exercise them. Even at present, when these entities have considerable resources available to manage at their discretion, results have not been encouraging. In many cases, funds are spent to the benefit of small groups in urban centers, neglecting the interests of surrounding rural areas, and in other cases, they are spent on luxurious public works and monuments.

It would be illusory to hope that local government efficiency will be achieved spontaneously. All these problems are linked to adverse characteristics of the power structure and the decision-making process. In backward and stagnant regions, as well as in those in which economic growth has occurred based on monoculture or exploitation of minerals, the dominant groups-landowners, merchants, political bosses, central government functionaries—have adapted to the situation and derive advantages from it which could disappear if development were accompanied by redistribution of power and income and expansion and diversification of the opportunities for social mobility. In the majority of cases, these are the only groups having effective links with national centers of economic and political power, and they are also the only ones capable of interchanging benefits with them. These groups are in position to monopolize whatever development aid flows from national centers. They can also frustrate application of national policies seeking the decentralization and democratization of power.

Mere statement of these problems does not signify that the situation of local governments in Latin America is irreversible or that nothing can be done for the moment. Local power structures are changing, as are national, and new forces ready to counteract such powers are emerging. Given the nature of the problem, however, it is necessary to insist on popular participation in regional development, in spite of the many complications that this involves, other than advocating technocratic models for development planning. Adequate consideration must be given to social factors if regional development is not to be frustrated and a mere panacea for problems presented by Latin American development.

NOTES

1. For an extension of this theme see Stöhr (1969).

2. "The justification for a regional-development policy appears clear if it is considered as an instrument of multiple objectives oriented toward improvement in the conditions of integration. Basically, regional-development policy must act through spatial ordering of activities (in terms of a hierarchy of central locations) to promote greater physical integration by means of adequate management of certain controlling variables (investment, migration, location, etc.) in order to cause economic decentralization, and by means of such decentralization policy to permit accentuation of regional participation in the decision-making process. The 'region' thus appears as an instrument of action for development policy and as an instrument of participation for the individual, object and subject of planning" (ODEPLAN, 1968: 35).

3. "To achieve improved distribution of the population of the nation's economic space, avoiding in this way present tendencies toward growing concentration in coastal zones, particularly in the metropolitan center, through formation of compensatory development poles in strategic regions clustered around a constellation of integrated resources" (Instituto Nacional de Planificación, 1968: 4). This strategic concept of regional development also appears in the same document when, on referring to state government reform initiated by the Peruvian government, it is affirmed that: "It constitutes the point of departure for a national development strategy leading to the transformations necessary to accelerate growth, distribute income, and generate and consolidate internal self-propelling forces, based on achievement of solid national integration assuring the incorporation of Peruvians from all the nation's regions into the benefits of progress" (Instituto Nacional de Planificación, 1968: 3).

4. The content of such proposals appears very clearly in the words of the President of the Venezuelan Republic when he affirms: "I shall never lose sight of the fact that development, to be integral and harmonious, must be regional. The regionalization conscience in Venezuela has accentuated in the past ten years. Study of geographic, political, demographic, economic, and ecological factors defines the regions as units having certain determined characteristics and requirements. One of the first acts of the new government will be to adopt, at least as a provisional criterion, a regionalization standard in

harmony with analyses already made to propel the preparation, creation, and functioning of appropriate organs for development of the respective regions" (Caldera, 1969: 19).

5. In explaining the scope of the new system, the Argentine President declared: "National unity is an undertaking still to be fulfilled, our own great undertaking, which we may synthesize in this way: it is necessary that in every corner of the nation inhabitants have the same opportunities as in any other place in Argentina to achieve full human development, satisfy expectations, work with enthusiasm, and feel incorporated with passion and hope into universal life. We know that today this is not so; there are pockets of light and pockets of shadow, and they do not form an harmonious landscape but rather a discordant structure. Forgotten zones, uninhabited, which the State has not provided with services and stimuli, constitute a challenge to our imagination and are the principal entry in the list of our responsibilities as governing officials" (Secretaría de Estado de Gobierno, 1967: 9).

6. These contrasts have been described by some authors as *regional dichotomies,* for the purpose of contructing and analyzing regional typologies (see, for example, Higgins, 1969).

7. The term *independent* has, particularly in the case of Latin America, a relative sense. Its use may only be justified by the fact that it is the opposite of "dependent." In recent times, the thesis has been gathering momentum that industrialized regions—and the modern sector in general—of certain countries like Brazil, Argentina, Mexico, and Peru may continue to grow indefinitely, relatively speaking, based on their own internal markets.

8. "The patterns of economic growth . . . characterized by a high degree of concentration of technical progress, in some sectors, with very pronounced effects on the structure of productive capacity, income distribution and labor absorption, may also be clearly appreciated in the regional distribution of economic activity. In effect, the marked geographic concentration and the strong disparities between different regions of each country which characterized Latin American economic structures at the end of the nineteen sixties are not unrelated to this scheme of growth. Certain historical antecedents of this problem suggest the existence of circular relationships in that these regional characteristics derive certain characteristics from the development process and tend in turn to reinforce them" (see ECLA, 1969b: 1-87).

9. "In effect, later industrial development modified this locational pattern only to a small degree. The import-substitution industry was oriented principally toward the market for common manufactured consumer goods already in existence in order to exploit the growing consumption demands of urban agglomerations constricted by rigidities in import capacity. Consequently, this industry attempted to install itself near the centers of consumption. At these points an industrial concentration was created which continued to attract new capital and population. Only when the possibilities of import substitution were exhausted were other locations nearer to certain natural resources imposed, but even in these cases administration and often the final stages of transformation continued to be located in traditional poles. To a certain degree, strictly industrial activity came to replace handicraft production which was more aptly suited to regional dispersal. This explains the relative loss of importance of many secondary urban centers located in a wide geographic area. First to be replaced were traditional handicrafts, like textiles, which succumbed to similar fabrics imported at lower price, and, once suppressed or reduced to a folkloric art, their importation was replaced by the domestic production of modern zones. Thus, with heavily-protected industrial development and without great pressure to maximize efficiency and productivity, extra-economic factors, such as the personal advantages of living in the largest urban centers, exerted great influence on locational decisions" (see ECLA, 1969b: 1-89).

10. For example, the great Venezuelan petroleum wealth of Zulia has not provided that region's population with either the necessary social and community services or the required employment. Instead, it financed the modernization, luxurious public works, and the high incomes of Caracas. Analogous is the relationship of Chilean nitrate and copper regions to

the capital, Santiago. The great productive effort of the coffee planters of Brazil's Minas Gerais or Colombia's Caldas did not substantially modify the life of the peasants, but it did permit financing of large urban public works in São Paulo and Bogotá, respectively.

11. For greater development of this topic, see ECLA (1965) and Utria (1969b).

12. In this regard, Luis Vera (1967) states: "An analysis of the social evolution of the Brazilian Northeast leads to the conclusion that, during all stages of its historic development, it was not drought but rather the endemic feudal system which opposed its progress. The great masses of population were considered exclusively labor reservoirs and, consequently, remained on the margin of the existing plantation economy. The continuous absence of a middle class, caused by the lack of social mobility, maintained the gap between élite and oppressed groups and permitted only the dominant minority to prosper and progress."

13. Such is the case with "free ports" and "duty-free industrial zones" which compete with the other regions, awarding exceptional concessions (tax exemptions, subsidized services, custom preferences, and the like). These mechanisms are useful and convenient when they respond to loyalties to the national interest and interregional competition.

REFERENCES

CALDERA, R. (1969) Discurso del Presidente de La República, Dr. Rafael Caldera, En El Acto de toma de Posesión del Cargo. Caracas: Publicación de la Presidencia de la República.

Departamento Nacional de Planeación (1969) "Modelo de regionalización: informe preliminar presentado al Comité Organizador del Seminario sobre Regionalización de la Política del Desarrollo." Document DNP-334-UDRU, Bogotá, September 5.

Economic Commission for Latin America (ECLA) (1969a) "Los aspectos sociales del desarrollo regional en América Latina." Document ST/ECLA/Conf.34/L.1.

— — (1969b) "La Economía de América Latina en 1968." XIII Período de Sesiones, Lima, April.

— — (1969c) "Aspectos básicos de la Estrategia del desarrollo de América Latina." Document E/CN.12/836. XIII Período de Sesiones, Lima.

— — (1965) "La participación popular y el desarrollo de la Comunidad en la Aceleración del desarrollo Económico y social." Boletín Económico de América Latina 9,2.

FRIEDMANN, J. (1969) Políticas Urbanas y Regionales para el desarrollo Nacional en Chile: El desafío de la próxima década. Santiago: Fundación Ford, Programa de Asesoría en Desarrollo Urban y Regional.

FURTADO, C. (1969) La Economía latinoamericana desde la conquista ibérica hasta la Revolución Cubana. Santiago, Chile: Editorial Universitaria.

HIGGINS, B. (1969) The Scope and Objectives of Planning for Underdeveloped Regions. Rio de Janeiro: Comisión de Geografía.

ILPES (1968) "Informe de avance sobre los trabajos para la formulación de una estrategia de desarrollo venezolano en el marco de la integración subregional." Preliminary Report. Caracas, August.

Instituto Nacional de Planificación (1968) "Estrategia del desarrollo nacional a largo plazo: resumen." November, Lima.

MATUS, C. (1969) "El espacio físico en la política de desarrollo." Reference Document 21, Seminario sobre Aspectos Sociales del Desarrollo Regional. November, Santiago: ECLA.

NEIRA ALVA, E. (1969) "La regionalización de las políticas de desarrollo en América Latina." Reference document 7, Seminario sobre Aspectos Sociales del Desarrollo Regional. Santiago: ECLA.

ODEPLAN (Oficina de Planificación Nacional) (1968) Política de desarrollo Nacional: Directivas Nacionales y Regionales. Santiago: Presidencia de la República.

Secretaría de Estado de Gobierno (1967) Dirección General de Provincias. Regionalización: Instrumento operativo del cambio. Buenos Aires.

STAVENHAGEN, R. (1969) "Seven erroneous theories about Latin America," in I. L. Horowitz et al. (eds.) Latin American Radicalism. New York: Vintage.

STOHR, W. (1969) "Regional development in Latin America: experience and prospects." Presented to the Seminario sobre Aspectos Sociales del Desarrollo. November, Santiago: ECLA.

UTRIA, R. D. (1969a) "La naturaleza social del desarrollo y sus implicaciones en la política social a nivel regional." Geneva: Instituto de Investigaciones de las Naciones Unidas para el Desarrollo Social.

— — (1969b) Desarrollo Nacional, participación popular y desarrollo de la comunidad en América Latina. Pátzcuaro, Mexico: Ediciones del CREFAL, UNESCO.

VERA, L. (1967) "El proceso de desarrollo regional en el Nordeste de Brazil." Primer Seminario sobre Definición de Regiones paro la Planificación del Desarrollo, Hamilton, Canada.

ZIOLKOWSKI, J. A. (1969) "Problemas metodológicos en la sociología del desarrollo regional." Document UNRISD/69/C.2, GE69-11 1. Geneva: Instituto de Investigaciones de las Naciones Unidas para el Desarrollo Social.

Chapter 4

REGIONAL POLICY
THE INTEGRATION OF SPACE IN LATIN AMERICA

ENRIQUE RUBEN MELCHIOR

THE CONCENTRATION OF ECONOMIC ACTIVITY

Latin America as a whole constitutes vast, poorly integrated multinational space. The situation is rooted in the characteristics of Latin American nations' historical growth processes, based on the dynamics of external demand for primary products. The production structure derived from this process gave rise to export nuclei, which constituted large reception centers for the exogenous influences of the growth of the economies. The transportation and communications infrastructure has developed in turn so as to improve the access for primary products to the port of export.

After the Depression of 1929, a majority of countries experienced a decline in exogenous growth impulses, reflected in relative stagnation of exports or deterioration in their purchasing power. These circumstances gave rise to industrialization oriented toward import-substitution. In general, there was a tendency to locate such industries in the thriving regions within each national space, concentrating in or near the traditional export nucleus.

Industrial location gravitates, of course, to these areas to take advantage of external economies existing within the privileged region due to greater development of the region's infrastructure, and because of the relative concentration of consuming population with greater purchasing power. The nature of industrial activities established (in general, in a first stage, consumer goods industries) favors closeness to the market. An appreciable proportion of imported, intermediate goods (chemical, metallurgical, and so on) are used here so that the port of export also becomes the most important source of essential industry inputs. The need to import capital goods, due to internal insufficiency

Editor's Note: English translation by Alejandro Vélez Gómez.

of basic industries, reinforces the port's importance. Thus, from the beginning, decisive gravitational force over location of Latin American industry was exercised by the export nucleus in three ways: as a consumption center, as a center for supply of imported essential inputs, and as a center for economic activities capable of generating economies of scale.

Under the conditions, the Weberian scheme of industrial location has clearly been fulfilled. The relevant vectors of locational polygons in Latin America lie in great proportion outside its political limits, giving rise to locational configurations largely outside its geographic space. The only significant vectors within Latin American space are formed by consumption centers coinciding with urban agglomerations surrounding export nuclei.

The production of intermediate and capital goods has increased the process of concentration in already industrialized areas. In some cases, these industrial concentrations occurred along industrialized strips, in order to avoid the problems accompanying excessive concentration in cities not designed for such functions. This is the case with the expansion of Buenos Aires toward La Plata and Santa Fe on the Argentine coast, the strip uniting São Paulo with Rio de Janeiro and the stretch linking Caracas, Maracay, and Valencia. These "lineal" expansions of industrial nuclei do not constitute examples of regional decentralization. Industrial activity continues to concentrate in a few nuclei in already predominant regions of each country. There are, however, important steps taking place toward greater regional articulation in Córdoba, Argentina, Concepción, Chile, and Guayana, Venezuela.

One of the most important consequences of the process of industrialization in Latin America is the rapid growth of urban population, which now represents about 50 percent of Latin America's total population.[1] Four Latin American countries demonstrate the highest rates: between 1950-1960, urban population in Venezuela, Brazil, Guatemala, and Colombia increased 87, 74, 70, and 69 percent, respectively. Countries such as Argentina, Chile, and Uruguay also show high "macrocephalic" indices (Dorfman, 1967: 259). This accelerated urbanization process is due to the gravitational pull of industrial nuclei, especially over the most highly qualified human resources; expectations nurtured by such industrial centers regarding the possibility of better-paying jobs, better living conditions, greater opportunities for social mobility, access to higher cultural levels, and the freeing of labor from the primary sector, particularly agriculture. There is thus a shift of human resources from the countryside and smaller cities to the large, important ones.

These shifts are connected to one of the basic characteristics of Latin American underdevelopment: structural unemployment in the labor force which cannot be absorbed by the productive apparatus. To make matters worse, year after year, new groups are incorporated into the labor force. There are, however, mechanisms through which this gap may be closed. One is absorption by the public sector, giving rise to a margin of hidden unemployment and making more rigid the portion of governmental budgets devoted to current expenditures. The other is employment of part of the labor surplus in unproductive jobs and services. These mechanisms are insufficient to resolve the problem and are irrational allocation of resources.

To these mechanisms are added the internal migratory movements from depressed regions to industrial centers in each country. In a first stage of industrialization, based upon labor-intensive activities, these centers performed their roles effectively as absorbers of surplus labor, but at the same time drained the human resources of the rest of the regional system. After this first cycle of expansion was over, the industrial nuclei's gravitational pull over human resources tended to diminish. However, since labor force continues to be freed from primary activities and the expectations associated with industrial nuclei continue to exist, although with lesser intensity, the migratory flow toward urban centers persists. Consequently, the industrial nuclei are converted into importers of a portion of the structurally unemployed.

Structural unemployment not only constitutes one of the outstanding characteristics of Latin America's underdevelopment, but is also one of its more serious short-term problems. Solution to this problem cannot be achieved without altering the mechanisms through which the labor surplus is allocated. Insufficient internal saving and the slight rate of capital formation, the principal obstacles to Latin American development, are also due to these deficiencies.

The location of economic activity in Latin America is influenced by the network of existing locations causing the prevalence of static locational criteria. These criteria are based on considerations of an existing market, distribution and endowment of resources, and the transport and communication infrastructure. Regional inequalities tend to be accentuated in cumulative form, both within a particular country and within Latin American space in general.

A community's decision to interfere in the behavior of the system in order to achieve a different structural and spatial configuration leads instead to consideration of dynamic locational criteria. In this way, certain magnitudes previously considered as givens now become variables. The decision to introduce changes in the productive structure leads to modification in the rules and composition of demand. Therefore, demand projections based on parameters of historical behavior should give way to consideration of potential demand. The degree of compatibility of both static and dynamic criteria will depend on the state of economic integration. The more regionally disarticulated the economy, and the greater the inadequacy of its spatial configuration in relation to the requirements of economic development, the greater will be the incompatibility of these two criteria.

INADEQUACY OF INFRASTRUCTURE

In a process in which changes in the productive structure establish the prerequisite of a restructuring of space, the infrastructure network of transportation and communications ceases to be a given and is converted into a variable of singular importance. Its modification will be essential to transformation of the system's spatial configuration.

One of the outstanding characteristics of Latin American space is the unequal evolution of transportation networks. This is a consequence of the form followed by historical growth oriented toward the external market, and of concentration of economic activity in a few important nuclei. The transportation infrastructure has generally evolved radially, converging on exporting nuclei, to such an extent that only certain zones of each country have benefited. These are usually those tied to export activities. The rest of the regional system has remained marginal to this exogenous economic growth.

Import-substitution industrialization aggravated the problem of economic concentration, giving rise to growing disparities between regions and, at the same time, between countries. In spite of attempts to launch an endogenous development process, Latin America's polarized structure continues to show characteristics similar to those of the earlier, so-called "outward-directed growth" stage. A study of Latin American transportation (ECLA, 1965: 7) notes that:

> even though expansion of transportation networks has partially modified the general picture, the network as a whole continues to be, to a great extent, complementary to axes of ocean transport uniting Latin America and the large centers of the world economy.

This orientation of Latin American infrastructure has created a drain of human and financial resources to the benefit of dominant national nuclei, depressing peripheral regions and zones even more. It is these regions which form the political borders separating the Latin American nations among themselves. Thus overland communications among them are scarce, and Latin America appears as a complex of national space more closely tied to exogenous decision-making centers than to itself. Commercial relations are more intense with countries outside Latin America than with those within. These characteristics of the evolution of Latin America's economy and infrastructure have also given rise to the formation of empty areas, like Patagonia in Argentina, and depressed areas, like the Brazilian Northeast or the Argentine Northwest.

Regarding the railroad network, not only are there problems of orientation but also of unequal distribution through Latin American space. Three-fourths of Latin America's railroads are in Argentina, Brazil, and Mexico. Within these countries, railroads are concentrated in a few states or provinces (São Paulo and Rio de Janeiro in Brazil, and Buenos Aires and Santa Fe in Argentina). Mexico is an exception. Here railroads are more uniformly distributed among the different states. Another problem of basic importance is the railroads' high degree of obsolescence.[2] Obsolescence appears in varying degree in the different countries, with exceptions like Mexico, which in the postwar period has been modernizing its lines. In addition, certain countries like Colombia, Chile, and Brazil have begun vast programs of improvements in their railroad networks.

Similarly, highway networks in Latin America show considerable disparity in geographic distribution, notably at the national level. Within each country, the highway network is particularly concentrated in the most developed regions, serving to magnify the polarizing effects of existing nuclei. Statistics reveal that Latin American highway density indicators are the most unfavorable. In 1962, Latin America had only 4.6 kilometers of paved roads per 1,000 square kilometers, as compared with 3.0 for Africa, 15.6 for Asia and the Middle East, 15.8 for Oceania, and 27.3 for the world[3] as a whole (ECLA/CEPAL, 1965: 37). With respect to permanent, all-weather roads, the comparison is equally unfavorable. Latin America had 21 kilometers per 1,000 square kilometers, while the world as a whole had 130 kilometers, or 2 kilometers per 1,000 inhabitants, as compared to 6.3 kilometers for the world as a whole (ECLA/CEPAL, 1965: 37). Some steps are being taken, however, to improve highway infrastructure. One is completion of a Pan-American highway system, which by 1963 covered 45,658 kilometers, 92 percent of which was permanent road. Important interconnecting road projects have recently been undertaken by neighboring countries, Argentina-Chile, Colombia-Venezuela, Colombia-Ecuador, and Brazil-Uruguay, and the rapid development of the highway network in Central America is outstanding (ECLA/CEPAL, 1965: 41). Two other projects of great breadth will also contribute to change in the configuration of Latin America's infrastructure: the jungle peripheral road *(carretera marginal de la selva)*, stretching 6,500 kilometers from Puerto Carreño to Corumbá and uniting peripheral regions of Colombia, Ecuador, Peru, and Bolivia; and the East-West Highway *(carretera transversal panamericana)* linking Brazil, Paraguay, Bolivia, and Peru. Yet, in spite of the rapid expansion of Latin America's road system since World War II, its deficiencies in terms of low density and uneven geographic distribution persist.

Although South America possesses two of the world's largest international river systems—the Río de la Plata and the Amazon, with their respective tributaries—river navigation has not attained its proper importance, given the size of its navigable resources and their potential for exploitation. The communications infrastructure has similar characteristics. An eloquent indication is the fact that people in Latin American countries make more than three times as many telephone calls to the United States as to other Latin American countries.[4] Geographic distribution of telecommunications is very uneven. There is a low degree of interconnection among the Latin American countries, except in the case of neighboring countries in which there is more intense traffic, particularly the southernmost countries (Argentina-Uruguay, Chile-Argentina, Paraguay-Argentina, and Brazil-Uruguay). Communications between Uruguay and Argentina amount to more than 70 percent of all communications among the Latin American countries. If communications between Chile and Argentina are added, this figure rises to more than 80 percent. Thus, with the exception of Argentina, Bolivia, Chile, Paraguay, and Uruguay, which have relatively intense communications between neighboring countries, the remaining Latin American countries maintain more communications with the United States than with the rest of Latin America. Outstanding is the case of Mexico, bordering the United States, whose communications with the United States are 100 times greater than those with the rest of Latin America, and, in turn, represent 85 percent of the

United States' communications with Latin America. Similar disequilibria occur within the Latin American countries. The most intense traffic takes place in the few dominant centers of each country. In addition, a high degree of obsolescence characterizes the communications infrastructure in Latin America.[5]

The characteristics paramount in this summary of Latin America's transport and communication are their relatively sparse density, uneven geographic distribution, low quality, and obsolescence. Given these characteristics, Latin American infrastructure is converted into an important factor in the disintegration of Latin American space.

THE PROBLEM OF LOCATIONAL INERTIA

Excessive concentration of economic activity in a few important nuclei and allocation of insufficient and inadequate infrastructure interact, in cumulative fashion, to cause consolidation of existing nuclei and their respective areas of influence within Latin American space and even within component national space. Nevertheless, as the process of industrialization advances, new relocation problems arise, making the ordering and organization of space into a dynamic problem. New techniques are discovered through an accelerated process of technological development, and, consequently, locational criteria tend to be modified. However, as Isard (1956) has noted, historical inertia exerts resistance over this dynamic process, contributing to the persistence of existing spatial configurations. This locational inertia may lead to the same locations which would arise through consideration of technical or economic factors. Yet, on the other hand, locational inertia reinforces the cumulative development of existing locations in such a way that unsuitable places may be chosen because of the influence of the network of existing locations (Ponsard, 1954).

This problem creates the need to introduce modifications in traditional techniques of project evaluation, above all in the case of disarticulated national or multinational space. What is needed is to move from individual analysis, project by project, to joint evaluation of a group of projects concerned with highly interrelated activities. For instance, individual analysis of an important project such as a hydroelectric dam or a petrochemical plant could, if considered in isolation, lead to unfavorable conclusions regarding location of such project or activity in a depressed area, favoring its location in relatively more advanced zones, especially where there is already an existing network of locations. Yet, if this evaluation were made through joint consideration of projects concerned with highly interrelated activities, then the conclusions drawn from individual analysis might be reversed.[6] A criterion of individual yield does not lead to a social optimum in economies in which the price mechanism does not operate effectively as an optimum allocator of resources. Similarly, in disarticulated economies, traditional locational criteria do not function effectively as mechanisms for the spatial allocation of resources. From the point of view of individual yield, the cost of "relocation" may appear greater than the advantages, due to the fact that the price system does not reflect the endowment of existing resources or their underutilization.

The inefficacy of both the price mechanism and traditional locational norms establishes the need for a reallocation of resources not only sectorally, but also spatially. This action is intimately related to transformation of the productive structure as well as modification of the spatial configuration, two fundamental aspects of what has been called, from the economic point of view, "structural change."

NATURAL RESOURCES

The influence of the importation of essential inputs (such as metallurgical and chemical) on the behavior of the location of Latin American industry has previously been noted. Importation has favored the relatively limited number of nuclei already in existence, especially the export centers. This situation has been a consequence of the paucity of basic industries in Latin America, whose development constitutes one of the pillars of Latin America's economic progress.

Exploration of natural resources is thus essential to new patterns of development. Latin America possesses 28 percent of known and suspected iron-ore deposits; its potential holdings may raise this to 41 percent. Moreover, Latin America has 22 percent of the world's bauxite, 35 percent of the copper, 10 percent of the lead, and 15 percent of the zinc. Indicators reflecting the importance of Latin America's mineral reserves must be interpreted in light of the inadequate prospecting and exploration which characterize estimates of its mineral wealth.[7] This shortcoming opens the possibility of greater availability of such resources as mineral prospecting and exploration improve. These advances would permit a more solid supply base for Latin America's industrial development.

Even though Latin America is endowed with vast natural resources, these resources are very unevenly distributed from a regional point of view. For example, Brazil at present holds two-thirds of Latin America's iron and manganese reserves; Chile has three-fourths of the copper reserves; Mexico owns more than half the zinc and lead; Bolivia, most of the tin; and Venezuela, more than 70 percent of the petroleum (Herrera, 1965). Nevertheless, regional supply of these resources could meet the needs arising as the result of creation of new dynamic nuclei or development poles within a scheme of articulation of Latin American space. In this way, certain minerals whose exploitation is destined to nourish development of great extrazonal industrialized centers could be shifted to creation of new Latin American industrial centers. This would introduce efficacious stimuli to the process of integration which Latin America has decided to follow.

The importance of energy resources must be mentioned, particularly hydroelectric potential. The report of the Latin American Seminar on Electric

Energy held in Mexico City in 1961, and published by the United Nations (1962: 488) affirms that Latin America could count on more than 22 percent of the world's hydroelectric potential. Its hydroelectric resources are equal to those of Europe (including the Soviet Union) and those of the United States. These resources are, however, unevenly distributed geographically. It was estimated in 1960 that 70 percent of Latin America's economically exploitable hydroelectric potential was concentrated in four countries: Colombia, Brazil, Chile, and Venezuela. Only 4.5 percent is being exploited by the region as a whole.

Together with hydroelectric energy, the possibilities of nuclear energy should also be considered. By February 1966, there were 46 nuclear energy plants in the world with an installed capacity of 5,700 milliwatts, and 44 plants under construction with a potential capacity of 17,700 milliwatts. One of the most important endeavors upon which Latin America should embark is exploration for reserves of nuclear materials,[8] a task still not adequately undertaken. With respect to the energy sector's role in the process of Latin American development, it is fitting to quote J. M. Martin's (1967: 153) observations.

> Attempt can be made, from the first moment, to construct the energy sector as an industrializing sector, that is, as a sector which itself creates part of its own markets as a function of general industrialization objectives, without yielding to the requirements of the existing market, a notoriously bad guide, especially in economies dominated from abroad and poorly integrated nationally. From this perspective, the region attempts to maximize the benefits from articulation and propagation of its energy centers.

In spite of Latin America's relative dearth of knowledge of its own natural resources, it is undeniable that these resources, even at present levels of prospecting, constitute one of the most relevant factors in the process of Latin American integration, based on industrialization and regional articulation of the multinational space under consideration. Exploitation of these natural resources can serve as a way to guide Latin America toward eliminating structural unemployment, foreign dependence, and the disarticulation characterizing its space.

In accordance with the characteristics of component national space, Latin America may be defined as a grouping of polarized regions in which a few dynamic centers and their respective areas of influence are truly privileged areas, and in which the greater part of economic activities is concentrated. These privileged zones also drain resources away from the rest of the regional systems. Thus, global indicators of the economic situation in the different Latin American countries represent, essentially, the condition of the economic structure of each country. Disguised by these global indicators is the reality of vast, depressed, empty regions, completing the physical configuration of each national space. Economic policy decisions have been oriented traditionally toward solution of immediate problems affecting prevailing economic structures in the most advanced areas. In this way, peripheral regions in many Latin American countries are taken into account only as a function of this orientation, and not to the end of assuming a role of relative importance in the process of national development, or in participating in its benefits.

Within this orientation of economic policy in favor of dominant areas, one may conceive of present-day Latin American space as a set of planning regions in which, instead of conciliation of interests of component zones of each national space, there is real subordination of the empty or depressed peripheral zones to the interests of developed areas in each country. In general, the polarized structure of Latin American space is the prolongation of a far more significant polarization proceeding from large foreign industrialized centers. The planning regions making up Latin American space form part of a planning region of major importance in which foreign decision centers are prevalent. These characteristics, sharpened by Latin America's growth patterns, have resulted in notable disconnection of the Latin American economies and have become important disintegrating factors.

INTERNATIONAL ECONOMIC INTEGRATION AND ECONOMIC SPACE

From the point of view of spatial articulation, international economic integration constitutes a problem in modification of the spatial configuration of a multinational region, and creation of new spatial relationships and new development poles, for the purpose of achieving communitarian objectives impossible to attain within individual national space considered in isolation. It is for this reason that Erbes (1966) conceives international economic integration, not in terms of abolishing national borders, but, following Myrdal's (1958) concept of integration, as "a widening of the community of interests." In accordance with Christaller's (see Ponsard, 1954) theoretical scheme, a hierarchy of economic functions is established, which as the functions increase in importance, requires larger cities as well as an expanding hinterland or field of action. Applying this functional analysis to current spatial distribution, we find that numerous national spaces are not in a position to offer a hinterland with the dimensions compatible with the highest-priority functions required by the present era. Thus, in many cases, such economic size will only be attained through integration of these national spaces into a multinational space. Integration becomes the only mechanism by which diverse nations may gain access to the most relevant functions, and, therefore, to a more preponderant relative position in the field of international relations.

This functional scheme acquires unsuspected importance when we consider that economic progress is closely linked to scientific and technological progress in an interaction we can consider cumulative. Scientific and technical knowledge constitutes an increasing share of the price of goods and services produced by the community. Scientific and technological research becomes one of the highest priority functions of a particular system and requires great economic size for development. For this reason, such functions can only be carried out by a few countries of great economic size, or, in other words, by economic spaces not only of large proportions geographically, but economically. Other countries find themselves, to a greater or lesser degree, in a dependent relationship with them. The advance of technological progress makes the differences between these two kinds of countries increasingly great.

There are, therefore, two alternatives open to least-favored countries: (1) renunciation of the possibility of having a decision center permitting access to performance of highest-order functions and either seeking to attain the greatest possible advantages within their dependent relationship or trying to attenuate their drawbacks; or (2) integrating their national spaces into a multinational region for the purpose of participating in a large center of joint decision-making, inaccessible at the national level, through which they can perform highest-order functions and jointly improve their relative position on the international scale.

TWO ALTERNATIVES FOR INTEGRATION OF LATIN AMERICAN SPACE

Policies of regional development, within national or multinational space, are an essential requirement for integration policies. Regional disarticulation and foreign dependence are two basic characteristics of underdeveloped economies. Economic integration of a multinational space whose national spaces present the above-mentioned characteristics should be analyzed in light of two distinct alternatives offering sharply different results as much for multinational as for component national space:

Spontaneous Integration

One approach is to encompass the process of integration within the framework of what may be called the spontaneous behavior of economic forces acting on multinational space. Integration implies, in this case, articulation of national space through a greater and more efficient interrelationship of prevailing structures within each national space—that is, greater and more efficient interconnection among dominant regions within each nation. The dominant regions in each country will tend to "draw near" in economic terms by means of greater development of the transportation and communications infrastructure. In turn, an improved information network will make possible greater functional integration of the predominant structures, contributing, too, to improvement in infrastructure and elimination of trade barriers.

Interrelating the regions prevailing within each national space implies the formulation of a development policy for infrastructures interconnecting the dominant poles. This process will cause widening of the disparities existing between developed and depressed regions in each national space, and, in addition, a tendency toward sharpening the inequalities between more and less advanced countries within the multinational space under consideration.

Dominant poles within each country will see a strengthening of their decision-making power and command over the respective national spaces over which they exert their polarizing action. Ascendancy of highest-order poles will take place at the expense of less-important ones, establishing greater dependency in favor of the most-developed countries, which also contain the highest-order poles. Even in the European case, the consequences of spontaneous integration may be foreseen. Erbes (1966) notes that in the concrete case of European integration there are many reasons to fear reinforcement of regional disparities. All polarized structures propagate from their poles and in accordance with their rank what Barre (1964) has called propelling and retarding development of effects. To the extent that a great degree of disarticulation or regional differences exist, retarding influences would tend to be superior to propelling ones. This disequilibrium of forces is always prejudicial to depressed or peripheral regions.

Retarding developmental factors are reinforced in depressed regions due to the existence of a little-diversified industrial structure whose sectors are weakly interrelated. This reflects the nonexistence of development poles within these regions, that is, the lack of motive industries. In the most advanced regions, the agglomeration mechanism tends to act cumulatively around development poles due principally to existence of motive industries. Within this method of growth and integration, the mechanisms of trade liberalization will result in intensification of the flow of goods to the most-advanced areas within the multinational space being integrated. Greater mobility of capital will mean that its flows will also basically be directed to most-advanced regions. As obstacles to migratory flows within multinational space are eliminated, displacements of human resources will tend to favor existing urban nuclei in the most-developed zones. In the case of economies with great regional disarticulation, this complex of polarization effects will mean a real drain of the human and financial resources of peripheral or depressed areas to the most-developed regions.

Erbes (1966: 95) has expressed his skepticism over policies by the European Six to correct regional disparities in their countries. "Almost nothing," he writes, "can be expected from these national policies, except minor corrections in interregional disequilibria resulting from development of the Common Market." If these problems have occurred in the integration process of nations experiencing a relatively high degree of development, as is the European case, it is reasonable to infer that they will be even more severe in the process of integrating disarticulated national space with a much lower degree of development, as occurs in Latin America.

Integration as an Instrument of Structural Change

The process and pattern of integration must be analyzed and evaluated as it relates to the mutual objective of the self-sustained development of the national spaces whose integration is sought. When integration is converted into a fundamental requisite for self-sustained development of participating countries, integration is elevated to the category of a communitarian objective. On the other hand, conceived as a solution to the problem of underdevelopment, it should be formulated in a manner compatible with the structural nature of this underdevelopment.

Economic integration can become an effective instrument of structural change when profound disarticulation of national space and growing regional inequalities have ceased to be a mere matter of adjustment or regional reequilibrium, as in the European case, and have become instead fundamental obstacles to the development process. There should be consensus in the multinational community regarding the adoption of decisions of a structural nature; establishment of free-trade zones and customs unions, as well as coordination of monetary and fiscal policies, do not alone lead to solving the problem of underdevelopment, which is essentially structural.

Joint decisions should have a much more widespread effect and should imply a certain degree of mutual interference in the spontaneous behavior of economic units acting in multinational space, so as to achieve reallocation, sectoral and spatial, of resources. Transformation of the multinational area's spatial configuration into a mechanism capable of originating a process of structural change assuring initiation of a development process, becomes, in this case, an intrinsic objective of economic integration.

INTEGRATION AND CHANGE IN REGIONAL STRUCTURE

The characteristics of Latin American space and the structural nature of its problems make necessary careful selection of the goals to be achieved through integration, and the pattern which this process of integration should follow. Economic integration should be oriented toward solving problems such as structural unemployment, foreign dependence deriving from attachment to foreign markets, foreign supply of essential inputs, direct foreign investment, and technological and regional disarticulation. Finally, an integration project should consider distributive problems, both among the social sectors of participating countries and among participating countries themselves.

The decision of a group of underdeveloped countries to integrate makes sense when the objective sought is to begin a process of sustained and *independent* development. Formulation of this goal implies advance recognition that its attainment will not be achieved solely by means of the spontaneous behavior of the different national economies. Participating countries must recognize that such a goal cannot be achieved in isolation from the level of possibilities of each national economy. Given that the structural and spatial configuration of Latin America presents great disparities among component national space, mechanisms tending only to favor spontaneous, more rational, and efficient behavior of the economic units involved will aggravate such disequilibria to the detriment of less-developed or more-depressed national economies.

It should be clear, then, that change in Latin America's spatial configuration is being advocated as an intrinsic part of the integration process. Latin America's regional structure, developed as a function of the growth of national economies, based on the strong pressure of exogenous impulses, is wanting in the face of the requirements of a process of industrialization which should be based on the creation of new endogenous impulses.

The location of economic activity, oriented toward minimizing transportation costs, cannot be based, under this new scheme, upon a transportation and communications infrastructure designed to maximize the efficiency of traditional export activity. On the contrary, the transportation and communications infrastructure should be reoriented in accordance with the need to interconnect new industrial nuclei or development poles, the motive factors of change in the productive structure and in the Latin American spatial configuration. Orientation of the labor factor cannot depend upon the supply of labor; rather, it will be necessary to permit spatial labor mobility and to consider a change in the direction of migratory flows as a function of new foci of attraction, given the decision to create new dynamic nuclei assuring a growing degree of regional integration of Latin American space. Finally, orientation toward economies of scale cannot be based upon the network of existing locations. Introduction of new industrial complexes as a function of energy and mineral resources, whose locations differ from those of the traditional export nuclei, will generate new economies of scale, strengthening the relative importance of new development poles as adequate channels of communication are established.

It is necessary, however, to clarify further the concept and content of economic integration as a mechanism for the structural transformation which Latin America's development requires. It is evident that, within Latin American space, there is a series of dynamic nuclei with wide differences in rank. Differences existing among these dominant poles result in equally marked differences in the level of development achieved by the respective countries. The interconnection of existing poles (equivalent to integration of prevailing structures in the different countries) will lead to aggravating the above-mentioned inequalities. When poles of similar rank are put in touch, a fertile interrelation is produced among them, as well as among their respective areas of influence. In this way, real integration among these zones forms what might be called an area of economic integration. When such areas lie within one country's national borders, the process is one of regional integration; when such areas belong to different countries, then the process is one of multinational integration, which will require, in addition, application of complementary measures tending to facilitate more fluid displacement of goods and factors among such nations.

If two poles of differing rank interrelate, a dependent relationship of the weaker pole to the stronger pole will inevitably result. Integration will not be fertile. It will consist of incorporation of the weaker's area of influence into that of the stronger. The greatest polarization effects originating in the more dynamic pole become suction effects on the weaker pole's resources and area of influence. There will be, consequently, a domination effect, conscious or unconscious.[9] If the respective areas of influence are found within a single national space, one area or region will prevail over others. If different countries are concerned, broadening of the inequalities existing between both countries will take place.

CONCLUSION

Certain conditions must thus be present for true integration. In order for integration to serve as an instrument for structural transformation within a multinational space to be integrated, it is necessary that the nations involved have a complex of regions serving as adequate hinterland over which existing development poles of similar rank exercise their influence. In some cases, the creation of new poles within Latin American space could be directed toward exploitation of energy and mineral resources, permitting resurgence of depressed or uninhabited zones, which, because of availability of these resources, could then play a leading role in the Latin American development process.

The process of integration as thus conceived signifies the creation of new spatial relationships. Consequently, a new Latin American spatial configuration will emerge, whose articulation will require new public works in transportation and communications infrastructure. No longer will these public works respond to present demand for infrastructure influenced by the polarization effects of dominant nuclei, but will be programmed and evaluated in accordance with the future configuration of a new, integrated Latin American space.

Yet this process cannot take place within a scheme of spontaneous behavior of economic forces. Joint action by national decision-making centers is required for gaining access to the most relevant and highest-order functions within the multinational space to be integrated—functions that, because of their magnitude, could not be performed by individual participating nations acting in isolation. Perhaps the most important of these functions today is that of scientific and technical research, which would permit creation of Latin America's own technology, and more efficient and rational exploitation of Latin America's own resources. This would also offer the possibility of removal of one of the fundamental characteristics of underdevelopment—foreign dependence, rooted in ignorance.

It must be made explicit that the process of integration, given its structural approach, affects "all" of Latin American space. Not only decisions to integrate two different countries are to be considered acts of integration, but also those national decisions tending to promote depressed or empty regions to the extent they are conceived for the purpose of creating new multinational areas of integration. The essential requisite here is that coordination of regional policies of the different countries exist, within the framework of transformation of multinational space.

Thus, for example, development of the Brazilian Northeast,[10] even though it is a national decision, will contribute effectively to articulation and integration of Latin American space. Analogous results will be produced by integration of two or more depressed regions in different countries, as well as of depressed regions and extremely underdeveloped countries which are themselves depressed national spaces.

NOTES

1. Dorfman (1967: 261) cites the fact that urban population grew annually by 3.5 percent between 1935 and 1945, and by 5 percent annually between 1955-1965, while rural population has grown annually by 1.5 percent.

2. The ECLA study (1965: 25) concluded that, "to synthesize in one sentence the most common condition of Latin America's railroads, as a whole they are obsolete, with old, light-weight rails, badly ballasted railroad beds, railroad ties in poor condition and generally deficiently maintained."

3. Excludes mainland China, the Soviet Union, and a few small countries.

4. See the interesting table in Calcagni (1967: 17) showing telephone traffic in minutes per day for 1964.

5. As Calcagni (1967: 20) notes: "Latin America's telecommunications system, both internal and the links one with another, is weak, and inadequate for the needs of an integrated Latin America. It may also be added . . . that it is the unanimous opinion of Latin American telecommunications engineers that, in general, the systems being used are, in addition to their other limitations, antiquated, inorganic, and anti-economic."

6. Isard et al. (1966) describe an interesting study of the location of industrial complexes, referring to petroleum refining, petrochemicals, and synthetic fibers in Puerto Rico.

7. Herrera (1965: 19) notes that "the figures with which the mineral wealth of a region is described, whether tons in reserve or potential deposits, do not reflect only physical reality; they also reflect, and at times to a greater extent, the degree of knowledge of this reality."

8. Martin (1967: 147) notes that, "in spite of their present weakness, reserves of materials suitable for use as nuclear fuels should not be an obstacle to development of this new form of energy. While exploration has not yet been begun in the bulk of the Latin-American countries, it is already known that Chile has reserves of some importance, Colombia has high-grade uranium and Brazil has available great quantities of thorium. Moreover, Argentina, a country which has made a special exploration effort, has discovered appreciable quantities of uranium."

9. For additional information regarding the domination concept, see Perroux (1964).

10. See the essay by Eduardo Neira Alva in this volume.

REFERENCES

BARRE, R. (1964) El desarrollo económico. Mexico: Fondo de Cultura Económica.

CALCAGNI P., H. (1967) "Integración de las telecomunicaciones en América Latina." Buenos Aires: Instituto para la Integración de América Latina (INTAL) (Cur. 4/dt.3) November.

DORFMAN, A. (1967) La industrialización en la América Latina y las políticas de fomento. Mexico: Fondo de Cultura Económica.

Economic Commission for Latin America (ECLA/CEPAL) (1965) "El transporte en América Latina." United Nations E/CN.12/703. Volume I.

ERBES, R. (1966) L'integration économique internationale. Paris: P.U.F.

HERRERA, A. O. (1965) Los recursos minerales de América Latina. Buenos Aires: Editorial Universitaria de Buenos Aires (EUDEBA).

ISARD, W. (1956) Location and space economy. Cambridge, Mass.: MIT Press.

— — E. SCHOOLER, and T. VIETORISZ (1966) Estudio regional de complejos industriales. Mexico.

MARTIN, J. M. (1967) "La política regional en el sector energético." Revista de la Integración (Banco Interamericano de Desarrollo-INTAL) (Buenos Aires) 1 (November).

MYRDAL, G. (1958) Une économie internationale. Paris: P.U.F.

PERROUX, F. (1964) La economía del siglo XX. Barcelona: ARIEL.

PONSARD, C. (1954) Economie et espace. Paris: SEDES.

TOSCHI, M. U. (1947) "Localization des industries et inertie." L'actualité économique et financial a l'étranger, April.

United Nations (1962) Estudios sobre la electricidad en América Latina. Volume I. New York.

Chapter 5

REGIONAL POLICY
DEVELOPMENT POLES AND RURAL MARGINALITY
IN BRAZIL: TOWARD A DEFINITION OF
REGIONAL POLICY

IVO BABAROVIC

This essay defines the conceptual framework and methodology with which to approach the problem of rural marginality in countries with strong interregional socioeconomic disparities. Special reference is made to Brazil. Applied to the Brazilian case, this methodology has led to results which may contribute to deeper understanding of the spatial structure of that country, and of the processes and conditions for integration of the country's marginated rural population into the national economy and into the benefits of development. The results and conclusions of this analysis have not yet been published, nor are they included herein as they are still subject to discussion and revision. Nonetheless, it has been considered of interest to present in this article an outline of the conceptual and methodological basis of the study.

Effects of Geographic Concentration of Development

As is well known, the process of economic and social development has been historically characterized, at a global level as well as at the level of individual countries, by strong geographic concentration of this development, a phenom-

Author's Note: The author alone is responsible for the points of view expressed in this essay. They are not necessarily shared by the Instituto de Planejamento Econômico e Social (IPEA), the Brazilian government agency for whom he undertook the study, or by the Bureau of Technical Assistance Operations of the United Nations, which sponsored his mission to Brazil. English translation by Alejandro Vélez Gómez.

enon due to the polarizing and centralizing forces which accompany this process. At the national level, it has been observed, furthermore, that this spatial concentration of development has assumed more acute forms in countries in which industrialization had a late start—that is, in the so-called developing countries. In these, the effects of this tendency are valued positively in the first stages of the process, being related to the utilization of external economies as well as economies of scale linked to the concentration of economic activity and population in large urban centers. In addition, there is the modernizing and unifying effect which these metropolitan centers often have over traditional societies still loosely integrated in the national state.

Generally speaking, given the locational requirements and the increasing economies of scale of the more modern and dynamic branches of industry, this geographic concentration is self-reinforcing. In developing countries, especially, it assumes increasingly more marked proportions as the country reaches more advanced stages of industrialization, entering what has been called the "transitional phase" (Friedmann, 1966: 7)[1] to a developed industrial economy.

Thus, in this phase, the spatial structure of the country is characterized by a marked duality between a so-called "center" or "national development pole," which concentrates more and more of the resources and propulsive activities of the economy at the expense of the "periphery," which includes those regions least favored or more impaired by this process. The extreme polarization characteristic of this phase implies the emergence of strong interregional disequilibria which have economic, social, and political repercussions.

In theory, and as the process of industrialization proceeds and the economy enters the so-called "industrial phase,"[2] the development process should begin to manifest a certain "diffusion effect" which would slowly bring about an increasing dynamization of the "periphery," its more effective incorporation into the national economy, and greater integration of national space (Friedmann, 1966: 35-37).[3] However, the general experience of presently more developed countries indicates that spatial diffusion of development and this eventual incorporation of the "periphery" occur at a very slow pace and are generally limited to territories more immediate to the "center." Countries like France and Italy, for example, whose economies are clearly in the "industrial phase," still have important peripheral regions whose development is being strongly inhibited by the "center." In the case of countries of late or recent industrial development, the centralizing forces act even more intensely in favor of the "center," preventing any real possibility of a spontaneous, gradual elimination of regional imbalance and the strong duality between "center" and "periphery." This duality is, indeed, a phenomenon characterizing to a greater or a lesser degree all developing countries. Furthermore, it constitutes an increasing cause for concern because of its negative implications, the solution of which cannot be entrusted to free or spontaneous mechanisms.

Notwithstanding the specific regional and local problems it generates, this increasing interregional disequilibrium affects the country as a whole and must, therefore, be focused from a national viewpoint.[4] The major negative national aspects of the problem are:

(a) Excessive growth of metropolitan areas beyond their critical size, which is evidenced by the diseconomies caused by congestion becoming greater than the external economies resulting from urban concentration.[5] This situation constitutes a growing hindrance to the dynamism of the national economy.

(b) Excessive concentration of economic activity in the center at the expense of the periphery's latent potentialities, which remain untapped, thus curtailing the expansion possibilities of the entire economy.

(c) Marginality with respect to the national economy of a large part of the population of the periphery, particularly its rural population, implying a limitation of the size of the country's internal market. This limited market size can become a serious obstacle to future economic development of the country.

(d) Intensity of interregional inequalities in economic and social well-being, chances for personal advancement, and the like, which constitute an unjust situation. This is particularly true in the case of marginated rural populations, scarcely deriving any benefit from progress and living a mere subsistence existence.[6]

(e) Growing tension between peripheral regions and the center, as a consequence of strong contrasts in standards of living and development possibilities. If these differences become too acute, the possibility arises of more serious interregional and social confrontations, which may, in some cases, go so far as to compromise the political viability of the state.

(f) Isolation of certain thinly populated border territories far from the center or foci of regional development, which may lead to gravitation of these areas toward foci of attraction in neighboring countries, weakening the nation's territorial cohesion.[7]

It will be noted that the first three situations—(a), (b), and (c)—correspond to inefficiencies in the economy's spatial structure, which adversely affect its possibilities for expansion over the longer term. Situation (d), on the other hand, refers to a problem of social and interregional equity, while (e) and (f) deal with problems of national cohesion.

Since the degree of urgency of these problems varies, the most pressing ones will generally receive special attention. Nevertheless, these problems as a whole represent the kinds of regional problems characteristic of developing countries, whose integral confrontation requires a regional and urban policy conceived within national criteria and treating national space as a whole.

In the specific case of Brazil, the first four problems appear to be most relevant at the moment, while the final one, (f), could be potentially significant.

Regional Policy Objectives

In view of the negative effects a highly polarized spatial structure may have upon economic and social development (if we look upon this development with a certain perspective), it is evident that national development plans need to encompass not only global and sectoral objectives, but also spatial aspects of development, stating specific goals in this area and defining a *national policy of regional development.*[8]

The general objective of such a policy will naturally be to reduce as much as possible the negative effects previously mentioned. More specifically, however, *this regional policy should respond to and be in agreement with the national objectives judged to be of highest priority in each stage of the development process.* Given that in developing countries the first priority among national objectives is generally the achievement and maintenance of dynamic and self-sustained economic growth, regional policy will tend to be conditioned and oriented basically by "economic efficiency" criteria, notwithstanding that wider and more general objectives (social or political) may also be served by such a policy.

Placing, in this manner, regional objectives within the framework of global economic objectives, a regional policy must then be defined that, in the first place, contributes to *"the achievement of that spatial structure of the economy which, at any point in time, is judged to be satisfactory for promoting and sustaining an efficient process of economic growth"* (Friedmann, 1966: 54).[9] Thus, concentration will appear, in the case of a nation that has just begun industrialization, as an economically positive element, and regional policy, generally implicit, will work to consolidate the budding national "development pole." In the later stages of industrialization, it will be necessary—as negative aspects of concentration sharpen, and greater concern for the more long-run perspectives for economic expansion emerges—to make explicit specific regional objectives which will contribute to the maintenance of economic dynamism in the future.

In the advanced stages of the "transitional phase" toward an industrial economy, as is the case with present-day Brazil, a regional policy taking into account the strong polarization of Brazilian economic space should be concerned with the following objectives:

(1) Effective occupation, settlement, and incorporation into the national economy of peripheral or "frontier" regions, rich in natural resources or unexploited (or barely utilized at the level of restricted local markets) economic potential.

(2) Incorporation of marginated or poorly integrated populations of "traditional" peripheral regions into the national economy. These regions, primarily agricultural, have dense rural populations constituting a potential market for national industry.

(3) Reducing the rate of economic, demographic, and physical growth of the center's large metropolitan areas, in which problems of urban congestion have reached critical proportions.

Attainment of these objectives will require a certain degree of geographic decentralization of future economic development, whether on an interregional level, to the benefit of peripheral regions and at the expense of the central region, or on an internal level within the central region, decentralizing metropolitan growth in favor of satellite centers, or on both levels simultaneously. Specific features of a decentralization policy will depend, nevertheless, on the one hand, on possible restrictions and requirements of higher-priority global economic goals,[10] and, on the other hand, on the degree to which the community is willing to sacrifice efficiency to remedy social, political, and territorial situations judged urgent or unjust. Without underestimating the importance of these restrictions imposed upon regional policy, restrictions which may be determined and justified by the limitations of underdeveloped economies and by the requirements of an economic "take-off" stage, it must be emphasized that, within the long-term perspective that must dominate all regional policy, there is a convergence of greater social and interregional equity and a path of economically efficient development, guided by the objectives previously expressed. In effect, a policy responding effectively to these objectives (in particular objective 2) needs to promote, among other conditions, a gradual correction of interregional differences in socioeconomic level. This corresponds to a noneconomic "equity" objective.[11] It may be said, then, that progressive achievement of all the aforementioned regional objectives must be translated, over the long term, into an economically efficient and more socially equitable spatial structure.

Given the above-mentioned regional goals, which are basically aimed at assuring both economic dynamism in the future and complementary, noneconomic objectives, it may be said, in general, that a regional policy conceived from a national perspective and arising from the growing dichotomy between center and periphery should favor the *economic, sociocultural, political, and physical integration of national space.* In the case of Brazil, the general outlines of such a policy are contained in the Strategic Development Program (Programa Estratégico de Desenvolvimento–PED) for the period 1968-1970, which includes strategies in diverse areas of action, responding in general terms to the broad regional objectives previously discussed.[12]

Integration of Rural Population as an Objective of Regional Policy

As previously noted, one of the most negative expressions of the marked spatial polarization of economic and social development in developing countries is the persistent marginality of a large part of the periphery's population, essentially its rural population, with respect to this development.

As we have seen, this marginality is manifested, on the one hand, in strictly economic terms. First, in the persistence of isolated agrarian economies, almost of mere subsistence, without ties to the national market, and, in the best case, with minimal participation in local markets. The *campesinos* of these areas for natural,[13] economic,[14] or sociocultural[15] reasons, produce only the bare minimum necessary for family survival or that and a little more. Marginality may also be the result of the land tenure structure, particularly in areas of more commercialized agriculture whose products supply regional or national markets. In the case of *minifundia,* the uneconomic size of plots and primitive methods of exploitation limit family income. In the case of the traditional *latifundia,*[16] marginality arises because farm-workers (as well as other farm people associated in different ways with production) receive a minimum wage which only covers their subsistence.

In all the above examples, members of the rural population remain marginal to the market insofar as their income does not permit them to participate in it as consumers of industrial products. On the other hand, the economic marginality of rural populations goes hand in hand with social marginality—that is, they have no or only minimal participation in the benefits of development such as health, education, and opportunity for personal advancement.[17] The marginality of a large part of the periphery's population, especially the fact of their marginality with respect to the market, may represent, in terms of long-term economic development, an important limitation on national expectations of sustained economic expansion.[18]

During the "import-substitution" stage, the relatively small size of the internal national market did not constitute an obstacle to development of industries based on relatively simple technology which could operate economically either on a small scale (for regional or local markets), or a medium scale (for the limited national market). In later stages, however, market size becomes crucial. As the possibilities of economic expansion have shifted to industries requiring more complex technologies and presenting economies of scale, the need for a sufficiently large national market has become urgent.

This explains why *expansion of the internal market* is being articulated as an important objective for medium- to long-range national economic development. In the case of Brazil, for example, expansion of the internal market constitutes, for the above-mentioned Programa Estratégico de Desenvolvimento, the principal source of future industrial dynamism, together with promotion of exports and import-substitution in the sectors where this is still relevant (Ministério de Planejamento, 1968b: 12 n.).

This particular objective may be pursued on two sides. On the supply side, it may be achieved by increase in efficiency of production and the resulting reductions in costs and prices. On the demand side, it may be achieved by allowing a relative increase in income of middle and upper economic groups, whose marginal propensity to consume tends to favor durable consumer goods requiring larger-scale production and, therefore, larger markets.

Nevertheless, the latter approach implies greater concentration and inequalities of income and lesser absorption of labor force. In addition, besides these negative social implications, it offers only limited possibilities of expansion of the internal market, since it is predicated on a restricted population base. An income redistribution approach seems more in order. If the longer term is considered, a more adequate (and socially more just) policy would appear to be income redistribution to least-favored economic groups, including a policy to absorb greater amounts of unemployed, underemployed, or unintegrated labor force (abundant in underdeveloped countries) so as to widen the production and consumption base of the national economy with a view to gradual creation of a mass market.

This mass market, by virtue of the marginal consumption structure of the lowest income levels, implies enlarged demand for generic consumer goods corresponding to the so-called "traditional" industries, such as foodstuffs, textiles, clothing, shoes, housing.[19] Yet, in subsequent phases, it should represent a growing and potentially larger market for more complex industrial products.

At this point, the regional dimension of the national goal of internal market expansion emerges. Integration of the periphery's marginated or poorly integrated rural population into the internal market becomes an important aspect of national long-term economic development policy, especially in countries like Brazil, whose large unincorporated rural population represents, in this context, enormous development potential.[20]

The process of incorporation into the market would lead, at the same time, to a rise in the standard of living of rural population being incorporated, an increasing need for technical training and education, changes in traditional behavior patterns, and the like. Economic integration into the market implies a process of sociocultural integration into "urban" living patterns and a general process of social change and development, which is, also a generally proclaimed national objective.

From the above, it follows that the *social and economic integration of the periphery's still unincorporated rural population* is one of the most important objectives of a national policy of regional development conceived within and based on fundamental national development objectives. This specific regional objective fits perfectly within the more general objective of a regional policy in the "transitional phase" of national development, namely: *gradual integration of national space along economic, sociocultural, political, and physical lines, and eventual elimination of the duality between center and periphery.*

The methodology of analysis that will be presented in this essay will specifically explore possibilities and conditions for integration of this marginated rural reserve into the national economy and into the economic, social, and cultural benefits of development.

Development Poles as Instruments of Integration

Use of the idea of development poles has become generalized as a strategic approach and as an instrument of a regional policy directed toward national spatial integration under conditions of extreme polarization. Without attempting to examine in depth theoretical aspects involved, a brief review of the most essential characteristics of what has been called a "development pole" will be made in order to determine the concept's possibilities and its utility for a policy of national integration.

Development poles (or "core regions," as he calls them) have been defined by Friedmann (1967) as "areas of concentrated, highly interdependent economic activity which have exerted (or are capable of exerting) a decisive influence on the character and rhythm of economic development of a larger spatial system."

Two different kinds of development poles should be distinguished. There are *historical development poles* which have emerged spontaneously as a consequence of the process of polarization and concentration accompanying development, and *planned development poles,* deliberately activated in the periphery as instruments of regional policy. In the latter case, activation of the pole is, in general, based on an industrial complex located near an urban center of relative importance either already in existence or purposely created. This industrial complex is composed of a highly dynamic, "propulsive industry," and of industries of induced growth, integrated either vertically or horizontally with the former and located in its vicinity. In addition, existence of the complex also induces a series of complementary activities serving both other industries and the pole's population.[21]

Use of the "development pole" concept as an instrument of regional policy consists, in fact, of the planned activation of the eventual "diffusion effect" of development from the historic "pole" to the peripheral areas, a process which has been scarcely effective in presently developing countries. As we have seen, the influence of the national development pole on the economic development of its periphery (i.e., the rest of national economic space) may be visualized in terms of:

(a) concentration processes, by which economic activity is increasingly centralized at the pole, while the possibilities of the periphery[22] are more and more inhibited, especially with regard to more dynamic activities;

(b) diffusion processes, by which development spreads toward the periphery as a consequence of communication and human interaction in general, on the one hand, and of demand existing in the pole for certain raw materials, partly processed inputs, or final products the periphery can provide, on the other; corresponding extractive and manufacturing activities are thus induced at the periphery,[23] determining a degree of dynamism and increasing integration of regional economies into the national economy (represented by the pole).

It has also been said that a net "concentration effect" prevails during the first stages of industrialization, growing stronger as the economy enters the so-called transitional phase, and increasingly aggravating the duality between center and periphery and the problems this duality implies. A net "diffusion effect" of development from the historic pole to the periphery may appear, on the other hand, in the more advanced stages of the process; its intensity and range, however, are limited by factors inherent in the spatial structure itself, and particularly by distance, whose negative effect on interaction is well known;

consequently, the "diffusion effect" will generally reach only areas immediately adjacent to the pole, without penetrating the more distant periphery.

The idea of deliberate activation of new poles in the periphery proceeds from the premise that diffusion processes may be provoked and accelerated giving them, in addition, greater territorial reach. Thus, the very implementation of a new, *planned pole,* which is to act as a new focal point for the concentration of economic activity, implies already a degree of decentralization with respect to the *historic pole,* and, through interactions and interdependencies with it, represents a step in the integration of national space-economy.

By analogy with the spontaneous behavior of historic poles, new planned poles should constitute, as we have said, focal points of concentration at the regional level. This role should be deliberately reinforced during a period of consolidation of the pole, in order to maximize the external economies and economies of scale associated with concentration. Only in later stages, once a certain autonomous dynamism of the new pole (or poles) as well as its effective integration with the rest of the national economy, has been achieved, will the moment arrive to repeat the previously described process, activating additional poles within a predetermined sequence, until the objective of complete integration of national economic space has been attained.[24]

We must emphasize the important role in this integration process of the country's system of urban centers and the transportation and communication networks linking these centers among themselves and to the poles. In effect, a well-conceived regional policy should contemplate, simultaneously with activation of new poles in the periphery, complementary action directed toward strengthening and structuring an urban system and its integrating networks in general (Bernard, 1969: 12-14). Specific urban centers should be reinforced in their function as "central places" and assigned a special role as *regional distribution and service centers* with broad regional influence. In addition, certain urban centers may be able to act as *secondary centers of industrial growth* and, therefore, of population concentration.[25] Last, transportation and communication networks constitute channels for exchange and interaction between the poles and the rest of the urban system, and their development will mean greater accessibility. Together, these elements facilitate the transmission of development poles' impact to the periphery, and, in the last analysis, to rural areas.

We may now ask how this process will affect rural population, especially the unintegrated rural population which concerns us here. Also at this level, the integrating role of new, planned poles with other transmission elements discussed above, presents itself as potentially effective. The periphery's rural population will now be within the range of impact of the new poles and the urban phenomenon in general, an impact which will in turn determine this population's gradual incorporation into the market along two possible paths:

(a) migration of rural population to new development poles or other urban foci of attraction, resulting in relatively better-paid employment in new industrial and service activities emerging in these foci, and in the consequent acquisition of a certain capacity to consume industrial products; or,

(b) modernization of agriculture and increase in agricultural productivity, which should represent greater income for rural population[26] and consequent creation of purchasing power for industrial goods.

Both paths are complementary and should operate simultaneously and gradually so that the process does not create either labor shortages in agriculture or unemployment in the cities. Specific local conditions and potentialities will determine the relative importance of these two modes of incorporation in individual regions and areas. As was previously mentioned, incorporation of these marginated masses of rural populations into the market will mean, besides their accession to better living standards, a process of social and cultural change and of integration into "urban" conditions of life.

ANALYSIS OF ACCESSIBILITY TO UNINCORPORATED RURAL POPULATION: METHODOLOGICAL STATEMENT

Purpose and Scope of the Analysis

If we accept that integration of unincorporated rural population constitutes one of the main objectives of a regional policy for a nation having the characteristics and stage of development of present-day Brazil, and if we consider that a policy involving activation of new development poles or "secondary growth foci" may serve well this particular objective (as well as other regional development objectives discussed earlier), an immediate question comes to mind, namely, the number, location, and characteristics (size, activity structure, and so on) such poles or "growth centers"[27] should have in order to serve this objective efficiently; in other words, in order that the "integration effect upon unincorporated population" be maximized.[28]

One of the conditions for this maximization refers to the location (macro-location) of the poles or growth centers that are to be activated with this objective in mind. Their geographic location should be such that accessibility from these growth foci to the total mass of unincorporated rural population be greatest, so that their impact reaches the maximum number of individuals categorized as marginated rural population. Given the weakening effect of distance on the interaction of points in space, the impact of a new pole (or growth center) which should be located at a great distance from the main concentrations of rural population will be significantly low, if not nonexistent. On the other hand, the maximum impact of a new pole or growth center will be felt by the rural population of its nearest area of influence.

Accessibility to the urban phenomenon by rural population appears to be an essential factor in the urbanization process. In a country of continental dimensions like Brazil, the inaccessibility of a greater part of its rural population to the attraction effect of the large national development poles appears as one of the causes of the persistence of a great mass of unincorporated rural population. This situation still characterizes Brazil in spite of its possessing two of the largest and most dynamic historic development poles in Latin America;[29] in spite of important industrial development promoted in certain regional poles in the more traditional periphery (the Nordeste), and in spite of the sizeable effort achieved in road development (which represents an increase in accessibility).

We shall here attempt to design a methodology for analysis permitting us to establish, in the case of medium- to-large urban centers in Brazil,[30] their degree of accessibility to unincorporated rural population. In this way, a criterion may be established ranking and selecting pole or growth center candidates in the light of our objective herein.[31]

The Concept of Potential

The methodological approach to this problem is based on the concept of the "potential" of a given point k in geoeconomic space with respect to masses located at all points in said space, including point k (Isard, 1960: 493-544). This potential measures the accessibility from said point k to all masses distributed in space (at points i, including k), and is expressed by the following general formula:

$$V_k = \sum_{i=1}^{n} \frac{w_i P_i}{d_{ik}^{\alpha}}$$

in which P_i is the mass (which can represent the population of points i, or their active population, or total income in i); w_i is a coefficient that weights the different masses P_i; d_{ik} is the distance from k to each and all i points;[32] and α is an empirically determined coefficient characterizing the "degree" to which distance affects the potential negatively.[33]

In this case, $w_i P_i$ should represent unincorporated rural populations located around specific urban centers (i). These urban centers should have a certain regional importance possessing the role of central places, i.e., providing goods and services to smaller urban centers within their respective nodal regions and, in varying degree, to the rural population of such regions. Using the regional breakdown of a study by the Instituto Brasileiro de Geografia (IBG; 1968: 177-208), second-order centers and their corresponding nodal regions identified therein will be taken as a basis, totalling 112 centers.[34]

We can thus obtain V_k values for all centers (points) considered, and, interpolating among them, a map of iso-potential curves. The urban centers encompassed by the "highest" curves will represent locations *with greater accessibility to total unincorporated rural population.*

Urban Impact and Incorporation of Rural Population

Given the fact that distance weakens the intensity of interactions and effects through space, it is possible to assume that activation of new development poles[35] or secondary growth centers at these points will have relatively greater total impact on the mass of marginated rural population it is desired to incorporate.

As has been seen, this impact is constituted principally by the *attraction* exercised on said rural population by the new pole or growth center finally translated into migration to the pole (or growth center), more productive employment therein, and eventual incorporation into the consumer market and urban culture. Given favorable conditions, however, part of this impact may consist of the *diffusion* of development toward the periphery, including the rural population remaining after migration, through rise in the technological and productivity levels in specific economic activities. In the last analysis, this will also imply a kind of "urbanization" of the above-mentioned populations, in the sense of their incorporation into the market and the urban social and cultural context.

At this point, an important matter should be clarified. Obviously, this impact (attraction/diffusion) of a new pole or growth center on rural population does not take place in an urban vacuum. These centers are already subjected to the impact of existing (historical) development poles or, in general, to the nation's urban system.[36] Thus, the new pole (or growth center) must compete, as a focal point of development, with already existing foci (historic poles and the existing urban system).

Thus, for a given point j, the rural population "available" for the action of one or more poles or growth centers is limited to a certain degree by:

(a) intensity of the impact exercised by the existing urban system on point j;

(b) "permeability" to urban impact (attraction/diffusion) characterizing rural population surrounding j.

The intensity of the impact exercised in j is related to j's access to the urban system as a whole, and may be measured, then, in principle, by the "urban potential" corresponding to point j and relative to the whole of the system's "urban" populations.[37] Given that these urban populations contain strong interregional differences in standards of living (especially in countries with strong dichotomies between center and periphery) and accepting that these differences imply different relative "weights" in their capacity to exercise impact at a distance, such population groups should be weighted by means of a coefficient related, for example, to per capita income or other variables of similar meaning. Thus, the "urban potential" in j is expressed as follows:

$$V_j = \sum_{i=1}^{n} \frac{r_i \cdot U_i}{(d_{ij})^{\alpha}}$$

in which r_i is an "income coefficient" and U_i is the urban population of i; $r_i \cdot U_i$ represents the weighted urban population which we shall call *"urban mass."*[38] Thus, V_j will be high in the case of metropolitan areas, and low for the points (centers) which are distant, peripheral or of limited "urban mass."

Once V_j have been calculated for all points of the system, they can be standardized on a scale from 0 to 100, associating to each center i an index E_i expressing the relative degree of "exposure" of center i with respect to the total phenomenon of urban radiation. We shall call E_i an *index of urban exposure.*

Accepting that the rural population around each center i (included within the corresponding nodal region) is functionally linked in some degree to its urban focal point, the "urban exposure" to which this center is subjected (measured by E_i) will also radiate toward its nodal region. However, the effect of this "urban exposure" on rural population may be lessened, to greater or lesser degree, by certain characteristics of this population. Thus, the effect will be mitigated in the case of populations greatly attached to traditional living patterns and little receptive to changes in their environment (cultural inaccessibility), or in the case of rural populations physically far removed from their regional focal point (physical inaccessibility). The effect, on the contrary, will be greater on rural populations more in touch with the market economy or partly incorporated into it, who have been receiving the impact of this "urban exposure" for some time and with a certain intensity. This leads us to formulate, for rural populations surrounding center i, an index m_i called *coefficient of rural permeability*, which may fluctuate according to conditions from 0 in the case of total impermeability of the rural hinterland (theoretical case) to 1 in the case of a rural hinterland physically or culturally predisposed to incorporation to urban conditions (or effectively assimilated to some degree).

Combining E and m, a *coefficient of rural accessibility* for each nodal region i can be formulated,

$$a_i = \frac{m_i \cdot E_i}{100}$$

representing *the degree to which the rural population of region i is accessible from the existing urban system,* and, therefore, *the degree to which it is receiving the urban impact radiated by the urban system.* The coefficient *a* can vary from 0 to 1, depending on the following situations (arbitrary values for purposes of example):

(a) Rural population near metropolitan areas (existing development poles) having complete permeability to urban impact:

$$E = 90, m = 1 \quad \therefore \quad a = 0.900$$

(b) Rural population relatively near metropolitan areas, but with strong traditional sociocultural ties:

$$E = 60, m = 0.20 \quad \therefore \quad a = 0.120$$

(c) Rural population relatively remote, located in colonization areas on the fringes of settled society, but which enjoys proximity to a focal point linking it to the urban system:

$$E = 30, m = 0.70 \quad \therefore \quad a = 0.210$$

(d) Traditional or primitive rural population settled in subsistence-economy areas far removed from the urban system (such as Amazonia or the interior of the Nordeste):

$$E = 5, m = 0.10 \quad \therefore \quad a = 0.005$$

As we have seen, the values of E_i are related to the potentials (in i) relative to the "urban masses" distributed in the system of centers considered, and may be established with these potentials as a point of departure. As for the values of m_i, they may be established, in principle, on the basis of relevant indicators reflecting these population characteristics of individual rural areas.[39]

Given the series of values m_i and E_i, once the "coefficients of rural accessibility," a_i, are calculated, they will affect the respective regional rural populations, R_i. Accepting that, in terms of probability, *the part of R_i that will respond to the impact of the urban system will be proportional, in each case, to the rural accessibility coefficient,* a_i, then this "receptive" and "responsive" portion of rural population will be:

$$R_i' = a_i \cdot R_i = m_i(E_i/100) \cdot R_i$$

This part of the rural population corresponds to those rural groups who eventually will migrate to the regional focal center i, and who, in the final analysis, will migrate toward national development poles (or other foci of expected employment). It also includes those rural groups who, without migrating, are employed in increasingly more productive local activities, agricultural or not. In both cases, these groups will be integrating or will be already integrated into national labor and consumer markets, as well as into urban social conditions and cultural patterns. It may thus be said in this sense that a_i represents a *"coefficient of rural incorporation."*[40] The rest of center i rural population will not respond to the impact of "urban exposure" and will remain marginated.

Accessibility to Unincorporated Rural Population

Given the existence of rural impermeabilities as measured by m_i, only a part of the unincorporated (marginated) rural population of nodal region i can effectively be incorporated as a result of the *additional* urban impact which represents the appearance of a new pole or growth center in the vicinity of i (or in i itself).[41] The incorporable part is:

$$R_i'' = m_i \cdot R_i - m_i(E_i/100) \cdot R_i = m_i(1 - E_i/100)R_i$$

Given the impermeability (m_i) of rural population in region i, the first term of the expression, $m_i \cdot R_i$, corresponds to the maximum rural population within nodal region i susceptible to incorporation, if E_i were to reach a maximum value of 100. The second term, $a_i R_i$, corresponds to the part of the population effectively incorporated, given the present value of E_i. The expression

$$b_i = m_i(1 - E_i/100)$$

represents, then, an "incorporability coefficient" affecting total rural population in region i, given E_i and m_i.

Optimum location of a new development pole or secondary growth center, in terms of maximum incorporation of marginated rural population, corresponds to that point (urban center) *with maximum accessibility to the total incorporable rural mass.* This accessibility is measured, as we have seen, by the "potential" in each point k with respect to this incorporable rural population, whose magnitude at any point i was expressed above; that is, by the expression

$$W_k = \sum_{i=1}^{n} \frac{m_i(1 - E_i/100) \cdot R_i}{(d_{ik})^\alpha} = \sum_{i=1}^{n} \frac{b_i \cdot R_i}{(d_{ik})^\alpha}$$

The center having a maximum W_k would then be the point for optimum location of a new, planned development pole or secondary growth center from the point of view of the impact (in terms of effective incorporation) that said pole or growth center would have on unincorporated rural population. For a given increment of the coefficient E_k of the new pole or growth center (this increment being a measure of its increased importance as a focus of urban radiation), impact on unincorporated rural populations will be maximized from said location since from the latter accessibility to these populations is also maximum.[42]

Given the geographic dispersion of marginated rural populations in Brazil and the limited reach of urban impact resulting from the negative effect of distance, the need for several poles or growth centers becomes evident. It will therefore be necessary to consider *a locational zone including a set of points (centers) whose W_k approach the optimum.* It will suffice to pick one of the iso-potential curves as an exterior limit, providing that it encompasses a convenient number of urban centers or represents a margin of suboptimization deemed adequate.

This procedure also allows the consideration of alternative locations within this zone and the use of combined selection criteria. It will permit, for example, selection of locations which, while being within the optimum (or suboptimum) zone in terms of their "integration effect" on rural population, also fulfill other requirements such as having a higher-order urban infrastructure or a better resource base and other favorable preconditions for eventual economic dynamism.

An important point now arises with reference to fulfillment of the objective of economic and social integration of marginated rural population, which should be kept in mind in defining a regional development policy serving this objective effectively. We have proceeded to this stage in our analysis on the basis of the existence of rural impermeabilities, expressed by means of the coefficient m_i, which clearly are a limiting factor in the total potential impact of new poles or growth centers on the marginated rural mass.[43] These impermeabilities, a reflection of traditional socioeconomic and cultural structures, are barriers difficult to penetrate through the mere impact of urban exposure judging by the persistence of important "pockets" of underdevelopment near large metropolitan regions (such as the Ribeira valley in the state of São Paulo). While intense urban exposure (high E index) might in principle result in gradual incorporation of marginated rural masses (implying gradual modification of m coefficients), we must accept in the face of existing evidence that this process requires considerable periods of time *unless the socioeconomic and cultural root of the problem is attacked.*

It follows, therefore, that for a development poles policy to have maximum integrating effect, it will be necessary to proceed simultaneously with determined action at the local community level, aimed at achievement of deep changes in the economic, social, and cultural structures of the countryside.[44] Such measures would improve the receptivity, among rural populations in impermeable areas, of the impact radiating from both the existing urban system and from future new poles and growth centers to be activated. This would correspond to a rise in the low m values for such areas to values closer to 1.

Clearly, relatively rapid increase in m_i values will imply increases in the values of "rural incorporation coefficients" (a_i), and "rural incorporability coefficients," (b_i)—that is, increased accessibility to rural populations previously considered unincorporable. Increase in incorporable rural masses in the more traditional regions ultimately implies increase in the potentials in each of centers k with respect to such masses and change in the ranking of these centers, improving the relative position of those centers located in the more traditional regions.

For the purpose of measuring the importance of the above-mentioned effects, the proposed model's sensitivity to variations (increases) in m_i parameters will be tested by assigning them values bringing them gradually to unity.[45]

Definition of Parameters

One of the problems that emerges in applying the proposed gravity model to a concrete case is the exact definition of the basic parameters which compose the above-stated general mathematical expression. In the preceding sections, tentative definitions of some of these parameters have been advanced in very general terms, which we shall now complete and make more precise.

To begin, the term "population," generically called "mass" in the basic mathematical expression, should be examined. In principle, the terms "urban masses" and "incorporable rural masses" were defined as a derivation of "urban" and "rural" populations respectively affected by "income coefficients" (r_i), and "incorporability coefficients" (b_i). This makes it necessary to stipulate precisely what is meant by "urban" population and "rural" population.

An obvious criterion would be to accept the census definition; however, in the case of Brazil, this would seem to be too all-inclusive, since the census classifies certain small localities as urban which are more realistically part of the rural world. A better alternative would be to consider urban only those centers having more than 20,000 inhabitants, a limit generally accepted as a standard for international comparison of levels of urbanization.

On the other hand, given the regional breakdown of the IBG (1968) study with its 112 focal centers and respective nodal regions, and having accepted this regionalization as the basis for this study, a practical criterion would be to define the populations of these regional foci as our urban population.[46]

While the latter criterion assures inclusion of all centers of a certain regional importance (influence) independently of their size, we should somehow consider the mass of those larger urban centers (of over 20,000 inhabitants), which, even though they are not foci of regional influence (and are not therefore included in the above-mentioned 112), imply by their size the presence of an urban infrastructure and urban activities (manufacturing and service) of a certain importance. These centers, many of which possess considerable economic dynamism, clearly constitute part of the urban mass that exercises impact on rural populations.

The most practical solution appears to consist in a combination of both criteria, taking as "centers" of the urban system the 112 "central localities" (regional foci) of the IBG (1968) study (with the advantages that this implies) and assuming as concentrated within these centers an urban population composed of the "central locality's" population *plus the population of all localities of 20,000 or more inhabitants included in the respective nodal regions.* This will reinforce the weight of centers or regional foci heading industrialized or metropolitan regions, which also contain other cities of considerable size but without "central place" functions. Such cities are generally centers of manufacturing concentration or metropolitan expansion. As has been said, this urban population (as defined above) "weighted" by an "income coefficient" (r_i), constitutes the urban mass of each center.

Simultaneously, the rural population of each nodal region is thus defined as the difference between total population of the region and urban population as already defined. The incorporability coefficient (b_i), applied to this rural population defines, finally, the incorporable rural mass.

The values of these weighting coefficients of masses will have to be expressly established: the values of the first can be based on surveys of family budgets taken by the Instituto Brasileiro de Economia (IBRE) (1961-1962, 1962-1963); the values of the second, on estimated values of the rural permeability coefficient (m_i) and the "urban exposure index" (E_i), the latter in turn based on the urban potentials (V_i) to be computed.

In addition, "distance" should be expressed in terms of "virtual distance" by existing roadways, weighting different sections according to the type of road (paved, gravel, or dirt). Naturally, other means of transportation also have importance if one wishes to obtain a more exact measure of the relative "accessibility" of the individual centers to the urban system. In particular, air travel brings centers distant overland into proximity, and, in certain areas, river transportation may be the only means available. In addition, communications systems (newspapers, telephones, radio, and television) are important means for approximation and the diffusion of urban impact. Yet, if we consider that urban impact is translated, for our purposes here, into integration of marginated rural populations through their rural-urban and interurban migration, or through changes in productivity in these same rural areas, the most relevant "accessibility" will be that determined by the most widespread, generalized, and massive medium of interaction. This medium, with all its well-known restrictions and exceptions, is the highway network.

Finally, we should define the value of the exponent α, which affects distance and indicates the degree with which distance influences negatively the level of interaction between points (in this case, the potential).[47] This exponent is characteristic in each case and should be determined empirically. Studies of migrations[48] undertaken in different countries reveal a variation in α of between 0.4 and 3.3. The lower values are more typical of contemporary migration in developed countries, while the higher values correspond more to nineteenth-century migrations or those in less-developed countries (Haggett, 1965: 37).

On the other hand, studies of the process of innovation diffusion indicate that this aspect of urban impact occurs more slowly and within a smaller geographical radius in less-developed countries,[49] which corresponds to a strong negative effect exerted by distance and therefore to a higher α. The opposite occurs in more developed countries in which α will in general have low values.[50]

For the purpose of our analysis, and given that this study is attempting to obtain highly aggregated indicators in which greater or lesser accuracy will not cause results to vary substantially, computations can be made with three values for α (1, 1.5, and 2), obtaining in this way results for each hypothesis. In simplified terms, we may accept that $\alpha = 1$ will correspond to interactions in a relatively more advanced country in which urban impact is transmitted by the system with a certain ease; $\alpha = 2$ may additionally correspond to the case of a slightly developed country in which urban impact is strongly restrained by distance and has less geographic range. An examination of these results will permit an approximation of Brazilian reality to one of the three hypotheses (or to intermediate ones).[51]

Limitations of the Proposed Methodology

One of the obvious limitations of the proposed methodology derives from its static character. In effect, the general gravity model, on which our analysis is based, permits description of a situation that presumably exists at a given moment—1970, in this case. It does not permit representation of the temporal evolution of the structure described. This time dimension can only be incorporated by comparing static situations corresponding to consecutive moments (comparative static method).

Spontaneous evolution of the spatial structure of the nation will consist of:

(a) variation in spatial distribution of rural and urban populations as a consequence of the process of urbanization and interregional migration; this variation will mean, in terms of the model, change in the values of U_i and R_i, modifying the values of both "potentials" calculated, V_i and W_i;

(b) decrease in virtual distances between regional foci, as a consequence of new roads and additional paving; this variation will modify the d_{ij} matrix and will result in positive variation of the "potentials" (increase in the "accessibilities");

(c) gradual, although slow, increase in "rural permeability" (m_i), in areas more exposed (accessible) to urban impact;

(d) possible change in the hierarchy of central places and consequently in the polarizations they produce; this may imply increase in the number of regional foci (and nodal regions) under consideration and reassignment of certain municipalities from one region to another.

To the extent that these changes can be foreseen and quantified for a future time period, it will be possible to establish in what measure these changes will cause variation in the rankings of centers obtained for the present situation. It seems probable, however, that these spontaneous changes will not come to affect fundamentally the relative positions of centers, given the known stability of regional structures.

Meanwhile, it will be of interest to test the sensitivity of the proposed model to deliberately introduced changes aimed at substantially modifying the structure in the sense of more harmonious spatial development, in accordance with a National Plan for Regional Development.[52]

Another limitation of the methodology, to the extent it has been developed herein, lies in the fact that even if it permits ranking regional foci in accordance with the stated objective, determining zones of suboptimal location, it does not directly resolve the problem of the number of poles or growth centers to be activated, or the size, structural characteristics, and exact location of each of them, within the set of preferential locations.

Nevertheless, the zones of suboptimal locations delimited by descending iso-potential curves, constitute a frame of reference for consideration of possible alternative combinations of size, number, and location of poles or growth centers. Subsequent elaboration of the methodology used should permit estimating and comparing the total impacts that each of these alternative solutions represents in terms of incorporation of marginated rural populations.

Definition of these alternatives should involve consideration of regional specific characteristics, economic potential of individual centers and regions, volume of industrial and urban investment required in each case, and other factors and objectives which may impinge upon the number of poles and growth centers to be activated and the size, location, and activity structure of each.

In summary, we may say that, in spite of the limitations noted above, the proposed approach and methodology can deliver results useful for definition of a national policy of regional development for Brazil. Such results, however, insofar as they represent *a partial approach, oriented toward a specific objective,* are not sufficient in themselves to define all elements of a regional development policy and should be considered jointly with other defining factors.

NOTES

1. This phase is characterized by relatively important participation of industry in gross national product (10 to 25 percent), accompanied by a strong tendency toward spatial concentration of industry and population in a dynamic region functioning as a development pole.

2. In this phase, industry contributes between 25 and 50 percent of gross national product and tends to be replaced by the tertiary sector as the most dynamic factor (see Friedmann, 1966: 7). Note that Brazil, with 29.2 percent of its gross internal product originating in industry (1966), is apparently in the beginning of this phase. Nevertheless, it is believed that this figure is overestimated (Ministério de Planejamento e Coordenação Geral, 1968a: vol. I: 3, 21, 22).

3. Friedmann here describes an ideal outline of the process of spatial diffusion of development, as it may have taken place in countries of older industrial development.

4. Local and intraregional problems will find true solution only within the broader context of an ordering of national space.

5. Studies to date do not permit precise definition of this critical size, which should correspond to large cities of several millions of inhabitants. Similarly, it is not easy to establish the optimum size of a metropolitan center, through which net external economies are maximized. Yet it is estimated that this size might occur above 500,000 inhabitants and within a more or less broad range, according to the particular characteristics of each center.

6. While emigration may alleviate this situation, the strong attraction exercised by the "central" region implies an increasing population concentration accompanied by the negative effects seen in point a, as well as increases in marginal urban population. Besides, diverse sociological and cultural factors, as well as distance, may limit the exodus from less-integrated rural regions.

7. While international complementarity on local and regional levels may be desirable and beneficial, it should generally not imply a weakening of the bonds of local areas with their respective national entities.

8. Subsequently in this essay, the term "regional development" will also include development of the "urban system," since the latter is an inseparable element of the former.

9. It should be kept in mind that "economic efficiency" should be understood here in a *long-run* perspective, with respect to *a global process of economic development,* and not as the sum of efficient decisions in the short run, applied to individual projects.

10. It should be recalled that a decentralization policy, even when it represents an efficient approach in the long run, usually implies short- and medium-run inefficiencies resulting in a lower growth rate of gross national product. Global development objectives, however, may impose minimum national growth rates.

11. On the other hand, the paramount objectives of planning, whose nature is essentially social, will be better served in the long run by a strategy assuring dynamic and efficient development for the future.

12. It does not, however, define a regional and urban policy as such, explicitly and in sufficient detail (see Ministério de Planejamento e Coordenação Geral, 1968a: vol. II, chs. 18-19; for a condensed version, see Ministério de Planejamento e Coordenação Geral, 1968b).

13. Low soil fertility, irrigation, and erosion problems, and the like.

14. Lack of access to possible markets, high demographic density per hectare cultivated, and so on.

15. Family structure and traditional culture, ignorance of more productive techniques, and so on.

16. Whose exploitation is based on methods of low productivity and use of cheap labor.

17. A similar situation characterizes marginal urban populations in the large metropolitan areas of developing countries. These groups will not be relevant to this study, however, since they are populations already urbanized and in the process of being integrated and therefore not available for the development of peripheral regions.

18. In addition to the negative implications for the regional economies themselves, it must be remembered that urban population, supposedly incorporated into the market, represents a generally low percentage of the total population of traditional peripheral regions (whose economies are predominantly agricultural), this implying almost nonexistent regional markets.

19. And also, to some degree, to certain durable goods (such as transistor radios) within reach of these income groups.

20. A pertinent discussion of the role of the internal market in economic development is that of Magalhães (1968). In this paper, the author relates the need for widening the internal market to a regional development policy based on activation of development poles.

21. It should be noted that historic poles have not necessarily emerged around industrial complexes, but also through gradual concentration of increasingly interdependent diverse activities.

22. More specifically, of certain areas of the periphery which Friedmann (1966: 39-44) has called "downward-transitional areas."

23. More precisely, in the so-called "upward-transition areas" or "frontier regions" (Friedmann, 1966: 39-44).

24. The number, selection, and implementation sequence of planned poles, as well as the duration of consolidation phases, are specific aspects of the design of a regional development plan, and should be defined on the basis of concrete conditions.

25. These secondary *growth foci* may, in successive phases of a regional development program, become candidates for additional development poles, since they will show a certain industrial dynamism and possess relatively advanced urban infrastructures.

26. And, indirectly, for urban populations in the smaller service centers in agricultural regions, which for this purpose may be considered as rural.

27. Henceforth, the term pole will be used to designate development poles proper, and the term growth center to refer to secondary foci of industrial growth.

28. A question that remains open is the degree of conflict that may arise between a solution believed to be optimal from the viewpoint of this particular objective and the solutions (location and characteristics of the poles and growth centers) required by other objectives. We shall not concern ourselves herein with criteria for final selection, for the most part determined by economic policy options.

29. Note that, in spite of this fact, Brazil's rate of urbanization was barely 39.4 percent in 1960 (United Nations, 1963: 80) while a country like Uruguay, with a more modest national pole, is almost completely urbanized (70.9 percent in 1960), due to the fact that the Uruguayan pole acts upon a much more restricted and accessible hinterland.

30. Since these larger centers must possess a relatively developed urban infrastructure, they constitute preferential sites for location of possible new poles or growth centers.

31. It should be made clear that this cannot be the only criterion for final selection of poles or growth centers to be activated. In this final selection, the economic potential of "candidates" (the relative dynamism of their economies, the existence of specific natural resources, their access to national markets) as well as physical and service infrastructure available (level of urban facilities) play decisive roles.

32. Including the distance d_{kk} to which, in order to avoid a quotient of infinite value, it is necessary to assign a value different from 0 (zero), usually 1.

33. Note that in more traditional formulations of the potential concept (Stewart), as well as in its more usual applications, distance is given the exponent 1. Nevertheless, empirical evidence has led to generalization of the model, introducing an exponent α, varying with socioeconomic context and whose value may be determined empirically (see Isard, 1960: 508-509).

34. This includes first-order centers (metropolises) and their more immediate areas of influence corresponding to second-order nodal regions.

35. It should be remembered that this activation implies not only investment in specific industrial sectors but also supplementary investments which are not directly productive.

36. It should be recalled that medium-to-large urban centers, whether development poles or not, are in any case focal points of urban attraction or urban influence, insofar as they constitute either secondary growth centers or service centers for dependant areas (nodal regions). In this regard, it should be noted that the migratory process from rural to urban areas occurs in stages. Generally, rural migrants, before reaching metropolitan areas (development poles) spend more or less long periods in medium-sized cities closest to their original homes. Similarly, the diffusion process (of innovations or of development in general) to rural areas or toward the more distant periphery proceeds through intermediate steps down the urban hierarchy.

37. It remains to define what is meant by urban population (and consequently by rural) in this study. This will be discussed in the section entitled "Definition of Parameters."

38. Note that the urban potentials thus defined are in reality "income potentials." That is, they are potentials relative to the purchasing power concentrated in the foci under consideration. They therefore represent the accessibility from such foci to the consumer market.

39. An adequate indicator might be some measurement of the intensity of intraregional interaction (relationship) between the rural hinterland and the urban focal point of each nodal region j. Note that if this differentiation were to be of little relevance, as if, for example, m_j were highly correlated with V_j, it would suffice to establish that $m = 1$ for all j regions Nevertheless, the regional reality of the developing countries demonstrates strong rural impermeabilities in regions with more traditional socioeconomic structures, including pockets near metropolitan areas.

40. To stress this assumption, the above definition of a_j will be used preferentially henceforth, rather than the previously mentioned "coefficient of rural accessibility."

41. Or, also, because of spontaneous growth of existing poles and growth centers, or because of improvement in their accessibility to center i. This will all be translated into an increase in urban potential V_j, and, therefore, in the urban exposure index, E_j.

42. As we have seen, for a maximum increment of E_k to a value of 100 on the relative scale, incorporable rural population in region k would become totally incorporated; at the same time, total impact on neighboring points would be maximized.

43. We have seen that in a given region i, for a total rural population, R_i, maximum incorporation is given by $m_i R_i$ and unincorporable rural mass by $(1-m_i) R_i$. In so-called traditional periphery regions, with large rural populations and low m_i, this impermeability can seriously impede realization of the objective sought.

44. This action could include implementation of programs and measures of agrarian reform and modernization of agricultural activity; construction of access roads and rural infrastructure in general, with active participation of local population; consolidation of a hierarchy of central places which could provide rural areas with different services and manufactured goods, while also acting as marketing centers for local products; literacy campaigns, promotion of community organizations, and so on.

45. Note that m's new, increased values represent the introduction of a normative element into the model, inasmuch as these increases respond to a policy decision conducive to facilitating achievement of the objective proposed.

46. This criterion has the advantage that urban masses would coincide with the focal points (centers) of nodal regions, from which urban impact presumably radiates over the encircling rural population; this would facilitate calculating the two potentials (relative to urban and rural populations).

47. A low α indicates weaker negative influence of distance and therefore a wider field of attraction; contrarily, a higher value of α indicates a more limited field of attraction due to the stronger negative effect of distance.

48. As we have seen, migration is one of the results of urban impact on rural populations.

49. In these countries, the diffusion effect expands more easily through areas immediately surrounding the point of origin of the diffusion (the national pole), than through the urban system to regions in the more distant periphery.

50. An interesting analysis of these processes is found in Pedersen (1970).

51. For hypotheses with $\alpha > 1$, a refinement could consist of distinguishing, within the country's urban system, a metropolitan level formed exclusively by centers of this character, among which interactions would occur on the more favorable basis of $\alpha = 1$.

52. Relevant parameters for introduction of regional policy (policy variables) are: (a) the distances, affected by road development programs bringing the periphery closer to great national and regional poles; (b) the urban masses (populations), modified as a consequence of the activation or introduction of new poles or growth centers; and, (c) rural permeabilities, increased by means of agrarian reform and local development programs.

REFERENCES

BERNARD, P. (1969) Les pôles et centres de croissance en tant qu'instruments du développement regional et de la modernisation. Rapport Preliminaire. Geneva: UNRISD.

FRIEDMANN, J. (1967) "Regional planning and nation-building: an agenda for international research." Economic Development and Cultural Change 16 (October): 119-129.

—— (1966) Regional Development Policy: A Case Study of Venezuela. Cambridge, Mass.: MIT Press.

HAGGETT, P. (1965) Locational Analysis in Human Geography. London: Edward Arnold.

Instituto Brasileiro de Economia (IBRE) (1961-1962, 1962-1963) Pesquisa sobre orçamentos familiares. Rio de Janeiro: Fundação Getúlio Vargas.

Instituto Brasileiro de Geografia (IBG) (1968), Subsídios à Regionalização. Rio de Janeiro: Fundação IBGE.

ISARD, W. (1960) Methods of Regional Analysis. Cambridge, Mass.: MIT Press.

MAGALHAES, J. P. d'A. (1968) "Sugestão para uma política de desenvolvimento econômico em condições de escassez de mercado." Internal working paper. Instituto de Planejamento Econômico e Social, Ministério de Planejamento do Brasil.

Ministério de Planejamento e Coordenação Geral (1968a) Programa estratégico de desenvolvimento, 1968-70. Volumes I and II, June, Rio de Janeiro.

—— (1968b) O desafío brasileiro e o programa estratético. Rio de Janeiro.

PEDERSEN, P. O. (1970) "Innovation diffusion within and between national urban systems." Geographic Analysis 2 (July): 203-254.

United Nations (1963) El desarrollo económico de América Latina en la postguerra. New York: Comisión Económica para América Latina (CEPAL) (ECLA).

PART 2

CASE STUDIES

OF URBAN

AND REGIONAL

DEVELOPMENT

PROGRAMS

A series of case studies form the second section of this volume. All refer to ongoing programs in Latin America in different stages of implementation. The case studies are designed to provide pictures of different kinds of programs for solution of urban development problems on a national, regional, metropolitan, or subcommunity *(barrio)* scale, in countries with varied human, capital, and technical resources. Argentina, Bolivia, Colombia, and Chile are represented here by two examples each; Cuba, Mexico, Peru, Brazil, and the Dominican Republic by one. The first three cases discuss regional planning and development projects. The next cases concern national urban reform laws, particularly land reforms, and metropolitan organization. The remainder of the case studies are focused on programs and philosophies associated with the problems of marginal populations.

We do not consider these case studies an ideal selection, nor as necessarily representative of the best examples of urban and regional development programs under way in Latin America today. We had originally hoped to include also studies of national urban policy in Brazil, of regional development in the Venezuelan Guayana and the Cauca Valley of Colombia, of metropolitan planning in Cali, Colombia, and in São Paulo, Brazil, and of the experience of the Urban Improvement Corporation (Corporación de Mejoramiento Urbano-CORMU) in Chile.[1] We also regret our inability to include more studies of Central America. Many such cases had to be excluded because authors were unable to meet publication deadlines.

In order to unify the presentation of cases, we have attempted to organize each case submitted according to three themes: (1) an explanation of the problems that spurred creation of the program; (2) a historical or descriptive discussion of objectives and characteristics of the program; and (3) a personal evaluation of the success of the program. We have asked each author to emphasize particularly the effectiveness of the programs they discuss, rather than simply describing institutions and measures.

The authors of almost all the case studies have participated or are now participating actively in the programs described. Thus, for example, Achurra was, until November 1970, a subdirector of the National Planning Office and in charge of Chile's regional development program; Cárdenas is participating in implementation of key aspects of the development of the Río Balsas basin; Neira is at present a consultant to the state government of Bahia for implementation of the Recôncavo Baiano project; Pérez Montás is an active member of the rural community-development program in the Dominican Republic; Basaldúa and Moreno designed the legal and institutional structure of metropolitan Rosario; Labadía has served as director-general of planning in the Chilean Ministry of Housing and Urban Development; Sanjinés organized the communal action program of La Paz and is at present Director-General of Urban Development for the Municipality of La Paz; Robles Rivas is with the Peruvian Oficina Nacional de Desarrollo de Pueblos Jóvenes (Barriadas); Pineda is a former head of the

Instituto de Crédito Territorial's Planning Office; and Morcillo is Secretary for Public Administration of the Colombian Presidency. Even in cases in which authors have not been directly involved in the programs they discuss, their relationship with these programs as researchers of the central problem or as urban specialists active in their own countries has permitted them direct knowledge of these programs. That most authors are practitioners involved with the programs in question provides them with a special viewpoint regarding the experiments they describe, and with a more pragmatic approach to the problems faced than is characteristic of the authors of the more general analytic essays with which the volume opened.

Although these case studies form a very flimsy base for generalization, it is worthwhile to comment on their common themes, given the absence of much systematic analysis on comparative administration affecting local areas,[2] particularly that emphasizing the performance outcomes of different kinds of devices and structures. Taken as a whole, these reports suggest a number of working notions concerning the implementation of urban and regional development policies in Latin America. First, it is clear that spatial planning at the national or even the regional level is very difficult to implement. Yet at the same time, urban problems cannot be attacked with fragmented solutions of limited range. The example of the urban situation in the United States clearly demonstrates that it is not through investing large sums of money without greater coordination that "urban life with quality" is achieved. Freeways, massive parking lots, and programs of urban renewal are not substitutes for collective systems of rapid transit or public control of land. Neither do they constitute a solution to racial and social discrimination. In the Latin American countries, corresponding sums of money to create jobs and construct housing and urban services do not exist; yet these countries are confronting much more accelerated and disorganized urbanization.

Both Achurra and Cárdenas emphasize the difficulties of imposing the standards of the planning agency on ministries involved in making investments in specific functions not controlled by the planning body. The Mexican Rio Balsas Commission, which has operating powers, seems more powerful than the national planning agency, but as Achurra emphasizes with regard to regional development corporations in Chile, its concerns affect only a small portion of the nation's total land area or population. Neira pinpoints the key role of a modernizing elite in this process. Anthony Downs, summing up the experiences of planners in Ciudad Guayana, concludes that a good starting rule is that "area development agencies must be run by leaders who have a significant political following and are extremely skilled in political negotiations" (Rodwin et al., 1969: 376). The need for these talents is clearly illustrated by the negotiations with national ministries the Chilean and Mexican case studies imply, as well as by the potential for competition among area development agencies and among programs for "balanced" growth and the growth of older core cities in both instances.

Cuba, according to Acosta and Hardoy, is embarked on a decentralization effort not dissimilar in its outlines to the Chilean strategy. It has had more success to date in actually redirecting growth. Breaking up an established pattern of urban settlement presumably requires a continuing level of political support normally unobtainable by national or area planning agencies in other Latin American countries (Acosta and Hardoy, 1971). John Friedmann has emphasized that in order to succeed, regional and national planning efforts must in other countries be "joined to effective power for implementation" and urbanization policies must be "embodied in new institutions capable of outlasting periodic changes in the government," constitutional, administrative, or corporate. The success attributed to the Cuban reforms as compared with the problems of implementing urbanization policies in other countries without radical institutional change seems to prove his rule (Friedmann, 1971).

A second general conclusion is that legislative measures for urban land reform are only a first step in the actual solution of national urban problems, though land distribution is fundamental to change. Three case studies present pictures of efforts to reach this point. Colombia has since 1966 been in the process of considering laws dealing with land expropriation. But it has not, according to the analysis herein, squarely faced the issues of land ownership and low-income housing construction. We do not believe that the draft housing and urban development bills presented to the Colombian Congress in 1969 and 1970 will serve, if one is approved, as anything other than a simple palliative. The 1969 draft bill proposes a tax on unimproved or improved lots exceeding 850 square meters, and in the case of ruined or dilapidated buildings (Article 44) suggests control of leasing in relation to assessed valuation (Articles 99 to 101), insists upon the right of expropriation with partial payment in bonds, establishes measures to speed this process (Article 64), and proposes a bond issue (Articles 23 and 25). This bond issue, however, in spite of its unprecedented scale, is insufficient in relation to actual and potential demand for housing and urban services over the years, and the source of other resources is not specified. Payment of expropriation in bonds, because of the stable value of Colombian currency, represents issuance of money and payment at high price which limit the program's range. As Morcillo suggests, the market for urban and suburban lands is left in apparent freedom, and these lands, because of the way they are fragmented and subject to speculation, constitute one of the impediments to planned and less costly urban development. Speculative operations of urban developers are financed, without imposing limits on their time periods or on possible gains. The present rent-control system is replaced with imprecise systems of regulation. And the draft bill does not incorporate new legal concepts regarding the use of private property.

Cuba now has the legal base for overcoming its housing and service deficit under legislation far more encompassing than anything Colombia has yet considered. The Cuban urban reform law was authorized to combat the acute housing crisis aggravated by the intervention of speculative factors in the price of lots, rented buildings, and urban buildings in general, and rentals themselves, and in order to end the practice of exclusive and luxurious residential districts coexisting with malnutrition, crowding, and poverty. The Cuban reform also attacked the use of loans with mortgage guarantees. The law declared null and void leases of agricultural estates and urban real property, collection of rents derived from leases, mortgages, pending leasing debts, and placed an embargo on real property and eviction proceedings. The law foresees a state plan in three stages whose final objective is the granting of a house with permanent usufruct and at no cost to each family.

Metropolitan Rosario also has a legal base for areawide planning. We are given no data on the outcome of these legislative programs, presumably because they are too new to be assessed as yet, although the evaluation in the Argentine and Cuban cases is positive. In this situation, it is hard not to read larger principles into the report on Bolivia. Bolivia has worked with an admittedly "anemic" urban reform law since 1954. The reform was only partially applied and within a short time lost a great deal of its value. It was based upon control of urban property according to extensions established within predetermined urban administrative limits: 10,000 square meters per landowner. Since the Bolivian currency was undergoing rapid devaluation when the law was promulgated, and landowners possessing properties larger than 10,000 square meters in size were indemnified with bonds of fixed value, the government was able to acquire significant amounts of urban and suburban lands in the city of La Paz. But, in ten years, the limits of the urban areas affected by the law were surpassed by the city's physical growth, and it was not then attempted to expand them. The Bolivian government could not, or was unaware how to, complement its action in the field of urban and suburban lands with credits, technical assistance, and the indispensable institutional and legal organization. Thus the law has not halted land speculation in La Paz, nor overcome the tendency to expand via uncoordinated squatter settlement. It has had a useful positive effect in housing a tiny group of stable low-income workers, however. One suspects that legislation for urban reform is a useful device for focusing the attention of political elites on a critical problem area, but is unlikely to prevent land speculation or alter the housing situation without other instruments for urban development coordinated with reform. Calvimontes calls for the addition of a scheme to hold lands in reserve in La Paz, as well as for an urban development plan which foresees the likely direction of the extension of the city's boundaries, alongside land reform. It is noteworthy also that, compared to regional or subcommunity programs, the need for metropolitan planning or interjurisdictional programs below the regional level is relatively unemphasized, despite the existence of large numbers of jurisdictions within major metropolitan areas.

Six of the case studies concern the operation of programs affecting the poor. In this set of studies, there are a number of underlying disagreements and uncertainties. Both the definition and numbers of poor people are debated. There is no doubt that Latin American cities contain large groups of people not accepted as equal in the market, and found in poor housing, poorly paid employment, and inferior positions in the educational system. But is this because such persons are victims of the way economic growth occurs? Or are they actually a separate enclave, "marginal" to the national economy as a permanent condition of a class or group in society? It appears that the poorly housed population is increasing rapidly as a consequence of accelerated urbanization.[3] But how numerous are the people in this group? Tobar graphically demonstrates the unreliability of most estimates in comparing *villa* population figures from official agencies for greater Buenos Aires. The imprecision of our knowledge of migration is also suggested by Pineda. Despite the common notion that housing problems arise from the pattern of migration to cities, Pineda attributes Colombia's low-income housing problem to natural increases,[4] though all authors also emphasize the impact of rural-urban and interurban flows.

Authors of the case studies discuss responses to the problems of the varied poor, ranging among attention to low-income housing only (Pineda), programs integrating community facilities and services with housing for sectors at or below subsistence (Labadía), efforts at community organization and social education (Sanjinés, Pérez). Tobar and Labadía suggest that land acquisition is more important than housing construction itself in overcoming the conditions and distortions created by uncontrolled urban settlement, while others emphasize provision of housing and community facilities.

An interesting and fundamental division of opinion appears in evaluations of the utility of community organization and action as a strategy. Pérez endorses the program in the Dominican context; Tobar is skeptical of the uses of civic education in groups whose homes have been eradicated by public order; Robles believes that barrio organizations are inevitably weak, and brands community action as a tool consciously used by national elites to capture the poor. Clearly, one set of evaluations rests on the notion that poor persons can be helped to assimilate into society and that civic education and housing programs will lead to integration into the economic and social system. Opponents of this view suggest that these people are already "integrated" in a venal system; the economic and social structure of society must be altered radically if the poor are to rise. Without such structural changes, government programs might somewhat ameliorate but will always also reinforce and perpetuate the unfavorable condition of certain groups in the cities.[5] Under this assumption, only radical alteration of the system of production and consequent urban domination will change the course of barriada development, since the situation of its population is largely dependent on structural forces external to the communities.

G. G., J.E.H.

NOTES

1. See Rodwin et al. (1969), Friedmann (1966, 1965), and Stöhr (1969) for discussions of important regional programs, including Brazil's SUDENE and the Foundations for the Development of Amazônia and Brasília.

2. Notable exceptions include the studies of comparative field administration at Yale University. See, for example, Fesler (1949) and Fried (1963) and the urban studies of the Comparative Urban Administration and Politics group within the Comparative Administration Group of the American Society for Public Administration (Daland, 1969).

3. Turner (1969) has formulated a working hypothesis about the relationship between the volume of autonomous settlements and stages or levels of economic and demographic development. He indicates that cities with the highest proportion of autonomous settlement are those of countries with the highest rates of urbanization. He points to a parallel between the demographic curve of increasing and decreasing urban growth rates described by Wingo (1967).

4. Davis (1965) indicates that the basic worldwide problem will be caused by population growth within cities even as rural-urban migration decreases.

5. Recent analyses supporting this view include Eckstein (1971) and Pearlman (1971).

REFERENCES

ACOSTA, M. and J. E. HARDOY (1971) Reforma urbana en Cuba revolucionaria. Caracas: Ediciones Síntesis Dos Mil.

DALAND, R. T., ed. (1969) Comparative Urban Research: The Administration and Politics of Cities. Beverly Hills, Calif.: Sage Pubns.

DAVIS, K. (1965) "The urbanization of the human population." Scientific American 213 (September).

ECKSTEIN, S. (1971) "Theory and methods in the study of poverty and the politics of poverty: the substitution of a socio-economic structural approach for an individualistic cultural approach in Mexico." Presented at the American Political Science Association meeting, Chicago.

FESLER, J. (1949) Area and Administration. University: Univ. of Alabama Press.

FRIED, R. (1963) The Italian Prefects. New Haven, Conn.: Yale Univ. Press.

FRIEDMANN, J. (1971) "The implementation of urban-regional development policies: lessons of experience." Los Angeles: University of California, School of Architecture and Urban Planning. (mimeo)

–– (1966) Regional Development Policy: A Case Study of Venezuela. Cambridge, Mass.: MIT Press.

–– (1965) Venezuela: From Doctrine to Dialogue. Syracuse, N.Y.: Syracuse Univ. Press.

PEARLMAN, J. E. (1971) "Search and research: learning from fieldwork on Brazilian migrants." Presented at American Political Science Association meeting, Chicago.

RODWIN, L. et al. (1969) Planning Urban Growth and Regional Development: The Experience of the Guayana Program of Venezuela. Cambridge, Mass.: MIT Press.

STOHR, W. (1969) "Materials on regional development in Latin America: experience and prospects." Prepared for the Curso de Planificación Regional del Desarrollo, Seminario sobre Aspectos Sociales del Desarrollo Regional, UN/ECLA (CEPAL). Santiago: CEPAL.

TURNER, J.F.C. (1969) "Uncontrolled urban settlement: problems and policies," pp. 507-534 in G. Breese, ed., The City in Newly Developing Countries: Readings on Urbanism and Urbanization. Englewood Cliffs, N.J.: Prentice-Hall.

WINGO, L. (1967) "Recent patterns of urbanization among Latin American countries." Urban Affairs Q. 2 (March): 81-110.

Chapter 6

REGIONAL PROGRAMS

A. CHILEAN REGIONAL DEVELOPMENT POLICY

MANUEL ACHURRA LARRAIN

THE PROBLEM

In Chile, as in most Latin American countries, there is a concentration of population and economic activity in a few centers. In 1960, 40 percent of gross regional product was generated in the province of Santiago, rising to 46 percent in 1970, and a projected 54 percent in 1980. Santiago had 34.6 percent of Chile's total population in 1970 and has the highest rate of immigration. Indicators show even greater concentration when dealing with the industrial sector and services in general. In 1967, 64.4 percent of industries employing more than fifty workers were located in Santiago, and Santiago collected about 70 percent of the taxes and accounted for about 65 percent of all banking transactions in Chile. In addition, the chief public administrative activities are located in Santiago. Financial activities are also controlled by Santiago, which explains why a majority of businesses have their headquarters in the capital, even though their plants may be located elsewhere. Simultaneously, higher-level service activities related in some way to economic, social, political, and cultural change—such as higher education, scientific research, exhibitions, art lectures, and political party headquarters—are all basically located in Santiago. The chances for growth and diversification are more varied in the capital, as are communications and transportation, which converge and radiate outward from Santiago to the rest of the nation and abroad.

This concentration has taken place at the expense of other Chilean regions,

Editors' Note: A number of discussions of Chilean regional development policy are available in English. See John Friedmann and Walter Stöhr, "The Uses of Regional Science: Policy Planning in Chile," *Papers of the Regional Science Association,* 18 (1966); Mariano Valle, "Planning Regional Development in Chile: Achievements and Perspectives" (Cambridge: Special Program on Urban and Regional Development, 1969—typescript); and John Friedmann, *Urban and Regional Development in Chile* (Santiago: The Ford Foundation, 1969—offset). Chapter IX of the latter appears as "Urban-Regional Policies for National Development in Chile" in *Latin American Urban Research,* Vol. I. English translation by Leonidas F. Pozo-Ledezma.

whose populations have migrated to the more dynamic centers. The counterpart of Santiago's predominance is the weakening of peripheral regions. The problems generated by this regional imbalance are of a social, economic, and political nature. Economically, the lack of new investments, especially in industry, weakens regional markets and income. Socially, the problems of unemployment and lack of opportunities cause migration, which further debilitates peripheral regions. Politically, the central government becomes heavily pressured to aid the development of backward regions having a standard of living lower than that of the most developed urban areas. Unbalanced regional development also manifests itself in the widening gap that separates less- from more-developed regions. The Chilean government has therefore put into operation a regional development policy which seeks to close the gap separating levels of development in different regions of the nation, as well as to achieve more balanced growth throughout Chile.

A HISTORY OF REGIONAL DEVELOPMENT EXPERIENCE

The best-known regional development efforts in Chile involve programs for the frontier zones. Because of the nation's elongated shape and the great distances between its northern and southern limits and the capital city, little development has occurred in the frontier regions. The government has provided unusual stimuli to attract population and develop economic activity here. The establishment of Arica, near the Peruvian border, as a free port in 1953, and its subsequent industrial growth, beginning in 1958 with the creation of its Junta of Progress (Junta de Adelanto), represents one of the first regional development experiments. Arica's development was characterized during early years by trade in imported articles that could not be commercially distributed to the rest of the nation. Later, an automotive industry developed, consisting mainly of assembly with little value-added. In both cases, development had an artificial character. These activities could be maintained only because they were exclusive to Arica and were protected by sweeping tax and customs exemptions. The Arica experiment has been costly for the rest of the nation because of the foreign exchange allocated for imports in this department, the taxes that went uncollected by the government, and the high price and low quality of Arica products. During the past two years, because of the application of national planning criteria coordinated with the central government, Arica's development has begun to be given new orientation.

Another experiment in regional planning dates from 1956. In that year, special import privileges were granted to the southern provinces of Magallanes, Aysén, and Chiloé. Since the foreign exchange in dollars allocated to those provinces amounted to much smaller sums, the trade of this region did not develop as spectacularly as did Arica's. In 1968, the Corporación de Magallanes was created to stimulate regional development. Development Corporation (Corporación de Fomento—CORFO) institutes were also formed in Chiloé and

Aysén, but these institutions do not possess sufficient resources to promote large-scale development in their regions.

The approximate budgets of the regional corporations were as follows (in U.S. dollars):

Junta de Adelanto de Arica	16,000,000
Corporación de Magallanes	7,000,000
Instituto CORFO Aysén	500,000
Instituto CORFO Chiloé	500,000
Instituto CORFO Norte	9,000,000

The northern zone has benefited from the 1955 copper law, which allocates a portion of copper tax revenues to investment in provinces in which copper mines owned by large companies are located. Traditionally, these funds have not been part of a program of regional development, but rather have served to set the minimum level of state spending in those zones. In 1967, the Instituto CORFO Norte was created, which uses its share of copper tax revenues to promote industrial, mining, fishing, and agricultural development.

In 1962, as a result of the earthquakes of May 1960, which caused great damage in the southern part of Chile, the government created new Provincial Development Committees (Comités Provinciales de Desarrollo). These were composed of representatives from public and private sectors, presided over by the intendent of each province, with CORFO regional agencies serving as technical secretariats. The provincial committees failed dismally because power was not delegated to them, nor was expeditious communication with national agencies provided.

The weakness of autonomous regional development corporations and the centralization of Chilean government made it possible in 1965 to redirect regional development policy again from the top. The first thrust was the incorporation of all planning into the Office of National Planning (Oficina de Planeamiento Nacional—ODEPLAN), thus breaking with the traditional pattern of considering only global and sectoral planning by adding a geographic dimension.[1] ODEPLAN began its work by redefining Chile's territorial divisions. The central idea was to regroup Chile's twenty-five provinces into regions capable of generating self-sustained development. In each region, one or more development poles would serve as dynamic agents and as integrating centers of regional development. The size and relative importance of each region would be such that it could be governed by a regional authority.

Using these criteria, a classification based on two types of regions was developed—colonization regions and consolidated regions. The first are located in the southern and northern extremes of the nation. They have low population densities, problems of access and communication with the rest of the nation, and economic activities subject to fluctuation because of depletion of natural resources or changes in price and demand for raw materials. These regions contain about 60 percent of Chile's total land area, but only about 15 percent of the population. In the second or consolidated type are those regions located in the central part of Chile, where exploitation of resources and generation of economic activities have led to population stability and permanence. Density here permits settlement of cities and the building of an infrastructure which makes them endure and integrate among themselves.

Within this consolidated region, two subgroups may be distinguished: the Central Macro-zone, and Peripheral Regions. More than 50 percent of the nation's population lives within the Central Macro-zone. It generates approximately 60 percent of gross regional product, and more than 70 percent of industrial production. Santiago is located in this zone, with nearly 2,500,000 inhabitants. It is linked by highway—within two hours' drive—with the metropolitan area of Valparaíso-Viña del Mar and other smaller urban centers, such as Rancagua, San Felipe, and Los Andes, noted for their industrial dynamism. In the peripheral regions, economic activity is primarily agricultural, with the exception of the Concepción area, which contains a metropolitan center of importance and is developing basic steel, petroleum-refining, and petrochemical industries under government sponsorship. The grouping of the twenty-five provinces into eleven regions and one metropolitan zone is summarized in Table 1.

Once the regions in Chile were defined, a regional development policy was formulated to set regional priorities, rank development poles, and regionalize sectoral development. In the four contiguous regions in the central valley, from the Maule Region to that of Los Lagos, agriculture is predominant, though there are centers which will permit support of new industries and creation of more specialized services. What is sought here is integral development on a multisectoral basis, including agriculture, fishing, forestry, and manufacturing industry coupled with the development of a transportation and communication system, which would facilitate the linking of development poles with their areas of influence. Basic raw material-processing industries whose transporation costs

TABLE 1
CHILEAN REGIONAL DEVELOPMENT CLASSIFICATIONS

Colonization Regions	North	I	Tarapacá
		II	Antofagasta
		III	Atacama-Coquimbo
	South	X	Los Canales
		XI	Magallanes
Consolidated Regions	Peripheral Regions	VI	Maule
		VII	Bío-Bío
		VIII	Cautín
		IX	Los Lagos
	Central Macro-zone	MZ	Santiago
		IV	Aconcagua-Valparaíso
		V	O'Higgins-Colchagua

are high could be installed in these regions. Examples include paper and cellulose plants, beet-sugar mills, fruit and vegetable canneries, meat-packing, and refrigeration. The encouragement of small- and medium-sized industries which could substitute for regional imports or use the semi-finished products of basic industries located in those regions (mainly steel and oil) would have an important decentralizing effect on future industrial development. This policy affects 30 percent of the national population in an area in which 23.5 percent of gross regional product is generated and in which 18 percent of industries employing more than 50 persons are located.

In the Central Macro-zone, natural but disorderly growth exists, particularly in Santiago. The Central Macro-zone, which runs from Aconcagua Province on the north to Colchagua Province on the south, generates 60 percent of gross regional product and accounts for 70 percent of industries employing more than 50 persons. The policy dictates that new industries should be located in places other than Santiago, unless they require advanced technology and a variety of services that only Santiago can offer. In the colonization regions in the extreme North and South, it is necessary that the government apply a development policy with special incentives and create development corporations enjoying financial autonomy.

Adequate ranking of development poles as priority locations for integrated urban-regional development and particularly for new industries is a basic instrument of the regional development policy, since urban centers account for almost 70 percent of the nation's population, and, even more importantly, will account for almost all population growth in coming years. Almost all secondary and tertiary activities are located in the development poles, so their influence is exerted over an area whose size is larger than the center; this permits integration of the national territory through the interrelation of these development poles. Development poles have been ranked as follows:

(1) *national development poles:* Santiago, as the seat of administration and institutions serving the entire nation;

(2) *multiregional development poles of national importance:* Antofagasta, Valparaíso, and Concepción, cities which in the North, center, and South of the nation should constitute effective counterpoints to Santiago's growth, creating a dynamism which can be self-sustaining;

(3) *regional development poles:* Areas with populations approaching or above 100,000 inhabitants, relatively distant from poles of national importance. These poles are differentiated according to the areas they serve and fulfill different roles in accordance with their size and location. They include Arica, Iquique, Serena-Coquimbo, Rancagua, Talca, Temuco, Valdivia, Osorno, Puerto Montt, and Punta Arenas.

EVALUATION

The results of the policy adopted are not yet known. The integration policy has had great success in the Bío-Bío region, in which growth rates higher than the national average were achieved from 1965 to 1968. This, together with continuing large investment in industrial development, suggests the region's future dynamism. Nevertheless, this policy has not been successfully applied in the Maule, Cautín, and Los Lagos regions because of the lack of strategic industrial projects which could make the local economies more dynamic.

Meanwhile, the Central Macro-zone has continued enjoying natural growth. Here there is also no metropolitan or regional authority supervising the municipalities in planning and executing programs in housing, urban facilities, and transportation or determining the uses to which available physical space will be put. A decision on this matter is important, since the government allocates about 50 percent of its investment expenditures to the Central Macro-zone, in which half the nation's population lives. The results of the policy of barring new industries in the Santiago metropolitan area are also not considered satisfactory. No other city can yet compete with Santiago as the country's magnet for manufacturing.

The policy applied to colonization regions in the extreme North and South has led to the creation of new stimuli for the development of these regions. In the far North, Arica continues its spectacular growth, increasingly sustained by more solid and dynamic bases, such as development of the electronics industry. The resources of Arica's Junta de Adelanto and the activities of established industries ensure sustained growth in the future. But the economies of the departments of Iquique and Pisagua have stagnated, due to the crisis in the fishing industry beginning in 1965. The province of Antofagasta has felt the favorable impact of expansion programs involving the copper industry, because of increased production and activities of related manufacturing industries. In the far South, the provinces of Llanquihue and Chiloé have grown relatively slowly and do not have projects that could modify the present trend. In the provinces of Aysén and Magallanes, however, there have been some sizable investments which have created more favorable conditions for the development of both provinces.

The most important gap is not in plan formulation but in the mechanisms for implementation of these plans. The National Planning Office (ODEPLAN), which is in charge of formulating regional plans, has only an advisory role vis-à-vis executive agencies of the public sector. Even though everyone accepts the idea of planning, plans are rejected when they modify traditional systems of decision-making. They are also rejected by those who do not wish to subject their decisions to a national planning system, which inevitably imposes restrictions.

A whole series of measures has been used to try to carry out ODEPLAN's regionalization policy. These include regionalization of planning and development institutions, direct investments, location incentives, and regional development corporations. The creation of regional planning offices (ORPLAN) in Magallanes, Puerto Montt, Valdivia, Concepción, and Talca was the first effective step toward implementation of the regional policy. The ORPLAN's role is to forge a regional conscience and stimulate personnel from public and private sectors to organize on a regional basis.

The President of Chile recently also signed a decree ordering all government service offices to adjust their territorial jurisdictions to the regionalization scheme proposed by ODEPLAN. This has been approved by the Ministry of Housing and Urban Development, and Zonal Coordinating Committees (Comités Zonales de Coordinación) have been created in the agricultural sector. National ministries have also begun delegating greater authority to their regional offices (Delegaciones Zonales). Among the organizations delegating most authority are the National Development Corporation (CORFO), which increased the amount of credit its provincial agencies can lend without consulting Santiago. The Ministry of Education has begun a pilot experiment in the Bío-Bío region, as has the Ministry of Interior, with regional committees of intendents in the Bío-Bío and Maule regions. The Housing Ministry has moved to create fully decentralized regional offices to coordinate with the regional ORPLANS. Other ministries, including Agriculture, the Tourism Directorate (Dirección de Turismo), which has created regional tourism councils, the Armed Forces, and the Ministry of Foreign Relations have also begun to organize for decentralization.

Devices affecting the location of industry are another basic instrument for regional development policy implementation. Industrial location policies geared to regional growth have been applied with relative success, thanks to the coordination established between ODEPLAN, CORFO, the Ministry of Housing and Urbanism, and the Ministry of the Economy. For the first time, the policy–of not permitting installation of industries in the Santiago area–is being applied more strictly, thus creating a series of stimuli to attract new industries to the provinces. These stimuli include both direct investments like the construction of industrial parks and barrios–such as those in Arica, Antofagasta, Coquimbo, El Belloto, and Concepción–and location incentives like the special customs exemptions for importation of machinery and equipment earmarked for provincial regions. The same criteria are followed by CORFO, and the National Bank (Banco Nacional) in granting credit. Application of these policies has favored Concepción, Arica, Valparaíso, and other urban centers in the Central Macro-zone, such as Rancagua and San Felipe-Los Andes.

Regional development corporations, like Arica's Junta de Adelanto which enjoys important financial resources and ample autonomy,[2] constitute another powerful mechanism for regional development. It is not possible, however, to distribute this type of corporation throughout the entire nation both because of a scarcity of resources and because a national blanket of corporations would diminish the central direction of national development. Development corporations were originally justified only as exceptional cases in the extreme North and South. Arica's Junta de Adelanto has signed an agreement with ODEPLAN to link its regional plans to the national development plan. In the South, Magallanes province has a recently created corporation which, although it serves a population of equal size and geographic area larger than that of Arica's Junta de Adelanto, has available only about one-tenth the budget enjoyed by Arica's Junta. The Magallanes Corporation also dovetails its plans with recommendations made by ODEPLAN through its regional office.

The experience of Arica's Junta and the Magallanes Corporation whetted the appetites of neighboring regions for similar treatment.[3] Regional political pressure forced the government to grant a greater degree of decentralization to depressed zones relatively distant from the nation's center. This autonomy was granted by means of creation of decentralized departments of the Corporación de Fomento through the Instituto CORFO Norte. Regional CORFO departments have less autonomy than Arica's Junta de Adelanto or the Magallanes Corporation, since their budgets must be approved by the council of CORFO, but they do assure that CORFO must invest a minimum amount in these zones. In addition, allocation of specific expenditures is decided upon by a regional council. Recently, the Chilean Parliament also approved a law creating the Regional Investment Programming Council of Tarapacá (Consejo Regional Programador de Inversiones en la Región de Tarapacá), composed of heads of the public sector's service agencies and representatives of the private sector. They will decide upon investment priorities in their region, having at their disposal funds budgeted directly to them or those derived from taxes collected in the region.

Regionalization of the public-sector budget is another mechanism for implementation of regional development policies which has been applied during the past two years. Since the traditional system of budgeting has a sectoral and institutional approach, difficulties have been encountered in attempting to make innovations. And it would be unrealistic to expect extremely encouraging results from regionalization of the budget since many annual investments are part of projects already begun which take years to complete, thus making the amounts available for regionalization at times very small.

Regionalization of international technical assistance is another instrument for implementing regional planning. This assistance is ODEPLAN's responsibility and its ORPLANs are used for regional action. Recently, an agreement was signed between the Chilean government and UNICEF to carry out a social-development program in coastal and foothill zones of the Los Lagos region. This program represents a pilot experiment in Latin America which went to Chile because of the availability of regional-level decentralization.

At present, regionalization of decisions of central agencies of government is of vast importance, since Chile's system of government is so highly centralized. The majority of governmental institutions have councils and committees to approve programs and projects, and ODEPLAN has been trying to make its presence felt in these councils and committees. ODEPLAN has representatives in the Economic Committee of Ministers, where the highest-level decisions are made; in the Council of CORFO, which dominates industrial development, agriculture, fishing, and mining; the Development Council of the National Bank (Consejo de Fomento del Banco del Estado), which approves credit for financing new investment in the fields of industry, agriculture, fishing, and tourism; and in the Committees of Foreign Investment, External Credit, Tariff Policy, Transportation, Coordination of Tourism, Customs, Electronics, Fishing, Easter Island, and the Institute of Natural Resources.

ODEPLAN's relative success in these endeavors is due in large part to its holistic view of Chile's development, and to the wealth of information it has available from studies carried out by its different departments and regional offices. This permits ODEPLAN to incorporate both a national and a more selective regional view into the implementation of planning and development policies in Chile today.

NOTES

1. Under the Director of ODEPLAN is the National Under-Directorate of Planning, which is basically in charge of formulating the global plan as well as making sectoral plans compatible. Also under the Director is the Regional Under-Directorate, which oversees the Department of Regional Planning (Departamento de Planificación Regional) in Santiago, and Regional Planning Offices (Oficinas Regionales de Planificación—ORPLAN), in a majority of regions into which Chile is divided.

2. Arica's Junta de Adelanto has available a total of about 150 million *escudos* annually, of which about 45 million can be lent directly to encourage economic development.

3. This expansion of development corporations from region to region has also occurred in Venezuela and Colombia.

B. REGIONAL RURAL DEVELOPMENT: THE MEXICAN RIO BALSAS COMMISSION

CUAUHTEMOC CARDENAS

THE PROBLEM

The Mexican Río Balsas basin, particularly the "hot country" zones of the states of Guerrero and Michoacán, was traditionally an economically backward region. Its inhabitants' livelihood was meager. Its climate was unhealthy and malaria-ridden, its agriculture weak—devoted to corn-growing and extensive cattle-raising with poor yield—and its mines were largely uneconomic. As Mexico's communications system modernized, this rugged region was left isolated from the more developed areas of the country, in spite of the region's proximity to such areas.[1]

The population was dispersed in many small localities. Centers on the periphery of the region's "hot country" were old settlements which had formerly served as mule-driving centers. These centers acquired, and in some cases later maintained, local commercial importance. In the late nineteenth century, textile and sugar mills were also established on the upper Balsas basin, where the river rises near Mexico City.

In the late nineteenth and early twentieth centuries, the first large private irrigation works were built. In addition, the main railroad tracks traversing the region were laid during this period. Beginning in the late 1920s, main roads were built, the railroad network was expanded, and the Comisión Nacional de Irrigación built several dams which began important hydraulic projects. The commission began operation in 1926, and in late 1946, its functions were assumed by the Ministry of Water Resources (Secretaría de Recursos Hidráulicos).

Although the Balsas basin bordered the most developed area of Mexico, that of the capital city, it received only minor benefit from this proximity. The region was densely populated, though, as previously mentioned, its population was dispersed in a large number of small settlements and a few important centers, and suffered from the urgent need to improve the standards of living of its people.

On May 14, 1947, in the face of the need to stimulate the region's development, the government created the Comisión del Tepalcatepec, which was to carry out a development program in the basin of the Tepalcatepec River, 18,000 square kilometers in length and the Balsas' most important tributary. The commission proposed to construct hydroelectric plants, exploit copper deposits in Inguarán, silver in Oropeo, and iron ore in Las Truchas, construct a Pacific seaport adjacent to the Las Truchas steel plant, build a paper mill to

Editors' Note: English translation by Alejandro Vélez Gómez.

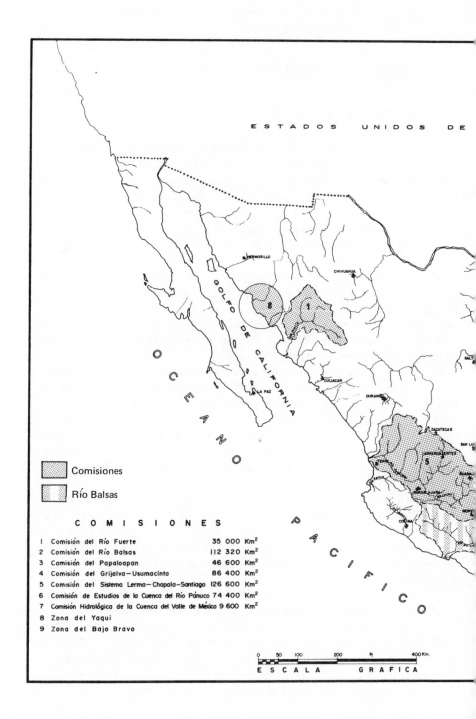

Comisiones

Río Balsas

C O M I S I O N E S

1 Comisión del Río Fuerte   35 000 Km²
2 Comisión del Río Balsas   112 320 Km²
3 Comisión del Papaloapan   46 600 Km²
4 Comisión del Grijalva—Usumacinta   86 400 Km²
5 Comisión del Sistema Lerma—Chapala—Santiago   126 600 Km²
6 Comisión de Estudios de la Cuenca del Río Pánuco   74 400 Km²
7 Comisión Hidrológica de la Cuenca del Valle de México   9 600 Km²
8 Zona del Yaqui
9 Zona del Bajo Bravo

exploit the upper basin's forests, construct the railroad line from Nueva Italia to the Pacific coast, and control the Tepalcatepec River and its tributaries in order to irrigate unproductive lands or those of very low yield which could only be cultivated during the rainy season or under irrigation.

In the fourteen years the commission was in operation, 97,000 hectares, mostly in *ejidos,* were irrigated; an interconnected network of roads of more than 800 kilometers was created; three hydroelectric plants with an installed capacity of 160,000 kilowatt hours were constructed in coordination with other government agencies; and projects for and studies of the hydroelectric exploitation of the Balsas' course, below its confluence with the Tepalcatepec were initiated. In addition, studies were undertaken of how to exploit rationally existing forests and their industrialization, and of the proposed steel works utilizing ore from Las Truchas.

In 1959, the Balsas River Basin Studies Committee (Comité de Estudios de la Cuenca del Río Balsas) was formed with the Minister of Water Resources as president with a view to expanding the radius of action which had been limited to the Tepalcatepec basin.

In response to the committee's report, the Río Balsas Commission was created in November 1960. The Río Balsas Commission, like its predecessor, was established as a technical-administrative organ to supervise the functioning of all water-use and flood-control projects, irrigation works, generating plants, water supply to centers of population, sanitary engineering, communications and transportation, including roads, railroads, telegraph and telephone services, ports, and the like, and also to create and expand centers of population. It also has power to dictate measures regarding agricultural, industrial, and colonization matters touching upon the execution of projects for the integral development of the basin.

THE PROGRAM

The commission has from the beginning considered it necessary to expand the basin's communications network to integrate the area physically, culturally, and economically. Whenever possible, new schools have gone hand-in-hand with new roads, given the area's high rate of illiteracy and the serious lack of schools and teachers. In the realm of electrification, an almost permanent campaign has been mounted to electrify communicating towns and the countryside in general by means of programs in which the local population participated along with the Río Balsas Commission and the Comisión Federal de la Electricidad.

Special importance has been given to irrigation in the commission's programs. Lands benefited are largely ejidal or owned by proprietors whose holdings are within legal limits (a maximum of 100 hectares of irrigated land, even though in certain irrigation districts recently put into operation outside the Balsas region, 20 hectares has been set as the maximum). The new wealth generated by irrigation is consequently widely distributed. Irrigation is the first step in economic improvement, and the intervention of official credit institutions in these new areas has been sought in order to provide financial aid to farmers and ranchers. In this way, the economy of these *campesino* sectors is strengthened, although the basin's great demographic increase and hostile physical environment make it necessary also to continue integrating the region and intensifying activities in other sectors of the economy.

The Balsas Commission has played a relatively small role in general development efforts with the exception of infrastructure and agriculture, but the idea of stimulating Mexico's basic industry and creating a development pole in the region has also led the commission to promote the Las Truchas steel project. This involves construction of a plant having an annual finished-product capacity of 1,000,000 tons. The Las Truchas plant is intended to complement the nation's existing steel industry and to serve as a first pole of the planned development of the Balsas basin. In order for the local population to benefit directly from new industry, urban development and housing programs are contemplated, as well as port development (construction of the Pacific port has already begun), railroad construction (still in the planning stages), and construction of schools of different grades and specialized training centers.

The commission has not considered intervening more actively in industrial matters or in the resolution of problems of the basin's urban areas, since, in general, other governmental agencies are so engaged. In addition, preference has been given to the basin's most depressed areas, primarily rural, because their problems are so vast, their needs so pressing, and their resources so limited.

Faced with an extensive region having numerous problems of the most diverse kind, the commission has used two criteria in selecting areas in which to carry out its activities. The first is that areas are to be economically depressed, with harsh living conditions, isolated, mountainous, and heavily eroded. They are also to be areas in which the possibilities of irrigation or short-term improvement are limited, and those in which preferential attention has been given to roads, education, electrification, and, whenever possible, to small irrigation systems. On this basis, work has been initiated in the basins of the Mixteco and Tlapaneco rivers, tributaries of the Balsas, in the states of Oaxaca, Puebla, and Guerrero.

The second criterion for selection was that an area, even though equally isolated and offering only a meager livelihood, offer the possibility of more rapid development. The extensive plains along the Balsas in Guerrero and Michoacán met this criterion, since some 100,000 hectares are suitable for irrigation, of which approximately 40,000 hectares will be irrigated on completion of systems now under construction. Other areas having potentially exploitable mineral or forest resources are found all over the basin. Minerals are primarily concentrated in the mid-river region, where deposits of gold, silver, and copper are known to exist. Forest resources are found in the basin's higher areas. Their exploitation is being attempted for the purpose of benefiting property owners, primarily Indian communities and ejidos, and of preserving and increasing this resource, as well as safeguarding projects already constructed by preventing erosion and silting.

The capability to control the water of the Balsas and its tributaries has been established by means of various irrigation works with which 230,000 hectares more could be brought under irrigation (irrigation in progress at present will benefit 70,000 hectares). Eventually, the Balsas basin irrigation system will cover almost half a million hectares. There is also the possibility of significantly increasing hydroelectric output. At present, the capacity is 1,000,000 installed kilowatts. The La Villita hydroelectric plant now under construction will add 300,000 kilowatts, and it is hoped to increase the area's total capacity to 2,500,000 kilowatts.

EVALUATION

It is difficult to evaluate the work accomplished in the Balsas basin, since studies made were not translated into a political program or plan implying a commitment to the region's inhabitants or to the nation as a whole. The commission acts on the basis of budgetary appropriations authorized annually by the Ministry of the Treasury and Public Credit (Secretaría de Hacienda y Crédito Público) through the Ministry of Water Resources, whose minister is president of the Río Balsas Commission. Each year, moneys are spent to conclude or proceed with ongoing programs or to initiate new, high-priority programs in each area of the basin.

Given the limitations noted above, the work performed in the Balsas basin has brought conclusive improvement in the standard of living of the region's inhabitants and has increased economic activity. Although the Tepalcatepec Commission's program set no deadlines, major works have been initiated or completed, including hydroelectric projects, road-building, and irrigation. The projected Las Truchas plant is also in the planning stage. The Balsas port works alongside the proposed steel plant have begun, and the mining and smelting of copper in Inguarán is beginning. In addition, the region's agriculture is modernizing and becoming more technical, while its output is increasingly finding its way into export markets. Finally, regional planning was extended, in theory, to cover the entire Balsas basin, although in practice it encompasses only the hot-country valleys of mid-basin, the mouth of the Balsas, and the upper Mixteca.

The balance is favorable and work is proceeding, although great needs and pressing problems are pitted against limited budgets. With this in mind, the commission has brought benefits to the region through participation of other agencies in the basin's programs. The commission has outlined specific basin problems in which these agencies have competence, sought mutual collaboration, and granted them assistance. The commission is not empowered to act in certain matters, particularly agrarian reform. Yet there are problems affecting important nuclei of the population and solution could be accelerated if direct collaboration with the Department of Agrarian Affairs (Departamento de Asuntos Agrarios) were established, permitting on-the-spot decisions as problems arise, and consideration of development projects in the presence and with the participation of the interested population.

The work of all the commissions—Papaloapan, Grijalva, Fuerte, and Balsas—constitute an example of what can be accomplished by decentralizing activities and functions, bringing together problems and the population affected by development programs, and decision-making centers.

NOTE

1. Located in south-central Mexico, the Balsas river basin covers 112,000 square kilometers, is generally mountainous, with little flat land, and has a torrid climate with rain concentrated from July to September almost throughout the entire basin.

The region's population is estimated at 5,000,000 inhabitants, giving it a mean density of 45 inhabitants per square kilometer, a figure higher than that for Mexico as a whole, 25. Population settlement is dispersed. According to the 1960 census, there were the following urban areas: Puebla, Pue. (1960, 289,049 inhabitants; 1970, estimated at 392,000); Uruapan, Mich. (45,727; 67,000); Cuernavaca, Mor. (37,144; 44,000); Iguala, Gro. (26,485; 38,000) and Zitácuaro, Mich. (23,883; 29,000). In addition, prior to 1970, Apatzingán, Mich. (estimated 1968 population, 49,000) and Ciudad Hidalgo, Mich. (24,000) had achieved the status of urban areas. Preliminary data from the January 1970 census were not available at time of writing.

The region's principal economic activity is agriculture. Production is secure only in the 240,000 hectares under irrigation: 97,000 hectares irrigated by the Tepalcatepec Commission, approximately 40,000 under large-scale irrigation, and the remainder under small-scale irrigation or aging, relatively rudimentary systems. In a large part of the basin, agricultural production is confined to the rainy season, with accompanying great risk and low yield. Agriculture is also sometimes practiced on steep slopes with antiquated techniques, causing erosion.

Similarly, cattle-raising in the region leaves something to be desired. Dairying has been developed near large population centers and in those parts of the basin in which important public-works programs have been carried out. Nonetheless, in a large part of the region cattle production is still extensive, and suffers from poor sanitary conditions, lack of scientific breeding, and deficiencies in livestock and ranch management. It is worth noting that, due to the combined efforts of campesinos, official credit institutions, and the Río Balsas Commission, a good number of cattle ranches managed by campesinos have been developed with technical and credit assistance, which are achieving satisfactory results.

Industrialization has preferentially clustered around large population centers, which, in turn, are near Mexico City. Of importance are the textile mills of the state of Puebla; the cotton mills in Apatzingán, Michoacán; and the wheat and sugar mills at certain points close to the basin's watershed. Recently, industries have increasingly settled in the city of Puebla, outstanding among which is a steel plant with an annual capacity of 300,000 tons, and in Cuernavaca, Morelos, where medium and light industries of various kinds have been established.

REFERENCES

BASSOLS, A. (1967) La división económica regional de México. Mexico, D.F.: Universidad Nacional Autónoma de México.
BUENROSTRO, C. (1965) La Región del Río Balsas y su desarrollo. Santiago de Chile: Seminario Latinoamericano sobre Aspectos Sociales del Desarrollo Regional.

— — (1964) "Organismos del desarrollo regional. Algunas experiencias mexicanas," in Organismos de desarrollo regional. Ahuacatitlán, Morelos, Mexico: Comisión del Río Balsas.

CARDENAS, C. (1965) La Villita-Las Truchas. Industrialización de la Costa del Pacífico. Melchor Ocampo del Balsas, Michoacán, Mexico: Comisión del Río Balsas.

— — (1964a) Planes regionales actualmente en ejecución en México. Ahuacatitlán, Morelos, Mexico: Comisión del Río Balsas.

— — (1964b) "Desarrollo integral de Cuencas Hidrológicos. Regiones por desarrollar en México," in Organismos de desarrollo regional. Ahuacatitlán, Morelos, Mexico: Comisión del Río Balsas.

Comité de Estudios de la Cuenca del Río Balsas (1962) Estudios del Río Verde. Mexico, D.F.: Secretaría de Recursos Hidráulicos.

— — (1961) Estudios para el aprovechamiento de los recursos de la Cuenca del Río Balsas. Mexico, D.F.: Secretaría de Recursos Hidráulicos.

DURAN, L. (1965) Los indígenas del Balsas. Ahuacatitlán, Morelos, Mexico: Comisión del Río Balsas.

Plan Lerma Asistencia Técnica (n.d.) Información Regional. Guadalajara, Jalisco, Mexico.

C. DEVELOPMENT STRATEGY AND THE RECONCAVO BAIANO OF BRAZIL

EDUARDO NEIRA ALVA

THE PROBLEM

This study describes historical factors and future perspectives in the development of the Recôncavo Baiano, a subregion of the state of Bahia in the Brazilian Northeast. At present, the region is in a process of transition from traditional exploitive to industrial activities and from largely spontaneous development to a deliberate process of rational development. In this transition process, three factors are dominant: the presence since the 1950s of an innovative spirit in both government and private sectors; reversal of adverse economic trends in Bahia after a long period of stagnation; and the decision of the state government to direct this process through a coordinated development strategy.

Manifestations of these factors are found in certain concrete accomplishments: establishment of the Industrial Center of Aratú, which since 1965 has been acquiring most industrial installations located in the Recôncavo; creation of the Recôncavo Development Council (Conselho de Desenvolvimento do Recôncavo—CONDER), a state agency which promotes and coordinates public-sector policy within the Recôncavo; construction of the Port of Aratú which will complete and strengthen the industrial estate; and the forthcoming petrochemical complex of Camaçari which will serve as a second industrial development pole of this industry in Brazil.

It is difficult, however, to determine the chronology of the process. In 1967, a mission organized by the Inter-American Development Bank and composed of members of other international and national organizations visited Bahia and proposed the formulation and application of a global development strategy for the Recôncavo Baiano. This proposal, however, was in effect a reflection of ideas and projects existing in Salvador, rather than an exogenous suggestion. Yet some of the Mission's proposals, such as the study on petrochemicals, have already effectively served as a basis for the state government's political actions, ensuring its position as an instrument for the coordination of investment, and strengthening its capacity for negotiation.

While the Recôncavo's process of development is still in its initial phases, it is considered of interest to discuss the potentialities of a rather different approach to the planning of regional development.

Author's Note: Paper presented to the Congress of the Inter-American Planning Society held in Salvador, Bahia, Brazil, September 1970. Two noncommercial publications of a slightly different version have been made, one in Portuguese by the Conselho de Desenvolvimento do Recôncavo da Bahia (CONDER) and the other in Spanish by the Organization of American States (OAS) after presentation at a seminar in Caracas in December 1970. English translation by Felicity M. Trueblood.

The Internal Evolution of the Recôncavo

The zone extending along the coast of the Bahia de Todos los Santos in the state of Bahia in the Brazilian Northeast is known as the Recôncavo Baiano. The word "recôncavo" means the internal side of a circle or a curving surface. In this case, it describes the most salient morphological characteristics of an area covering a half-moon-shaped coastal plain of some 6,500 square kilometers of fertile clay soil, limited on the West by the *sertão*, a rather dry ecological environment completely different from that of the Recôncavo.

The area has considerable physiographic homogeneity. As L. A. Costa Pinto (1958) has written, it is a large amphitheatre in which the slope of terrain makes rivers and landscapes descend gradually to the large gulf which is the epicenter of the region. In this amphitheatre, a process of cultural settlement developed 400 years ago, when the Portuguese found the region a natural focus for trading activities and, later, exceptional conditions for the cultivation of sugar cane. The antiquity of the settlement process and the relative isolation which followed have produced considerable sociological unity.

> We may understand the Recôncavo as a regional society structured on the basis of an
> ecological synthesis, formed and developed historically around activities by means of
> which its population, which occupies the land and uses its resources, produces and
> reproduces the material conditions of its existence and forms the social environment
> in which it lives (Costa Pinto, 1958: 21-22).

Regional unity comes from just this permanent process of adjustment, and not only from identities or similarities among the region's different social or economic sectors which could become antagonistic under certain conditions.

The Recôncavo's economic and social history can in fact be described by tracing the relationships created by different forms of production (Costa Pinto, 1958). Historically, the Recôncavo had many economically different cultures: fishing and maritime navigation; tobacco and subsistence agriculture; sugar, and, more recently, petroleum. Fishing and navigation in the Gulf are traditional or even primitive activities.[1] Navigation in Bahia is still based on the *saveiro*, a primitive sailboat which transports a considerable portion of intraregional cargo. It has not yet been replaced by other means of transportation, even though its predominance has been affected by the truck, whose use was promoted by federal government's road-building efforts during the past thirty years.

For centuries, tobacco has been present, together with sugar, in the history of the Recôncavo; it still constitutes the central activity of an important subarea. It has functioned in two ways: the traditional artisan production and processing of leaves, and the modern methods associated with export of selected leaves and local manufacture of cigars. In the former, the *fazendeiro* (farmer) produces tobacco on his own land, buys the production of his sharecroppers *(parceiros)* and sells both to the *armazenista* or *trapicheiro* who processes, often through rudimentary techniques, leaves for sale to export enterprises or local cigar plants. The *armazenistas,* who began by financing the small farmer, have become intermediaries who tend to control this mode of production. In the modern process, introduction of standards and quality control required by foreign trade forced the large tobacco enterprise to modernize. Modern production methods and greater availability of financial resources have reduced the relative importance of the *"armazenista-fazendeiro"* system and, consequently, of the peasants involved. The reduced ability of export and manufacturing enterprises to influence the international tobacco market limited the sector to a secondary position and stagnated production levels long ago. Technologically and economically limited, industrial production of tobacco represents, nevertheless, a factor of change vis-à-vis primitive forms of artisan manufacture and has served to introduce new types of social and economic relationships promoting the development process of the Recôncavo.

For centuries, sugar was the reason for being of the Recôncavo. Traditionally grown on *massâpe* lands (a characteristic soil formation of the lowest part of the Recôncavo, synonymous with lands rich in clay), sugar cane gave rise to a social structure based on the lord-and-the-slave sytem which has been described by Gilberto Freire in *Casa Grande e Senzala*. The result of this culture was, as in Pernambuco, the presence of *sobrados* and *mocambos*, material structures reflecting a traditional and highly stratified society.[2]

The cost crisis originated by the appearance of substitutes for sugar cane and by the abolition of slavery brought about the end of the integrated producing system, creating the conditions for the factory sugar mill *(engenhos centrais* or *usinas)* and the intermediate function of *usineiro,* the sugar industrial entrepreneur in the Recôncavo. Disassociated from agriculture, he was closely related to the financial functions of Salvador. The usineiro, in turn, was converted into a supplier of raw material for the large export enterprises.

The intermediary phase in the sugar economy of Bahia began approximately with the twentieth century. Cane production and the manufacture of sugar became from that time onward two separate activities. Cane is the main input of sugar production, but the characteristics of its cultivation differ markedly from the industrial factors associated with the manufacture of sugar and its commercialization.

The usineiro, the system's innovating agent, became the financial agent of the large wholesale firms of Salvador which concentrated in one subsidiary firm more than sixty percent of the sugar production of the state of Bahia. The need to adopt new agricultural techniques in order to resolve problems originating in the clay soil predominant in the sugar area began a process of land accumulation that should end in creation of another integrated system if only because of government intervention. In 1958, four sugar mills produced sixty percent of the Recôncavo's total production; of these, one contributed half this percentage. As in the case of tobacco, the agent of change was converted into a factor of stagnation.

A new external factor appeared with oil exploitation, which brought greater possibilities for industrial development. The Recôncavo Baiano produces ninety percent of Brazil's petroleum. Since PETROBRAS oil fields occupy a large proportion of lands formerly devoted to the production of sugar cane, transformation overtook the Recôncavo in the very epicenter of its traditional economic activity. Nevertheless, the two economies coexist, showing once again the recurring contradictions observed in tobacco and sugar production.

The modern petroleum economy has not been able to penetrate the life of the Recôncavo, remaining in great measure an exogenous activity. In fact, PETROBRAS policies are directed from Rio de Janeiro and Brasília with little participation, if any, by the state government of Bahia. Furthermore, the technological effects that a modern and efficient activity like oil exploitation could have fostered in the economic environment have penetrated the Recôncavo only superficially. Petroleum exploitation is an enclave, exerting its influence in the region almost exclusively by means of payment of royalties to the state government, and by acquisition of goods and services locally produced. And even this is considerably reduced by PETROBRAS's capacity to produce many of its required technical and personal services.

Petroleum exploitation has not had important consequences for the urban environment. Towns and small cities where petroleum production occurs have not been transformed by the presence of this activity and continue to languish. Even Salvador has only minimally benefited from the relative increase in commercial activity generated by the salaries of PETROBRAS personnel, and from the demands for technical services in the enterprise's local offices. An internal system of commissaries, social assistance for its workers, and its own infrastructure services maintain the petroleum sector in isolation from the rest of the Recôncavo's economy.

Yet petroleum does contribute totally new elements which could exercise an important innovating function. First, PETROBRAS is a large enterprise.[3] This implies the potential introduction of modern methods of management and administration necessarily influencing the rest of the region. Second, it is a public enterprise, and while it behaves as if it were private due to its independent charter, it does represent a diversification factor vis-à-vis private enterprise, particularly in the possibilities of integrating its regional and national activities. Finally, petroleum does carry with it the possibility of modern industrial development, as opposed to mere exploitation of natural resources and agricultural activity. With oil in the picture, the doors for petrochemicals and derivative industries are open, which could, in turn, begin a new stage in the development of the Recôncavo.

New Factors of Change

The Recôncavo today has all the characteristics common to underdeveloped regions: acute problems of unemployment, badly used resources, undernourishment, low-productivity agriculture, high mortality and infectious disease rates, dependence on foreign markets, profound social inequalities, a hypertrophied tertiary sector, low educational levels with marked illiteracy, a high rate of demographic growth, lack of services, and deficiencies in infrastructure. Yet the Recôncavo was the setting for economic activity over many centuries which caused a considerable accumulation of wealth, based on a structure of natural resources favorable to the production of export raw materials and on the availability of extremely low-cost labor. This phenomenon is not limited to the Recôncavo, but has different causes and effects in each location.

For reasons which may be explained by the economic history of Brazil, the internal situation of the Recôncavo evolved differently from those of other regions of Brazil. While the southern states, especially São Paulo, were able to begin capital accumulation, creating conditions for industrial development, Bahia and Pernambuco continue to be centers of low yield agricultural activities. The appearance of other crops, such as cacao in the southern part of Bahia, did not modify the Recôncavo's economy. Its agriculture is still characterized by low capitalization of crops and in general, limited exploitation of agricultural land. The inability of Bahia's economy to retain the savings generated by the export system may be a factor of great importance in explaining the backwardness of the Recôncavo's regional development. While São Paulo was developing as an industrial center producing consumer and capital goods and originating a process of import substitution, Salvador continued as an export center of raw materials and contributed, by means of purchases and transfers, to the capitalization of industrial areas of the Central-Southern regions of Brazil.

As Fernando Pedrão has noted (1963: 4):

> Internally, the type of relations with other regions of Brazil transformed the State (Bahia) into an importer of products of the industrial complex located in the states of Guanabara, São Paulo, and Minas Gerais (the Center-South region). The purchasing power to sustain this flow of imports came from exports and was a result of the dollar exchange established by the National Exchange Control. Meanwhile, these imports transferred to the region raised prices as a result of the cost inflation affecting principally the Central-Southern industrial complex where the goods consumed in Bahia originated. In this way, an intra-regional transfer mechanism of purchasing power was established. And this mechanism would end in conditioning the process by which Bahia contributed to acceleration of the concentration of capital in the Center-South, a region which had created the conditions to retain it.

In addition, the dual socioeconomic structure existing in Bahia determined a form of reinvestment favoring Salvador and only marginally the rest of the Recôncavo, if and when export profits had not been transferred to Rio or São Paulo. This reinvestment mainly took the form of luxury goods or was limited to basic agricultural investment. The local financial system has served principally as a drain mechanism for the region's savings, as often occurs in less-developed regions. As a consequence, capital investment was maintained at a very low level and could not create sufficient employment opportunities for a population whose rate of growth has been notably accelerating during recent decades. Under these circumstances, displacements of population of considerable magnitude occurred with numbers of unemployed going to southern regions of Brazil. Nevertheless, migrations could not diminish sufficiently the number of unemployed laborers; thus population increase neutralized in part the growth of industrial production in Bahia.

The presence of a large mass of unemployed in the Recôncavo has created economic and social problems sufficiently important to indicate the need for change by themselves. Extensive unemployment aggravates the marginalization of a considerable sector of the population, and therefore, by accentuating income inequalities, works against the region's social integration—a first-order condition for the process of inward-oriented development. If conditions permitting wider social mobility are not created, the Recôncavo's future development, whatever the orientation adopted, could be significantly bottlenecked.

Unemployment and social distortions do not pose the only restrictions observable today to development of the region. In addition to the lack of adequate savings and investment mechanisms, other institutional deficiencies are apparent which obstruct development of productive activities, supply of services, and integration of marginal sectors of the population. These deficiencies, inter alia, have delayed introduction of a progressive tax system. Sharp increases in the cost of living resulting from additional demands for food and shelter in the face of inelastic supply also reflect the extent of the disadjustment. Accentuated deterioration of urban structures, observed primarily in housing and in the system of transportation and communications, may seriously endanger Salvador's function as the economic center of the Recôncavo and of the state of Bahia.

The situation described arises from conditions prevailing in the past which molded economic and social structures too rigid to adapt successfully. Nevertheless, in recent years new factors have appeared; their effects cannot yet be fully evaluated, but their presence does give momentum to the Recôncavo's economic development. The first of these factors is the energy-generating plant at Paulo Afonso, which created the conditions for industrial development of the Northeast. The second is establishment of the Banco do Nordeste do Brasil (BNB), the initial framework for coordinated action by the federal government in the Northeast. It both represents a fresh source of capital for long-term financing and innovating techniques for analysis and evaluation of economic development projects.

The institutional matrix was also altered by creation in 1955 of the Economic Planning Commission (CPE) of Bahia, later the CPE Foundation, designed to program the state's economic development. In addition, in 1956, the exchange rate system for cacao and other products was modified. Other institutional changes were the creation of the Superintendência do Desenvolvimento do Nordeste (SUDENE) and application of fiscal and financing incentives favoring transfer of capital from central and southern Brazil to the Northeast. Communications have been improved, too, by the paving of the Rio de Janeiro-Bahia highway, ending the isolation produced by the stagnation of maritime transport after World War II.

Also significant is the growth of the city of Salvador, reaching at the present time more than a million inhabitants, a fact that in itself represents continuous pressure for new employment opportunities and, at the same time, offers the indispensable urban environment for development. External economies originating from PETROBRAS's action in the region and in the existence of conditions for establishment of industries derived from petroleum, especially petrochemicals, help, too, as does creation of the Industrial Center of Aratú, which has begun to provide the infrastructure and services necessary for establishment of a large industrial estate. Finally, and perhaps most importantly, Salvador and, in general, Bahia, have a modern elite which has assumed an innovating posture in both private and public sectors. Experience appears to demonstrate that even though a region may enjoy all other elements favorable to development, lack of modern, dynamic elites may neutralize even the best opportunities for development.

Certain observations regarding the above factors should be made. First, although some of the existing locational advantages apply to the whole Northeast, the most benefited areas are Salvador and the Recôncavo. Of the three largest centers of the Northeast, Salvador is the closest to the most developed part of Brazil and is the only center linked to this area by paved highway. Locational advantages are, in the case of Salvador, probably the strongest force pushing for its development, since the Recôncavo's natural resources, as varied and important as they may be, do not appear to be sufficient per se to justify permanent development.

Second, most of these advantages are external to the area and outside the political control of the state's government. Therefore, there is a sense of urgency in utilizing factors which may be altered by national policy decisions or by technological modifications. And, finally, the survival and resistance to change of structures created by the traditional economy should be noted.

The Recôncavo's development possibilities depend, therefore, on the skill with which these new elements are exploited and combined with existing structures. There is little doubt that it is in the industrial sector that the Recôncavo must maintain a continuous process of economic growth, but industrial growth requires, in addition to substantial social change, expansion of the agricultural sector, not only because it constitutes an important source of food and industrial raw material, but also because the transformation of regional agriculture can become, through expansion of local consumption capacity, the link assuring that impulses generated in the industrial sector are transmitted to the rest of the Recôncavo's economy and do not end only in creating new enclaves.

POSSIBLE PROGRAMS FOR RECONCAVO DEVELOPMENT

The Recôncavo's history shows the presence of a socioeconomic constant: the coexistence of anachronistic and frequently contradictory forms of production. Maintenance of stability under these conditions indicates the existence of a compensatory system capable of absorbing surplus tensions. While this system may be explained in various ways, it is clear that a relationship exists between it and the absence of a regional mechanism for reinvestment which has led to a continuous weakening of the Bahian economy, causing its dependence upon other, more developed regions. In many respects, tobacco, sugar, and petroleum have acted as enclaves of local social groups or of economic interests external to the region. The effects of the forces encouraging development could promote creation of a new type of dependence contributing only marginally to the Recôncavo's development through increases in the absorption of unemployed labor and through unspecialized tertiary services. This is compounded by the capital-intensive nature of industry found in the Recôncavo and accentuated by the fact that the ICM (Imposto a la Circulação de Mercadorias) sales tax derives its revenue from the merchandise-exporting states, thus making the economy dependent on the business cycles in those regions.

A great deal of the new economic growth of the Recôncavo is directly related to the application of tax exemptions under Article 34/18 of the law establishing SUDENE. The comparative advantages of the Recôncavo relating to the location of basic industries and the local capacity of the public and private sectors to attract investments to the region have been responsible for this growth in recent years. Yet this development has been occurring as a function of the Center-South's economy. Dependence on a powerful center is perhaps unavoidable and necessary for an economy such as that of the Recôncavo. But whether it could be congruent in the future with the need for development of an internal market is questionable, especially if capital-intensive techniques must be applied. The best prospects for inward-oriented development appear to be related to the creation of mechanisms for reinvestment and increase in local consumption capacity.

It has already been noted that agricultural activity should be increased as a means of counteracting further rises in the cost of living, which could impair the comparative advantages of locating industries in the Recôncavo. Yet, if the need to widen the regional market is recognized, an increase in the food supply could possibly be insufficient. What is required is an increase in the purchasing power of the Recôncavo's population, which is still largely dependent upon agriculture. To do this, it would be necessary to augment the production capacity of the agricultural sector, which, in turn, would require changes in the structure of production and distribution. Basically, the Recôncavo would have to increase its rate of fixed capital formation. An increase in capitalization presupposes (1) expansion of productive activities, (2) maintenance of the comparative advantages the Recôncavo enjoys vis-à-vis other northeastern zones, protected by the laws administered by SUDENE, and (3) a better relationship between elite groups and the Recôncavo's population.

The immediate prospects for expansion of the Recôncavo's economic activities appear to be related to production-goods industry. The Recôncavo's traditional agricultural export products, tobacco and sugar, face highly competitive and slow-growing markets. The possibilities for introduction of substitute products (palm oils, tropical fruits, cacao) are confined to a limited area of the Recôncavo and could not represent anything more than a secondary measure to obtain additional capital. Food-crop cultivation represents a potential for development limited by the urban demand of Salvador and possibly by that of certain other nearby northeastern centers. In reality, agricultural development in the Recôncavo would have greater impact socially than economically. To the extent that transformation of the agricultural structure produces an increase in local consumption capacity, it would change attitudes in a considerable part of the population and would expand Salvador's food supply.

The existence of petroleum, natural gas, important mineral deposits (manganese, lead, salgema, and copper), and abundant energy represent, on the other hand, development possibilities already confirmed by the recent establishment of several industrial plants and the nearby installation of many others. These potentialities should, however, be considered over the long term and integrated within a development policy to assure the most adequate utilization of the Recôncavo's resources and location. This is well illustrated by the case of petroleum.[4]

Mineral resources appear to be the Recôncavo's second source for development, as indicated by the existence of two already-producing iron alloy plants, and another of titanium oxide (TIBRAS). Feasibility studies were recently completed for an iron works plant using natural gas (USIBA), and for an aluminum plant (ALCAN). Other projects are under way: an investment of approximately $120 million (U.S.) in a copper reduction plant (CARAIBA METAIS); a project to produce magnesium by Dow Chemical, and other smaller projects. All this indicates that metallurgy and possibly metal-working may constitute other leading sectors for the Recôncavo's development.

Finally, the historical and scenic attractions of Salvador and of the Recôncavo, in general, offer exceptional conditions for the development of tourism. This is indicated by the results of a recent study sponsored by the Bahia Development Council (CONDER) and is confirmed by the increasing tourist activity observed in recent years. Development of this activity will not only be an effective means of preserving and defending historical and artistic monuments and natural beauty, but also will force expansion of urban services, especially transportation and recreation, which would have beneficial effects on the whole regional economy.

Maintenance of locational advantages is a second necessary step. The Recôncavo has been able to attract an important portion of investments in the Northeast as a result of federal government stimuli created by Article 34/18, but nothing will guarantee its continuation if comparative locational advantages are not maintained. Among these advantages are three of exceptional importance: the area's natural resources, the advantages offered by the present level of labor remuneration, and the favorable transportation rates between the Recôncavo and center-south markets.

Development tends to increase employment opportunities and to raise wages. If the fruits of development are to be retained within the region, it will be necessary to make real increases in family income compatible with the need to maintain the previously mentioned advantages. An effort to raise the productivity of social investments may provide a means of improving real income without disproportionate increases in wages. If production of food and basic consumer goods is stimulated, the tendency toward increases in the cost of living could be partially checked.

At present, transportation costs also favor the Recôncavo. The normal overland transportation rate to the South is equal to fifty or sixty percent of the rate in the opposite direction. This advantage could disappear as transportation flows from the Northeast increase. To maintain this comparative advantage, action by the public sector is necessary. Finally, the Industrial Center of Aratú provides an important attraction for investments, as has been demonstrated by the rise in the number of firms located there. The recent approval of a 26 million *cruzeiro* loan by the National Economic Development Bank (BNDE) and the financing by the Inter-American Development Bank of the first stage of the Recôncavo's new industrial port assure that this advantage will be maintained in the future. It will be necessary, however, to assure an adequate water supply for industries located in the Aratú industrial park, as well as consolidation of road networks linking the industrial estate and Salvador with the rest of the Recôncavo.

One of the most important factors in the Recôncavo's recent development is the presence of a local elite of entrepreneurs and public servants who have understood the need for change and introduced innovations in organization and technology. The role of this elite is illustrated by the case of Empreendimentos da Bahia, a firm specializing in the creation of enterprises which has already contributed to the establishment of many industries in the Recôncavo. The social sciences still do not completely explain how the elites described by Schumpeter, Hagen, and Lerner are created. Yet it is known that in all successful development processes there has always been a group of men who have deliberately introduced innovations in the social and economic order destined to free productive forces and modify obsolete structures. The motivation of these groups has been associated with a desire for fulfillment and with a vocation for power. The groups of the "Schumpeterian" elite arise from the transformation of individuals who, belonging to the old privileged strata, can comprehend the need for change in order to maintain certain class privileges. Lerner's innovating elites are composed of "new men with new ideas" who seek new fields of action when their original means do not offer maximum possibilities. Both cases involve intellectually capable and functionally efficient groups operating from motivations tied to economic success, the use of power, and class privilege.

If these elite group functions cannot be combined with greater popular participation, there is risk of repeating the old models and of causing stagnation of the region after a short period of economic growth. The most powerful mechanism for social integration is provided by the degree of participation and vertical mobility that a society is capable of offering to its members. This not only means collective participation in the formulation of political decisions, but also effective participation in the processes of production and consumption.

Industrialization offers the best channels through which principal social changes proceed, and yet industry's capacity to absorb labor is limited.

Development based solely upon industry cannot alleviate social tensions overnight, especially when the low cost of labor is one of the Recôncavo's comparative advantages. Consequently, the possibility of participation will remain far from the reach of the largest popular sectors if the capacity to absorb labor is not increased by public works or services. The public sector can always intervene through redistribution mechanisms which can compensate for inequalities in income. Increase of public sector investment in social infrastructure and services may provide a particular form of redistribution, as well as a means to increase absorption of labor, especially if new investment comes from additional state government revenues (after its revenue increase resulting from expansion of industrial activity), and, most importantly, if regressive distribution is avoided in the allocation of new investment. Improvement in the quantity and quality of public services may provide a real increase in salaries and wages and may upgrade the population's standard of living without disproportionate increases in labor. This would reduce the social burdens devolving on households.

A traditional resistance to widening the channels to social mobility based on the old class structure must still be overcome. The characteristics of Brazilian civilization, however, are favorable to wide mobility, and this should not, therefore, be a serious obstacle. Nevertheless, a great effort to improve the population's educational level rapidly is necessary. It will also be necessary to maintain the motivation of elite groups, accentuating their identification with the region, and, at the same time, opening access to collective participation. Universal education and improved communication among the different social groups, as well as an increase in social investment, may aid integration of the population. In this way, a sound policy of social overhead investment would serve not only to improve the Recôncavo's comparative advantages in the location of economic activity, but also to achieve greater popular participation in the development of this process. Moreover, as popular economic participation widens, the risk of flights of capital out of the region should be reduced.

EVALUATION

Is it possible to develop the Recôncavo, achieving both an increase in capitalization and greater participation of the population in production and consumption? Can mechanisms of reinvestment and participation be established and enclave economies avoided? Can effective coordination of public and private sectors be achieved in the face of competition from other regions and other countries? These questions are eminently political and to deal with them realistically one must consider the political and economic capabilities of the state government to conduct a development process of this type.

Under Brazil's system of political organization, the individual state enjoys greater autonomy than any other subnational unit in Latin America. Brazilian states dispose of their own resources and are able to conduct regional policies if compatible with national policies. In the case of Bahia, the state's main sources of income are provided by ICM tax revenues and oil royalties paid by PETROBRAS. State resources are administered by two different financial bodies, the State Bank of Bahia and the Development Bank of Bahia. The federal government acts through the national executive system (ministries) and a series of decentralized autonomous entities (autarkies), some of which behave like private enterprises, as in the case of PETROBRAS, but whose policies are tied directly to the federal government.

In the Northeast, in addition to ministries and decentralized public agencies, there are two powerful public sector organisms created to aid the nation's poorest states. One is SUDENE, created to administer the resources resulting from enactment of Article 34/18 of the SUDENE law. SUDENE is the administrative organism regulating the transfer of resources from the developed center to the underdeveloped periphery of the Northeast. The other organism is the Banco do Nordeste do Brasil (BNB), the financial agency specializing in financing development supporting the incentives of Article 34/18. It also lends technical assistance to public and private sectors in the Northeastern states. Capital resources and technology in the hands of the private sector originates primarily in São Paulo and Rio de Janeiro, and local investment capacity is severely limited. As a matter of fact, local private banks act principally as a source of short-term finance capital.

The state government does not have all the political and economic power necessary to formulate development policies with sufficient autonomy, and these policies depend ultimately on the federal government. Nor can the state control private initiative, which depends in large part on enterprises and financial groups from outside the region. Under these circumstances, the public sector's effectiveness will depend on its capacity for negotiation with centralized and decentralized agencies of the federal government, and on its ability to attract private-sector investment to the state of Bahia, and the Recôncavo. A large part of the future characteristics of the Recôncavo's development will therefore depend on the state government's capacity for negotiation with federal government agencies in Fortaleza (BNB), Recife (SUDENE), Rio de Janeiro (PETROBRAS), and Brasília.

It may be that the best way to support the Recôncavo's economic development is by endowing the private sector with a development strategy and a stock of investment projects. This strategy could maximize use of natural resources, exploit present and long-term opportunities, and intervene with greater security in the political processes which concern the region's destinies. It could also permit integration of the Recôncavo's development into the rest of the state's economic space. The state government would thus expand its capability for action and its ability to apply its own resources with catalytic power. It could also concentrate its own financial capabilities through the state's banks in the most important sectors, stimulating the efficiency and activities of the private sector. In this way, too, the state government would be able to create a supporting infrastructure, which could combine social with economic growth.

Such a strategy represents an alternative to traditional concepts of development planning, in which objectives and goals are fixed, and complex mechanisms are established to impose normative order on action. Traditional planning approaches are often too rigid, especially in less-developed regions, and cannot always anticipate changes originating primarily through external forces. A static position is not suited to the extraordinary dynamism characterizing the development process of rapidly expanding growth poles. A strategy of development based on general objectives and flexible instruments will always be able to orient action along the lines of least resistance toward these foreseen objectives. It is possible that a strategy concept, instead of a normative, all-embracing approach, may best serve the development of a region having the characteristics of the Recôncavo Baiano.

The efficacy of such an approach seems already demonstrated. In fact, the existence of the study of the Recôncavo's petrochemical potential has been of great importance to the state government in its dealings with federal agencies when the location of a second petrochemical growth pole was under discussion. It was on the basis of the economic analysis contained in this study that a declaration from the federal government was obtained to secure construction by PETROQUISA of the basic petrochemical plant initiating the Camaçari complex in the Recôncavo. A general scheme of this type was recommended in 1967 by a mission organized by the Inter-American Development Bank and was acted upon by the state government. In addition, as a result of the missions's recommendations, the Recôncavo Development Council (CONDER) was created in the same year, and basic studies were begun in sectors considered strategic at that time. To date, the previously mentioned study of the petrochemical industry, a general examination of the Recôncavo's tourist potential, and a preliminary study of the Metropolitan Area of Salvador have been completed. Other sectoral studies, especially in agriculture and industry, are also in process for the purpose of identifying other economic growth poles.[5] At the present time, a technical assistance agreement between the state government of Bahia and the Inter-American Development Bank is being initiated. This operation is intended to consolidate previous aid and should result in new investment projects as well as in strengthening of CONDER's technical capabilities.

Since the region's development process has not, however, eradicated the Recôncavo's traditional social problems, it may be assumed that this pattern of development is not socially effective, and that only the application of greater rationality can achieve the objectives of greater social integration and faster economic growth.

Finally, a development strategy for a region like the Recôncavo should contain a definition of the most important economic activities, and an analysis of the conditions that should determine their location. Such definition should be based on the leading (matrix) activities concept, in accordance with the theory of polarized growth.[6] Definition of leading activities should also serve in programming public sector investment in infrastructure and orienting the functions of public credit financing destined for development activities. If infrastructure and the financial aid of the state of Bahia are shaped in this way to support leading activities, the state's public sector would be augmenting the region's comparative advantages over other economic spaces.

The next step in formulating the development strategy must be selection of leading activities. These leading or matrix activities represent, within an economic system determined by external factors over which no real capacity for intervention exists, capital-intensive technologies and forms of production. This would tend to maintain the region in a dependent condition with respect to other regions of Brazil. The need to reduce dependence constitutes, therefore, a key aspect of the strategy. If it is not possible to reconcile the presence of the large enterprise applying foreign capital resources and technology with rapid expansion of the internal market and greater local participation, the present development of the Recôncavo could result in the perpetuation of social and cultural dualism. The problem of finding production techniques permitting competition in the national and even in the international market, and, at the same time, broadening employment opportunities, remains as the basic bottleneck in relating economic growth to social development. Thus, the problem is basically that of creating a technology and a form of entrepreneurial organization adequate to the needs of underdeveloped countries and regions. To date, no solution has been proposed. Yet it must be recognized that massive efforts have not been made in the sciences and in technology to investigate these possibilities. Until a solution is found the alternatives are the absorption of unemployed labor by other sectors of the economy, or the transfer of surplus labor outside the region.

In the search for sectors which can increase their capacity to attract surplus labor, governments have frequently resorted to public works and services. Yet these policies have not had permanent effects. Techniques used in the construction of public works have also tended to be capital-intensive; it could be argued that this is more of a demonstration-effect from the industry than an economic need. Urban services are, with the exception of the most specialized, not transferable and therefore not subject to competitive pressures. If this holds true, investment in infrastructure and services could result in considerable expansion of employment if labor-intensive techniques were applied. Streets, housing, water supply, sewerage, and even electrical installations can be built, largely through use of the marginal labor force. Small and medium-sized businesses could also aid in widening employment opportunities. The increase in allocations for social investment that this requires because of the rapid growth of urban population would be additionally justified as a mean of increasing labor opportunities. At the same time, a greater volume of unemployed labor could be absorbed by intensifying general and, especially, vocational education. An increase in the number of persons being trained for technical and handicraft jobs could lead to a net reduction in unemployment for relatively prolonged periods of many persons of working age. In this way, demand for employment could be reduced and labor's skills increased.

NOTES

1. Fishing is linked to the family subsistence economy. Fishermen enjoyed relative prosperity before refrigeration ended the traditional fishing-boat system. The scale of economic exploitation of fishing boats with refrigeration systems appears to be, nevertheless, disproportionate to local economic capacity; thus, fishing has not been able to become a regionally important activity.

2. Production of sugar began in the Recôncavo in colonial times. It developed because of the extraordinary fertility of the *massâpe* soil and the presence of slave labor imported by the Portuguese in the earliest days of the colony. The formation of large properties, a consequence of the occupation of lands without known owners, dictated the rise of a plantation system for the production of sugar cane and sugar. Sugar production was initially an integrated activity including the cultivation of cane, the actual production of sugar, and trade with external markets. Every sugar plantation had its own *engenho* or elementary sugar mill and every *fazendeiro* was an exporter of sugar.

3. PETROBRAS is one of only four Latin American companies included in the 200 largest businesses in the world outside the United States. The others are PEMEX, Yacimientos Petrolíferos Fiscales de la Argentina, and Bunge & Bohr of Buenos Aires.

4. A study (1969) identifying investment opportunities in the petrochemical industries, conducted recently by CLAN, a Salvador consulting local firm, proposed petrochemical development in two stages: first, a basic complex located in Camaçan, based on already existing units, those in the process of being established, and those projected by the public sector; second, expansion of the basic complex. For the first stage, thirty basic products could be manufactured from the combination of the Recôncavo's raw materials (petroleum, gas, salgema, potassium) and a small quantity of inputs imported from outside the region. The most significant are ethane, propane, BTX (benzene, toluene, and xylene) and ammonia. PETROQUISA, a national mixed-economy enterprise, has begun the installation of an ethane plant, and the Ypiranga industrial group proposes to build a large ammonia plant. More specifically, the CLAN study recommends immediate installation of an ethane plant of 70,000 tons based on ethane produced by existing Recôncavo natural gas plants. This plant could later be complemented by a new unit of 120,000 tons; adaptation of the PETROBRAS refinery to produce 60,000 tons of propane; execution of an existing project for a BTX plant of 40,000 tons; installation of two ammonia plants (one by PETROBRAS, the other by Ypiranga) to serve national export markets, based on the natural gas abundant in the region; and installation of a dicholoroethane plant based on salgema from the Recôncavo and on chlorine from the neighboring state of Alagoas.

5. The Recôncavo's development process was not initiated by the Inter-American Development Bank mission. Actually, creation of the Aratú Industrial Center in 1965 is the most significant factor in the Recôncavo's economic transformation. This accomplishment was in part the result of previous action such as the work of the Economic Planning Commission, which as early as the 1950s examined the area's industrial potential and identified concrete opportunities for new investment. Many of the commission's plans were converted into actual projects resulting in enterprises now in operation.

6. Identification criteria for these leading activities should include the capability to generate derivative activities, and among them, those having a large proportion of value added.

REFERENCES

Clan, S.A., Consultoria y Planejamiento (1969) Desenvolvimento da indústria petroquímica do Estado da Bahia. Salvador.

COSTA PINTO, L. A. (1958) Recôncavo: Laboratório de uma experiência humana. Rio de Janeiro: Centro de Pesquisas em Ciências Sociais.

PEDRAO, F. C. (1963) Política de desenvolvimento do Estado da Bahia. Salvador: Economic Planning Commission.

Chapter 7

URBANIZATION POLICY AND LAND REFORM

D. URBANIZATION POLICIES IN REVOLUTIONARY CUBA

MARUJA ACOSTA and JORGE E. HARDOY

THE PROBLEM

Like all other countries of the world, Cuba has a serious housing deficit and complex urban problems. Cuba inherited a pattern of urban settlement from the colonial period reflecting an economic system oriented toward export of agricultural products and import of foodstuffs, equipment, machinery, and consumer goods in general. With the exception of the sugar industry, manufacturing was little developed and, in addition, was preferentially concentrated in Havana. Exports of sugar and other agricultural products contributed to development of a regional port system, but imports were concentrated in Havana, the capital city, which was also the principal political-administrative, financial, industrial, and cultural center of the nation. The settlement scheme reflected an almost undiversified agriculture of low yield, based on extensive sugar plantations and cattle ranches. The concentration of land ownership (see Table 1) and the system of agricultural exploitation were the principal causes of seasonal unemployment and the rural population's low standard of living.

In January 1959, when the Revolution assumed control of the Cuban government and administration, its leaders were forced to confront the uncoordinated action of public and private organizations and traditional bureaucratic inefficiency and impose systematic and coordinated programs upon agencies and businesses accustomed to resolving problems on a day-to-day basis. The process that the revolutionary leaders had to begin was that of changing the mentality and organization of multiple institutions, imposing a planned system, and encouraging the population to define and accept new values. The pre-Revolutionary situation was in large part a consequence of the limited opportunities of the mass of the Cuban people to participate in decisions

Authors' Note: This case study is based on a monograph by the authors entitled "Urban Policies and Urban Reform in Cuba" to be published by the Institute of Latin American Studies, Yale University. English translation by Felicity M. Trueblood.

TABLE 1
CUBA–TOTAL AREA OF AGRICULTURAL UNITS
CLASSIFIED BY SIZE

Units	Number of Units	% of Total Units	Area in Hectares	% of Total Area
Small (less than 100 hectares)	147,189	92.57	9,077,086	58.48
Medium (100-500 hectares)	10,475	6.59	2,193,599	14.13
Large (500 hectares or more)	1,336	0.84	4,253,632	27.39
Total	159,000	100.00	15,524,327	100.00

SOURCE: National Agricultural Census, 1946.

defining the political and economic orientation of their country, and the result of the social and physical environment in which they lived.

The scheme of urban and rural settlement in Cuba did not adequately serve the nation. The concentration of decision-making and the major part of industrial, commercial and cultural activities in Havana deprived the rest of the nation of opportunity.

Cuba is an elongated and narrow island with a length of 760 miles and a width varying between 25 and 125 miles. Its total land area is 44,204 square miles and its population, in September 1969, was estimated at 8,360,395 (see Table 2). The city of Havana is located in the western part of the island. A few years before the Revolution, in 1953, its population of 1,217,674 inhabitants was 7.46 times larger than that of Santiago (163,237 inhabitants) and 3.46 times larger than the combined population of the three other principal cities: Santiago, Camagüey (110,388 inhabitants), and Santa Clara (77,398 inhabitants). It was 1.54 times larger than the combined population of the twelve principal Cuban cities: Santiago, Camagüey, Santa Clara, Guantánamo (64,671 inhabitants), Matanzas (63,916 inhabitants), Holguín (58,776 inhabitants), Cienfuegos (57,991 inhabitants), Cárdenas (43,750 inhabitants), Manzanillo (42,252

TABLE 2
CUBA–URBAN-RURAL POPULATION AS PERCENTAGE
OF TOTAL POPULATION (in percentages)

Year	Total Population	Urban	Rural	In Centers of 20,000 or More
1889	1,572,797	47.1	52.9	–
1907	2,048,980	43.9	56.1	–
1919	2,889,004	44.7	55.3	24.3
1931	3,962,344	51.4	48.6	27.6
1943	4,778,583	54.6	45.4	30.7
1953	5,829,029	57.0	43.0	35.5
1969	8,360,335	57.0	43.0	43.0

SOURCE: National population censuses of 1889, 1907, 1919, 1931, 1943, and 1953. For 1969, estimate of the Junta Central de Planificación.

TABLE 3

CUBA–POPULATION OF FIFTEEN PRINCIPAL CITIES IN
1969. INDEX OF PRIMACY: TWO CITIES, FOUR
CITIES, AND TWELVE CITIES

Cities	1919	1931	1943	1953	1969[a]
Havana	434,721	653,823	857,495	1,217,674	1,737,954
Santiago	62,083	101,508	118,266	163,237	286,523
Camagüey	41,909	62,581	80,509	110,388	186,980
Matanzas	41,574	–	54,844	63,916	87,721
Cienfuegos	–	50,250	52,910	57,991	76,129
Santa Clara	–	–	53,981	77,398	124,127
Guantánamo	–	–	42,423	64,671	152,749
Manzanillo	–	–	36,295	42,252	73,091
Holguín	–	–	35,865	58,776	123,492
Pinar del Río	–	–	26,241	38,885	73,319
Cárdenas	–	–	37,059	43,750	51,489
Sancti Spíritus	–	–	28,262	37,741	56,483
Ciego de Avila	–	–	23,802	35,178	59,540
Bayamo	–	–	–	–	74,625
Victoria de las Tunas	–	–	–	–	50,283
Index of 12 cities	–	–	1.65	1.60	1.31
Index of 4 cities	2.98	3.05	3.38	3.46	2.61
Index of 2 cities	7.01	6.44	7.25	7.46	6.15
Percentage, Greater Havana, of national population			19.57	20.76	20.76
Percentage, 12 principal cities, of national population			12.30	13.44	13.78

SOURCE: National population censuses of 1919, 1931, 1943, and 1953.

a. For 1969, estimates of the Junta Central de Planificación.

inhabitants), Pinar del Río (38,885 inhabitants), Sancti Spíritus (37,741 inhabitants), and Ciego de Avila (35,178 inhabitants; see Table 3).

Cuba is and has been since colonial times one of the most urbanized countries in Latin America and one with a high index of primacy. Cuban urbanization in general, and that of Havana in particular, was continuously nourished by rural migration, and until a little before World War II by foreign migration. As we have seen, in Table 3, with the exception of Havana, Cuba had and has no large cities. Nevertheless, the existing cities were adequately distributed throughout the national territory in relation to resources under exploitation prior to the Revolution. However, the wealth of the countryside was concentrated in the cities and especially in Havana. This situation of internal colonialism was accentuated by dispersal of the rural population and the difficulty of providing it efficiently with services.

The last population and housing census undertaken in the pre-Revolutionary period was that of 1953. This census determined that only 45 percent of urban population and 2.4 percent of rural had housing considered good or acceptable. In other words, only 27 percent of total population enjoyed good or acceptable housing. Belts of misery surrounded all Cuban metropolitan areas, in which the extensive population of unemployed and underemployed was crowded in slums and precarious housing constructed of perishable materials and lacking public services. In a country of 5,800,000 inhabitants, it was necessary to build almost 1,000,000 dwelling units for 73 percent of the total population, that is, for 4,255,000 persons. In addition, the construction industry, based on use of traditional systems or traditional systems with a few standardized components, could not solve the problems of production on such a vast scale. The situation was aggravated by speculation in urban and suburban land, which, by promoting continuous fragmentation, impeded massive solutions. Credit was out of reach for low- and lower-middle-income sectors of the population, who lived threatened by eviction if they did not pay their rents or meet their mortgage installments in the infrequent cases in which they were able to assure themselves of housing compatible with their means of payment.

REGIONAL DEVELOPMENT AND URBANIZATION POLICY

Until 1964, there was a Department of Physical Planning (Departamento de Planificación Física) in the Ministerio de la Construcción (MICONS) dedicated to developing industrial projects in Cienfuegos, Nuevitas, and other cities whose growth and economic diversification the government sought to encourage. Studies and economic plans were concentrated in the Central Planning Junta (Junta Central de Planificación—JUCEPLAN), which also lent its attention to other urban and territorial problems.

In 1964, the Department of Physical Planning was transformed into the National Institute of Physical Planning (Instituto Nacional de Planificación Física—IPF) with the objective of granting it greater authority and freedom of action. The principal role of IPF is that of giving a territorial dimension to JUCEPLAN directives and its sectoral plans. In order to achieve these ends, IPF proposed a different administrative system, attempting to strengthen intermediate and low levels. Thus, regions were created with the object of decentralizing central and provincial administration and achieving greater participation.

In the Cuban planning system, the provinces occupy an intermediate planning role, which is essentially that of coordinating and promoting certain sectors of the economy organized horizontally, like agriculture. The regions, on the other hand, are essentially executive and undertake analytical tasks at the same time. Their main preoccupations have been agricultural problems and urban regulating plans. Cuba has maintained its six traditional provinces, which are, from west to east, Pinar del Río, Havana, Matanzas, Las Villas, Camagüey, and Oriente. In the new system, the regions replace the *municipios*. The number of regions has varied since the system was created and will undoubtedly continue being modified in relation to practical needs and better knowledge of the characteristics of each one.

IPF is divided into a Division of Urban Planning (División de Planeamiento Urbaño), which is concerned with making demographic growth and its territorial distribution compatible with economic development plans, establishing urban standards and urban-design criteria, and studies of human resources in general; and into a Division of Regional Planning (División de Planeamiento Regional), which, being more decentralized, is concerned with agricultural plans and the industrialization of agricultural production, and with plans for industrial development and infrastructure. Both divisions are coordinated by a Directorate-General. Spatially, this organization is repeated in the provinces, which receive technical assistance from IPF's National Directorate. The provinces in turn provide technical assistance to the regions.

With the objective of achieving more balanced regional development and curbing excessive concentration of activities and population in Havana and its province, the government of the Revolution outlined a series of plans and projects whose strategy is synthesized below. Oriente Province, traditionally agricultural, with excellent natural resources and demographic growth 50 percent higher than the national rate, was selected for integrated urban-rural development. The plan envisions: (a) development of Nicaro-Moa on the northern coast as the principal center of heavy industry in Cuba, using the laterite and serpentine deposits; (b) the polyfunctional character of Santiago in the future (Santiago, located on the southern coast, is being converted into a center of industry—petroleum refineries, flour mills, rum production, cement, and so on—culture, and services); its new port will have regional importance; (c) industrial development of other smaller urban centers by means of extractive activities in their respective areas; in Manzanillo, industries derived from fishing, leather, and rice mills; in Bayamo, dairy and refrigeration industries; in Holguín, food and textile industries; in Guantánamo, textile and light metallurgical industries; (d) a highway plan which will unite all the above centers, and the province in particular, with the rest of the island; (e) the province's agricultural development plan whose outstanding features are expansion of sugar-cane areas in the north, diversified exploitation of the fertile Río Cauto basin, and development of dairy and rice production; (f) improvement in the standard of living of the rural population and in agricultural centers.

In other urban centers, diversified projects are being undertaken. Nuevitas, on the northern coast of Camagüey Province, is to become the principal sugar export port for the region, and an industrial center with one of the main Cuban cement plants, a fertilizer plant, a new thermoelectric plant, and a fuel terminus. Cienfuegos is being transformed into Cuba's second port and into a tourist and industrial center with a fertilizer plant, light metallurgical industries, and, in the future, a petroleum refinery and a thermoelectric plant. In Santa Clara, the capital of Las Villas Province, located in the geographic center of the island and astride the principal highways, will be located a textile plant for the production of sacks for the harvesting of cereals and factories for the manufacture of stoves, refrigerators, and so on. Camagüey, capital of the province of the same name, and Sancti Spíritus are to be transformation centers for agricultural production. In parallel fashion, a plan has been advanced to create more attractive conditions in the *"bateys,"* the small rural agglomerations developed near the sugar refineries, providing services and additional sources of employment by means of more rational and more complete exploitation of sugar cane and its derivatives. Rural projects like that begun in the Ciénaga de Zapata on the southern coast west of Cienfuegos constitute a different approach. In this swampy and isolated area, massive cultivation of citrus has begun, whose packing and industrialization will be complemented by a new scheme of settlement and training centers.

Little has been done, however, to attract new industries and population to Havana. The capital of the republic will continue to fulfill its traditional functions, but without the preponderance these functions enjoyed in the past. The advantages inherent in concentration of labor and greater specialization will be used to locate new industries requiring these conditions. An agricultural cordon around Havana has been partially developed for the purpose of provisioning the metropolitan area more efficiently and reducing transportation. This plan gave rise to a program of construction of new settlements, in which the dispersed rural population was relocated.

This policy of decentralization of productive urban investment and human resources in relation to natural resources, supported by decentralization of teaching and health centers, and new systems of roads and highways, has had the desired repercussions. The growth of Havana, after experiencing sharp advance in the years immediately surrounding the Revolution, is practically halted. Its percentage relation to total population of the island, and especially to the other twelve most populated centers, is in frank decline. Influencing this decline was the fact that a comparatively important percentage of Cubans who abandoned their country after 1959 lived in Havana. But the rates of growth of all cities having 20,000 or more inhabitants is much more accelerated than that of the national capital. This is particularly true of certain centers, like Holguín, Bayamo, and others, which had less than 100,000 inhabitants in 1966.

URBAN REFORM

In the face of the crisis in employment and housing created by the civil war, the Revolutionary government was faced with the need to develop national legislation to avoid injustice. By means of ratification of a series of urban reform laws analyzed here, order was introduced into the physical growth of cities, and practices like speculation in land and rents, which had been primordial factors in Cuba's chaotic urban expansion, were drastically eliminated. Legislation prior to the Urban Reform Law also served to organize the institutions responsible for guiding the process of urbanization at the local level.

A series of legislative measures, ratified during the first year of the Revolution, prepared the way for the Urban Reform Law. These laws are summarized in Appendix A. The legislation altered the housing market and eliminated the activities of private builders. Of the 10,200 dwelling units completed annually in Cuba between 1945 and 1958, only 1.02 percent were built by the government. During this period, only 400 rural dwelling units were constructed. Between 1959 and 1963, the production of housing jumped to 17,089 units annually; 30.4 percent were rural, constructed by government and cooperative organizations. Of the 59,397 dwelling units built in urban areas, the government and private initiative contributed almost equally. Beginning in 1963, private initiative in the housing construction industry disappeared.

The Urban Reform Law was ratified October 14, 1960. The principal reasons given for its passage were the housing deficit and general living conditions in the cities. The law's first chapters contain a declaration of principles and include the outlines of a three-stage program. During the first stage, the state must find a solution for tenants so that in a period of from five to twenty years these persons, by means of an investment which cannot exceed monthly rent paid, may acquire the housing they occupy. The emergency ordained, the state must begin massive construction of housing, which is to be given permanently to usufructuaries through payment of 10 percent of family income. This stage obtained during almost all the 1960s. In this decade, Cuba raised the annual average of urban and rural housing construction to approximately 30,000 units, which constituted about 75 percent of need caused by natural increase of the population. A third stage, which was to begin in December 1970, but which we believe has been delayed, foresees construction of housing by the state and its permanent ceding to families at no cost.

Another series of important articles defines criteria to be followed to indemnify owners of rented housing which has become the property of tenants. The sale price is related to age of housing and amount of rent. In addition, all unpaid rent is to be included in the sale price. No owner can receive compensation higher than $600 a month. A scale related to the amount of rent received was established as indemnity for life "after termination of receipt of the price of real property owned." The National Bank of Cuba (Banco Nacional) assumed responsibility for payment of indemnities. Tenants were to pay their contributions to the Urban Reform Council (Consejo Superior de la Reforma Urbana) or to their provincial urban reform councils. The Councils were created by the same law and the National Council received the ultimate responsibility to act on all questions of a civil or social nature arising from the law's application.

The law declared null and void all leases and rental contracts, as well as transfer of total or partial use of real property, with the exception of hotels, motels, guest houses, and houses and apartments in summer-resort and rest areas. Slums, rooming houses, and similar lodging were expropriated without compensation. Rent paid by their occupants was to be credited in determining the housing they were to be given. The law prohibited the exchange, conveyance, sale, or transfer of any real property without authorization of urban-reform councils. Legislation regarding inheritance modified the traditional system of transfer of real property. The Urban Reform Law stipulated that occupants of dwellings were the owners thereof; on the other hand, the system of their transmission was modified. Successor legislation established a difference between ownership of housing and the right to occupancy. In addition, different criteria were applied to urban housing which was a social service complementary to production or isolated dwelling units used for recreational purposes. In the former case, after death of the owner, the dwelling was transferred to other occupants, regardless of whether they were related to the former owner; in the latter case, children were to have priority over other relatives in succeeding to this property.

EVALUATION

Comparative research regarding the relation between national development and urbanization is infrequent. Nevertheless, the example of Cuba, in comparison with what is taking place in other Latin American countries, reveals that schemes of urban settlement, as well as ecological characteristics of the cities which compose them, began to differ in Cuba from the moment the measures of the government of the Revolution started to take effect. A first evaluation might be summarized as follows. The values of societies differ in accordance with their sociopolitical systems, and, therefore, their institutions and the foci they favor for solution to problems limiting their development possibilities are also different. In terms of urbanization, it is obvious that a society favoring planned development and collective and collaborative effort and attempting to organize itself horizontally, encouraging equality and participation, is in the process of producing and attempting to produce very different and more satisfactory national-regional settlement schemes and human groupings than a society organized vertically and hierarchically, favoring unplanned development subordinated to market forces, competition, and speculation.

The Cuban experience in problems of urbanization and housing is very new. In this brief case study, we have pointed out some of the objectives pursued, the organization of the system responsible for analysis and implementation, and certain results which are beginning to appear. The Cuban experience is, in our view, positive. To evaluate the input of urban policies and the urban reform attempted in Cuba fully would require far longer study than we have been able to achieve. Certain additional conclusions, however, although limited, may be useful.

The Urban Reform Law and legislation which preceded it cannot, alone, solve the housing and urban-services deficit and the general deterioration of cities and other urban centers. The body of legislation analyzed here constitutes measures to overcome factors which traditionally have influenced negatively the physical growth of urban centers and the urban environment, such as speculation in land and rental values, and uncontrolled subdivisions—badly designed and lacking services—low densities, badly integrated land uses. It also tends to equalize opportunities for residence and the services of urban society, eliminating the influence which in pre-Revolutionary decades certain socioeconomic groups enjoyed over delimitation of ecological areas in Cuban cities and it permits effective use of zoning and other urban regulations, as well as public investment in solving problems of housing, services, industrial and recreational locations, and transportation routes.

Present-day urban legislation in Cuba is essentially a prerequisite for an integrated solution in the future and an instrument with which to minimize in the short term the social differences of the past. It must, therefore, be considered a step toward creating the conditions for solving urban problems and not the solution itself. Overcoming the deficit in housing and urban services is intimately linked to overcoming the problems limiting development of the nation. Fundamental to this is incorporation of a technology permitting massive housing solutions, using to the maximum degree Cuba's natural and human resources. This process is reflected to an extent not seen in any other country of Latin America in the experimentation with new building techniques and in the adaptation of technology imported from Yugoslavia, Denmark, and other countries to Cuban climatic conditions, availability of certain building materials, and scarcity of labor.

APPENDIX A: URBAN LEGISLATION PRIOR TO THE URBAN REFORM LAW

Law 26. Ratified January 26, 1959; suspended for 45 days all legal decisions and eviction proceedings then under way.

Law 86. Ratified February 17, 1959; created the National Institute of Savings and Housing (Instituto Nacional de Ahorro y Vivienda; INAV); directed toward eliminating gambling, institutionalized through the National Lottery, and soliciting new funds for housing construction by means of substituting bonds for lottery tickets.

Law 135. Ratified March 10, 1959; established a reduction of 50 percent in urban leases not exceeding $100 a month, 40 percent in those between $100 and $200, and 30 percent in those over $200 a month.

Law 218. Ratified April 7, 1959; provided for forced sale of vacant lots; its objective was to limit the action of speculators and monopolizers of urban and suburban lands and establish bases for orderly urban growth.

Law 691. Ratified December 23, 1959; clarified concepts and regulations advanced by Law 218. Its objective was to regulate the price of vacant lots and establish the procedure for their forced sale. Law 691 charged the Junta Nacional de Planificación with delimiting the urban perimeters of cities and determining zones for the purpose of obtaining the best social land use. The law permitted private urban builders to operate, but limited the average legal price to a maximum of $4 a square meter. In addition, the law automatically reduced by

30 percent the price of lots sold on the installment plan prior to ratification of Law 691. INAV was empowered to acquire by means of forced expropriation properties necessary for the construction of low-cost housing. The law also stipulated that every Cuban citizen could request forced sale of a vacant lot at the established price if its owner had not built on the lot within a certain time period. Vacant lots were also subject to a tax rising from 3 percent annually. Law 691 has two very clear purposes: full and efficient use of urban and suburban land, and deterring land speculation. The first purpose cannot be achieved without achievement of the second. The law respected ownership of lots, but forced their sale if their owners did not within a short period of time provide for their definite use, and if there were other Cuban citizens who needed lots and who could use them constructively.

REFERENCES

ARRINDA, A. (1964) "El problema de la vivienda en Cuba." Cuba Socialista 4, 40: 11-21.
AZZE, E. (1967) "Plan Director del Distrito José Martí (San Pedrito)." Arquitectura 337: 54-61.
BALANDRON, J. (1967) "Plan Director para el desarrollo urbano de Levisa en la región de Oriente." Arquitectura 337: 23-31.
CASTRO, F. (1970) "Discurso en conmemoración del 26 de julio en La Habana." Granma (July 28).
−− (1967a) "Discurso en conmemoración del 26 de julio en Santiago de Cuba." Granma (July 30).
−− (1967b) "La historia me absolverá," pp. 31-106 in Siete documentos de nuestra historia. Havana: Ediciones Políticas.
−− (1966) "Discurso en el VI aniversario de la fundación de los C.D.R." September 8.
−− (1965) "Discurso en la Reunión con los Secretarios Generales de los 25 Sindicatos Nacionales."
−− (1963) "Discurso en el cierre del VII Congreso de la Unión Internacional de Arquitectos." October 8.
Cuba Socialista (1966) "El desarrollo industrial de Cuba." Volume 6, 56: 128-183.
DARIAS, R. (1966) "Las tareas en el sector de la construcción." Cuba Socialista 6, 62.
GUTELMAN, M. (1967) "L'agriculture socialisée à Cuba." Maspero (Paris).
GUERRA Y SANCHEZ, R. (1944) Azúcar y población en las Antillas. Havana: Cultural.
HUBERMAN, L. and P. SWEEZY (1969) Socialism in Cuba. New York: Monthly Review Press.
Junta Central de Planificación (JUCEPLAN) (1968) "La planificación económica en Cuba," pp. 117-166 in United Nations, Aspectos administrativos de la planificación: Documentos de un Seminario. New York.
−− (1967) "La Habana, 1944." Resumen de estadísticas de población 3.
LE RIVEREND, J. (1967) Historia económica de Cuba. Havana.
LOCKWOOD, L. (1969) Castro's Cuba, Cuba's Fidel. New York: Vintage.
Ministerio de la Construcción (1964a) "Viviendas urbanas, experiencia sobre prefabricación en Cuba." Dirección de Investigaciones Técnicas 1 (July).
−− (1964b) "Viviendas rurales." Dirección de Investigaciones Técnicas.
RABELLA, O. and M. PULIDO (1967) "Planeamiento urbano de bateyes de centrales azucareros." Arquitectura 337.
RODRIGUEZ, C. R. (1967) "La Revolución cubana y el campesinado." Panorama Económico Latinoamericano (Havana) 6: 270-301.

SALADRIGAS, R. (1963) "Criterios para una restructuración político-administrativa de Cuba." Cuba Socialista 2, 17: 40-53.

SANCHEZ ROCA, M. (1960) Estudio y orientaciones sobre la Ley de Reforma Urbana. Havana: Editorial Lex.

SEGRE, R. (1970a) "Vivienda y prefabricación en Cuba," in Arquitectura Cubana. Cuadernos Summa-Nueva Visión 46 (March) (Buenos Aires).

—— (1970b) "Diez años de arquitectura en Cuba Revolucionaria." Cuadernos.

Séptimo Congreso de la Unión Internacional de Arquitectos (1963) La arquitectura en los países en vías de desarrollo: Cuba. Havana.

VEGA VEGA, J. L. (n.d.) La reforma urbana de Cuba y otras leyes en relación con la vivienda. Havana.

E. URBAN LAND REFORM IN BOLIVIA DURING THE VICTOR PAZ ESTENSSORO ADMINISTRATION

CARLOS CALVIMONTES ROJAS

THE PROBLEM

One of the consequences of the Bolivian Revolution of April 1952, was the establishment of a maximum amount of unimproved urban property which could be owned by any one individual. This act was based upon the idea that large, unimproved urban lots did not perform a social function, and that their owners sought only to benefit themselves by speculating in and hoarding an increasing number of such lots—thus raising their value without the addition of any effort on the owners' part. This in turn escalated the already extremely high value of urban property. Further, it was argued that this situation made solving the urban housing problem more difficult, and that it constituted an obstacle to the rational growth of Bolivian cities.

Although the principle of the social function of property enjoys a certain tradition in the nation, only recently, in 1954, was Article 17 of the Constitution of 1947[1] used to achieve a series of legal acts,[2] which constituted the so-called Urban Property Reform. The immediate antecedent of the Reform[3] provided for reassessment of urban real property in Bolivia, based upon the need to bring its value up to date for tax purposes, since the five-year reassessment established by a 1928 law had not been regularly applied. Nevertheless, the provisionally proposed method did not achieve up-to-date revaluation of urban property, leaving it at a value much lower than its true worth. By so doing, such property could be expropriated in the future at low cost.

Although Reform legislation applied to urban radii within the city limits of departmental capitals,[4] it was implemented only in the cities of La Paz and Cochabamba, and only in the former to any significant extent. This essay, therefore, describes pertinent national legal norms, measures implemented by the municipality of La Paz, and results achieved in that city.

THE PROGRAM

The target of the Reform was privately owned urban property of any kind, unitary or fragmented, larger than one hectare in size. Subject to expropriation, therefore, were single-owner properties that exceeded the maximum size allowed, even if in widely scattered areas of the city, so long as they were unimproved or contained only unimportant construction. If a lot, or lots, owned

Editor's Note: English translation by Leonidas F. Pozo-Ledezma.

by a single proprietor, were larger than one hectare, and contained one or more buildings, the improved area would be subtracted from the total quantity of land owned. The unimproved remainder would be resurveyed for the purposes of expropriation, leaving the owner with unimproved land equal to one hectare in size.

The Reform law stipulated that the city limits of La Paz would be those established ten years before.[5] Areas not included within these limits would be subject to Agrarian Reform laws.[6] Property located partially within urban areas would be affected in accordance with Agrarian Reform and Urban Reform laws operative in the corresponding areas.

Exempted from Urban Reform were dairy and industrial installations, athletic fields, sanatoriums and clinics, railways, airlines, and educational and social-welfare establishments. Campesino renters within the city limits could retain, after paying for the land, up to 900 square meters for housing, and, in addition, enjoyed the right to be indemnified for any lost income.[7]

After a survey determining the eligibility for expropriation of properties larger than one hectare (generally those pinpointed by persons interested in being granted such lands after expropriation), the municipalities had to file for expropriation of the affected lands, citing reasons of public need and utility, and notifying the affected property owners that they should appear within thirty days to establish the price, manner, and conditions of payment for their lands. After a municipal resolution of expropriation,[8] there could be no further appeal, except before the Ministry of Public Works.

Once expropriation proceedings had been completed, urban-planning studies would be undertaken, their cost being paid by the affected property owner, to determine net residential areas and areas of public use: unimproved reserve lands, parks and green belts, construction for public benefit, school districts, and commercial and industrial buildings.

After these studies were completed, and areas for public use in general set aside, property owners affected by expropriation could choose the one hectare which would remain in their possession. The indemnities for expropriated lands, which were very low, were to be paid within a maximum of one year in twelve equal payments. Campesino renters were to be indemnified for lost income at the time they were notified to vacate their lands.

The municipality was then and only then authorized to regulate the manner, price, and condition of sale, and to distribute lots of a size sufficient for housing construction to workers and middle-class persons, either individually or as members of a group, who did not own urban real property. Those granted land had the obligation to build housing within a firm deadline of three years after the installation, in their respective zones, of public services for drinking water and sewage.

The almost exclusive application of urban reform to the city of La Paz was due to many factors: La Paz is the seat of government, has the largest population, and a high rate of growth. It also suffers an impressive shortage of urban lands because of its geographic setting.[9]

EVALUATION

To date, lands expropriated in the city of La Paz amount to 95 hectares. This area, omitting property devoted to public use (although not all such property established by law), was distributed among the members of 26 groups of workers and public employees. They form a population which fluctuates between 15,000 and 20,000 persons. This group represents from 4 to 6 percent of the population of La Paz in the mid-1950s—the time of the most important expropriations—and between 3 and 4 percent of the present population.[10] The Reform, with its territorial range of application thus restricted, achieved only moderate success in halting the speculation that affected approximately 2 percent of the urban land of the nation's most important city.

The objectives related to improving the housing conditions of disadvantaged sectors had no possibility of being accomplished,[11] due to the lack of financial and technical resources. There was no national housing plan. When the appropriate institutional mechanisms finally were created,[12] the Reform had already, in the case of La Paz, practically ceased to be applied. In addition, the low incomes of those granted land did not permit, in most cases, their constructing suitable housing. Thus, to date, part of these lots remain unbuilt, others with buildings half finished, and still others with poor or badly finished construction. Since these buildings were contructed without technical advice, housing conditions are substandard, and, further, according to municipal regulations, most of them are illegal or clandestine.

There was also no relation between expropriation and urban planning in general, to such an extent that, the Reform's anemic legal provisions notwithstanding, expropriated lands were not supplied with indispensable public services, all the areas earmarked for public use were not so reserved, and the facilities necessary for community minimum needs were not provided.

Finally, another problem exists, caused by the lack of foresight manifest in the legal procedures discussed above, and by the absence, chronic in the case of Bolivia, not only of planning, which should have emphasized the necessity of holding lands in reserve, but also of an urban development policy. The cities have expanded their urban radii without prior detailed studies, thus creating cases in which lands covered earlier by the Agrarian Reform could today be affected by the Urban Reform—encountering the natural resistance of owners who would suffer double expropriation in a relatively short period of time.[13]

In conclusion, the Urban Reform, for lack of resources of all kinds, has in practice been inoperative, when it might have become a first-class instrument for urban planning in Bolivia. It is perhaps not too late to correct its errors, but a great deal of precious time has already been lost.

NOTES

1. Article 22 of the Bolivian Constitution of 1967 in force today (the sixteenth in Bolivian history), states: "Private property is guaranteed when and if its use is not

prejudicial to the collective interest. Expropriation is imposed for reasons of public utility, or when the property does not fulfill a . . . social function, in accordance with the law and with prior just compensation." In addition, as an innovation to the present Constitution, Article 206 establishes that: "Within the city limits *(radio urbano)* owners may not possess extensions of unimproved land greater than the amounts fixed by law. Lands in excess of these amounts may be expropriated and devoted to the construction of public housing" *(viviendas de interés social).*

2. These laws were the following: Executive Decree *(Decreto Supremo)* 03819 of August 27, 1954, which established the bases of the Reform; Executive Decree 03826 of September 2, 1954, which complemented the previous decree principally for the purpose of curtailing fictitious transactions designed to reduce the size of properties and thus make them ineligible for reform; and Law of the Republic *(Ley de la República)* of October 29, 1956, which elevated to the status of laws the preceding decrees.

3. Executive Decree 03679 of March 25, 1954.

4. At this time there were already cities with populations larger than those of certain departmental capitals.

5. Municipal Ordinance of July 13, 1944.

6. Executive Decrees 03464 and 03471.

7. Up to an amount equivalent to five times their average income, based upon the final two years of work on the affected rented lands.

8. Drafted in the Dirección General de Afectación de Tierras Urbanas, the office created to administer the Reform in the city of La Paz.

9. La Paz is located in a canyon surrounded by the Altiplano and the Cordillera Oriental of the Andes.

10. The groups granted lands deposited as payment therefor approximately U.S. $45,000, which amounts to about U.S. $13.00 per lot.

11. *Cuadernos de CONAVI,* No. 1 (August 1964), page 63.

12. Executive Decree 04385 of April 30, 1956, which established the people's housing system (Régimen de Vivienda Popular) and the National Housing Institute (Instituto Nacional de Vivienda) to carry out the system. Executive Decree 06916 of July 3, 1964, reorganized the National Housing Institute and created the National Housing Council (Consejo Nacional de Vivienda, CONAVI), one of whose functions is that of "defining and classifying housing and urban residential districts of social interest." Its directorate is charged with, among other functions: "carrying out expropriations under the Urban Reform law."

13. At present, the Municipality of La Paz is in the advanced stages of expropriating an extension of land of approximately 100 square kilometers for reserve purposes. This area, on the inhospitable Altiplano, is the site of the city's present growth with zones housing the population having the most limited financial resources, and zones devoted to industrial, customs, and transportation establishments. It was beyond the city limits when the urban property reform was put into effect.

F. URBAN REFORM LAWS IN COLOMBIA

PEDRO PABLO MORCILLO

THE PROBLEM

Three major pieces of urban reform legislation have been considered in Colombia to May 1971, one in 1966, one in 1969, and another in 1970. Although none has become law, they indicate likely future directions, and probable future limitations of the urban reform program which will be undertaken.

In 1966, a group of congressmen presented to the Congress of the Republic bill 45, which concerned urban social reform and public housing policy. The bill, which did not gain approval, proposed (1) to make tenants owners of the urban housing in which they lived; (2) to program and execute in orderly fashion official housing plans, coordinating the resources and efforts of the public sector; and (3) to stimulate the private sector's housing activities.[1] The bill met with almost immediate opposition among urban landowners and builders primarily because it envisioned powers of emergency expropriation to acquire properties at prices not exceeding more than 10 percent of assessed valuation, and because it prohibited the construction of housing with a unit value of more than 400,000 pesos.

It also contained a number of flaws which were likely to make its implementation impossible, whether palatable to large landowners or not. First, it empowered the municipalities to issue bonds in payment for expropriated properties, but it did not provide them with appropriate financial resources nor indicate how they might be obtained. Second, it induced owners and builders to sell through tax exemptions, but it did not expressly finance the buyer, who had available only the usual limited means. It revealed an apparent contradiction between the goals of transforming tenants into owners and of stimulating renting by freeing controls. It also guaranteed that properties destined for housing (whose value was not in excess of 200,000 pesos) would not be expropriated for ten years, condemning urban development needs to lack of solution during this period. In addition, it authorized the formulation of national housing plans by the Instituto de Crédito Territorial (ICT)[2] and the National Housing Council (Consejo Nacional de Vivienda), which were not to be subject to, or coordinated with, the nation's economic development policy drafted by the office of national planning. Neither were they to be subject to regional development policies attempting to direct or stem the flow of migration, or to local development policy.

Finally, it fostered the belief that housing is subject to expropriation, leading to contraction in construction activity due to the risk of investing in housing

Editors' Note: English translation by Leonidas F. Pozo-Ledezma.

183

which might later be expropriated. Since a socialized economy was not substituted for the present system of private property, the effect was counterproductive. Thus, dependence on the private economy continued, but it became a private economy threatened with expropriation. The law would have made payment a condition of expropriation, but if financing were not available—in sufficient quantity and deliberately programmed by municipalities—how could expropriation be carried out? And it was based upon the false premise that in Colombia, at least in the large- and medium-sized cities, the total population is already housed and enjoys a decent roof overhead. In this view, the problem is, rather, the injustice of being a tenant instead of an owner. Thus, expropriation was necessary to distribute real wealth; in this urban reform bill, outright ownership was more important than facilitating the income which would permit renting or even buying a house.

The bill was also based upon another false premise—namely, that municipalities could expropriate without regard for the local power structure, which determines municipal councils' behavior. This power structure is characterized by the predominance of traditional groups since political participation is still precarious in Colombia.

In late 1969, the national government presented to Congress another bill—65—dealing with housing and urban development. This bill also did not win approval before the legislature recessed in December 1969.

So far as urban land ownership is concerned, the bill declared that acquisition of urban and rural lands by the nation, departments, the Special District of Bogotá, municipalities, and the ICT were of "public utility" and "social interest" when these entities required such real property for execution of urban renewal or development plans, construction of housing in urban areas, execution of public works necessary for development of the community, segregation of lands destined for water supply and protection of watersheds, segregation of zones on the periphery of cities in order to control or regulate urban development, solution to problems created by de facto occupation of urban or suburban lands, eradication or prevention of the construction of *tugurios, barrios,* or buildings not subject to the respective municipal codes, or construction of satellite and new cities. The bill also contemplated measures to accelerate expropriation proceedings which, at present, are slow and expensive. Specifically, in order to appraise properties to be expropriated, the basis to be used was the official assessed valuation, if one existed. If not, the voluntary appraisal of the owner or possessor was to be taken as the basis. Payment in the case of expropriation was to be partly in cash and partly in urban development bonds. As for de facto occupation of private real property (the so-called invasions), the bill established that the ICT could buy directly, or expropriate, urban or suburban properties occupied before September 1, 1969 (just prior to the date the bill was presented), provided that the courts, in trying to regularize such situations, did not rule in favor of the occupiers. In large cities, the bill substituted for the urban development tax *(impuesto de acción urbana)* another tax equivalent to 8 percent of the assessed valuation of unimproved lands, buildings in ruins, or those built in violation of urban codes.[3]

The bill's provisions concerning expropriation for housing and urban development actually already existed in prior laws, even though this particular bill was of far wider and more specific application. Withal, expropriation will depend, as formerly, on public initiative, which remains subject to the financial capabilities of the public agency interested in the particular expropriation. Thus, the newly proposed urban reform bill was limited in matters of urban land ownership and did not attempt to introduce into national legislation new legal norms governing the use of private property, norms which could meet the requirements of direction and control of the urban real estate market.

When the above two proposed urban reforms are compared, both coincide in using the mechanism of expropriation of urban property. The first bill used expropriation primarily to facilitate the acquisition of housing by present tenants, while the second promotes urban development and construction of housing through expropriation. The bills also coincide in their stimulation of housing construction, but they employ relatively different means. The first would put the Savings and Housing Bank (Banco de Ahorro y Vivienda) into actual operation, while the second would order nationalization of the Central Mortgage Bank (Banco Central Hipotecario).

Finally, both bills fail to control or regulate the private urban land market, in which price speculation, vacant lots in urban areas, clandestine urban sub-divisions, and the legal and administrative impotence of municipal authorities to subordinate the physical growth of cities to already-drafted land use plans are ever-present phenomena.

EVALUATION

Urban reforms being proposed today in Colombia cover only partial aspects of the urban problem. As a consequence, the measures will not have real impact on obstacles which at present complicate orderly development of the cities and equitable allocation of housing to their inhabitants. Urban reform takes place in a local physical environment, in an expanding urban area bound by forms of private ownership. This local physical environment has a government, the *municipio,* which must be given (or permitted to expand) power to direct and control urban development. This government requires financial resources to be able to provide the diverse urban services demanded by the population. The population needs housing, which it should secure on its own initiative, but the latter is conditioned by income and credit facilities.

Thus, urban reform in Colombia must include laws dealing with municipal aspects, both administrative and financial, physical development and land ownership, financing of housing, regional development and training of specialized personnel for municipal planning and administration.[4] But Colombians are already launched on a new revision. On October 22, 1970, Congress received yet another urban reform bill—91—of 1970—from the national government, differing from the 1969 one in not nationalizing the Banco Central Hipotecario but converting it into a central mortgage bank for housing loans and urban development. A new institution, to be known as the National Urban Reform Council, was suggested, which will concern itself with the problems of utilization and tenancy of urban property. An executive technical secretariat in the National Institute of Urban Development and Housing is to replace the older ICT. In addition to the urban development tax, which is retained with an interest rate of from 8 to 15 percent per annum, a new presumptive tax on rented housing is introduced and a tax of 5 percent per annum on assessed valuation for luxury housing of more than 250 square meters is added, plus 1 percent per annum for housing whose assessed valuation is more than Col. $500,000 (U.S. $25,000). Measures concerning urban renewal zones are also included, together with a price freeze and the creation of a space category as "reserve" in or outside urban areas. While these measures are suggested, however, the regulations concerning the expropriation of lands for urban development needs are to remain as stated in the 1969 bill.[5]

NOTES

1. To achieve these ends, the bill established the following:

(1) *Acquisition measures:* (a) Acquisition of property by public agencies for housing and urban development by means of direct negotiation and purchase at a price not to exceed 10 percent more than the assessed valuation. In the event the owner were to resist sale of his property, the administrative authorities could sue for its expropriation. (b) Emergency expropriation to acquire properties for the above ends. This involved the judicial authorities' decreeing the surrender of properties immediately, without awaiting the results of court decisions, after payment of a deposit in the amount of the assessed valuation. If the court ruled in favor of the owner of properties so expropriated, he was to receive compensation for damages, but not return of his properties. (c) The price of improved lands acquired either by negotiation or by expropriation was to be paid partly in cash and partly in Class A bonds, redeemable in fifteen years and bearing 8 percent annual interest. The price of partially or completely unimproved lands was to be paid partly in cash and partly in Class B bonds, redeemable in twenty-five years and bearing 6 percent annual interest. In the case of properties which were the habitual residence of the owners or those which were the owners' sole rental property, up to the first 200,000 pesos of total value was to be paid in cash and the balance according to the above-mentioned provisions. (d) Authorizing the Instituto de Crédito Territorial (ICT), departments (states), and municipalities to issue public-housing and urban development bonds in payment of negotiated or expropriated properties destined for such purposes.

(2) *Inducements to transforming tenants into owners:* Owners selling houses to their occupants on long-term mortgages within the first three years of passage of the law were to enjoy the following benefits: (1) exemption from income taxes on occasional profits derived from the sale of houses; (2) exemption from sales taxes where applicable; and (3) exemption from inheritance, allowance, and gift taxes. Once the three-year period expired, the established laws dealing with negotiation or expropriation were to apply in full again.

(3) *Rent control:* Three years after passage of the law, all rent controls were to cease. In no instance, however, could monthly rents exceed 1 percent of assessed valuation.

(4) *Inducements to construction:* (a) Putting into actual operation the Savings and Housing Bank (Banco de Ahorro y Vivienda) created, though not activated, by a previous law. (b) Authorizing financial corporations to provide rediscountable credit to enterprises manufacturing building and urbanization materials and constructing housing, either for sale or rent. (c) Guaranteeing that buildings constructed within six months before and ten years after passage of the law would not be expropriated for twenty years. (d) Exempting from all national, departmental, and municipal taxes nonprofit organizations specifically dedicated to collaborating in solving the problem of housing for the poor.

(5) *Action agencies:* (a) The ICT was to formulate national housing programs and to coordinate them with national and municipal public agencies in rural as well as urban areas. (b) The ICT was to decentralize its functions, creating joint societies with departments, municipalities, and other official or semi-official organizations for housing and urban renewal. (c) The National Housing Council (Consejo Nacional de Vivienda) was to be created, composed of representatives of public and private sectors, to serve as an advisory agency to the ICT in programming its activities. (d) The municipalities were to be empowered to join among themselves to achieve the same ends.

(6) *Maximum value of new construction:* Prohibited was the construction of housing, in single- or multifamily buildings, which when completed or repaired would have, according to estimates, a unit value of more than 400,000 pesos.

(7) *Urban renewal:* Agencies in charge of advancing plans for low-income housing were to give preference to urban renewal projects in order to prevent further deterioration and improve the use of urban property.

2. See the study by Roberto Pineda in this volume.

3. The above were the only provisions regarding urban land ownership contained in the bill. Other provisions of the bill concerned financing of housing through nationalization of the Central Mortgage Bank (Banco Central Hipotecario) to convert it into the mortgage market's central bank, reorganization of and greater financing provided to the ICT, organization of mutual savings and loan associations for housing, governmental issue of certificates for the development of housing to encourage the construction of low-income projects, and elimination of all rent controls over urban buildings not in use as housing, such as commercial sites.

4. For more detail, see the author's "Del deterioro de Cali a una política urbana," a monograph presented to the United Nations' interregional seminar on shantytowns and uncontrolled settlements in Medellín, Colombia, in February of 1970.

5. This bill did not gain approval by the Congress during the 1970 sessions. The government planned to present to the Congress in July 1971 a new bill including the changes introduced in the former bill by a commission convened by the President of the Republic.

Chapter 8

METROPOLITAN GOVERNMENT

G. THE LEGAL AND INSTITUTIONAL ORGANIZATION OF METROPOLITAN ROSARIO, ARGENTINA

RAUL OSCAR BASALDUA and OSCAR MORENO

THE PROBLEM

Rosario and its surroundings have felt the impact of accelerated urbanization, a phenomenon which has been repeated in other coastal cities of Argentina. An urban economy has been established and has expanded in direct relation to productive activities serviced by the port of Rosario. Rosario's growth is also fomented by its role as the center of one of the most important Argentine grain regions integrated by railway and highway. Historically, and until the advent of industrialization in Argentina, Rosario was the keystone of communication between the interior and the outside world, during a time in which Latin America's role was limited by the international division of labor to that of primary production.

The important influxes of immigrants into Argentina between 1870 and 1920 also had an impact on Rosario, setting off rapid, uncontrollable, and disorderly expansion of the city. The 1940s and 1950s were a period of great industrial growth in Argentina, structurally based on a policy of import substitution which caused large population shifts. This produced changes in Rosario which, in addition to its function as a port, now also served as an important industrial center, basically in the field of metallurgy.

These circumstances, coupled with the physical suitability of the environment and the lack of institutional controls over urban growth, worsened preexisting problems. Rosario's disorderly growth has produced well-known deficiencies, among which are serious defects in the network of highways, access roads, and railways, location of important industries in residential areas, and insufficient essential urban services.

Editors' Note: English translation by Roberta W. Solt.

THE PROGRAM

Argentina and the Latin American countries in general lack experience in the organization, institution-building, and implementation of metropolitan programs. This has forced us in Rosario to attempt to elaborate an original model designed at the same time to avoid elements that might impede the necessary adjustments to the existing legal system.[1]

We propose an organization for the Prefectura del Gran Rosario which has as its principal objective integration of areawide planning and programming. Such action, however, must not include strictly local affairs. Rather, overall action is confined to the functioning of urban services in and the socioeconomic development of the subregion as a whole. The Prefectura del Gran Rosario cannot itself assume the powers of a municipal or super-government since limits cannot be modified or constitutional and political powers changed. For these reasons, it was decided to attempt a solution institutionalizing a planning agency rather than an administrative or governmental one. Otherwise, the program

TABLE 1

POPULATION DENSITIES AND MUNICIPAL AND
COMMUNAL BUDGETS OF GRAN ROSARIO

Locality	I Number of Inhabitants	II Area Km. 2	III Population Density/ Km. 2	IV Annual Budget (U.S.$)	V Budget Per Capita (U.S.$)
Rosario	594,063	198.4	2,835.3	22,307,569	37.55
Puerto San Martín	4,262	47.0	90.7	54,581	12.81
San Lorenzo	22,057	38.6	571.4	737,051	33.42
Fray Luis Beltrán	5,167	8.2	630.1	41,434	8.02
Capitán Bermúdez	13,053	20.7	630.6	202,390	15.51
Ricardone	690	94.0	7.3	5,816	8.43
Ibarlucea	878	47.0	18.7	18,326	20.87
Gdro. Baigorria	5,965	24.0	248.5	179,681	30.12
Roldán	5,470	114.0	48.0	129,880	23.74
Funes	4,484	100.5	44.6	63,346	14.14
Zavalla	3,406	167.5	20.3	13,147	3.86
Pérez	7,702	67.0	115.0	70,517	9.15
Soldini	1,875	76.5	24.5	23,505	1.87
Piñero	812	87.5	9.3	47,808	58.87
Alvarez	3,278	66.0	49.7	23,904	7.29
Villa Gdor. Gálvez	18,418	31.0	594.1	484,382	26.30
Alvear	1,975	60.0	33.0	13,147	6.66
Villa Amelia	1,503	81.5	18.4	9,721	6.47
Gral. Lagos	2,399	75.0	32.0	18,725	7.81
Arroyo Seco	10,663	140.0	76.2	426,693	40.02
Fighiera	3,149	145.0	21.7	41,434	13.16
Total	711,266	1,639.44	433.8	24,913,057	35.03

SOURCES: I: 1960 census; II: Data provided by the Dirección de Catastro of the Provincia de Santa Fe; IV: 1965-1966 budget at a rate of exchange of 251 to the dollar.

would be far from implementation because of political tradition and an administrative-legal framework which to date has been impossible to modify.

The new agency's statement of purpose declares that it has the specific responsibility for unifying criteria in investment in services of common concern, and integrative action in the planning and programming of the area's development as a whole. This common action, coordinated or areawide, would not render inoperative specific local responsibility, except that an operational policy of common concern would be established for *municipios* and *comunas*.

The area included in Metropolitan Rosario is determined by following the criterion of functional relationships[2] (for more detailed information, see Figure 1, in which the total area, urban centers, access routes, railway networks and stations, and ports are delineated; in Figure 2, the geographical relationship of Rosario in comparison with the other metropolitan areas of Argentina is shown for 1947-1960-1970; Table 1 indicates the land area, population, density, the general annual budget and per capita budget of Rosario).

The proposed agency would be headed by a Directorate in which technical responsibilities would reside. The Directorate would be composed of experts elected as representatives of the different decision-making levels in the metropolitan area. The body itself would function as a typical technical mechanism for plan formulation in which resolutions are not adopted by member vote.[3] In the case of differing positions, the Prefect would bring these differences to the attention of the Assembly, together with reports on the distinctions between positions.

The Assembly is the primary organ charged with evaluation and political ratification of action taken by the technical Directorate. The Assembly is composed of intendents and presidents of the area's communes. The Prefect serves as Secretary. The Assembly would convene twice a year as a minimum. Voting in the assembly is designed so that each vote both reflects the total voting population of each zone of the metropolitan area, and also the equilibrium of its socioeconomic forces.

The value of the vote of each member of the Assembly is proportional to the number of inhabitants, budget, and geographical location of the problem being treated. In addition, a technical secretariat is suggested, which supports the work of the Directorate. The Prefect is the dominant officer representing the Prefecture, serving as secretary of the Assembly, president of the Directorate and Director of the Technical Secretariat for planning. The ordinary annual budget would be proportional to the budgets of the communes and municipalities now making up the metropolitan area.

EVALUATION

Establishing an institutional structure for a metropolitan area makes it necessary to distinguish two features: the programming and coordination of services of common concern, and the rationalization of urban growth in relation

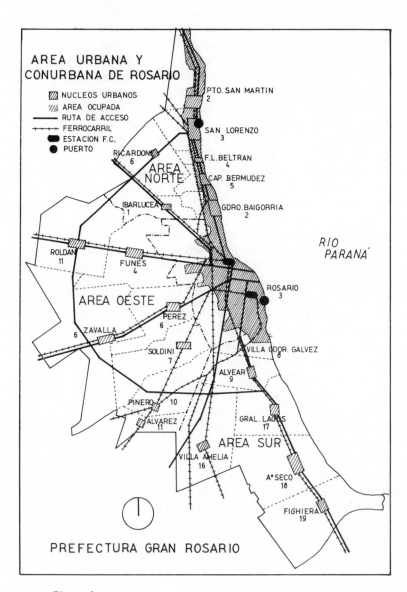

Figure 1

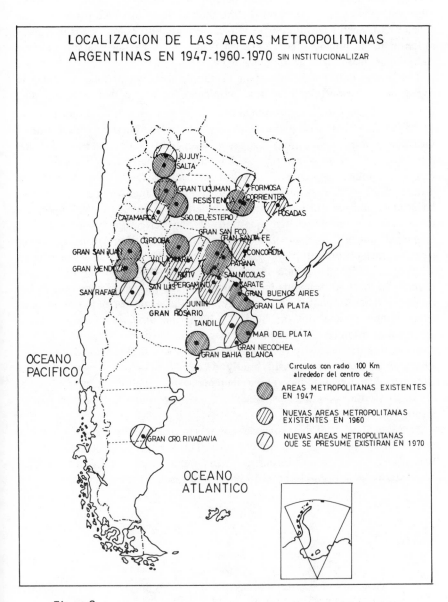

LOCALIZACION DE LAS AREAS METROPOLITANAS
ARGENTINAS EN 1947-1960-1970 SIN INSTITUCIONALIZAR

Círculos con radio 100 Km
alrededor del centro de:

AREAS METROPOLITANAS EXISTENTES
EN 1947

NUEVAS AREAS METROPOLITANAS
EXISTENTES EN 1960

NUEVAS AREAS METROPOLITANAS
OUE SE PRESUME EXISTIRAN EN 1970

Figure 2

to the area's socioeconomic system. In the developed countries, the duties of a metropolitan unit could be limited to the programming and achieving of services of common concern. In Latin America, the lack at a centralized level of a general strategy of economic and social development involving definition of an urbanization policy is the norm. In the limited cases in which regionalization policies have been tried, they have not incorporated bases for the institutionalization of urban policies. These circumstances require that such deficits be made up by inputs from lower decision-making levels.

The implementation of a system of subregional metropolitan planning in Argentina must confront three basic problems. The first is that of determining where the decision to organize the system arises and what is its authority to do so. In the case of Rosario and its zone of influence, the initiative for creation of the agency must come from the area's municipios and comunas. This was formally declared in a meeting held in the headquarters of the Granadero Baigorria comuna on August 3, 1967. This meeting was the first step toward metropolization. The resolution passed by municipal intendents at this meeting involved express recognition of the area's functional reality. It was also necessary to resolve the much-debated question of the delegation of powers since municipal powers, as has often been reiterated by the Argentine courts, represent delegations of power by the province. This problem became more acute after 1966, the period in which legislative powers of the deliberative councils of local governments were assumed by the provincial governors or the President of the Republic. Consequently, after the signing of an intermunicipal-intercommunal agreement on June 30, 1968, the province of Santa Fe was requested to establish the prefecture in view of the needs of the region. The final problem was the necessity of determining the area's organizational form. The structure proposed, previously briefly described, was one of an interjurisdictional order based on a common planning agency, whose objective or goal is the maximization of efficiency in actions, relatively diluted to date because of incomplete efforts.

In September 1969 the provincial law was signed, on the basis of the above agreement among municipios and comunas. This law was ratified by a National Executive Decree (Decreto Ejecutivo Nacional) in October 1969, and the system described has now begun to be established in Rosario.

NOTES

1. The model described is that developed by the authors of this essay as *Investigadores* of the Centro de Estudios Urbanos y Regionales (CEUR) of the Instituto Torcuato de Tella in Buenos Aires under a contract with the municipality of Rosario.

2. The geographic limits of the designated area are precise: it is bounded on the north by Puerto San Martín where the Paraná River separates National Route Number 11, causing a radical change in the zone, since it is here that the urban network disappears. To the east,

the boundary is the Paraná River; to the south, the Arroyo Pavón. To the west, physical and socioeconomic determinants clearly delimit the area's boundaries.

3. It is within the power of the *Directorio* to: (a) formulate the area's development plan, its different operational stages, and prepare the annual programs of labor and investment; (b) solicit from the Secretaria Técnica de Planificación those studies considered indispensable to facilitating decisions; (c) analyze, advise, and propose to the *Asamblea* the approval of projects, studies, evaluations, and plans; (d) advise the provincial government, by means of studies pinpointing problems, diagnoses, or prognoses of the area; (e) prescribe the general norms to which the area's zoning laws must be adjusted in matters affecting the area's structure; (f) coordinate and control the execution of the master plans of the area's municipios and comunas in matters affecting structure; (g) orient actions of the private sector to the end of promoting its participation in the formation of corporations to execute economic and social development.

Chapter 9

COMMUNITY DEVELOPMENT, HOUSING,
AND MARGINALITY

H. THE COLOMBIAN INSTITUTO DE CREDITO TERRITORIAL:
HOUSING FOR LOW-INCOME FAMILIES

ROBERTO PINEDA

THE PROBLEM

The growth pattern of Colombian cities,[1] with its distortion of the polarization of social classes caused by prolific increase of the lowest class, has determined the policies of the Colombian Instituto de Crédito Territorial since 1957. A high proportion of people in this lower urban stratum do not earn incomes above the family subsistence level. This potentially excludes them as recipients of credit from financial institutions in programs requiring complete recovery of investment.

At the same time, housing production costs increase by some 20 percent annually, while family income increases only between 5 and 8 percent. Urban public works are directly responsible for increases in costs, partly because of inadequate design, and partly because of extremely demanding urban standards set by municipalities. The housing construction industry in general operates with traditional building materials and systems. Unskilled construction labor is abundant and attractive because of its low wages. (The construction industry employs barely 4.3 percent of the total economically active population of Colombia according to the 1964 census, but it plays an important role in absorbing migrants, even though unemployment among the economically active population is in excess of 12 percent.) Under these circumstances, Colombia faces a housing deficit exceeding 600,000 units. The present rate of construction, both public and private, is not sufficient even to keep this deficit from growing.

Editors' Note: English translation by Alejandro Vélez Gómez.

THE PROGRAM

The job of the Institute is to bring housing programs to the lowest section of the population. It does so by financial action.[2] The Institute receives funds from appropriations in annual national budgets, repayment of its investments, internal credit resources, foreign credits (expiring in 1970), and proceeds from the sale of bonds. On the average, these funds cost 10.10 percent interest a year. Interest rates charged by the Institute in its programs for lowest income groups, however, range between 4 and 8 percent. Thus, the interest rates paid by low-income families include a subsidy, particularly if monetary depreciation and the system of constant, amortized installments are considered. The transfer of income from one socioeconomic group to another through the public sector by means of such subsidy is a policy maintained as one of the systems of income distribution. In a certain sense, therefore, the Institute's national budgetary appropriations annually cover this transfer and even leave a margin of capitalization. "Losses" are also compensated by investment of remaining capital in programs for higher socioeconomic strata, with interest rates ranging from 10 to 12 percent yearly.

Financial action, which is in any case insufficient, is alone not enough. It is complemented by other action directed toward seeking architectural and construction solutions to the problem of reducing the excessive costs which have been the rule in Colombia's building industry. Increasing population density is one means of achieving this end. Traditional multifamily housing projects carry relatively great weight today in the Institute's whole program, as compared with previous years, and the tendency is to increase their share. In addition, an effort is made to encourage the introduction of new construction techniques. Prefabricated housing for low-income groups is a popular new direction. Its application is limited to one-family dwellings, however, and almost exclusively to self-construction programs.

The need for designs increasing urban density, reducing urban development costs per housing unit, and introducing industrialized techniques at an accelerating rate is also being met with modular housing. It is not possible to establish a prototype house for all programs in the many cities of the nation due to differences in climate, topography, economy, and social patterns. The problem has been reformulated in terms of the functions of housing—service, sleeping, permanence—on the premise that these elements can be used to form a prototype adaptable to different regions without losing their differentiating characteristics. Prototypes may be differently laid out, and may be either single- or multifamily. The modular pattern permits each housing nucleus (a three meters by three meters size is being tried) to be combined with others of equal size, horizontally or vertically, to form compact dwellings with multiple uses. Urban designs facilitating vertical stacking of modules will permit devoting only one-third of a project's total cost to urban public works and services and indirect costs, and the remaining two-thirds "to housing and to providing families with more complete solutions, at less cost."

In order to construct dwellings (between 30,000 and 39,000 units have been announced for 1970), the Institute has also used many other procedures, including construction contracts with specialized firms through public bidding; construction by the Institute itself in places where specialized firms are not available; self-construction, with donation of lots, materials, plans, training, and technical and social assistance; loans in cash or materials to houseless owners of urbanized lots who wish to build; and special plans or programs in which there is financial participation by the Institute, the recipient of housing, and a third party, whether individual or entity.

EVALUATION

The Institute's involvement in the process of ordering urban development has been gradual, through its housing and barrio improvement and rehabilitation programs. The Institute is limited, at the moment, to housing and infrastructure such as public urban services and roads, and community facilities complementing residential life. The Institute legally operates in 104 cities with more than 10,000 inhabitants, causing its programs to be extremely dispersed. The

TABLE 1

INSTITUTO DE CREDITO TERRITORIAL COMPLETED
DWELLING UNITS BY CITY: YEARS 1942-1969

City	Total to 1965	1966	1967	1968	1969[a]	Total
Total	107,650	9,069	12,082	12,148	3,485	144,434
Armenia	2,428	173	64	379	8	3,052
Barranquilla	7,504	234	1,151	1,062	195	10,146
Bogotá	26,593	1,666	4,367	3,554	1,432	37,612
Bucaramanga	5,472	818	749	892	169	8,100
Cali	19,054	1,903	1,486	1,685	320	24,448
Cartagena	2,920	95	133	442	46	3,676
Cúcuta	4,534	10	171	269	231	5,215
Ibagué	4,754	297	307	265	301	5,924
Manizales	3,709	255	387	488	151	4,990
Medellín	10,651	1,697	717	1,333	139	14,537
Montería	3,465	185	46	124	56	3,876
Neiva	3,193	192	445	164	6	4,000
Pasto	2,826	336	361	142	117	3,782
Pereira	3,446	491	688	467	15	5,107
Popayán	2,525	74	283	160	2	3,044
Santa Marta	1,576	171	142	183	5	2,077
Tunja	1,693	226	311	270	78	2,578
Villavicencio	1,307	246	274	269	174	2,270

SOURCE: Oficina de Planeación, Sección de Investigaciones y Estadística.

a. First six months.

tendency of the National Planning Department and the Institute has been to consider only cities having 30,000 or more inhabitants, which reduces the area of action by more than half.

Involvement, however limited, in such a vast field as public urban services and housing improvement requires, in addition to an elaborate and costly technical staff, financial capability which is beyond the resources available at present to the Institute. For this reason, its policies seek coordination of other institutional mechanisms, national and local. The Institute itself allots its limited funds not in proportion to priorities suggested by the magnitude of the problem, but in inverse proportion to the financial capability of the cities experiencing housing problems.

The Institute has achieved very low average unit costs and a total production of dwelling units which in 1963 was sixteen times greater than the annual average to 1957. Evaluation of many of these programs yields a balance more positive than negative. Nevertheless, the capital invested in acceptable completed housing leaves only a bare margin for a very few dwelling units. Under these circumstances, experience has been gained in planning, but little headway has been made in industrial design, mechanization of construction processes, use of new materials, and adoption of prefabrication of an important number of materials and components.

The Institute is challenged by the urgency of increasing the production of dwellings and the new housing requirements connected with urban growth. It has tried to promote industrialization with accompanying mechanization, while maintaining its objective of preferentially serving the lowest urban classes. While in theory, at least, mass production and industrialization in its widest sense should bring about reduction in costs, this does not affect marginal classes, which for economic reasons can obtain only the most elementary housing, even with existing subsidies in the form of installments, interest rates, and other mortgage features.

Modular housing is a valuable illustration, even though the modular-housing design has not yet been put into practice. There is only one experimental unit constructed for exhibit and analysis. An experimental unit is projected in the vicinity of Ciudad Kennedy in Bogotá.[2] It will consist of more than 200 units built by three different systems: traditional materials and systems; industrialized procedures—i.e., the Outinor system; and a transitional system combining traditional procedures and materials with prefabricated components. But a solution in terms of housing for the lowest strata will not be the result, given the unit costs involved.

High capital costs will not contribute to lowering unit costs, nor can investment below levels necessary for recovery of principle be continued indefinitely. Three measures are therefore needed: (1) placing with the Institute the least expensive domestic funds, leaving to the Central Mortgage Bank (Banco Central Hipotecario), a private institution which finances housing for middle-middle sectors and above, the more expensive funds; (2) constantly increasing the Institute's financial resources[3] in order to maintain an appreciable and rising volume of construction;[4] and (3) determining the percentages of investment to be allocated at different interest rates in order to maintain the income transfer from social sector to social sector, thus aiding marginal classes without impairing the Institute's capitalization.

NOTES

1. In 1964, Colombia had 57 urban centers of over 20,000 inhabitants, distributed as follows: 22 centers with 20,000 to 49,999 inhabitants; 13 centers with 50,000 to 99,999 inhabitants; 9 centers with 100,000 to 499,999 inhabitants; and, 3 centers with over 500,000 people. The tendency is toward concentration of population in the two largest categories.

2. The most important residential complex built by the Institute. It has 12,000 units.

3. The institute at present has the financial capability to produce approximately 30,000 dwellings per year.

4. The Institute recently inaugurated the piggybank plan *(plan alcancía),* a kind of temporary substitute for the system of savings and loans, in order to channel family savings.

SUGGESTED BIBLIOGRAPHY

Historical Background

Instituto de Crédito Territorial (1958) El problema de la vivienda en Colombia: Planteamientos y soluciones. Bogotá.
–– (1955) Una Política de vivienda para Colombia. Bogotá.

Policies and Achievements

Departamento Nacional de Planeación (1969) Plan Quinquenal de Inversiones. Bogotá. (This is noteworthy for its statement of general urban development and housing policy and the investment plan.)
Instituto de Crédito Territorial (annual) Reports to the Minister of Development (Fomento) for his yearly accounting to the National Congress, 1958-1970. (The report for 1965 includes a study of modular housing for low-income groups.)
–– (n.d.) Report to the Second Inter-American Housing Conference (Congreso Interamericano de Vivienda). (Covers the Institute's administrative organization, methods of operation, financing, achievements, policies, and projections.)
Instituto de Crédito Territorial (1970) Untitled pamphlet. Begins with "Basic conditions for solution to the housing problem." (The most recent statement of policy.)

I. OPERACION SITIO: A HOUSING SOLUTION FOR PROGRESSIVE GROWTH

ANTONIO LABADIA CAUFRIEZ

THE PROBLEM

"Houseless" people are a typical situation in Chile and in all Latin America. In Chile, we find *callampas, conventillos,* houses rented by the room, *allegados,* and, finally, squatter settlements. Whether they are called *favelas, villas miserias chabolas, bidonvilles, ranchos, tugurios,* or *casas de vecindad,* the fact remains that cities have not been able to adapt their structure to the growing requirements of the population. The number of urban inhabitants is growing at such a fantastic rate that the availability of housing and services, as well as the entire urban structure, including food supply, networks of transportation and infrastructure, open spaces, and educational and health services, keeps falling farther behind.

In Chile, with an average population growth rate of 2.3 percent per year, rural zones are not growing at all. The rate for urban areas is 2.8 percent. In the extreme case, the city of Santiago is growing at a rate of 3.8 percent annually and receives 76 out of every 100 persons deciding to change residence in the remainder of the nation. Santiago has thus succeeded in accumulating 40 percent of the entire urban population of Chile. In the metropolitan areas of Peru, the number of marginal inhabitants rose from 45,000 in 1940 to 958,000 in 1965, and in Caracas they comprise more than 35 percent of the total population. Brasília is another classic case. While the specialized magazines continue to extol the city's magnificent architecture, a sea of favelas has begun to surround it. According to statements of the former mayor of Brasília, Paulo de Tarso (*AUCA,* 1970; Secrétariat, 1969) half the city's population, some 35,000 families, 200,000 people, live in favelas.

In Chile, a study undertaken in December 1964 by the Housing Corporation's (Corporación de la Vivienda—CORVI) planning department revealed 105,000 families living in urban callampas throughout the entire nation. Through a plan of regional development which has been initiated in Chile in recent years,[1] some of the present disequilibrium can be corrected, but it is probable that the tendency to overurbanization will continue. Regardless of the shape of future evolution, a considerable number of families lacking housing are living in the cities at the present time, and their needs must be met.

The problem consists of an insufficiency of resources vis-à-vis the magnitude of investment required by a housing plan. Even if governments were to grant housing a high priority, only with great difficulty could they have at their disposal investment funds sufficient to keep pace with yearly growth and to

Editors' Note: English translation by Charles J. Savio.

amortize the accumulated deficit in some way. In fact, approximately 40 percent of the urban population, and 50 percent of the rural, of Latin America live crowded together in unhealthy conditions. To confront population growth and eliminate in 30 years the existing housing deficit as well, some 3 million dwelling units per year would have to be built, or, about 11 1/2 units for each 1,000 inhabitants (United Nations, 1963). When it is kept in mind that Chile, undertaking one of the most ambitious programs in Latin America, has barely succeeded in building 4.9 dwelling units per 1,000 inhabitants, one begins to understand the impossibility of achieving a solution by traditional means.

It is necessary, then, to adopt other strategies and simultaneously to employ unused resources. The new policy rests on two fundamental premises. The first is that marginal settlers generally do not aspire to build their own homes, but rather to have an urban lot assuring them of definite settlement. For decades, their most urgent problem has been instability—the permanent sensation of stealth, the continual life of the outsider, always subject to suspicion and expulsion; in sum, to be second-class citizens. The site is the first and most basic step toward normality. Later, they will know how to construct their housing to their own taste, as they have done through the years.

The second premise is the settlers' aggressive and progressive attitude, which contrasts with that held by callampa-dwellers of former years. Callampas were once conglomerates without organization or hope. Their dwellers occupied public lands surreptitiously, trying to remain inconspicuous, living their lives with resignation. Today, the callampa has been conquered. The settler installs himself in the city, not expecting mere toleration, but rather to live actively there, improving his working conditions, educating his children, and satisfying his many aspirations. By demanding his right to live in the city, he is demanding his right to a certain way of life, a culture expressed in city life. This attitude in itself represents an additional resource of incalculable value which is lost in the callampa or coventillo.

THE PROGRAM

The name Operación Sitio has been given to a Chilean government credit program enabling the acquisition of one-family urban lots along with basic utilities and community services. The program aims to integrate community facilities with housing projects by beginning urbanization with land title and services, not houses. It is also based on the idea of prior savings as the criterion for government-sponsored housing.

This program is the first of five options contained in the Popular Savings Plan (Plan de Ahorro Popular) for housing, put into effect by *Decreto Supremo* 553, September 26, 1967, by the Ministry of Housing and Urbanism. Until that date, an abundance of individual and collective loans for the construction of housing and urban subdivisions existed, all with diverse amounts of down payments, rates of monthly payments, dividends, and periods of amortization. The extraordinarily ambitious Popular Savings Plan served to rationalize the spectrum of existing loans, establishing a series of five options for loan programs on the basis of a unitary savings plan and noncontractual credit: semi-urbanized sites; completely urbanized sites; self-built basic housing; one-story housing of 45 square meters; and four-story apartment buildings. No person who owns real estate, or whose immediate family does, can sign up for the program under penalty of sanctions. For those owning lots, the People's Savings Plan provides—in addition to the basic operations already outlined—seven alternative forms of credit for improving or completing improvements, or for building and enlarging up to 40 square meters an existing housing unit. Operación Sitio, like the People's Savings Plan's other features, is fundamentally a governmental program of individual or collective credit. Those interested can use this credit to acquire lots provided by government programs, though they may also take advantage of lots offered by private enterprise.

The Plan is administered by the Corporación de Servicios Habitacionales (CORHABIT). The applicant must, at the time of registration, have at least twenty savings payments in his State Bank (Banco del Estado) savings book. These savings accounts may be opened individually or collectively. Funds deposited in such accounts are labeled savings payments at the time of deposit and cannot be withdrawn for three years except to acquire or build a dwelling. The value of savings payment is increased monthly according to the rise in the cost of living. Thus, deposits are protected against inflation. In addition, deposits earn 2 percent interest from the Bank.

Once an applicant is enrolled, he must deposit four payments monthly during the year, at the end of which time he will have accumulated in his account 68 payments and earned the right to receive a semi-urbanized site. Once living on the site, he must continue depositing 5 savings payments a month for 15 months, raising this initial savings to 143 payments and giving him the right to a loan of 787 savings payments. The total of the loan and initial saving—with the latter's value determined at the time of signing the credit application—is the amount applied toward payment for land and basic utilities and equipment. The loan must be liquidated in 14 years, at a monthly payment rate of 5 savings units and at 5 percent interest per year. The above procedure is Plan 1, which contemplates two stages in the process. Plan 2 requires 50 payments as initial savings and a somewhat longer waiting period to obtain the credit necessary for acquisition of a lot having complete urban utilities and services.

Plan 1 in its initial stage distributes single-family lots of 160 square meters, with wire mesh enclosures, and in complexes supplied with roadbeds, networks of drinking-water troughs and electricity and street lighting. In cases certified by the social welfare service, a *"mediagua,"* i.e., a temporary wooden dwelling of 20 square meters, is granted. In most cases, residents own their own *"mediagua"* or *"mejora"* which they can transport to their assigned sites. If they do not have temporary housing, they generally obtain it from the "Hogar de Cristo" Housing Foundation, a private charitable organization which produces such units on an industrial scale and sells them at cost. Participants in the program may also take advantage of a special line of credit at the Banco de Estado permitting them to acquire—under CORHABIT's control—siding and materials necessary for preliminary installation.

In this first stage, there is no provision for sewage, meaning that hygienic services are reduced to privies, whose superstructures can be obtained on credit from the National Health Service. As community facilities, the program includes temporary or permanent schools, community centers, and commercial sites. Each project follows the outlines of avenues, streets, and alleys, as well as open spaces and those reserved for community activities and other land uses established by area-regulating plans.

In the second stage, construction is completed: electricity and water services begin and meters are installed, the sewage system is constructed and dwellings connected, and the paving of streets and sidewalks is completed. In practice, there is no precise division between stages because different situations may establish different priorities and because each project usually demands its own special treatment. In fact, the climatic differences presented by the regions of Chile establish varying priorities, to such a point that in the southern region projects must often include paving and sewage in the first stage.

The fundamental objective is the installation of a family—albeit in a temporarily precarious way—in its future social and physical environment and community. This goal rests on several preconditions. In the first place, the areas in which projects are developed must be well located and adequately connected in relation to the rest of the city. This helps counteract the natural tendency of a new social group to segregate itself, forming a barrio in disequilibrium cohering internally only through common origin, socioeconomic homogeneity, and initial low level of achievement. From this point of view, it is also important that projects be distributed throughout the different residential districts of the city and that the size of projects enable analysis and control of the sociological phenomena taking place within each project.

The essential process follows the settling-in. What is required is a clear financial program, correct initial evaluation of the possibilities for urbanization, and the technical and administrative assistance necessary to guide the nascent community and channel its efforts. The final stage is construction of actual housing, which may be achieved by means of individual or cooperative credit through the People's Savings Plan or by do-it-yourself projects. In the latter, the application of industrialized building systems opens new perspectives. In numerous Operación Sitio centers, CORHABIT has installed factories turning out panels and parts under an industrial patent whose rights it has acquired, and in which residents themselves, voluntarily working 18 hours a week with adequate supervision, manufacture the materials necessary to construct their own dwellings. In 1970, it is hoped to begin about 20,000 dwelling units of 36 square meters each. Once this has been accomplished, factories will remain in the hands of neighborhood residents, who will thus be able to continue their productive activity, helping other groups and obtaining additional profit.

The fact of receiving a piece of land produces an immediate reaction in "houseless" families. Those who have lived for generations in unhealthy callampas, often located in river beds, garbage dumps, or along open sewers, glimpse for the first time the possibility of a dignified dwelling. From that moment, they organize, save, and work, transforming the neighborhood with their efforts in less time than could be expected. Many begin building housing on their own, acquiring the necessary materials little by little. In addition, the number who buy wooden dwellings on credit from the Hogar de Cristo Foundation is quite high.

Operación Sitio began in 1965, with acknowledgment of the need to complement traditional housing programs with a program aimed primarily at the large "houseless" sector. In an initial enrollment held in Santiago to determine demand, 65,000 families registered during the first two weeks. By the end of 1970, 110,000 lots will have been distributed among almost all of Chile's urban communities. At present, there are about 50,000 families, representing some 60 percent of the total CORHABIT registry, enrolled in People's Savings Plan programs of partially or completely urbanized sites.

To date, it has been the state, through CORVI, which has acquired lots, elaborated plans, and executed through public bidding the appropriate public works, according to guidelines laid down by the Housing Ministry. The Corporación de Servicios Habitacionales, following People's Savings Plan registers, is promptly assigning lots and administering the program, whose stages are being completed according to conditions presented by each project, with the participation of settlers themselves and the collaboration of different agencies of the Housing Ministry, national government, municipal education, public promotion, institutes, and private foundations.

Enrollment preference has been given to Settler's Committees (Comités de Pobladores) and other organizations, which, although they do not possess legal stature, constitute bodies which can later collaborate effectively in the particular community's development. These groups will eventually give rise to Juntas de Vecinos (Neighborhood Councils), Centros de Madres (Mother's Centers), and many other community activities.

It is hoped that among the 100,000 lots granted, about 40,000 permanent dwellings will have begun by December 1970. Gradually, in this manner, temporary dwellings will be replaced, the community's structure will be completed, and networks of public services will be provided so that the entire complex will be converted into a complete residential neighborhood incorporated into the rest of the city. In order to facilitate the latter, the projects of Operación Sitio generally consult sectors in which there is housing and building earmarked for other People's Savings Plan registrants, so as not to produce too homogeneous a stratification with possibly stifling effects. Moreover, projects are distributed in different zones of each city, taking into consideration areas in which petitioners live or work.

The provisions of Decree 103 of February 16, 1968, are applied in connection with acquisition of necessary properties. The decree states that in order to set a fair price, the increase in the land's value, when due to public works or public or municipal services or remodeling in contiguous areas within the five years prior to the decree or accord ordering expropriation, would be eliminated. In addition, the law permits acquisition to be paid in installments and actual possession of property as soon as 20 percent of its established value has been deposited.

EVALUATION

There have been many adverse judgments of the program. For example, it has been stated that Operación Sitio is nothing more than a callampa made official. This statement reveals profound ignorance of the reality of life in marginal settlements as well as of the essential aspects of the solution proposed. It is difficult to imagine what it means to a family to live among trash and garbage, suffering heat and cold, waterless, besieged by flies and infection, without hope of any kind, for years and even generations. Operación Sitio limits itself to an initial point of contact with the callampa. Only an extremely myopic vision could fail to note the possibilities for a dignified life it fosters.

It has also been objected that Operación Sitio tends to spread the city over a greater area, that it leads to reduction in neighboring agricultural areas and to the growth of demand for urban services. With regard to such criticism, it is important not to confuse cause and effect. The cause of growth is the rise in urban population, which will only be limited to the extent that the demographic explosion is arrested and internal migration (rural-urban and city to city) controlled. Migration control would probably require an extremely strict set of laws alien to the Chilean character. If this growth cannot be absorbed by high-rise buildings because of their high initial cost, the inability to meet payments, or low aspirations, it will have to be solved by means of gradual development. In fact, if the state were not to offer Operación Sitio, marginal settlers would extend the cities anyway, acquiring properties by simply invading them illegally.

Many families, acting in good faith, bought lots lacking urban services from unscrupulous realtors, paying exorbitant prices in the process. The situation reached such crisis proportions that it was necessary to promulgate Law 16, 741 of March 23, 1968 (Ley de Loteos Irregulares) which made the seller responsible for promised improvements. In addition, the seller's properties could be sold in order to defray the cost of water, sewage, electricity, and paving. To appreciate the magnitude of the situation, one should note that, in the first two years the law was in effect, about 400 communities (totaling 53,000 families) throughout Chile had recourse to it. These communities, accounting for a sizable segment of the poorest elements in urban areas, generally produce the most disastrous problems of city extension. Those who are most scandalized by Operación Sitio have never had recourse to the law, which is really a form of anticipating the problem—i.e., channelling its effects positively. Today many service cores are completed even before housing is finished, reversing the previous pattern.

Other criticisms refer to the problems not covered by housing planning, such as the relation of Operación Sitio complexes to new centers of employment and the work status of inhabitants. These signal the need for intersectoral treatment. It has also been said that prospective applicants' initial payments do not really equal the cost of Operación Sitio. A subsidy exists, but it is the cost which should logically fall to the state because of the responsibility it assumes when it recognizes that every family, regardless of financial status, has the right to minimal housing. Even when, in terms of the total debt, the normal cost of land and allied public works is paid, other costs and associated investments are absorbed by the state. Moreover, a bonus mechanism which is applied to ensure that payments do not exceed 20 percent of monthly income also affects the financial picture.

There is no doubt that imperfections exist. Yet, basically, Operación Sitio constitutes a key to solving Chile's urgent housing problem through the transfer of legal title to land, the provision of basic community services, and the building of housing in stages.

NOTE

1. See the essay by Manuel Achurra Larraín in this volume.

REFERENCES

AUCA (1970) Santiago. April.
Secrétariat des Missions d'Urbanisme et d'Habitat (1969). Number 54. Photograph. Paris.
United Nations (1963) Report of the Grupo Especial Experto en Vivienda y Desarrollo Urbano. New York.

J. THE ACCION COMUNAL PROGRAM:
LA PAZ, BOLIVIA

GUILLERMO SANJINES ROJAS

THE PROBLEM

The most rapidly growing population sector in many Latin American cities is urban squatters. The infrastructure and social problems created by internal migration are therefore a frequent starting point for inquiries into modern Latin American urbanization. Community organization and action programs are usually advocated as strategies for improving living conditions, stimulating migrant adaptation, and strengthening the leadership of migrant groups. How do such programs actually work?

Community action in La Paz provides a partial portrait of the current state of these programs. The Bolivian Urban Reform Law of 1954 provides that no person may own more than 10,000 square meters of land within the city limits. All lands in excess are expropriated for redistribution to the landless. Since 1954, expropriations of large areas next to the industrialized zones in the higher parts of the city have occurred.[1] But land distribution does not suffice to meet the demand for housing created in La Paz by internal migration. Zones bordering the city have therefore been systematically invaded. The need for shelter forces migrants to build wherever they settle. The migrant prepares good adobe, roofs his house with corrugated sheetmetal, and uses wood or cement for his floors. Even though this housing, given its solid structure, may well be classified as permanent, lighting, ventilation and design are often poor. These trends have prompted a search both for ways to prevent haphazard growth and to improve and channel the house-building efforts of migrants.

A HISTORY OF EFFORTS TO DEAL WITH
SQUATTER PROBLEMS

The first effort to deal systematically with the housing problem of migrants involved the creation of a municipal Department of Public Housing (Departamento de Vivienda de Interés Social) in March 1959. The La Paz department, modeled after proposals from the Inter-American Housing Center (Centro Interamericano de la Vivienda—CINVA) in Bogotá, Colombia, was a subunit of the central planning offices (Oficinas del Plan Regulador). Its goal was to educate and organize the community until after housing was completed. Its program primarily involved lending technical assistance in preparing blueprints for houses to be built in stages by owners.

Editors' Note: English translation by Leonidas F. Pozo-Ledezma.

The department's efforts to use rationally the large areas affected by the Urban Reform Law were thwarted, however, by social and political pressures which allowed persons to occupy land simply by drafting sketchy plats. The new zones were soon filled with housing constructed clandestinely and built in the traditional style. The department's large-scale plan could not therefore be executed.

As a response to the weakness of the department, programs for persons living on the city's outskirts were taken over by the Dirección General de Afectación de Tierras Urbanas (DGATU) of the municipality of La Paz. DGATU was selected because it had already organized an active program which provided heavy machinery and tools on Sundays and holidays to complement residents' efforts in the *barrios* of La Paz. Residents of *villas* and barrios on the city's outskirts were very receptive to the program, but the new zones expropriated under the Urban Reform Law continued to lack basic public services.

On August 3, 1964, a more direct response to the problem was made through the creation of the Dirección General de Acción Comunal (DGAC or Acción Comunal), whose task was to organize popular participation in providing basic public services, particularly on the outskirts of the city. In addition, Acción Comunal was asked to combine the initiatives of neighborhood organizations with those of community government, so that citizens could solve their own problems with the municipality's technical assistance. To implement the self-help housing program, and promote integrated land distribution, DGATU and the Department of Public Housing were placed under the Directorate General of Acción Comunal. In 1967, an auxiliary agency, the Department of Reforestation, was added to carry out reforestation of the La Paz watershed with public participation.

CURRENT ACTIVITIES UNDER ACCION COMUNAL

The earliest Acción Comunal effort involved the promotion of neighborhood emergency squads which deal with rainy season landslides until further help arrives. Little by little, the neighborhood councils *(juntas vecinales)* of the barrios on the city's outskirts joined a Sunday self-help program which worked at cleaning and leveling streets, constructing small tanks for storage of drinking water, planting trees, remodeling and constructing parks, and clearing the beds of streams and ravines.

In 1966, the program received a notable boost with the formation of a Civic Action Committee (Comité de Acción Cívica-Programa Comunal—CAP-PC) which included representatives of the Civic Action group of the Ministry of the Economy and the U.S. Agency for International Development (USAID) in Bolivia, as well as Acción Comunal. This committee, with financing from the USAID mission, carried out twenty-six projects with the community contributing labor and materials. Social centers were built, as well as a school, drinking-water reservoirs and distribution systems, sewage systems, public latrines and restrooms, and athletic fields. The municipality contributed heavy machinery and fuel. The neighborhoods handled the total cost. Since 1967, the program has received additional funds from the municipality of La Paz through appropriations in municipal budgets for social infrastructure projects on the city's periphery.

Acción Comunal is still faced with problems resulting from the increasing migration from rural areas to the city, fostering invasions of private property and the continued proliferation of illegal housing. Housing continues to be built on hillsides surrounding the city, in physically dangerous zones, in zones reserved for reforestation, and on steep slopes permanently subject to landslides which create added difficulties for lower zones because of the earth-moving involved in construction.

One strategy for dealing with this problem has been the extension of the expropriation law. The plains of El Alto, the area destined to be the site of the city's future expansion, were not within the 1944 city limits of La Paz and therefore did not originally come under the Urban Reform Law. A municipal ordinance of July 1968 provided for the additional expropriation of 100 square kilometers of land in this area. Acción Comunal is attempting to promote the growth of a satellite city, Huayna Potosí, here. The hope is that the agricultural and industrial zones will provide employment sufficient to encourage decongestion of the peripheral belt of La Paz. At present, the municipality acts as intermediary between the associations of those granted lands, groups interested in acquiring lots, and owners of lands subject to expropriation. Planning and layout are done by Acción Comunal, which has established a scheme based on neighborhood units of 1,000 lots each. Acción Comunal also hopes to make available blueprints for housing to be built in stages. The first cell, a room with kitchen and bathroom, would be built immediately by the owner or by housing institutions financing the program by occupational groups. Later, as the owner's economic situation improves, additions would be built with Acción Comunal's technical advice.

To date, approximately 5,000 applicants have registered to receive land and have made deposits to a local bank. Lands have already been partially laid out for distribution. The first stage involves housing a large group of municipal workers.

EVALUATION

All evaluations of social development programs must take into account the basic notion that community development depends on popular participation. It is encouraging, therefore, to be able to say that in the marginal areas of the city of La Paz, where Acción programs are being carried out, a majority of neighborhoods now participate. Public participation is organized through neighborhood councils or by the public works committees of the area. It is estimated that these groups have met in each neighborhood on the average of

TABLE 1

CONTRIBUTIONS TO COMMUNITY ACTION PROGRAMS,

1966-1970 (in percentages)

	Contribution		
Years	Community	Municipal	Acción Cívica
1966-1968	54	1[a]	45
1968-1969	66	34	–
1969-1970	56	44	–

a. The municipality's contribution represents financial disbursements only. It does not include contributions of heavy equipment, dump trucks, inspection vehicles, salaries of administrative and technical personnel, and so on.

forty times per year. The president, secretary-general, treasurer, and secretary of public works of each neighborhood council participate actively.

The monetary value of residents' contributions to projects executed under the program is as shown in Table 1. The community also contributes sand, stone, gravel, cement, and other local materials to projects.

Acción Comunal projects have had the additional side benefit of providing information, through public works committee registration records, with which programs other than those under the jurisdiction of this agency could be better administered. On this basis, a program of food and clothing distribution was carried out for the first time in July 1969 under the aegis of the Servicio Nacional de Planificación y Promoción Social (SENDEP).

The program has also succeeded in encouraging the municipality of La Paz to give more attention to community development. Since 1966, the municipality has allotted resources for the payment of personnel and the acquisition of materials for specific projects and contributed heavy machinery and equipment to the Sunday self-help days.

The most vulnerable part of the program is the lack of personnel, particularly environmental-health technicians, social workers, and community leaders who can transact the neighborhoods' business with government offices.

NOTE

1. See the article by Carlos Calvimontes Rojas included in this volume.

REFERENCES

Alcaldía Municipal de La Paz (1967) Recomendaciones y conclusiones de la II Reunión Nacional sobre Desarrollo de Comunidades. August, La Paz.

RIVERA F., R. (1967) "Informe de la Dirección General de Acción Comunal ante la Comisión Nacional Coordinadora de Movilización Social." November, La Paz.

SANJINES ROJAS, G. (1970) "Estructura y objectivos de la Dirección General de Acción Comunal." August, La Paz.

—— (1968) "Informe de la Dirección General de Acción Comunal a la 4a. Reunión Regional Bolivariana sobre Desarrollo de la Comunidad." October, Bogotá.

—— (1959) "Departamento Municipal de Vivienda de Interés Social. Antecedentes, Reglamentos de Urbanizaciones Mínimas, Reglamento de Viviendas Económicos." Ordenanzas. March, La Paz.

EUGENIO PEREZ MONTAS

THE PROBLEM

In the Dominican Republic, programs directed toward advancement of rural as well as urban sectors of the Dominican people are under way.[1] The majority of programs follow the same line of attack. Nevertheless, conflicts are beginning, as much on a national, institutional level as on a rural community one, due to lack of a coordinated policy. As a consequence, the executive branch ordered a commission especially created for the purposes of formulating legislative instruments to shape the process of community development. Recently, the commission submitted a draft bill for community organizations (Anteproyecto de Ley de Organizaciones Comunitarias) which embodies the findings of the two years of work and experience of this commission.

THE PROGRAM

The program's philosophy is based on the premise that in order to achieve development, government efforts alone are not enough. It is necessary to awaken the initiative of those affected by poverty for the purpose of incorporating them into active community life. For some people, community development in the Dominican Republic should consist of a general plan of tasks achieved by means of mutual aid and self-help. For others, the program should involve long-term coordination of the needs of different communities with the services of traditional government agencies. Though we are aware that community development is all these things, we are also convinced that it is a great deal more. The community development program in the Dominican Republic is based on the notion that the creation of modern societies depends upon development of their populations and upon systematic organization of their activities. Serious problems in organization and administration of community-development programs arise because this premise requires us to accept, ideologically, several new criteria.

Community development involves a new concept of government. A well-conceived community development program necessarily involves developing the awareness of individuals and organizations so that they may begin to participate in their own development, becoming in this way active protagonists in the mechanisms of production and decision-making on the local level. Community

Editors' Note: English translation by Felicity M. Trueblood.

development includes not only the activities of a particular public agency or department, but also channeling of programs through all existing public entities.

It is necessary, therefore, to establish new mechanisms which, on the one hand, harmonize national development plans with perceived needs of the communities, and, on the other, avoid the duplication of effort which unnecessarily swells the development and national administration budget. Thus, the goals of the Office of Community Development are stimulation and organization of the community for the purpose of undertaking and completing public works (infrastructure); education of community leaders in the organization and function of "territorial" associations; promotion of a national plan of permanent community organization in order to establish a community structure of submunicipal governments; study and promotion of structural and administrative reforms supporting community structures; and promotion of financing for integral community development.

EVALUATION

As of December 31, 1971, the Office of Community Development had participated in 2,681 projects covering 1,128 communities throughout the nation. Of these projects, 2,098 have been completed, leaving 583 in different stages of execution: 169 under way; 158 which for various reasons are temporarily stalled; 105 not yet begun; 151 cancelled. The 1,128 communities in which the Office of Community Development has acted have a total population of approximately 2,250,000. An estimated 1,720,000 persons, largely rural, have received benefits from the different projects carried out by the Office of Community Development. These run the gamut of activities from public works (roads, sewers), agriculture (irrigation ditches, wells), education (schools and other facilities), health (medical dispensaries, provision of drinking water), social well-being (athletic fields, community centers), and industry (sewing centers, driers) to housing.

In addition to physical projects undertaken, it is important to consider the qualitative achievements the communities have made. Each community has organized a committee to carry out the projects undertaken with the cooperation of the Office of Community Development. The organization of a local committee is required by the Office of Community Development in return for its cooperation in the project. Even though the majority of these committees survive only with great difficulty after termination of the particular projects for which they were organized, they provide experience in democratic procedures. They are also a demonstration of communal collective effort dedicated to the task of satisfying needs or solving communal problems.

At the same time, Office of Community Development organizers have contributed to stimulating organizations of more lasting character. A census carried out recently by the Office of Community Development indicated that somewhat more than 800 functional groups existed throughout the nation, a great majority of which had been organized or were being aided by the Office of Community Development. Athletic or cultural clubs and mothers' centers constituted the largest number of these groups, which also included various agricultural associations. More than 2,000 community leaders have been trained this year under the 1971 educational program, probably the most ambitious of Latin America.

The need for structural changes to facilitate popular participation in development is being advocated with increasing intensity. In the Dominican Republic, popular sectors have taken a basic first step. The absence of structures of participation is waning, and this organization of popular sectors is becoming important in labor unions and cooperatives, functionally and, of course, politically. Increasingly, a greater number of associations are structuring to seek answers to the demand of groups of *campesinos* for community, or of urban dwellers who form an impoverished sector of rural migrants.

NOTE

1. The most relevant social goals which the Dominican National Development Plan is attempting to attain are the following: (a) achieve by 1974, a per capita income of 316 pesos, or an increase of 10.8 percent over the present level of 287 pesos per capita, in 1969 figures; (b) create 211,500 new jobs, causing total employment to grow 22 percent during the period 1970-1974; (c) provide education to the entire obligatory school-age population (from 6 to 14 years of age). It has been projected that 90 percent of this population will be at primary-school level and the remaining 10 percent in middle-school and special programs; (d) build 27,050 housing units to satisfy the increase in demand; (e) build and rehabilitate water mains to benefit some 803,000 persons; (f) increase the number of hospital beds, as well as the efficiency of their use, and construct new hospitals.

As objectives not subject to quantification, but of vital importance to the social advancement of the Dominican Republic, the National Development Plan contemplates, in addition, the following results: (a) redistribution of income by means of a process of resettling 30,000 campesinos within an agrarian reform program, the most important strategic factor in reducing the level of unemployment; (b) reorganization of health services, consisting principally of integration of preventive and curative services in hospital installations existing at present, and of their regionalization; (c) establishment of conditions of organization and stability in the urban settlements in which marginal sectors of the population reside, with a view to their future improvement; (d) adoption of a law of incentives for the communitarian organization of the population; (e) expansion of the school-age population in the provision of social services of transportation, food, textbooks, and other indispensable items.

In order to fulfill these social objectives, annual growth of the gross national product at a rate of 6.6 percent will be required, according to the following growth rates by sector:

	1970-1974 Cumulative, Annually
Agriculture	5.5 percent
Sugar industry	3.4
Manufacturing industry	8.9
Construction	7.2
Energy, fuels, and lubricants	14.1
Mining	39.6
Services and other	5.8

L. THE ARGENTINE NATIONAL PLAN FOR ERADICATING *VILLAS DE EMERGENCIA*

CARLOS TOBAR

THE PROBLEM

The *villa miseria* (shantytown) does not constitute a problem in and of itself. Rather, it is a manifestation of a larger problem—the development and marginality of growing population groups in systems unable to provide for the needs of such groups. This does not imply that the existence of villas is peculiar to any particular type of society. But their transformation into an endemic ill is characteristic of Latin American countries, or of those which have not yet begun the process of transforming their structures and the pattern of distribution of wealth.

The housing problem is a consequence of the way the housing market operates in Argentina. There is no filtering process, as in the case of moveable goods, such as automobiles or home furnishings, which, after a period of use by higher socioeconomic classes, pass to lower classes. In the case of housing, two factors are involved: land and the dwelling unit itself. The tendency in urban areas is for the value of land to increase as the dwelling unit depreciates. As a result, some dwelling units that might remain in stock are replaced, even though they are not obsolete, because they do not provide the living conditions demanded by those population sectors which could acquire them. Those sectors who would find the living conditions acceptable are unable to acquire such housing due to the distortion which land values create in market price.

The availability of housing for sale is determined by private and public sectors. The former conditions its investment on the demand of the middle- and upper-class population. Insofar as the profit requirement is not met, investments will be transferred to another sector of production. In the public sector's case, other factors come into play. The government's assumption of a role in the housing market presupposes that its objective is to act indirectly as a redistributor of income. That is, it subsidizes or sells housing to a group which does not have access to that offered by the private sector. For this reason, the government's policy is oriented toward lower-middle and lower-class groups.

The oldest and still dominant public agency in the field of housing in Argentina is the National Mortgage Bank (Banco Hipotecario Nacional—BHN).[1] The BHN conducts its activities principally by direct action. The bank assigns the construction of housing to applicants with financial plans at interest rates

Author's Note: This essay is based on a study undertaken in collaboration with architects Rubén N. Gazzoli and Julio Silva Torres in 1968 by the Centro de Estudios Urbanos y Regionales (CEUR) of the Instituto Torcuato di Tella, Buenos Aires. English translation by Lucy T. Briggs.

significantly lower than those of the private sector. It also makes loans with down payments, whereby the borrower must have accumulated between 25 and 50 percent of the total loan sought before credit is granted.

The plans of the BHN and the actions of other public agencies have been very significant in the housing market, especially during inflationary periods. The system of nonadjustable credit permitted access to housing for large sectors of the middle class. This policy nevertheless produced a loss of capital by governmental credit organizations, which, in combination with other factors, resulted in a tightening of credit from 1958 onwards. This left activity in the field of housing almost exclusively in the hands of the private sector (see Table 1).

Beginning in 1964, the Municipal Housing Commission (Comisión Municipal de la Vivienda) became active along with the BHN in housing in Buenos Aires. The commission is an economically independent agency of the municipality of Buenos Aires which, with the support of the Inter-American Development Bank, carries out housing programs. These are primarily large urban renewal projects.

In all the cases mentioned, public-sector activity in the housing market to meet the needs of the lowest-income groups reaches only a portion of those needing assistance. The threshold is set by the need to assure the government a minimum saving capacity which will guarantee the return of its investment, although at low interest and over the long term. The impact of this limitation

TABLE 1

Total Housing Investment, Total Public Investment in Housing,
and Percentage of Total Investment by Private and Public
Sectors (in millions of Argentine pesos, 1960)

	Investment		% of Total Investment		
Years	Total Housing	Public	Public	Private	Total
1950	32,576	11,498	35.3	64.7	100
1951	34,390	9,731	28.3	71.7	100
1952	32,002	11,212	34.1	65.9	100
1953	30,050	15,705	52.3	47.7	100
1954	31,993	21,044	65.8	34.2	100
1955	36,165	20,025	55.4	44.6	100
1956	36,027	16,180	44.9	55.1	–
1957	40,778	16,102	29.7	70.3	–
1958	37,302	13,675	36.7	63.3	–
1959	32,952	3,034	9.2	90.8	–
1960	29,407	3,243	11.6	88.4	–
1961	30,247	2,635	8.7	91.3	–
1962	31,122	3,058	9.8	90.2	–
1963	26,683	2,258	8.5	91.5	–
1964	26,166	2,849	10.6	89.4	–
1965	31,345	4,253	13.6	86.4	–
1966	34,184	5,695	16.6	83.4	–

SOURCE: Consejo Nacional de Desarrollo (CONADE) Housing section, 1969.

may be estimated more clearly if it is realized that 35 percent of Argentina's population has no savings and underconsumes, and that it is this 35 percent which bears 65 percent of the housing deficit, according to a National Development Council (Consejo Nacional de Desarrollo–CONADE) study in 1968. If to this is added the fact that housing is a basic need, it is possible to understand the reason for the rapid spread of villas, *inquilinatos, tugurios,* and *viviendas precarias* that characterize our cities, while on the Buenos Aires housing market alone there are more than 40,000 dwelling units unsold and unrented.

THE PROGRAM

In October 1967, the Reconquista and Matanza rivers in the metropolitan area of Buenos Aires flooded, inundating 120 square kilometers of land and affecting 500,000 persons. The magnitude of the flood, and the flimsiness of the dwellings in the area, resulted in their almost complete loss. This disaster shocked the government and public opinion, and led to the National Plan for Eradicating Squatter Settlements (Plan Nacional para la Erradicación de las Villas de Emergencia). When it became known that flood victims were mostly impoverished squatters who had built dwellings on unused private or public land, the government responded with a plan to begin the eradication of squatter zones. The plan also took into account the need to provide land, at present occupied by shantytowns, for public works near the capital.

Eradication is undertaken by means of two programs to be completed at different periods. These are the "program of eradication and provisional housing" and that of "definitive housing solutions." The plan projects a seven-year period to accomplish both construction of 56,000 dwelling units and total eradication of the villas. The latter is conditioned on the success of "Operation Freeze" (Operativo Congelamiento), the name given to the official decision to prevent the growth of villas. Toward this end, municipal authorities will adopt measures designed to impede construction of new villas, construction of new dwelling units in existing villas, and installation of new individuals or families in existing villas.

Two estimates underlie the plan. One refers to the affected population and the other to alternative housing solutions available to the population. There are no precise figures of population living in villas. Estimates fluctuate between 300,000 and 600,000 persons living in the capital and greater Buenos Aires. The figure used by the plan at its inception is 280,000 *villeros* comprised of 80,000 persons (20,000 families) in the capital and 200,000 (50,000 families) in greater Buenos Aires.

Another of the initial assumptions is that "on the basis of income 60 percent requires some subsidy in order to obtain housing; 20 percent could obtain it with amortized long-term credit at moderate interest, and the remaining 20 percent would find its own solutions without taking advantage of the Plan, or

TABLE 2

	Percentage of Distribution		Number of Families	
Type of Group	Partial	Total	Partial	Total
Spontaneous elimination	–	20	–	14,000
Requiring loans	–	20	–	14,000
Shell housing	10	–	7,000	–
Completed housing	10	–	7,000	–
Requiring subsidy	–	60	–	42,000
Total	–	100	–	70,000

SOURCE: Plan de Erradicación de las Villas de Emergencia de la Capital y del Gran Buenos Aires. 1968. P. 7.

else would leave the villas and accept special solutions included in the Plan." The resulting picture may be seen in Table 2.

The plan specifies three cases of "spontaneous" elimination: "Whoever owns his own land may obtain credit to build a dwelling on it"; "whoever wishes to move to another part of the country may obtain free passage"; and "those who own their own land or are in possession of land and have a movable dwelling will be assisted in moving." The plan proposes rehousing 56,000 families—42,000 in rented housing and 14,000 in owned dwellings—over a period of seven years. This involves construction of 8,000 dwelling units per year during the period.

In order to achieve its objectives, 8,000 temporary dwelling units will be constructed for as many families to occupy until they can move into permanent housing. The temporary nature of the dwellings is not only determined by the use to which they will be put in keeping with the plan's stages, but also by their construction. Materials going into their construction are to be recovered at the end of the seven-year period required by the plan. Construction of temporary housing nuclei (THN) requires an area of 64 hectares of public land. The plan establishes, further, that lands occupied by villas are declared to be of "public use and subject to expropriation." Construction of infrastructure for THN will be undertaken by the public sector through the Army Engineering Command, the Ministry of Public Works of the Province of Buenos Aires and of the Municipality of Buenos Aires. The nuclei for which bids have been accepted cover barely 22.5 square meters for a family of four. The construction is in sections so that several units may be joined to accommodate larger families. The units are on individual plots of land and are provided with water and sewage systems.

The plan originally required that occupants of THNs understand that their residence was only temporary, in order to facilitate their adaptation to the permanent program. "No improvements will be permitted, so that the inconvenient living conditions they experience will encourage them to want, and to exert themselves to acquire, the advantages offered by the permanent dwellings foreseen in the second part of this plan" (Ministerio de Bienestar Social, 1968: 11).

The permanent housing program provides for construction of 8,000 units per year, 75 percent to be rented and 25 percent to be privately owned. Construction of dwellings is undertaken by private enterprise, which is free to plan projects. Location of barrios is made according to the availability of public land in different parts of the greater metropolitan area, and without regard for urban development criteria. Barrios under construction or bid fluctuate between 60 and 300 family units. The permanent housing project comprises, in Buenos Aires, a significant number of dwellings forming part of the Parque Almirante Brown, an urban renewal project of the Municipality of Buenos Aires with Inter-American Development Bank financing. Dwelling units financed by the latter are more costly than those of the plan, but this is the only project in which the location of barrios is an integral part of a larger urban development project.

EVALUATION

Villa population data are basic to the plan's structure, especially since one of its objectives is "total eradication of villas." There are no precise figures in this respect, but the most reliable estimates are considerably higher than those upon which the plan is based. Table 3 shows various estimates of the villa population in the capital and in greater Buenos Aires. All except one of the estimates are from official sources.

The divergence of data demonstrates the weakness of the plan's estimates. Of the data given, the most reliable on the basis of the method used are those of the municipal censuses of Buenos Aires and of the Diagnóstico Sanitario Aglomerado Bonaerense (DISABO) Plan for the greater urban area.

Apart from reliability of the estimates, it is necessary to evaluate the villa concept itself. Lack of anthropological and sociological studies has hindered recognition of the differential characteristics of the universe of villeros. It is for this reason that a general term is used which really defines only a situation of illegal land occupancy. This lack of knowledge concerning the differential characteristics of villeros has generated a series of stereotypes that underlie most policies relating to these groups. Technicians dealing with the problem, however, recognize that there are differences among villas, whether stemming from the inhabitants' places of origin or the physical characteristics or age of the villas themselves.

Elaboration of a villa typology is required for implementation of a realistic plan, as well as for evaluation of former policies which have attempted to deal with the problem. The argument against these objections is that the problem's urgency does not permit the time necessary for studies of the situation, and that plans will be modified as they go along. This argument is fallacious. First, failures of policies attempted until now have been due precisely to ignorance of villa types. Second, the urgency of the situation has existed for a very long time (and is independent of official sensitivity as a result of the floods), and any delay

TABLE 3

Source or Estimate	Year	Total Urban Population	Federal Capital	Greater Buenos Aires Alone	Total Capital and Greater Buenos Aires
1960 census	1960	51,565 / 200,000	6,180 / 22,700	19,555 / 72,000	25,735 / 94,700
Billorou[a]	1963	500,000 families / 1,750,000 inhabitants			
Comisión Nacional de la Vivienda	1959				112,000
Plan Nacional de Erradicaciones	1967		20,000[d] / 80,000	50,000[d] / 200,000	70,000[d] / 280,000
Municipal Census of Buenos Aires	1963		10,663 / 42,400		
Municipal Census of Buenos Aires	1968		22,924 / 102,534		
Plan DISABO[b]	1965			80,845 / 423,824	
H. Friedmann[c]					430,000
CONADE	1967		100,000	260,000	360,000

a. Julio Billorou, "Ante una Política de Vivienda," *Revista de la Sociedad Central de Arquitectos,* No. 63, Buenos Aires, 1969.

b. Plan DISABO, Diagnóstico Sanitario Aglomerado Bonaerense, Ministerio de Salud Pública, Buenos Aires.

c. Friedman, Herbert, Thesis proposal, "The role of community-development organizations in the integration of Villa Miseria inhabitants into modern urban life."

d. Families.

caused by a period of study would not aggravate the situation. Third, a study of this type can give short-term results which could be the basis of general program outlines. Fourth, changes once policies have been adopted are improbable, given the characteristics of government agencies and the amount of funds involved. Before undertaking any public works project, the government spends a significant length of time on feasibility and location studies and the like. Yet for a project involving moving a large sector of the population, whose lives will be profoundly affected, and introducing them into the urban structure of many sections of the city, and who furthermore represent a considerable investment, this all is undertaken with a high degree of ignorance of operational realities and without regard for future consequences.

The plan rests on four hypotheses: (1) The villas exist for historical reasons which have been eliminated or are in the process of being eliminated, and therefore when the plan is completed the villas themselves will have been definitively eradicated; (2) the freeze policy will paralyze the villa growth process; (3) the villa miseria is fundamentally a housing problem; and (4) the inhabitant of the villa is incapable of resolving his housing problem or of living in a *normal* dwelling.

In our view, the growth of villas is only one manifestation of a structural situation characterized by sharp differences in the degree of participation in the benefits of the production process by regions and social strata. To the extent that these differences do not disappear or tend to be reduced, the problems they produce, one of whose manifestations is the villa, will not disappear.[2] The decision to "freeze" the growth of villas by means of a law which does not provide other means toward that end beyond police control is therefore illusory. The proposed measures will, it is true, eliminate villas from those parts of the urban scene where control is exerted, but the potential population of the villas will settle in new areas.

We have previously mentioned the limited concept of the villa which exists, as well as the crucial role of access to land for solution of the housing problem. Both aspects are overlooked in the plan, in that there is no provision for different situations depending on the characteristics of each villa. The potential capacity of villeros to seek their own solutions with basic help and support, such as the acquisition of land and the provision of infrastructure, is ignored. Under the terms of the plan, villeros are converted into "passive" elements, a necessary adjunct of a paternalistic policy.

The provision of infrastructure services and access to land would probably have transformed the present villas into barrios not differing greatly from those of the stable low-income population. It would also require considerably less funding, which would permit transfer of part of the resources called for by the plan to those sectors which are more dynamic and capable of generating employment for that same population.

Another contradiction that arises from solutions proposed by the plan is that the anticipated spontaneous exit of 20 percent of the villa population, to the extent that it is directed to areas lacking sanitary facilities and infrastructure, will duplicate in some measure the present villa situation. The absence of a land law or other means of restricting the activity of land speculators is one of the elements that most endangers the chance of even a long-range solution to the lower-income housing problem.

The plan assumes that the villero comes from a place where the function of living in a dwelling is totally different from that characterizing his new milieu, meaning that he will require a period of adjustment before he can live in a "normal urban dwelling." This is one of the justifications for the temporary nuclei (THN). "Adapting" to new housing norms (the only active role given by the plan to the villero), will take place with the aid of social workers and will take approximately one year. The problem inherent in the THNs is that, due to their design, the only new elements they bring to the villa is running water and a bathroom, while other crowded conditions characterizing the old villa will persist, albeit to a reduced degree. The THNs are also furnished with an individual parcel of land for cultivation of a small family garden that, in the words of the plan, responds to "our peoples' need for pampa." However, the permanent dwellings for which the THNs will prepare the villero are high-rise apartments, with characteristics totally different from the THNs. In addition, insofar as the plan presupposes a freeze, it affects population nuclei which have already remained in the city for a length of time, managing more or less efficiently. These groups are really maintaining a level of adequacy higher than that required for adaptation to more comfortable housing. Yet, beyond this, if we accept the plan's premises as to the necessity of this adaptation period, it is nothing more than a period of education that could be undertaken in the *villa* itself, at much lower economic and social cost than that presented in the THN's program.

NOTES

1. We are not considering here the State Housing Ministry (Secretaría de Estado de Vivienda) inasmuch as its aims and objectives are implemented through the BHN. In addition to the activities of the Banco Hipotecario Nacional, other plans of different types are developed at the provincial level through local agencies. In general, these are of the first type mentioned and none is significant in level of funding.

2. Eradication of a villa is accomplished with the help of military personnel, who move the inhabitants to the new nuclei, after fumigating them and their effects and burning or bulldozing the eradicated villa.

REFERENCES

Ministerio de Bienestar Social (1968) Plan de Erradicación de las Villas de Emergencia de la Capital y del Gran Buenos Aires. Buenos Aires.

M. DEVELOPMENT ALTERNATIVES FOR THE PERUVIAN *BARRIADA*

DIEGO ROBLES RIVAS

THE PROBLEM

Existing literature has tended to glorify the process of self-help which is taking place in the *barriadas* of Peru and has created an image of possible self-development of these areas. My rather different evaluation is based on analysis of the series of actions the barriada settlers *(pobladores)* have been able to carry out for the purpose of improving their communities. I believe that, within the context of the capitalist economic system, the process of self-help has been incapable of integrating marginal settlers into national development. Rather, it has served to reinforce, through implantation of populist measures of a paternalistic nature via consumption, the existing system of domination.

The barriada represents one of the settlement forms which typify the process of urban domination and rapid dependent urbanization. The barriada is generated by the economic system. Capitalist forms of production are concentrated in urban areas, which are dependent on foreign power centers. This gives rise to expansion of economic activities in certain coastal towns and cities, without corresponding expansion in the interior of Peru, creating an unstable population equilibrium.

The form of industrialization in Peru also has a decisive influence on its labor force and occupational structure. Industrialization in Peru was not initiated as an internal expansion force. Since the 1950s, it has been oriented chiefly toward import substitution to satisfy select demand for immediate consumption goods. This production structure subordinates and conditions the behavior of less-developed classes by imposing disadvantageous conditions on economic satellite or dependent industries. They are forced to group together or go bankrupt and drive out their labor force. This in turn conditions the behavior of that part of the labor force which is not absorbed by or expelled from the production structure. For them, there remain only opportunities to take part in independent economic activities or work in unstable salary relationships for extremely low income.

The growth of marginality reinforces one of the basic contradictions of the capitalist production system: it opposes growing production and productivity with the decreasing ability of larger and larger population groups to consume. Nevertheless, by relegating to this marginal labor force those occupational roles of least social significance and lowest income, the system has been able to make this labor force functional for its own development.

Editors' Note: English translation by Eileen Welsh.

The degree of expansion and intensification of the urbanization process in Peru is directly related to the degree of penetration of capitalist forms of production. The cities constitute poles of a network of centralized domination, by their role in the process of social marginalization. In Peruvian cities, precapitalistic and capitalistic forms of production more or less accessible from the capital city coexist. Although the city acts as a core of technological expansion, this same technology initially generates a tendency toward marginalization of noncapitalistic forms of production.

The internal domination suffered by large sectors of the Peruvian population has been reinforced by the intervention of political factors. The capacity of social groups and classes to articulate their demands is directly related to their ability to sell their labor. Those with a greater degree of organization within the rules of the game established by the system have better opportunity to do so. In this way, dominant classes attempt to reproduce the conditions of their social position within the class structure. When the interests of the dominant group are endangered by the insurgence of groups from dominated sectors, such mechanisms as the raising of standards required and discriminatory actions based on deeply rooted prejudices are used to keep these groups out.

The subjective factors created around certain urban areas with a degree of selective industrial expansion have caused strong migratory flows of rural population to those urban centers. The objective factors of expulsion from rural areas characterized by low standards of living have forced peasants *(campesinos)* to move to the cities in proportions much larger than existing employment possibilities. This migratory process in turn is characterized by a high percentage of unskilled labor oriented toward urban areas having the highest rate of industrialization, and where service and commercial activities are concentrated. In addition, in such cities' basic infrastructure, there is heavy public or private investment.

These characteristics complete the complex picture of accelerated urbanization. In urban areas, disequilibrium is shown by nonincorporation and expulsion of the labor force from profitable sectors of the productive apparatus (the marginalization process). These processes have limited the income level of the population, giving rise to a situation in which the population is unable to participate in the urban land and housing market and is forced to form the barriada.

THE CAPITALIST PROGRAM

The barriada is not an isolated phenomenon or separate from the city in which it is located, but rather is dependent on the latter to achieve its development. Yet, the initial collective and insurgent nature of the barriada is transformed by the system into a totality of individual interests conditioned by the participation of external agencies.

Students of urban problems have interpreted the barriada in different ways. One is to consider it an anomalous form of urban development, a position implying application of assistance measures in health, housing, and education, and security measures through repressive action ranging from prohibition of barriada formation to massive eradication programs. Other studies concerned with formation of the barriada emphasize the positive aspects of the settlers' actions—their ingenuity, degree of acculturation, capacity for organization, ability to construct their own houses and necessary services, investment and savings capacity—but at the same time consider the barriada as marginal to the general urban context which conditions or limits the barriada's development possibilities.

Documentation exists showing that the barriada is not marginal geographically, economically, socially, or politically, and that it cannot ' ɔ considered to be a form of collective development even though in an initir' stage, the invasion of the site, collective interests are uppermost. Rather, once the poblador has assured tenure of his land, the initial process breaks up and evolves toward forms constituting a totality of individual interests. This does not differ basically from the achievements of other social groups experiencing similar conditions within the structure of urban domination.

The action of the barriada as a collective project is dysfunctional to the system whenever it involves confrontation with power groups. This is evident in the invasion stage in which private property, defined as one of the system's foundations, is attacked. The barriada is unable to follow a course of permanent rebellion, given that its population is economically, socially, culturally and politically dependent. In order to resolve the barriada's problems within the system, institutional support is chosen as the best strategy.[1]

Once this institutional support has been obtained, a consolidation process is initiated in the barriada. External agencies play an important role, acting as intermediaries between power groups and pobladores. The consolidation process consists of three stages: The first stage is in the barriada's initiation as a collective project located in the "legal" city, with prior action to organize groups participating in the project. The majority resides in deteriorated zones of the city, such as the *tugurios,* internal barriadas which are immensely overcrowded, and, to a lesser extent, other old, peripheral barriadas of high population density. These conditions produce a crisis leading to a position of insurgency. This is capitalized on by leaders who possess knowledge both of the situation of the group and the mechanisms of control of the "legal" city. The slow process of social mobilization begins with organization and identification of groups participating in the project, selection of the invasion site and obtaining of the economic resources necessary for the various negotiations.

The invasion usually takes place on a national or local holiday, preferably during the night or early morning, in order to give time to form an organization. Everyone assumes important roles such as those of defense, communal cooking, surveying and distribution of lots, identification of participants, diffusion of daily news, storage of materials, and construction of temporary shelters using light materials. The opportunity which appears to the insurgent group for invasion of lands on the urban periphery is closely related to the lack of intervention as a consequence of agreement among power groups, or their incapacity to assign new roles to external agencies and to implement action programs consistent with a policy of rapid urban development. Insurgence breaks into the mechanisms of control exercised by power groups, showing their flexibility in the face of apparent and momentary challenges. It arises from periods of internal crisis within the dominant elite and from its capacity for bargaining among power groups themselves or with the population making demands.

In order to achieve their objectives, pobladores take advantage of all possible resources in starting the new settlement, the barriada. In order to analyze costs incurred, it is necessary to distinguish among those concerned with organization and mobilization of the pobladores; investment of their savings in improvement of the area; and the contribution of their labor in housing construction and in installation of public services and other communal facilities.

The directing groups generate educational, consciousness-raising and organizational activities leading to establishment of the "Asociación de Pobladores" and work-groups. It should take advantage of the experience of existing associations, channeling them to the benefit of the new community seeking solution to its immediate problem, that of obtaining a stable residential site within the city itself or nearby. In order to organize, unite, and channel the community's immediate aspirations, and to be able to take advantage of the legal, administrative, commercial, and political mechanisms of the city, a great deal of effort, time, and ability is demanded of pobladores. This initial cost, in advance of formation of the settlement, is entirely borne by the pobladores.

Another contribution made by the pobladores is investment of individual savings, created by their labor and lack of consumption, accumulated long before formation of the barriada. These savings are invested by pobladores in the different stages of consolidation of the settlement. The greater part of these savings is invested in building materials offered by city markets.

Through various commercial mechanisms the pobladores are drained of their capital in favor of other urban power groups. In order to build his house and improve his settlement, the poblador's invested capital must be complemented by his own labor. This obligation in the form of a new investment in labor appears as the result of the poblador's decapitalization in buying building materials and tools. Yet, in this way, he is able to occupy and use his dwelling as it evolves in stages over a relatively long period of time. Since this process of building a house with only the poblador's individual contribution is extremely difficult and slow, pobladores are forced to obtain the help of relatives and to organize themselves in temporary work groups in order to take advantage of mutual aid and to make their own efforts more effective.

A second stage defined as transitional can be identified by the initiation of action by external agencies, public and private, which make contact with the community in order to satisfy the demands of the population in terms of immediate needs.

A third stage follows the point at which the collective nature of the project is disrupted and becomes, rather, the sum of individual actions channeled by certain external agencies. These agencies achieve a certain amount of penetration of and influence within the population and organize it according to their own criteria. These need not coincide with those of the population itself. The action of these external agencies consists mainly in social demobilization activities developed in the face of the possibility that the pobladores might unite, discover their basic interests, and organize for collective insurgence. The latter is linked to the persistence of the role of external agencies within the system and, more basically, to the persistence of the system itself.

External agencies have acted autonomously in the barriada in support of or in coordination with state agencies, according to the type of interest arising at the appearance and development of the barriada. These interests have been linked to the objectives of each power group and include assuring social peace, increasing popular consumption, making available an industrial reserve army in good condition, protecting high-priced urban land in the presence of possibilities for speculation, and attending to the demands of middle and upper social groups. External agencies have interpreted the phenomenon of the barriada in a restricted way—within a technical, social, economic, and political view not in harmony with pobladores' demands for productive means for their authentic mobilization. Instead, social strategies of external agencies are directed at promoting actions whose final objectives are softening the system's internal contradictions, lessening existing tensions, and retarding social change by reinforcing the status quo.[3]

The most general cause of the barriada's appearance as a form of collective insurgence is the deterioration in the exercise of power by the particular ruling political group. This gives rival groups the option of approaching the masses in search of new political loyalties based on promises of solutions to the population's immediate problems carried out in a climate of expectancy. These promises are confirmed by the new group's exercise of power through the use of populist measures of consumption. These measures take different forms in different settlements and in this way produce a demonstration effect which can be capitalized politically through reinforcement of popular loyalties.

The same thing occurs at moments of economic crisis or boom in Peru, localized in certain areas of the national territory and during which their wealth is either concentrated or consumed. Such a process changes some of the most important activities of the city and in extreme cases changes its incidence in the network of urban interrelations. Collective insurgence also occurs in periods in which external domination is accentuated. This translates into a policy of internal investment, and transfer of national capital abroad, swelling the bank accounts of a few. This situation is related to the impossibility of increasing Peru's internal consumption. Generalized poverty within the population is a direct result.

Three elements intervene in the barriada consolidation process: a power elite whose interests are linked to the production structure, commerce, and land-tenure system; external agencies which fulfill roles assigned to them by the power elite and which organize the population in terms of immediate needs which can be satisfied by consumption; and barriada pobladores who wish to be integrated and to improve their standards of living. Among these elements there is no possibility of agreement or dialogue, either between the power elite and pobladores or between the latter and external agencies. Their various development goals do not coincide, since within the system of domination the pobladores have been considered as not pertaining to the legal city.

EVALUATION

Given the form in which the self-help process operates in the barriada, it is impossible for the poblador to change the system of domination. The productive system does not allow the poblador to participate directly in the market for modern goods and services. As a consequence, the poblador is forced to resort to self-help. But the self-help system employed in welfare tasks directed toward community development decapitalizes the poblador through consumption.

Successive governments have carried out various measures for the purpose of responding to conditions created by the problem of insurgency. The responses have not been oriented toward policies of structural modification but rather have intensified the marginality and poverty of the majority of the Peruvian population. This is reflected in the migration process and in the accelerated urbanization of the nation's urban centers, which have, in a short time, been altered both qualitatively and quantitatively.

Power groups have attempted to manipulate with superficial palliatives the climate of expectancy created by population increase in these cities, by settlements on the urban fringe, and by the process of slum-building, because of their fear of losing social position and status to the dominated groups. As urbanization has become accentuated, the dominant elite, in search of "equilibrium," has imposed assistential-paternalistic measures on the marginal population based on solution of immediate problems.

Housing and other services or facilities which the marginal dweller "maintains" as permanent necessities have served to condition, within the view of the poblador, technicians, and external agencies, the need to solve the fundamental problems of the majority of the population. The housing-oriented view of the problem has served only to neutralize and demobilize. This distortion has allowed the system and the shifting political elite to incorporate the poblador in mutual-aid programs limited to assistance.

The poblador considers himself author of a "great work" in constructing his own community and in having his land tenure securely legitimized by provisional title. But mutual aid in the barriada is restricted to immediate action and is not oriented toward the poblador's basic interests, such as increase in income-levels, opportunity for stable occupation and active participation in the urban production structure. Self-help restricted to welfare increases the poblador's propensity to consume, distorted by the play of interests of the dominant production groups.

The added value represented by capital created by socially and economically dependent groups only partially benefits these groups. It does not produce a process of accumulation in their favor. Marginal workers, who can generally be classified as underemployed, create added value by their work in labor-intensive productive activities. The added value is transferred to dominant groups, and the depressed are then decapitalized.

This takes place, first, through consumption, pressuring these groups by means of systematic advertising and the opportunity for installment buying to widen the consumer goods market; second, through savings, capturing the savings of this population to the benefit of the banks of the dominant elite; and, lastly, through investment in which pobladores are oriented toward nonproductive activities and housing for the purpose of increasing consumption of products.

These rules of the game respond to the interests of the dominant class and not to the interests of the marginal population. For the dominant elite, the marginal population constitutes a reserve labor force for industry, a large mass of consumers who must be guided, and potential savers who could nourish the economic system. The cumulative effect of these relations has become an ideology of domination in which there is no development alternative for the dominated. While the pobladores make great efforts to increase their consumption, savings, and investment, the transfer of capital in favor of the dominant groups is much greater. In this way, the present system of domination continues to be reinforced.

The great question thus becomes: Is progress for the marginal population possible without altering the terms of the system and ending domination? It is clear that, while the system of domination which has created this unjust social order continues, development of large sectors of the population who do not actively participate in the task of national transformation is impossible. Although a phase of capital accumulation and of economic expansion could exist, a process of national development cannot take place without participation of these sectors in wealth generated and in management and control of the means of production. Only this will give rise to a new social order.

The process of development requires structural changes replacing the system of domination with a new social order allowing full participation of all the population. Within a scheme of domination, only negotiations can exist between the population of the barriadas, which is attempting to satisfy its immediate needs for water, lighting and housing, and external agencies, public and private, which act in accordance with roles assigned by the dominant elites.[4]

In order to overcome the system of domination, it is necessary to establish the possibility of direct negotiations between the population organized functionally by productive activities and the state, and replace the policy of technical assistance oriented toward community development with technical assistance in production. These actions should be incorporated into a national development plan, which coordinates measures taken at the community level with those on a national scale.

Once participation is assured, the population organized in terms of specific functions must have guaranteed access to the decision-making apparatus. This would imply powers of direct negotiation between this population and the state in terms of accelerated and self-supported development, primarily maintained by the internal potential of Peru. Increase in the participation of these populations in decision-making implies total transformation of the educational system, permitting a type of education suited to the structural change of society, to development, and to the workers. The rise in the standard of living of marginal populations will imply rational participation of workers in the management and profits of business and also the development and protection of new cooperative firms.

The strategy for incorporating the poblador into the process of national development depends on six steps. First, it requires definition of a population policy in order to resolve the problem of marked population disequilibria. Next, it requires establishment of orientation and control mechanisms for urban expansion which include programs of land distribution and provision of basic infrastructure for marginal groups, within a short- and medium-term urban development plan which contemplates integration of marginal groups into the socioeconomic development process of Peru.[5] Third, direction and organization of poblador participation in programs of urban living and housing, production and services, within a strategy leading to structural change is needed. Fourth, selection and implementation of technological levels guaranteeing high consumption of labor and allowing the poblador to qualify for integration into the process of socioeconomic development should follow. Fifth, introduction of financial mechanisms attracting the savings of organized pobladores and permitting them to finance programs according to their own interests and true abilities would occur. Finally, the establishment of training programs for leaders, volunteers, and technicians directed toward popular cooperation and social mobilization supported by public and private organizations is needed.

NOTES

1. It is significant that many barriadas have the names of prominent political leaders, saints, and the like.

2. Searching for a solution to the invasion of urban lands, the Peruvian government promulgated Law 13517—the Law of Marginal Barrios—in September 1961. It is a legal remedy which contemplates channeling human, technical, and economic resources in favor of pobladores of barriadas. In this way, pobladores obtained one means of requesting aid from the state in order to help solve their problems. This aid was made concrete by technical assistance in formulation of urban projects, housing, and installation of services and communal facilities. The population residing in those settlements classified as marginal by

Law 13517 have the right to buy land and to individual ownership of the lot occupied by the family.

3. An external agency financed by a group of industrialists would have as its goals, for example, intensifying consumption of certain products and organizing the population so as to achieve its participation in handicraft activities in the barriada.

4. An agrarian reform law and an industrial law have been passed. A Commission for Educational Reform has been established, whose recommendations are to become official.

5. In December 1968, the National Office for the Development of Pueblos Jóvenes (young towns), the name barriadas are now called, was established by the Peruvian government and is in charge of studying, planning, proposing, and coordinating needed solutions at the national level in order to intensify integration of the population of these barriadas into the socioeconomic development of Peru. This office is directly responsible to the President of the Republic.

REFERENCES

Instituto Nacional de Planificación (1970), Plan Nacional de Desarrollo para Los Años 1971-75: Objetivos genéricos de desarrollo. Lima.

JAWORSKI, H. (1969) "Políticas de vivienda popular y barrios marginales." Cuadernos DESCO. February, Lima: Centro de Estudios de Promoción del Desarrollo (DESCO).

NUN, J. (1969) "La marginalidad en América Latina." Revista Latinomericana de Sociología (Buenos Aires) 2.

QUIJANO, A. (1970) "Redefinición de la dependencia y el proceso de marginalización en América Latina." Santiago: UN Economic Commission for Latin America, División de Asuntos Sociales.

–– (1966) "Notas sobre el concepto de marginalidad social." Santiago: UN Economic Commission for Latin America, División de Asuntos Sociales. (mimeo)

ROBLES RIVAS, D. (1969) "El proceso de urbanización y los sectores populares en Lima." Cuadernos DESCO. Serie A., No. 1. February.

RODRIGUEZ, A. and H. JAWORSKI (1969) "Vivienda en barriadas." Cuadernos DESCO. Serie A, No. 4, August.

RODRIGUEZ, A., J. GIANELLA, and H. JAWORSKI (1969) "Aportes a la comprensión de un fenómeno urbano: la barriada." Cuadernos DESCO. Serie A, No. 2. April.

WELSH, E. (1970) "Bibliografía sobre el crecimiento dinámico de Lima, referente al proceso de urbanización en el Peru." Cuadernos DESCO. Serie A, No. 5. January.

APPENDIX

THE STATE OF THE ART: REGIONAL DEVELOPMENT PROGRAMS IN LATIN AMERICA AT THE END OF THE 1960s

WALTER B. STOHR

The present essay provides an overview of regional development programs around the end of the 1960s. It does so in synoptic form, distinguishing between programs for individual regions ("regional" programs) and programs for systems of regions ("interregional" programs). The rapidly changing spectrum of regional development programs in Latin America and their often rather ephemeral character make this a difficult task. It is not an attempt to cover the field completely, but rather to define types of programs which may be useful in the subsequent analysis of their genesis and of their major strategy elements.

DEFINITION OF THE SUBJECT

In view of the multiplicity of regional programs and the fact that ultimately all policy measures—even national ones in fields such as foreign commerce, taxation, housing, transportation—have implicit regional effects, it is necessary to define the type of policies and programs to be considered in this report. The following criteria have been used:

(1) When speaking of "regions," *subnational units* are referred to, not groups of countries or an entire continent, as is often done in current usage.[1] In some special cases (e.g., border development programs), a region as referred to in this study may also consist of subnational units of more than one country.

Author's Note: From a forthcoming study, *Regional Development in Latin America*, to be published in English by the UN Research Institute for Social Development, Geneva, and in Spanish by Editorial SIAP, Buenos Aires. Printed with permission.

(2) Only those regional policies and programs are considered which are *carried out or supported by official agencies.* It has not been possible to consider entirely private efforts for regional development, supported by informal citizen groups or individual firms, in spite of the considerable importance they sometimes have. Nor has it been possible to deal with the countless development proposals and studies elaborated by individual professionals or private consulting firms, except if they count with explicit official support.

(3) Only *multisectoral* development policies and programs will be considered, oriented toward the integral development of geographic areas. In general, this will mean a comprehensive approach and coordinated action along different sectoral—i.e., ministerial or agency—lines. In some cases, however, the comprehensive analysis of an area may come to the conclusion that inputs are feasible only in a very restricted number or even only in one sector. Although unisectoral in appearance, such a program (e.g., in transport investment) may still have been comprehensively conceived. The criterion of an integral development program therefore is not necessarily that inputs take place in all sectors (which often is neither feasible nor indicated) but that the sectors in which action takes place have been chosen after an integral analysis of the development potential and problems of the area.

(4) Programs included should in general represent a *medium- or long-term* approach. Pure stop-gap actions with a short-term view toward solving temporary emergency situations in general will not be considered. It will be shown, however, that emergency actions in such cases as natural catastrophes have often led to lasting institutional innovations which were of great importance for the decentralization of decision-making and for regional development.

(5) Only those policies and programs will be included which refer to geographic *areas of major size or importance within a national or continental context.* Local development programs or those dealing with community development for small areas will in general not be considered. Exceptions are cases where a local development program is undertaken explicitly in a regional context—for instance, a growth pole program intended to serve a larger area or to make use of its resources.

AN OVERVIEW OF CURRENT "REGIONAL" AND "INTERREGIONAL" DEVELOPMENT EFFORTS

The present overview is concerned with "regional" as well as with "interregional" programs and policies, respectively, depending on whether they deal with a single region in an isolated manner, or are conceived for a system of regions. Coverage has been as complete as available data permitted, given that from some countries no response was received to the survey made through the UN Economic Commission for Latin America (ECLA). For various of these countries, information could be compiled on the spot during two trips[2] and through personal contacts of the author. Sufficient coverage could not be obtained, however, in the time and with the means available, for the countries of the Caribbean areas, and for Costa Rica, Panama, and Bolivia. These countries, apart from the last-mentioned one, are comparatively small so that regional policies are likely to be of minor importance or to refer to very small areas only. In Peru, the present military government is in the process of a complete revision of the country's regional development policy, so that no clear picture of governmental intentions could be obtained (Waller, 1971). In this overview, emphasis has been placed on concentrating information on the more important regional development programs in each country, rather than on increasing the number of programs with only scarce information on each.

Programs for Individual Regions ("Regional" Programs)[3]

Development policies or programs will be considered "regional" (as against "interregional") if they are concerned with a specific region without being integrated either with programs for other regions or with national global or sectoral policies. This is the case with most programs motivated by problems of one specific region. It does not mean that national objectives cannot be involved. If they are, however, they are partial in that they are projected on one area of the country only, without considering similar problems of other regions or implications for them.

Table 1 gives the characteristics for some eighty major "regional" programs in Latin America.

Institutional form (columns 1-3 of Table 1). The following distinctions are made:

(1) *Executive organizations* which are charged with a full scale of attributions from planning through decision-making to executing their own programs. They are the most autonomous regional development organizations, usually in the form of regional corporations.

(2) *Coordinating, deliberative, or study organizations*, usually charged primarily with functions of planning. For decision-making and execution, they usually depend on other institutions. The more frequent forms are commissions, councils, or planning offices with advisory roles.

(3) *Noninstitutionalized programs* have been included in cases where implementation is guided informally or where institutionalization is likely to take place in the near future. Program propositions have been included in cases in which supranational financing institutions have shown interest, such as for several ongoing growth-pole studies.

TABLE 1
PROGRAMS FOR INDIVIDUAL REGIONS ("regional" programs)[a]

Program	Institutional Form			Guidance System				Major Orientation(s)									
	Executive	Coordinating, Deliberating, Study Organization	Noninstitutionalized	Regional	Coop. Regional/National	National	Bi- or Multinational	Decentralization of Decision-Making	Depressed Area Development	Coloniz. Agricultural Based	Coloniz. Mineral Resource Based	Metropolitan Area Development	Consolidation of Other Developed Area	New Growth Pole Development	Border Area Development	River Basin Development	
	1	2	3	4	5	6	7	8	9	10	11	12	13	14	15	16	17
A. Uninational Programs for Individual Regions																	
Argentina																	
1. Plan Noroeste		x				x			x								Integration of Bolivian immigrants
2. Plan Noreste		x				x											Agri. development
3. Plan Comahue		x				x					x		x				Generation of electricity for national consumption
4. Plan para la Patagonia		x				x									x		
Brazil																	
1. Superintendência do Desenvolvimento do Nordeste (SUDENE, 1960) and Banco do Nordeste (interrelated with São Francisco River development scheme)	x				x			x	x								

244

TABLE 1 (continued)

Program	1	2	3	4	5	6	7	8	9	10	11	12	13	14	15	16	17
2. Superintendência do Desenvolvimento da Amazônia (SUDAM, 1967, before SPVEA) and Banco da Amazônia	x				x			x		x							
3. Foundation of new federal capital Brasília		x				x								x			Creation of new national capital
4. Program for the development of the Recôncavo Bahaino			x	x										x			BID supported feasibility study
5. Priority border development areas (cf. Ministerio do Planejamento y Coordinação Geral, "Ação Coordinada do Governo Federal na Amazônia," Belem-Rio de Janeiro, 1968)			x			x									x		
6. Free zone of Manaos		x				x									x		
7. Interstate Commission for the development of the Bacia-Paraná-Uruguay areas		x		x												x	
8. Grupo Ejecutivo del Gran São Paulo			x	x								x					
9. Program of road construction in the interior						x				x					x		Unisectoral program with great significance for regional development
Colombia																	
1. Corporación del Valle del Cauca (CVC, 1954)b	x				x								x				Electrification, flood control, land reclamation
2. Corporación Regional de La Sabana y de los Valles de Ubaté y Chiquinquirá (CAR, 1961)b	x				x							x				x	Water regulation and distribution of electricity

245

TABLE 1 (continued)

Program	1	2	3	4	5	6	7	8	9	10	11	12	13	14	15	16	17
3. Corporación de los Valles del Magdalena y el Sinú (CVM 1960)c	x				x				x	x						x	Conservation of natural resources, management of natural parks
4. Corporación Regional del Guindio (1964)	x				x								x				Electrification and water regulation
5. Corporación Nacional del Chocó (1968)		x				x											Water transport and electrification
6. Corporación de la Meseta de Bucaramanga (1965)d		x			x				x								Erosion control and water regulation in outskirts of Bucaramanga
7. Free port of Leticia			x		x	x									x		
Chile																	
1. Junta de Adelanto de Arica	x				x			x									
2. Corporación de Magallanes	x	x			x			x							x		
3. Instituto CORFO Norte		x			x			x			x				x		
4. Instituto CORFO Chiloé		x			x			x	x	x					x		
5. Instituto CORFO Aysén		x			x			x	x	x					x		
6. Growth pole program for Concepción			x		x			x									
7. Metropolitan development study for Santiago and surroundings		x				x						x		x			
Ecuador																	
1. Corporación de Fomento del Norte (CORFONOR)	x				x			x					x				
2. Corporación de Fomento del Centro (CORFODEC)	x				x			x					x				
3. Centro de Rehabilitación del Manabí	x				x				x								
4. Plan de Colonización del Area de Santo Domingo de los Colorados	x								x	x							BID-support
5. Programa de Desarrollo de la Cuenca del Guayas	x				x								x			x	

246

TABLE 1 (continued)

Program	1	2	3	4	5	6	7	8	9	10	11	12	13	14	15	16	17
6. Centro de Reconversión Económica del Azuay, Cañar y Morona Santiago	x					x			x								
El Salvador																	
1. Metropolitan development schemes for San Salvador			x			x						x					
Guatemala																	
1. Empresa Nacional de Fomento y Desarrollo Económico del Petén	x		x			x									x		Considerable private sector guidance
Honduras																	
1. Colonization project Pulpa y Papel La Ceiba			x			x				x							
Mexico																	
1. Programa Nacional Fronterizo (PRONAF) (for Northern border area, 1960)		x				x									x		
2. Juntas Federales de Mejoras Materiales (for border and port cities)	x					x									x		
3. Comisión del Río Fuerte (1951)	x					x			x				x			x	Generation of electricity for national consumption
4. Comisión del Río Balsas	x					x			x							x	
5. Comisión del Papaloapan	x					x			x	x							
6. Comisión de Grijalva-Usumacinta (1951)	x					x			x	x						x	Generation of electricity for national consumption
7. Comisión de Estudios del Sistema Lerma-Chapala-Santiago		x				x							x			x	
8. Comisión de Estudios de la Cuenca del Río Pánuco		x				x							x			x	
9. Comisión Hidrológica de la Cuenca del Valle de México		x				x						x				x	Water supply for Ciudad Mexico

TABLE 1 (continued)

Program	1	2	3	4	5	6	7	8	9	10	11	12	13	14	15	16	17
10. Growth pole feasibility study for Monterrey	x																BID-support
11. Plan for the State of Oaxaca				x	x	x			x					x			Joint program State of Oaxaca-Nacional Financiera
Nicaragua																	
1. Programa Zona Puerto Cabezas	x		x			x				x							
2. Plan Prolacso	x		x			x							x				Overhead sprinkler irrigation
3. Plan Depto. de Rivas	x					x				x							
Paraguay[e]																	
1. Plan Eje Este			x			x				x							
2. Proyecto Integral de Desarrollo Rural Eje Norte de Colonización			x			x				x							
3. Colonia Presidente Stroessner (Entidad Autónoma)		x				x				x							
4. Plan de Colonización Saltos de Guaira			x			x				x							
5. Plan for the Chaco			x			x				x					x		
Peru																	
1. Departmental Corporations	x																
2. "Areas vitales" de colonización (under auspices of the Armed Forces)		x			x	x		x									BID-support
3. Feasibility studies for a series of growth poles						x									x		
4. Free port Iquitos		x	x			x									x		
5. Carretera marginal de la Selva			x			x				x					x		Unisectoral program with great significance for regional development

248

TABLE 1 (continued)

Program	1	2	3	4	5	6	7	8	9	10	11	12	13	14	15	16	17
Uruguay																	
1. Comisión Nacional del Río Negro		x				x										x	Water supply for Montevideo
2. Program for the Santa Lucia River Basin		x				x										x	
Venezuela																	
1. Consejo Zuliano de Planificación (CONZUPLAN 1964)[f]		x			x								x				
2. Fundación para el Desarrollo de la Región Centro-Occidental (1964)[f]		x			x								x				
3. Corporación de Los Andes (1964)	x			x				x					x				
4. Comisión para el Desarrollo de la Región Nor-Oriental (1966)[f]		x				x			x								
5. Corporación Venezolana de Guayana (CVG 1960)	x	x				x					x			x			
6. Free zone Isla Margarita		x				x									x		Tourist development
B. Multi-National Programs for Individual Regions																	
Central America																	
1. Project of new growth pole "Golfo de Honduras," feasibility study with BID-BCIE support (to benefit Honduras and Guatemala)			x			x	x						x	x			
2. Project of new growth pole "Golfo de Fonseca," feasibility study with BID-BCIE support (to benefit El Salvador, Honduras, and Nicaragua)			x			x	x		x				x	x			
3. Multinational development project Río San Juan de Costa Rica, feasibility study with BID-BCIE support (to benefit Nicaragua and Costa Rica)			x			x	x						x	x			

249

TABLE 1 (continued)

Program	1	2	3	4	5	6	7	8	9	10	11	12	13	14	15	16	17
South America																	
1. Colombian-Venezuelan border development program		x				x	x								x		
2. Colombian-Ecuadorian border development program		x				x	x		x						x		
3. La Plata Basin development program (Brazil, Paraguay, Bolivia, Uruguay, and Argentina)		x				x	x									x	
4. Development program for the Laguna MIRIM Basin (Uruguay-Brazil)		x				x	x									x	Water control, improvement of navigation and irrigation

a. Not all countries are covered. Dates refer to year of program initiation.
b. These corporations had autonomous character until the constitutional reform of 1968 when they were subordinated to the Ministry of Agriculture.
c. Most of the CVM's functions were recently transferred to the (National) Instituto de Recursos Naturales.
d. Predominantly local importance.
e. Based on exhaustive information supplied by Sr. Ivan Berger, at that time Advisor of the Interamerican Development Bank, Asunción, Paraguay.
f. Recently adapted to new national system for regional coordination and planning according to Presidential Decree 72 of 11-6-1969.

Guidance system (columns 4-7 of Table 1). The guidance system refers to the level at which objectives and criteria of regional development programs are defined. It corresponds in general to the degree to which a devolution of authority (Sherwood, 1969: 66 ff.) for development policy is granted to regional population groups.

The following distinctions have been made:

(4) *Regional guidance,* i.e., programs where the predominant initiative comes from the region concerned and where objectives and criteria are determined predominantly at the regional level. Usually these programs will correspond to A. R. Kuklinski's "Situation No. 2" (1968: 2) in which regional development activity is generated via the integration of local activities. These programs as a rule will be concerned with a single region only. Usually there will be little or no coordination with programs for other regions nor with national policies. At some stage, the national government may decide to support such programs to make them more effective, to share in their political benefits, or simply to gain control over them. They will then turn into one of the following categories.

(5) *Cooperative regional/national guidance* refers to programs where objectives and criteria are defined jointly between national and regional bodies. In most cases, they have not originated as such, but have rather become so after a maturing process from either a regional or a national guidance system. In other words, cooperation usually is not the initial stage, but may evolve from unilateral action at the regional or national level.

(6) *National guidance* refers to cases where the definition of objectives and criteria is made at the central government level. One would expect such programs to be mainly "interregional" in approach. In reality, with scarce national resources and differences in political power between regions, however, many of these nationally guided programs take into account individual regions only. In various highly centralized countries, only such nationally guided programs have been able to arise. They are usually fairly easy to coordinate with national, global, and sectoral policies or with interregional ones, although this possibility has been used only by very few countries so far. Nationally guided programs, however, usually suffer from a lack of local-regional initiative and cooperation.[4]

(7) *Bi- or multinational guidance* has been very scarce so far and usually has been facilitated only through the mediation of supranational organizations such as the Interamerican Development Bank, the Institute for Latin American Integration (INTAL), the Secretariat for Central American Integration (SIECA), the Bank of Central American Integration (BCIE), ECLA, and the Instituto Latinoamericano de Planificación Económica y Social (ILPES).

TABLE 2
PROGRAMS FOR SYSTEMS OF REGIONS ("inter-regional" programs)

Country[a]	National Technical Organism in Charge of Regional Development (as of 1969)	Regionalization of National Development Policy		Nationwide Coordinated Policy for Certain Types of Areas[b]				Regionalization of National Budget[b]	Official Physical Regionalization of National Territory for Integral Development Purposes[c,d]	Major Objectives		
		For Entire Country	For Certain Priority Regions in a Consistent National Framework[b]	Depressed Areas	Colonization Areas	Rural Areas[e]	Growth Poles		Type of Regionalization (no. of regions)	Decentralization of Decision-Making	Coordination of Central Government Action in Regions[c]	Others or Undefined
1	2	3	4	5	6	7	8	9	10	11	12	13
Argentina	Secretaría del Consejo Nacional de Desarrollo								I (8 regions)	C	O	
Brazil	Ministerio do Planejamento e Coordinação Geral, Sector Regional e Urbano		X (North-East, Amazonas)				P		I (5 macro-regions)	D	O	
Colombia	Depto. Nacional de Planeación, Unidad de Desarrollo Regional y Urbano						P		S	C	O	
Chile	Oficina de Planificación Nacional, Sub-Dirección Regional	X	X (extreme Northern and Southern periphery, growth pole Concepción)				(X)	(X)	I (12 regions)	D	O	

TABLE 2 (continued)

1	2	3	4	5	6	7	8	9	10	11	12	13
Ecuador	Junta Nacional de Planificación y Coordinación, Sub-División Planificación Desarrollo Regional								P (5 regions)		O	
El Salvador	Secretaría del Consejo Nacional de Planificación Económica						P		P (4 regions)		O	
Guatemala	Secretaría del Consejo Nacional de Planificación Económica Unidad Sectoral de Planificación del Ministerio de Comunicaciones y Obras Públicas						P		P (5 regions)		O	
Honduras	Secretaría del Consejo Superior de Planificación Económica, Depto. Desarrollo Urbano y Regional						P		P (10 regions)		O	
Mexico	Secretaría de la Presidencia, Dirección de Planeación Nacional Financiera Secretaría de Recursos Hidráulicos					X			P (8 zones, 104 regions)			O
Nicaragua	Ministerio de Economía y Comercio, Depto. de Planificación											

253

TABLE 2 (continued)

1	2	3	4	5	6	7	8	9	10	11	12	13
Paraguay	Secretaría Técnica de Planificación											
Peru[f]	Instituto Nacional de Planificación, Oficina de Programación Regional			P (Study INP 1960)			P		X (4 macro-regions, 7 regions)	D	O	
Uruguay	Oficina de Planeamiento y Presupuesto, Sector Programación Regional											
Venezuela	Oficina Central de Coordinación y Planificación División de Planificación Regional		X (Guayana)						X (8 regions)	C	O	

a. Not all Latin American countries are covered.

b. Interregional development programs: X = in execution; (X) = execution in trial stage; P = proposition by respective national agency.

c. Only regions for integral development are considered, not those used by sectoral agencies for their specific purposes.

d. Delimitation of regions: I = introduced officially; P = proposition; S = study by responsible agency in advanced stage. Major objectives of physical regionalization: C = controlling regional decision-making; D = delegation of decision-making powers to regional level (devolution of power); O = coordination of central government action in regions, other objectives or undefined.

e. Mexico: coordinated program of public investment in rural areas (for villages from 500-2,500 inhabitants).

f. Peru: refers to conditions up to 1969 only.

Major orientation (columns 8-16 of Table 1). The orientation of programs refers to the specific objectives and strategies pursued. The first category is concerned with decentralization of decision-making (column 8); the following five categories are related to specific problems and potentials of the area to which the program is applied (columns 9-13), while the last three categories (columns 14-16) refer to strategy devices such as growth pole development, border area development and river basin development, each of which can serve different problems or potentials referred to in the preceding columns.

Programs for Systems of Regions ("Interregional" Programs)[5]

Those policies and programs which apply a national system's approach to the treatment of all or some regions of a country are considered "interregional" programs.

The national technical organism in charge of regional development in the respective country is given in column 2 of Table 2 (state end 1960s).

A complete regionalization of the national development policy (column 3 of Table 2) has not yet been introduced by any country in Latin America. Such policy would mean that national development objectives, criteria, and targets would have to be disaggregated not only along sectoral lines but also along regional lines involving considerable technical problems (Mennes, Tinbergen, and Waardenburg, 1969). Chile at the moment seems to be the country most advanced in systematically regionalizing national development policy (Chile, 1968, 1970).

Partially regionalized policies are given in columns 4-8 of Table 2. Interregional policy does not necessarily require that concrete action for regional development take place in all parts of the country (which in developing countries will rarely be feasible). Action could take place only in certain priority regions, or in fact only in one region, but it would have to be derived from a national frame of reference and take into account the problems and potentials of the other regions of the country and the interrelations between them.[6] Such policies as a rule are nationally guided and national criteria are dominant. Venezuela, Chile, and Brazil seem to be furthest advanced in this sense (column 4 of Table 2). In Venezuela and Chile, the respective regional programs have been prompted by national considerations (incorporation of natural resources and national political integration, respectively); in Brazil, the interregional approach was superimposed upon regional programs as soon as it became evident that they were causing negative repercussions in other regions of the country.[7]

Interregional programs can also cover certain types of regions only, such as depressed areas, colonization areas, rural areas, or growth poles. Programs for these types of regions can be considered interregional—e.g., if a program for depressed areas is defined in a nationwide context and its application to one depressed area corresponds to an integral view of all the depressed areas of the country. There should exist objective criteria for applying a program to certain depressed areas and not to others. Such criteria could be that it experiences a particularly severe state of depression, that its potential for responding to development policies is particularly great, that its importance for national development is particularly great. Programs of this kind are still very scarce in Latin America and have hardly advanced beyond a preparatory stage (columns 5-8 of Table 2), with the exception of a program for the development of rural areas in Mexico.

Interregional policies may be partial also in that they refer only to direct public investment through a systematic regionalization of the national budget (column 9 of Table 2). This is a rather committing instrument of interregional policy. Probably due to the political sensitivity and the methodological problems involved, this instrument has hardly been applied so far in Latin America. Chile seems to be the country furthest advanced in this direction.

As a preparatory stage for the introduction of interregional policies may be considered the physical regionalization of a national territory—i.e., the definition of development regions on a nationwide basis (columns 10-13 of Table 2). The objectives of such regionalization may be, for instance, the decentralization of decision-making or the coordination of central government activities by regions. Other regionalizations lacking defined policy objectives are usually little more than an academic exercise. The great number of regional delimitations by sectoral agencies for their specific purposes are not considered here as they are usually responding only to sectoral criteria.

Interrregional policies are considered in Table 2 only if they are institutionalized or at least officially adopted. It has been impossible to include the vast number of official or academic propositions or studies of varying maturity on topics such as regionalization which are going on in practically all Latin American countries. Only at the supranational level, where an institutionalization of interregional policies is hardly feasible as yet, some major propositions or studies by international planning organizations such as ILPES or SIECA have been included. No doubt they have great potential influence both on the action of international financing institutions and on the policies of national governments.

NOTES

1. United Nations documents, for example, often refer to all of Latin America as a (world) "region."

2. January 1969: Honduras, El Salvador, Guatemala, Mexico. March 1969: Brazil, Venezuela, Colombia. The author was also stationed in Chile as Ford Foundation Senior Regional Planning Advisor.

3. See Table 1.

4. The "guidance system" refers to the level at which major objectives and criteria are formulated. This may be different from the level at which planning actually takes place. In Argentina up to about 1966, for instance, most regional plans were prepared by a national agency, the Consejo Federal de Inversiones, but with objectives and criteria defined primarily by the Provinces so that guidance essentially was regional (at best cooperative regional/national). On the other hand, in Chile's initial regional planning period (about 1964-1967) plans for various regions were prepared in a deconcentrated way at the regional

level. Since the respective regional offices were dependencies of the National Planning Office and practically all decisions were made at the national level, however, the guidance system was essentially a national one. I am grateful to Sr. Sergio Boisier of Chile for drawing my attention to this differentiation.

5. See Table 2.

6. We exclude from consideration here the general national policies of many Latin American countries which have implicitly led to the development of only the national capital region. This could constitute a perfectly justifiable interregional policy (particularly in early stages of national development), but in practice such patterns resulted from policies which had no deliberate spatial dimension at all.

7. Tax incentives for the Northeast of Brazil, e.g., led to excess capacity in certain industrial sectors and to forceful competition for established enterprises in the developed Southeast.

REFERENCES

Chile, Presidencia de la República de (1970) El desarrollo regional de Chile en la década 1970-1980. Santiago: Oficina de Planificación Nacional.

── (1968) A Model of Inter-Regional Programming and Compatibility. Santiago: Oficina de Planificación Nacional.

KUKLINSKI, A. R. (1968) "Trends in research on comprehensive regional development." Geneva: UNRISD. (mimeo)

MENNES, L.B.H., J. TINBERGEN, and J. G. WAARDENBURG (1969) The Element of Space in Development Planning. Amsterdam-London: North Holland.

SHERWOOD, F. P. (1969) "Devolution as a problem of organization strategy," in R. T. Daland, ed., Comparative Urban Research. Beverly Hills, Calif.: Sage Pubns.

WALLER, P. (1971) Problems and Strategies of Regional Planning in Developing Countries—A Case Study of Peru. Berlin. German Development Institute.

BIBLIOGRAPHY,

1969-1971

BIBLIOGRAPHY, 1969-1971

CAPITAL OR MAJOR CITIES

Asunción, Paraguay

MORENO, F. (1968) La ciudad de la Asunción. Asunción.
Municipalidad de Asunción (1969?) Memoria anual del Departamento Ejecutivo. Año 1968. Asunción.

Bogotá, Colombia

AMATO, P. W. (1969) "Environmental quality and locational behavior in a Latin American city." Urban Affairs Q. (September): 83-101.
–– (1969) "Patrones de vivienda en el desarrollo urbano." Revista de la Sociedad Interamericana de Planificación 3 (March-June): 44-50.
–– (1968) "Patrones de ubicación en una ciudad latinoamericana." Revista de la Sociedad Interamericana de Planificación 2 (December): 38-45.
–– (1968) "An analysis of the changing patterns of elite residential areas in Bogotá, Colombia." Ithaca, N.Y.: Cornell University, Latin American Studies Program Dissertation Series, No. 7.
HARKESS, S. (1971) "The pursuit of an ideal: Migration, social classes and women's roles in two Bogotá barrios." Presented at the Latin American Studies Association national meeting, Austin, Texas.

Editors' Note: Thanks are due to Amy Bushnell, Frederick V. Gifun, Leonidas F. Pozo-Ledezma, Alejandro Vélez Gómez, and Menno Vellinga who aided in the preparation of this bibliography. Please note that significant items from 1967-1969 which were not available at the time the bibliography appearing in Volume I, LATIN AMERICAN URBAN RESEARCH was prepared, have been included. Essays appearing in Volume I, however, have been excluded. The cutoff period for the present bibliography is the fall of 1971 for U.S. publications and the spring of 1971 for foreign. We make no pretense that this bibliography is exhaustive, however, given the difficulty of consulting all issues of serial publications, particularly foreign. Because of the size of the bibliography, it is divided into the following categories: Capital or Major Cities, Other Cities by Country, Countries in General, General Latin America, Regional Development and Planning, and General Urban Topics.

HAVENS, A. E. and W. FLINN (1970) "The power structure in a shantytown," in Internal Colonialism and Structural Change in Colombia. New York: Praeger.

LIPMAN, A. (1969) "The Colombian entrepreneur in Bogotá." Miami, Fla.: University of Miami Press. Hispanic American Studies, No. 22.

MARTINEZ, C. (1968) "Santa Fé de Bogotá." Buenos Aires. La urbanización de América Latina: Monografías de Historia Urbana, No. 1.

NEGLIA, A. and F. HERNANDEZ (1970) Marginalidad, población y familia: Estudio de un barrio de invasión de la ciudad de Bogotá (el barrio Quindio). Bogotá: Instituto de Desarrollo de la Comunidad.

OLIVARES, J. (1970) Proyecciones de la población del Distrito Especial de Bogotá, 1965-1985. Bogotá: Universidad de Los Andes.

REY REY, N. (1969) "Características y determinantes de la participación de la población en el mercado laboral de Bogotá." Revista de Planeación y Desarrollo (Bogotá) 1 (October): 81-108.

Universidad Nacional de Colombia, Centro de Investigaciones para el Desarrollo (1969) Alternativas para el desarrollo urbano de Bogotá, D.E. Bogotá: Editorial Andes.

Brasília, Brazil

COSTA, L. (1971) "Contra a revisão urbanística de Brasília." Revista de Administração Municipal 107 (July-August): 97-102.

PASTORE, J. (1969) Brasília: A cidade e o homen: Uma investigação sociológica sôbre os processos de migração, adaptação e planejamento urbano. São Paulo: Cia. Editôra Nacional, Editôra da Universidade de São Paulo.

— — (1968) Satisfaction Among Migrants to Brasília, Brazil: A Sociological Interpretation. Madison: Univ. of Wisconsin Press.

— — (1968) "A agricultura e o homen no Distrito Federal, Brasília: Relatório preliminar de uma investigação sociológica." Madison: University of Wisconsin, Land Tenure Center.

ROCHA, F. A. S. (1968) Determinants of Occupational Achievement, Income, and Level of Living in Brasília, Brazil. Madison: University of Wisconsin.

SILVA, E. (1970?) História de Brasília. Brasília.

TOYNBEE, A. (1970) Cities on the Move. New York: Oxford Univ. Press.

VAITSMAN, M. (1968) Quanto custou Brasília. Rio de Janeiro. Coleção Livro-Verdade, No. 1.

Buenos Aires, Argentina

BAULNY, O. (1969) "Buenos Ayres a la fin de l'époque coloniale." Cahiers des Amériques Latines 1 (January-June): 5-29.

ESCARDO, F. (1971) Nueva geografía de Buenos Aires. Buenos Aires.

FRIEDMAN, H. D. (1969) "Squatter assimilation in Buenos Aires." Ph.D. dissertation. Massachusetts Institute of Technology.

GUADAGNI, A. A. (forthcoming) Problemas económicos del sistema de suministro eléctrico del Gran Buenos Aires. Buenos Aires: Editorial del Instituto Torcuato di Tella.

MacEWEN, A. M. (1971) Stability and change in a shanty town. London: University of Essex, Department of Sociology.

MARONI, J. J. (1969) "Breve historia física de Buenos Aires." Buenos Aires: Municipalidad de la Ciudad de Buenos Aires. Cuadernos de Buenos Aires, No. 29.

Ministerio de Obras Públicas, Provincia de Buenos Aires (1971). Area Metropolitana. Buenos Aires.

Municipalidad de la Ciudad de Buenos Aires, Dirección de Estadística (1970) "Abastecimiento en la Capital Federal." Buenos Aires. Boletín No. 53.

— — (1969?) Buenos Aires: Publicación preparada por la Organización del Plan Regulador de la Ciudad de Buenos Aires para el XII Congreso Panamericano de Arquitectos, Bogotá, Colombia, 1968. Buenos Aires.

— — Dirección del Plan Regulador (1969?) Buenos Aires: Distribución espacial de la población y usos del suelo.

— — (1969?) Buenos Aires: Master Plan. Summary. Buenos Aires.

— — (1969?) Situación demográfica. Buenos Aires.

— — Dirección de Estadística (1969) Abastecimiento de la Capital Federal. Año 1968. Buenos Aires.

— — (1968?) Mortalidad en la Capital Federal, 1963-1967. Buenos Aires.

ROBIROSA, M. C. (1968) "Urban poverty and social change in Buenos Aires." Inter-American Conference on Poverty Leadership Styles. Philadelphia. November.

ROFMAN, A. B., O. YUJNOVSKY, et al. (1971) Diagnóstico preliminar del área sudeste de la Provincia de Buenos Aires: Metodología. Buenos Aires: Editorial del Instituto Torcuato di Tella.

SCOBIE, J. R. (1968) "Buenos Aires of 1910: The Paris of South America that did not take off." Inter-Amer. Economic Affairs 21: 3-14.

TORRE REVELLO, J. (1970) La sociedad colonial. (Páginas sobre la sociedad de Buenos Aires entre los siglos XVI y XIX.) Buenos Aires.

Caracas, Venezuela

Banco Central de Venezuela, Caracas (1968) Estudio sobre presupuestos familiares en el área metropolitana de Caracas para la elaboración de un índice de costo de vida. Caracas.

CELIS, J. P. (1969) "Movimiento migratorio del área metropolitana de Caracas." Universidad Central de Caracas, Estudio de Caracas 3: 207-241.

GASPARINI, G. (1969) Caracas colonial. Buenos Aires. La Urbanización de América Latina, No. 5.

Instituto Venezolano de Acción Comunitaria (1968) Estudio sobre barrios de Caracas. Caracas: Consejo Municipal del Distrito Federal.

KARST, K. L. (1971) "Rights in land and housing in an informal legal system: The barrios of Caracas." Amer. J. of Comparative Law 19 (Summer): 550-574.

MYERS, D. J. (1971) "Urban renewal in El Conde," in Readings in Latin American Studies. West Point, N.Y.: U.S. Military Academy.

— — (1969) "The political process of urban development: Caracas under Acción Democrática." Ph.D. dissertation. University of California.

PADRON, M. and R. BRASWELL (1969) "Planificación del sistema de tránsito rápido de Caracas." Revista de la Sociedad Interamericana de Planificación 3 (September): 43-48.

SEMPRUM, J. (1969) Visiones de Caracas y otros temas. Caracas: Corporación Venezolana de Fomento.

Ciudad Guayana, Venezuela

McGINN, N. F. and R. G. DAVIS (1970) Build a Mill, Build a City, Build a School: Industrialization, Urbanization, and Education in Ciudad Guayana, Venezuela. Cambridge, Mass.: MIT Press.

PROCTOR, N. (1968) "Economic developments in Guayana, Venezuela." Geography (London) 53 (April): 183-186.

RODWIN, L. (1970) "National planning of an urban growth region: the experience of Venezuela," pp. 32-69 in L. Rodwin, Nations and Cities: A Comparison of Strategies for Urban Growth. Boston: Houghton Mifflin.

Córdoba, Argentina

AGULIA, J. C. (1968) "La aristocracia en el poder. Estudio de un estrato tradicional en una comunidad en desarrollo." Aportes (Paris) 7 (January): 76-88.

CRITTO, A. (1969) "Análisis del campo y la ciudad, después de la migración campo-ciudad en Córdoba," in J. Hardoy and R. P. Schaedel, eds., The Urbanization Process in America from Its Origins to the Present Day. Buenos Aires: Editorial del Instituto Torcuato di Tella.

Dirección General de Estadística, Censos e Investigaciones, Facultad de Ciencias Económicas (1967) Encuesta sobre empleo y desempleo en la Ciudad de Córdoba. Córdoba: Consejo Nacional de Desarrollo.

FERRARI RUEDA, R. DE (1968) Historia de Córdoba. Volume II. Córdoba.

FLEUR, L. B. DE (1971) Delinquency in Argentina: A Study of Córdoba's Youth. Pullman: Washington State Univ. Press.

MILLER, D. C. (1970) International Community Power Structures. Bloomington: Indiana Univ. Press.

SCHULTHESS, W. E. and R. F. C. GIULIODORI (1968) Migraciones en la provincia de Córdoba: Período 1947-1960. Córdoba: Dirección General de Estadísticas, Censos e Investigaciones.

Guatemala City

MICKLIN, M. (1969) "Traditionalism, social class, and differential fertility in Guatemala City." América Latina (Rio de Janeiro) 12 (October-December): 59-78.

ROBERTS, B. R. (1970) "The social organization of low-income families," pp. 345-382 in I. L. Horowitz, ed., Masses in Latin America. New York: Oxford Univ. Press.

—— (1970) "Migration and population growth in Guatemala City: implications for social and economic development." Liverpool: University of Liverpool, Centre for Latin American Studies. Monograph Series, No. 2.

—— (1970) "Urban poverty and political behavior in Guatemala." Human Organization 29, 1: 20-28.

THOMAS, R. N. (1968) "Internal migration to Guatemala City, C.A." Ph.D. dissertation, Pennsylvania State University.

Lima-Callao, Peru

ADURIZ, J. (1969) "Así viven y así nacen (Estudio psicosocial de los condicionamientos de la fecundidad en los migrantes provincianos de Lima-Callao)." Lima: Centro de Estudios y Promoción del Desarrollo (DESCO). Cuadernos DESCO, Serie A, No. 3 (May).

ALMONTE, J. E. (1968) "Standard areas for housing and the selection of preferred sizes for government housing projects in Lima, Peru." M.S. thesis, Cambridge University.

ANDREWS, F. M. and G. PHILLIPS (1970) "The squatters of Lima: who they are and what they want." J. of Developing Areas 4 (January). Also in Ekistics 31 (1971): 132-136.

AUSTIN, A. G. and S. LEWIS (1970) Urban Government for Metropolitan Lima. New York: Praeger.

BEDINI, O. (1968) Análisis de la estructura comercial de Lima. Lima: Instituto de Planeamiento de Lima (October).

Centro de Estudios y Promoción del Desarrollo (DESCO) (forthcoming) Informe sobre la marginalidad social en el área de Lima metropolitana. Lima.

Centro de Investigaciones Sociales por Muestreo (1968) Información sobre sindicatos del área Lima-Callao: Encuesta de hogares. Lima: Ministerio de Trabajo y Comunidades.

CESPEDES ASCENCIO, Y. (1968) "La población inmigrante de Lima metropolitana: Tendencias en el tiempo, orígen geográfico, distribución en la ciudad." Ministerio de Hacienda y Comercio, Dirección Nacional de Estadística, Boletín de Análisis Demográfico (Lima) 7: 1-28.

COLLIER, D. (1970) "Urban marginality and the politics of cooptation in Peru." Urbana: University of Illinois, Department of Political Science. (mimeo)

Comisión de Coordinación de Desarrollo de los Pueblos Jóvenes (1968) Plan de acción inmediata. A ejecutarse en los pueblos jóvenes de los distritos de San Martín de Porres, Independencia, Comas, Surco y Chorrillos. Lima.

DELGADO, C. (1969) "Three proposals regarding accelerated urbanization problems in metropolitan areas: the Lima case." Amer. Behavioral Sci. 12.

DIETZ, H. (1971) "Assimilation and politicization of urban squatter migrants in Lima, Peru." Ph.D. dissertation, Stanford University.

Dirección Nacional de Estadística y Censos (1966-1968) Encuesta de inmigración, Lima metropolitana. Lima.

DOUGHTY, P. L. (1970) "Behind the backs of the city: 'provincial' life in Lima, Peru," pp. 30-46 in W. Mangin, ed., Peasants in Cities. Boston: Houghton Mifflin.

FOLAND, F. M. (1968) "Pampas de Comas revisited, Lima, Peru." Institute of Current World Affairs.

GARAY CASTILLO, A. (1969) Lima metropolitana: Acceso a la propiedad de la vivienda. Lima: Universidad Nacional de Ingeniería, Facultad de Arquitectura.

JAWORSKI, H. (1969) "Políticas de vivienda popular y barrios marginales." Víspera (Montevideo) 2 (January). Also printed in Cuadernos DESCO (Lima), Serie A, No. 1 (February): 27-46.

KOTH DE PAREDES, M. (1968) "Análisis ecológico del área metropolitana: aplicación del análisis factorial al estudio de algunas características socio-económicas distritales." (Plan de Desarrollo Metropolitano, Lima-Callao.) Lima: Oficina Nacional de Planeamiento y Urbanismo. Cuaderno PLANDEMET, Serie Violeta, No. 6.

LEEDS, A. and E. LEEDS (1970) "Brazil and the myth of urban rurality: urban experience, work and values in the 'squatments' of Rio de Janeiro and Lima," in A. J. Field, ed., City and Country in the Third World. Cambridge, Mass.: Schenkman.

LEEDS, E. (1969) "The myth of politicization: a comparison of urban proletarian political articulation in Rio de Janeiro and Lima." Austin, University of Texas.

LO CELSO, J. E. (1968) "Método para planeamiento del uso del suelo urbano: perspectivas de aplicación en la región metropolitana de Lima." Córdoba, Argentina: Talleres Gráficos de la Universidad Nacional de Córdoba.

LOWDER, S. (1970) "Lima's population growth and the consequences for Peru." University of Liverpool, Centre for Latin American Studies. Monograph Series, 2: 21-34.

LUTZ, T. M. (1970) "Self-help neighborhood organizations, political socialization, and the developing political orientations of urban squatters in Latin America: contrasting patterns from case studies in Panama City, Guayaquil and Lima." Ph.D. disssertation. Georgetown University.

McKENNEY, J. W. (1969) "Voluntary associations and political integration: an exploratory study of the role of voluntary association membership in the political socialization of urban lower class residents in Santiago and Lima." Ph.D. dissertation. University of Oregon.

MILLER, D. C. (1970) International Community Power Structures. Bloomington: Indiana Univ. Press.

MORSE, R. M. (1969) "The Lima of Joaquín Capelo: a Latin American archetype." J. of Contemporary History (London) 4 (July): 95-110.

Oficina Nacional de Planeamiento y Urbanismo (1969) Ocupación en el área metropolitana: Análisis del sub empleo. (Plan de Desarrollo Metropolitano, Lima-Callao.) Lima.

Peruvian Times (1968) "Port of Callao Supplement." Andean Air Mail and Peruvian Times (Lima) 18 (November 1): 7-28.

POLLITT, E. (1969) "Biological and social correlates of stature among children living in the slums of Lima, Peru." Ph.D. dissertation. Cornell University.

POWELL, S. (1969) "Political participation in the barriadas: a case study." Comparative Pol. Studies 2 (July): 195-215.

ROBLES RIVAS, D. (1969) "El proceso de urbanización y los sectores populares en Lima." Lima: Centro de Estudios y Promoción del Desarrollo (DESCO). Cuadernos DESCO, Serie A, No. 1 (February): 47-63.

RODRIGUEZ, A. (1969) "Vivienda popular y nueva política urbana." Amereida (Viña del Mar, Chile).

— and H. JAWORSKI (1969) "Vivienda en barriadas." Lima: Centro de Estudios y Promoción del Desarrollo (DESCO). Cuadernos DESCO, Serie A, No. 4 (August).

RODRIGUEZ, A., J. GIANELLA, and H. JAWORSKI (1969) "Aportes a la comprensión de un fenómeno urbano: la barriada." Lima: Centro de Estudios y Promoción del Desarrollo (DESCO). Cuadernos DESCO, Serie A, No. 2 (April).

ROEDER, M. (1969) "Informe descriptivo de una barriada, 'El Progreso.'" July, Lima.

SALAZAR, H. J. (1968) "La posible situación demográfica del Perú en al año 2,000." Lima: Ministerio de Hacienda y Comercio, Dirección Nacional de Estadística y Censos. Boletín de Análisis Demográfico, No. 8: 48-76.

— (1968) "Aspectos demográficos de la fecundidad en Lima metropolitana." Lima: Ministerio de Hacienda y Comercio, Dirección Nacional de Estadística y Censos. Boletín de Análisis Demográfico, No. 8: 1-33.

SANTISTEBAN LECCA, L. (1969) Transporte para recreación de verano en Lima metropolitana 1980. (Plan de Desarrollo Metropolitano, Lima-Callao.) Lima: Oficina Nacional de Planeamiento y Urbanismo. Cuaderno PLANDEMET, Serie Violeta, No. 3 (February).

SARAVIA, A. (1968) El gobierno metropolitano y Limatrópoli. (Publicado con el auspicio del Concejo Provincial y la Cámara de Comercio de Lima.) Lima.

SATTLER, R. S. (1969) "Lima squatter settlements: los pueblos jóvenes. Prospects for development." Lima.

Servicio del Empleo y Recursos Humanos (1969) Empleo, salarios y horas de trabajo en 1968. Informe de Lima-Callao. May, Lima.

STYCOS, J. M. (1968) "Empleo de mujeres y fecundidad en Lima, Perú." Lima: Ministerio de Hacienda y Comercio, Dirección Nacional de Estadística y Censos. Boletín de Análisis Demográfico, No. 8: 34-47.

Suceso. Suplemento del diario Correo (Lima) (1968) "¡Barriadas hasta el año 2,000!" March 17: 18-19.

TRIGOSO TRIGOSO, J. and E. CABRERA (1969) "Ocupación en el área metropolitana: Análisis del sub-empleo." (Plan de Desarrollo Metropolitano, Lima-Callao.) Lima: Oficina Nacional de Planeamiento y Urbanismo. Cuaderno PLANDEMET, Serie Azul, No. 1.

URIARTE, C. A. (1968) Encuesta de la actitud de los habitantes de la ciudad de Lima sobre el tamaño de la familia. Lima: Centro de Estudios de Población y Desarrollo.

VALLEJOS PAULET, E. (1967) "La asistencia hospitalaria a los asegurados de la Zona del Callao." Informaciones Sociales (Lima) 1-4: 3-10.

VELARDE, H. (1971) Lima City. Lima.

VILLA LUNA, M. (1969) Lima, 1535-1968: Un estudio de su evolución urbana. Lima: Universidad Nacional de Ingeniería, Facultad de Arquitectura.

WELSH, E. (1970) Bibliografía sobre el crecimiento dinámico del Lima, referente al proceso de urbanización en el Perú. Lima: Centro de Estudios y Promoción del Desarrollo (DESCO). Cuadernos DESCO, Serie A, No. 5 (January).

Mexico City

BATAILLON, C., M. ACEVES GARCIA, A. GUERRERO R., and H. RIVIERE (1968). Las zonas suburbanas de la ciudad de México. Mexico: Universidad Nacional Autónoma de México.

BERGE, D. E. (1970) "A Mexican dilemma: the Mexico City ayuntamiento and the question of loyalty, 1846-1848." Hispanic Amer. Historical Rev. 50 (May): 229-256.

BUTTERWORTH, D. S. (1970) "A Study of the urbanization process among Mixtec migrants from Tilantongo in Mexico City," pp. 98-113 in W. P. Mangin, ed., Peasants in Cities: Readings in the Anthropology of Urbanization. Boston.

CORNELIUS, W. A. (1971) "Local level political leadership in a Latin American urban environment." Presented at American Political Science Association annual meeting, Chicago.

COVO, M. E. (1969) Las instituciones de investigación social en la ciudad de México. Mexico: Universidad Nacional Autónoma de México.

Fortune (1969) "Mexico's subway is for viewing." (December): 105-109.

MACIAS, E. B. (1969) "Ordenanzas para el establecimiento de Alcaldes de barrio en la Nueva España. Ciudades de México y San Luis Potosí." Boletín del Archivo General de la Nación 1 and 2 (January-June): 51-125.

POZAS ARCINIEGAS, R. (1968) "El vago: un estudio de caso." Revista Mexicana de Ciencia Política 14 (October-December): 563-593.

SCHWARTZ, S. B. (1969) "Cities of empire: Mexico and Bahia." J. of Inter-Amer. Studies 11 (October): 616-637.

UNIKEL, L. (1971) "La dinámica del crecimiento de la cuidad de México." Comercio Exterior 21 (June).

WILKIE, J. W. (1971) "La ciudad de México . . . población economicamente activa 1930, 1965," in Historia y sociedad en el mundo de habla española: Homenaje a José Miranda. Mexico: El Colegio de México.

Montevideo, Uruguay

CSUKASI, M. et al., ed. (1968) Los rancheríos y su gente: Tareas, costumbres, historias de vida. Montevideo.

GRUNWALDT RAMASSO, J. (1970) Vida, industria y comercio en el antiguo Montevideo, 1830-1852. Montevideo.

PONCE DE LEON, L. R. (1968) La ciudad vieja de Montevideo: Trazado inicial y evolución en su primer cuarto de siglo. Montevideo.

RODRIGUEZ VILLAMIL, S. (1968) Las mentalidades dominantes en Montevideo (1850-1900). Volume I: La mentalidad criolla tradicional. Montevideo. Colección "Reconquista," No. 34.

SCHIAFFINO, A. et al. (1968) "Introducción a la investigación del medio social actual de los lactantes desnutridos hospitalizados provenientes de las zonas marginales de la ciudad de Montevideo." Boletín del Instituto Inter-americano del Niño 42 (December): 590-633.

Universidad de la República, Instituto de Ciencias Sociales (1969) La opinión pública de Montevideo. Montevideo.

— — (1969) La desocupación obrera en Montevideo. Montevideo: Publicaciones del Instituto de Ciencias Sociales.

— — Instituto de Estadística (1968) "Análisis de la ocupación y la desocupación en el Departamento de Montevideo." Revista de la Facultad de Ciencias Económicas y de Administración (Montevideo) 30 (December): 111-136.

VIDART, D. D. (n.d.) El gran Montevideo. Montevideo: Colección Enciclopedia Uruguaya.

Panama City

Instituto de Vivienda y Urbanismo (1968) Plan de Panamá. Panama City: De Diego y Fábrega, S.A.

LUTZ, T. M. (1970) "Self-help neighborhood organizations, political socialization, and the developing political orientations of urban squatters in Latin America: contrasting patterns from case studies in Panama City, Guayaquil and Lima." Ph.D. dissertation. Georgetown University.

Quito, Ecuador

CHIRIBOGA, C. G., ed. (1969) "Libro de Cabildos de la ciudad de Quito, 1650-1657." Archivo Municipal de Quito 33 (December).
McLEOD, J. M., R. R. RUSH, and K. H. FRIEDERICH (1968/69) "The mass media and political information in Quito, Ecuador." Public Opinion Q. 32 (Winter): 575-587.
NETT, E. M. (1971) "The functional elites of Quito." J. of Inter-Amer. Studies and World Affairs 13 (January): 112-120.

Rio de Janeiro, Brazil

Ação Comunitária do Brasil (1968) Catálogo de obras e recursos assistenciais do Estado da Guanabara. Rio de Janeiro: Ação Comunitária do Brasil. June 3.
BOMBART, J. P. (1969) "Les cultes Protestants dans une favela de Rio de Janeiro." América Latina 12 (July-September): 137-159.
BRASILEIRO, A. M. (1970) "A comparative study of 63 municipalities in the state of Rio de Janeiro, with special reference to decision-making." Ph.D. dissertation. University of Essex.
CANDIDO, A. (1970) "Dialética da malandragem." Revista do Instituto de Estudos Brasileiros 8: 67-89.
CHAMBERLAIN, L. (1969?) Rio antigo 1819. Rio de Janeiro.
Conjuntura Econômica (1970) "Construção de moradias na Guanabara." Volume 24: 51-54.
CONN, S. (1968) "The squatters rights of favelados." Ciências Econômicas e Sociais (OSASCO) 13 (December): 50-142. Also published in Cuadernos del Centro Intercultural de Documentación (CIDOC) (Mexico) 32 (1969).
CORRIE, J. C. (1971) "Umbanda, the syncretic cult as an aspect of favela society." Ph.D. dissertation. Oxford University.
Diario Oficial da União (1968) "Decreto No. 62.654 de 3 de maio de 1968. Criação de Coordenação de Habitação de Interesse Social da Area Metropolitana do Grande Rio (CHISAM)." Brasília, May 6.
Federação das Associações de Moradores em Favelas do Estado da Guanabara (1968) "Relatório do Segundo Congresso Estadual da FAFEG." November-December, Rio de Janeiro. (mimeo)
JERONIMO, P. (1968) "Governo ouvirá favelado para erradicar as favelas." Guanabara em Revista (Rio de Janeiro) 13: 14-18.
LANDERS, C. E. (1971) "The União Democrática Nacional in the state of Guanabara: an attitudinal study of party membership." Ph.D. dissertation. University of Florida.
LEEDS, A. and E. LEEDS (1970) "Brazil and the myth of urban rurality: urban experience, work and values in the 'squatments' of Rio de Janeiro and Lima," in A. J. Field, ed., City and Country in the Third World. Cambridge, Mass.: Schenkman.
LEEDS, E. (1969) "The myth of politicization: a comparison of urban proletarian political articulation in Rio de Janeiro and Lima." Austin: University of Texas.
MADEIRA, J. L. (1969) "Reformulação do crescimento demográfico da Guanabara no período 1940-1960 em face dos recenseamentos gerais." Rio de Janeiro: Fundação IBGE. Estudos e Análises, No. 5.
MEDINA, C. A. DE (1969) "A favela como uma estrutura atomística: elementos descritivos e constitutivos." América Latin 12 (July-September): 112-134.
PARISSE, L. (1969) "Las favelas en la expansión urbana de Rio de Janeiro." América Latina 12 (July-September): 7-43.
–– (1969) "Bibliografia cronológica sôbre a favela do Rio de Janeiro a partir de 1940." América Latina 12 (July-September): 221-232.
–– (1969) "Les favelas dans la ville: le cas de Rio de Janeiro." Revista Geográfica (Rio de Janeiro) 70 (June).

–– (1968) "L'assimilation des immigrants ruraux à Rio de Janeiro: hypothèses de recherche." Migrations dans le Monde (Geneva) 3 (July-September).

QUESADA, G. M. (1968) "A procura de informação em fontes burocratizadas com relação às características sociais de uma área rural no Estado do Rio." América Latina 11 (July-September): 105-112.

RENAULT, D. (1969) "O Rio antigo nos anúncios de jornais: 1808-1850." Rio de Janeiro. Coleção Documentos Brasileiros, No. 137.

SILBERSTEIN, P. (1969) "Favela living: personal solutions to larger problems." América Latina 12 (July-September): 183-200.

SOUZA, A. DE (1968) "Exposição aos meios de comunicação de massa no Rio de Janeiro: Um estudo preliminar." Dados (Rio de Janeiro) 4: 145-168.

VIEGAS, M. R. (1968) "Habitação popular na Guanabara." Commentário (Rio de Janeiro) 9: 106-111.

Salvador, Bahia, Brazil

Banco do Nordeste do Brasil S.A., Departamento de Estudos Econômicos do Nordeste (1969) "O consumo de produtos industriais na cidade de Salvador." Revista Econômica (Fortaleza, Ceará) Ano 1, 2 (October-December): 42-52.

PINHO, W. (1968) "História social da cidade do Salvador. Volume I: Aspetos da história social da cidade, 1549-1650." Salvador: Prefeitura Municipal do Salvador. Evolução Histórica da Cidade do Salvador, No. 6.

SCHWARTZ, S. B. (1969) "Cities of empire: Mexico and Bahia." J. of Inter-Amer. Studies 11 (October): 616-637.

Santiago, Chile

BEHRMAN, L. C. (1971) "The convergence of religious and political attitudes and activities among workers in Santiago, Chile." Presented to the American Political Science Association annual meeting, Chicago.

McKENNEY, J. W. (1969) "Voluntary associations and political integration: an exploratory study of the role of voluntary association membership in the political socialization of urban lower class residents in Santiago and Lima." Ph.D. dissertation. University of Oregon.

MERCADO VILLAR et al. (1968) La marginalidad urbana: Origen, proceso y modo; resultados de una encuesta en poblaciones marginales del Gran Santiago. Volumes I and II. Santiago: DESAL.

Universidad de Chile. (1970) Ocupación y desocupación: Gran Santiago. Santiago.

VARGAS, S. H. (1968?) "Estudio empírico de la oferta potencial de la mano de obra en el Gran Santiago." Economía 26: 161-167.

Santo Domingo, D.R.

CORTEN, A. and A. CORTEN (1968) Cambio social en Santo Domingo. Río Piedras, P.R.: University of Puerto Rico, Institute of Caribbean Studies.

FRANCO, F. J. (1968) "Gérmenes de una burguesía colonial en Santo Domingo, siglos XVI al XVIII." Revista de Ciencias Sociales (Puerto Rico) 12 (December): 527-541.

MORENO, J. A. (1970) Barrios in Arms: Revolution in Santo Domingo. Pittsburgh: Univ. of Pittsburgh Press.

São Paulo, Brazil

AMARAL, A. B. DO (1969) "O Bairro de Pinheiros." São Paulo: Prefeitura Municipal, Secretaria de Educação e Cultura, Série História dos Bairros de São Paulo, No. 2.

BERARDI, M. H. P. (1969) "Santo Amaro." São Paulo: Prefeitura Municipal, Secretaria de Educação e Cultura, Série História dos Bairros de São Paulo, No. 4.

BERLINCK, M. T. (1969) "The structure of the Brazilian family in the city of São Paulo." Cornell University, Latin American Studies Program Dissertation Series, Ithaca, N.Y.

— — and Y. COHEN (1970) "Desenvolvimento econômico, crescimento econômico e modernização na cidade de São Paulo." Revista de Administração de Emprêsas 10 (March): 45-64.

BIRKHOLZ, L. B. (1968) Planos diretores municipais no Estado de São Paulo e sua implantação. São Paulo: Separatas da revista DAE.

BOMTEMPI, S. (1969) "O Bairro da Penha." (Penha de Franca-Sesmaria de Nossa Senhora.) São Paulo: Predeitura Municipal, Secretaria de Educação e Cultura, Série História dos Bairros de São Paulo, No. 3.

Conjuntura Econômica (1970) "Custo de vida (total) e alimentação na cidade de São Paulo–Retrospecto, 1948-69." Volume 24, 5: 81-113.

— — (1970) "Construções não residenciais em São Paulo." Volume 24, 5: 53-55.

— — (1969) "Programa habitacional em São Paulo." Volume 23 (March): 51-64.

DEAN, W. (1969) The industrialization of São Paulo, 1880-1945. Latin American Monograph Series 17. University of Texas, Austin.

MARCILLO, M. L. (1968) "La ville de São Paulo: peuplement et population (1750-1850). Extrait des depositions des thèses de IIIe cycle. Annuaire 1967-1968," pp. 647-651 in IVe section, Sciences Historiques et Philologiques. Ecole Pratique des Hautes Etudes.

TORRES, M.C.T.M. (1970) "O Bairro de Santana." São Paulo: Prefeitura Municipal Secretaria de Educação e Cultura, Série História dos Bairros de São Paulo, No. 6.

OTHER CITIES BY COUNTRY

Argentina

ALISKY, M. and P. R. HOOPES (1968) "Argentina's provincial dailies reflect neutralism of mass media in country's political crisis (Rosario)." Journalism Q. 45 (Spring): 95-98.

AZEVES, A. H. (1968) Ayacucho: Surgimiento y desarrollo de una ciudad pampeana. Buenos Aires: Municipalidad de Ayacucho.

DI LULLO, O. and L.G.B. GARAY (1969) La vivienda popular de Santiago del Estero. Tucumán.

MARCO, M. A. DE et al. (1969) "Orígenes de la prensa en Rosario." Santa Fe: Universidad Católica Argentina "Santa María de los Buenos Aires." Serie Historia del Periodismo, No. 2.

PEDERNERA, J. A. (1970) Historia de la ciudad de Villa María. Buenos Aires: Escuela Normal Víctor Mercante.

Brazil

BALHAMA, Á. P. (1969) "Eleições em Santa Felicidade, 1945-1965." Revista Brasileira de Estudos Políticos 27 (July): 203-260.

CASTRO, C. DE M. (1970) "Investment in education in Brazil: a study of two industrial communities." Ph.D. dissertation. Vanderbilt University.

CINTRA, A. O. (1968) "Partidos políticos em Belo Horizonte: um estudo do eleitorado." Dados (Rio de Janeiro) 5: 82-112.

GONDIM, A.G.F. (1970) "Consumo de produtos industriais na cidade de São Luís." Revista Econômica (Fortaleza, Ceará) 2 (July-September): 55-64.

KELLER, E. C. DE S. (1969) "As funções regionais e a zona de influência de Campinas." Revista Brasileira de Geografia 31: 3-39.

LAUSCHNER, R. (1970) "Marginalização urbana na grande Pôrto Alegre: um estudo descritivo de duas vilas marginalizadas de São Leopoldo e sua autopromoção." Pôrto Alegre. Coleção Temas Filosôficos, Jurídicos e Sociais, No. 12.

Secretaria de Estado do Trabalho e Cultura Popular, Departamento de Habitação Popular (1966) Levantamento da população favelada de Belo Horizonte: Dados preliminares. Belo Horizonte.

SHIRLEY, R. W. (1971) The End of a Tradition: Culture, Change, and Development in the Município of Cunha, São Paulo, Brazil. New York: Columbia Univ. Press.

SILVA, M. L. DA, M. JUSTA, and F. A. DE LIMA (1969) "O consumo de produtos industriais na cidade de Recife." Revista Econômica (Fortaleza) 1 (July-September): 54-65.

SOUSA, H. R. DE (1970) "Delimitação e importância da área de mercado do Recife." Revista Econômica (Fortaleza, Ceará) 2 (July-September): 15-27.

SPALDING, W. (1967) Pequena história de Pôrto Alegre. Pôrto Alegre.

Chile

MASSEY, P. (1968) "Viña del Mar and Valparaíso, resort and port on the coast of Central Chile." Andean Air Mail and Peruvian Times (Lima) 18 (December 13): 9-12.

Colombia

DRAKE, G. F. (1970) "Elites and voluntary associations: a study of community power in Manizales, Colombia." Ph.D. dissertation. University of Wisconsin.

Gobernación de Antioquia, Departamento Administrativo de Planeación (1969) Plan piloto del Municipio de Turbo, sobre zonificación, división comunitaria y plan vial del sector urbana de la cabecera municipal, 1969. Medellín.

MORCILLO, P. P. (1970) "Del deterio de Cali a una política urbana." Presented at Inter-Regional Seminar on the Improvement of Uncontrolled Settlements and Shanty-towns. Cali: United Nations.

WALTER, J. P. (1970) "The economics of labor force participation of urban slum-barrio youth in Cali, Colombia: a case study." Ph.D. dissertation. University of Notre Dame.

ZAPATA CUENCAR, H. (1970) Historia de la parroquia de Copacabana (Colombia). Medellín.

Costa Rica

RICHARDSON, M. and B. BODE (1969) Urban and Societal Features of Popular Medicine in Puntarenas, Costa Rica. Baton Rouge: Louisiana State University Latin American Studies Institute.

Cuba

YGLESIAS, J. (1968) In the Fist of the Revolution: Life in a Cuban Country Town. New York: Pantheon.

Dominican Republic

GARCIA, C. (1968) Cómo se vive en un barrio de Santiago. Santiago de los Caballeros: Universidad Católica Madre y Maestra.

NORVELL, D. G. (1969) "Food marketing in an urban place in the Dominican Republic (Santiago)." Caribbean Studies (Puerto Rico) 9 (October): 104-110.

Ecuador

HAMERLY, M. T. (1970) "A social and economic history of the city and district of Guayaquil during the late colonial and independence periods." Ph.D. dissertation. University of Florida.
LUTZ, T. M. (1970) "Self-help neighborhood organizations, political socialization, and the developing political orientations of urban squatters in Latin America: contrasting patterns from case studies in Panama, Guayaquil and Lima." Ph.D. dissertation. Georgetown University.

Mexico

BROWNING, H. L. and W. FEINDT (1971) "Patterns of migration to Monterrey, Mexico." International Migration Rev. 5 (Fall): 309-324.
—— (1969) "Selectivity of migrants to a metropolis in a developing country." Demography 6 (November): 347-57.
BUTTERWORTH, D. (1971) "Squatter settlements in the city of Oaxaca: the structure of diversity." Presented at the Conference on Modernization and Urbanization Problems in Latin America, University of Illinois, Urbana.
DIAZ RAMIREZ, F. (1968) Historia del periodismo en Querétaro. Mexico.
DILLMAN, C. D. (1969) "Border town symbiosis along the lower Rio Grande as exemplified by the twin cities, Brownsville, Texas, and Matamoros, Tamaulipas." Revista Geográfica (December): 93-113.
FAGEN, R. R. and W. S. TOUHY (1972) Politics and Privilege in a Mexican City (Jalapa). Stanford, Calif.: Stanford Univ. Press.
FALCON DE GYVES, Z. (1970) Chilpancingo, ciudad de crecimiento. México: Universidad Nacional Autónoma de México.
FOSTER, D. W. (1971) "*Tequio* in urban Mexico: a case from Oaxaca city." Presented at the Central States Anthropological Society meeting, Detroit.
—— (1970) "From royalty to poverty: the decline of a rural Mexican community." Human Organization 29, 1: 5-11.
LOPEZ, B., comp. (1968) Cuernavaca: Fuentes para el estudio de una diócesis: Documentos y reacciones de prensa, 1959-1968. Cuernavaca: Centro Intercultural de Documentación (CIDOC).
LOPEZ GONZALEZ, V. (1969) Primer distrito de Morelos: Cuernavaca, Emiliano Zapata, Huitzilac, Jiutepec, Temixco, Tepoztlán. Cuernavaca: CEPES.
MIR, D. "Movilidad social, educación y grupos de referencia en Monterrey, México: un estudio sociológico." Revista Mexicana de Ciencia Política 14 (April-June): 281-286.
PASQUEL, L. (1969) Biografía integral de la ciudad de Veracruz, 1519-1969. Mexico: Editorial Citlaltepetl.
—— ed. (1968) Obras del Puerto de Veracruz en 1882. Mexico.
ROCKWELL, R. C. (1970) "Socio-economic status, values, and socialization: the case of Monterrey, Mexico." Ph.D. dissertation. University of Texas.
TORRES-TRUEBA, H. E. (n.d.) "Factionalism in a Mexican municipio." Sociologus (Berlin) NS 19, no. 2: 134-152.

Nicaragua

ARGUELLO ARGUELLO, A. (1969) Historia de León Viejo. León.
GUERRERO C., J. N. and L. SORIANO DE GUERRERO (1969). Monografía de Chontales. Managua.
—— (1968?) "Monografía de León." León. Colección Nicaragua, No. 10.

Peru

Centro de Investigaciones Sociales por Muestreo. Servicio del Empleo y Recursos Humanos (1968) Estudio de la ciudad de Iquitos: Movilidad ocupacional, educación, migración, encuesta de hogares de Iquitos. Lima.
DOZIER, C. L. (1970) "Peru's Chimbote Project: a government effort in desert development and colonization." Annals of the Southeastern Conference on Latin Amer. Studies (SECOLAS) 1 (March): 69-76.
Sociedad Geográfica de Lima (1968) "El tercer centenario de Puno." Boletín de la Sociedad Geográfica de Lima 87 (January-December): 7-34.

Puerto Rico

ROGLER, L. (1970) "To be or not to be political: a dilemma of Puerto Rican migrant associations," in E. Brody, ed., Behavior in New Environments: Adaptation of Migrant Populations. Beverly Hills, Calif.: Sage Pubns.

Venezuela

HOSKIN, G. (1968) "Power structure in a Venezuelan town: the case of San Cristóbal." International J. of Comparative Sociology (Toronto) 9 (September-December).
Instituto de Investigaciones Económicas (1969) Presupuestos familiares e índice de costo de vida de la ciudad de Valera, años 1966-1968. Mérida: Universidad de Los Andes.
── (1968) Presupuestos familiares e índice de costo de vida de la ciudad de Mérida. Mérida: Universidad de Los Andes Facultad de Economía.
── (1968) Incidencia de la Universidad de Los Andes en el desarrollo urbano de Mérida: Crecimiento físico. Mérida: Universidad de Los Andes.

COUNTRIES IN GENERAL

Argentina

BAILY, S. L. (1970) "The Italians and the development of organized labor in Argentina, Brazil, and the United States: 1880-1914." J. of Social History 3 (Winter): 123-134.
BASALDUA, R. and O. A. MORENO (1969) "Institucionalización de un área metropolitana en Argentina." Revista de la Sociedad Interamericana de Planificación 3 (March-June): 39-43.
CORTES CONDE, R. (1968) "Tendencias en el crecimiento de la población urbana en Argentina." Presented at the Thirty-Eighth Congress of Americanists, Stuttgart.
CORWIN, A. F. (1970) "Argentina's war on poverty: a lesson for Tío Sam? " Urban Affairs Q. 5 (June): 412-421.
GUAIA, E. (1969) "Política nacional de vivienda. Conferencia del Secretario de Estado de Vivienda pronunciada en el Centro Argentino de Ingenieros el 21 de mayo de 1969." Poder Ejecutivo Nacional, Buenos Aires.
HARDOY, J. E. and L. A. ROMERO (1971) "La ciudad argentina en el período precensal (1516-1869)." Revista de la Sociedad Interamericana de Planificación 5 (March-June): 16-39.
LLOSAS, H. P. (1969) "La política de promoción industrial y de desarrollo regional en la Argentina, 1959-1966." Económica 15 (January-April): 39-91.
LOPEZ, A. (1971) Historia del movimiento social y la clase obrera argentina. Buenos Aires.
Ministerio de Bienestar Social. Secretaría de Estado de Vivienda (1970) Acción pública y privada en vivienda: Datos al 31-12-69. Buenos Aires.
── (1969) Acción en vivienda, 1968-1969. Buenos Aires.
── (1969) Imágenes de vivienda. Buenos Aires.

— — (1969) Inversión en vivienda. Participación del sector público. Aporte a las Segundas Jornadas de Finanzas Públicas Organizadas por la Universidad de Córdoba. August.

— — (1969) Programas oficiales de vivienda en la República Argentina. Trabajo presentado por la Delegación Oficial Argentina al II Congreso Interamericano de Caracas. February, Buenos Aires.

PORTNOY, L. et al. (1967?) "Financiamiento de la vivienda." Buenos Aires: Universidad de Buenos Aires, Centro de Investigación Aplicada, No. 6.

RANDLE, P. H. (1969) "Estructuras urbanas pampeanas." Cahiers des Amériques Latines 3 (January-June): 87-123.

— — (1969) La ciudad pampeana: Geografía histórica. Mexico: Universidad Nacional Autónoma de México.

RATIER, H. E. (1969) "De Empedrado a Isla Maciel: dos polos del camino migratorio." Etnia (Buenos Aires) 9 (January-June): 1-9.

RECCHINI DE LATTES, Z. L. and A. E. LATTES (1969) Migraciones en la Argentina: Estudio de las migraciones internas e internacionales, basado en datos censales, 1869-1960. Buenos Aires: Editorial del Instituto Torcuato di Tella.

ROULET, E. (1969) "La red urbana en una región subdesarrollada: La región Nordeste de la Argentina." Desarrollo Económico 9 (April-June): 195-234.

VAPNARSKY, C. A. (1969) Población urbana y población metropolitana: Criterios para el relevamiento de información censal en la Argentina. Buenos Aires: Editorial del Instituto Torcuato di Tella.

— — (1969) "On rank-size distribution of cities: an ecological approach." Economic Development and Cultural Change 17: 584-595.

VILLASCUERNA, I. (1970) Bibliografía para el estudio histórico de la marginalidad en el Noroeste de Argentina. Buenos Aires: Editorial del Instituto Torcuato di Tella.

Bolivia

BUECHLER, H. C. (1970) "The ritual dimension of rural-urban networks: the fiesta system in the Northern Highlands of Bolivia," pp. 62-71 in W. P. Mangin, ed., Peasants in Cities: Readings in the Anthropology of Urbanization. Boston.

GUMUCIO GRANIER, J. (1968) Evaluación del desarrollo social en Bolivia." América Latina 11 (July-September): 124-137.

MARSCHALL, K. B. DE (1970) "La formación de nuevos pueblos en Bolivia: proceso e implicaciones." Estudios Andinos 1: 23-37.

— — (1970) "Cabildos, corregimientos y sindicatos en Bolivia después de 1952." Estudios Andinos 1: 61-78.

PRESTON, D. A. (1970) "New towns—a major change in the rural settlement pattern in Highland Bolivia." J. of Latin Amer. Studies 2: 1-27.

REYE, U. (1970) "Aspectos sociales de la colonización del Oriente boliviana." Aportes 17 (July): 50-79.

Brazil

BAILY, S. L. (1970) "The Italians and the development of organized labor in Argentina, Brazil, and the United States: 1880-1914." J. of Social History 3 (Winter): 123-134.

Banco do Nordeste do Brasil S.A., Departamento de Estudos Econômicos do Nordeste. (1969) Distribução e níveis da renda familiar no Nordeste urbano. Fortaleza, Ceará.

BECKER, B. K. (1968) "As migrações internas no Brasil. Reflexos de uma organização do espaço desequilibrada." Revista Brasileira de Geografia 30 (April-June): 98-116.

BYARS, R. (1971) "Culture, politics and the urban factory worker in Brazil: the case of Ze Maria." Presented at the Conference on Modernization and Urbanization Problems in Latin America, University of Illinois, Urbana.

CANO, W. (1968) "Industrialização e absorção de mão-de-obra no Brasil." Industria e Produtividade (Rio de Janeiro) 1 (June): 84-91.

Conjuntura Econômica (1969) "Housing program in Minas Gerais." Volume 23 (September): 58-63.

—— (1969) "Construções não residenciais no Nordeste." Volume 23 (April): 49-57.

—— (1968) "Real estate–apartments sought." Volume 22 (October): 41-44.

CORREA, R. L. (1969) "Os estudos de rêdes urbanas no Brasil." Revista Brasileira de Geografia 31, 4: 93-116.

—— (1968) "Contribução ao estudo do papel dirigente das metrópoles brasileiras." Revista Brasileira de Geografia 30 (April-June): 56-77.

COSTA, L. C. (1969) "Política de urbanização." Revista de Administração Municipal 97 (November-December): 637-654.

DALAND, R. T. (1970) Brazilian Planning: Development, Politics, and Administration. Chapel Hill: Univ. of North Carolina Press.

DIEGUES JUNIOR, M. (1968) "Las instituciones brasileñas: características originales y transformaciones actuales." Aportes 10 (October): 85-105.

FISCHLOWITZ, E. (1969) "Brasil em face do intercambio migratório internacional." Revista de Ciência Política (Fundação Getúlio Vargas) 3 (September): 83-104.

GARCIA-ZAMOR, J. C. (1970) "Social mobility of Negroes in Brazil." J. of Inter-Amer. Studies and World Affairs 12 (April): 242-254.

GORDER, Z. A. (1968) "Pelotas: uma experiência de Conselho Comunitário." Revista de Administração Municipal 15 (March-April): 181-188.

GRAHAM, D. H. (1970) "Divergent and convergent regional economic growth and internal migration in Brazil, 1940-1960." Economic Development and Cultural Change 18 (April): 362-382.

KUBAT, D. and F. A. MOURAO (1971?) "Optimum size of the Brazilian city-dwelling family." Ciências Econômicas e Sociais (São Paulo) 4.

KUBAT, D. and S. E. BOSCO (1969) "Marital status and ideology of the family size: case of young men in urban Brazil." América Latina 12 (April-June): 17-34.

LAMOUNIER, B. (1968) "Política e tensões estruturais no Brasil: teste preliminar de uma hipótese." Dados (Rio de Janeiro) 4: 186-198.

LELOUP, Y. (1970) Les villes du Minas Gerais. Paris: L'Institut des Hautes Etudes de L'Amérique Latine. Travaux et Memoires, No. 25.

MARTINS, F. H. et al. (1970) "Cidade e região no sudoeste paranaense." Revista Brasileira de Geografia 32 (April-June): 3-155.

MELLO, D. L. DE, and C. de BARROS LOYOLA (1970) "Aspectos institucionais da marginalidade urbana." Revista de Administração Municipal 102 (September/October): 7-32.

Ministério do Interior, Serviço Federal de Habitaçao e Urbanismo (1971). Organização administrativa das áreas metropolitanas. Brasília.

—— (1971) Orientação quanto à elaboração e à apresentação dos planos micro-regionais de desenvolvimento integrado. Brasília.

—— (1971) CIDUL: Informação para o planejamento. Brasília.

—— Serviço Nacional dos Municípios (1969). Plano municipal de desenvolvimento integrado. Brasília.

MORSE, R. M. (1969) "Cities and society in nineteenth century Latin America: the illustrative case of Brazil," in J. E. Hardoy and R. P. Schaedel, eds., The Urbanization Process in America from its Origins to the Present Day. Buenos Aires: Editorial del Instituto Torcuato di Tella.

MOURA, H. A. DE (1969) "Consumo alimentar no Nordeste urbano." Revista Econômica (Fortaleza, Ceará) 1 (July-September): 18-48.

OLIVEIRA, F. and G. BOLAFFI (1970) "Aspectos metodológicos do planejamento urbano no Brasil: Resenha bibliográfica." Revista de Administração de Emprêsas 10 (March): 155-162.

OLIVEIRA, R. C. DE (1968) Urbanização e tribalismo: a integração dos índios Terena numa sociedade de classes. Rio de Janeiro and São Paulo: Zahar Editores. Coleção de Etnologia Brasileira.

QUEIROZ, M.I.P. DE (1969) "Favelas urbanas, favelas rurais." Revista do Instituto de Estudos Brasileiros 7: 81-102.

REIS FILHO, N. G. (1968) Evolução urbana do Brasil. São Paulo: Editôra da Universidade de São Paulo.

RIOS, J. A. (1971) "The growth of cities and urban development," pp. 269-288 in J. Saunders, ed., Modern Brazil: New Patterns and Development. Gainesville: Univ. of Florida Press.

RIOS, P. L. (1969) "Urban-rural developmental interrelationships in Minas Gerais, Brazil, 1940-1960." Ph.D. dissertation. Iowa State University.

SAHOTA, G. S. (1968) "An economic analysis of internal migration in Brazil." J. of Pol. Economy (Chicago) 76 (March-April): 218-245.

SINGER, P. (1968) "Desenvolvimento econômico e evolução urbana: Análise da evolução econômica de São Paulo, Blumenau, Pôrto Alegre, Belo Horizonte e Recife." São Paulo: Universidade de São Paulo, Biblioteca Universitária, Ciências Sociais, Série 2, No. 22.

SOARES, M. T. DE S. (1968) "A organização interna das cidades brasileiras segundo seu estágio de desenvolvimento." Boletim Geográfico (Rio de Janeiro) 27 (March/April): 86-93.

SOUZA, W.P.A. DE (1970) "O planejamento regional no federalismo brasileiro." Revista Brasileira de Estudos Políticos 28 (January): 113-224.

TRINDALE, M. (1969) "O plano nacional de habitação." Revista de Administração Municipal 15 (January-February): 300-312.

TRUSKIER, A. "The politics of violence: the urban guerrilla in Brazil." Ramparts 9 (October): 31-34, 39.

WEFFORT, F. C. (1968) "Clases populares y desarrollo social: contribución al estudio del 'populismo.' " Revista Paraguaya de Sociología 5 (December): 62-150.

Caribbean

CLARKE, C. G. (1971) "Residential segregation and intermarriage in San Fernando, Trinidad." Geographical Rev. 61 (April): 198-218.

DUNCAN, N. (1970) "The political process and attitudes and opinions in a Jamaican parish council." Social and Economic Studies (Jamaica) 19 (March): 89-113.

GONZALEZ, N.L.S. (1970) Black Carib Household Structure: A Study of Migration and Modernization. Seattle: Univ. of Washington Press.

GRANT, C. H. (1971) "Company towns in the Caribbean: a preliminary analysis of Christianbury-Wismar-MacKenzie." Caribbean Studies 2 (April): 46-72.

LOPEZ TORO, A. (1970) "Migración y marginalidad urbana en países subdesarrollados (Trinidad)." Demografía y Economía 4, 2: 192-209.

MACK, R. W. (1968) "Race, power and class in an urban plutocracy: Barbados," in S. Greer et al., eds., The New Urbanization. New York: St. Martin's Press.

MILLS, G. E. (1970) "Public administration in the Commonwealth Caribbean: evolution, conflicts and challenges." Social and Economic Studies 19 (March): 5-25.

SEGAL, A. (1969) "Politics and population in the Caribbean." Río Piedras, P.R.: University of Puerto Rico, Institute of Caribbean Studies, Special Study No. 7.

Trinidad and Tobago, Central Statistical Office (1968) "Housing report: existing accommodations." CSSP, No. 10 (January).

Chile

ALZAMORA K., P. "Estructura político-administrativa para la planificación urbana en Chile: Limitaciones y perspectivas." Revista de Planificación (Santiago de Chile) 5 (March): 69-84.

BEHRMAN, L. C. (1970) "Political development and secularization in two Chilean urban communities." Prepared for delivery at American Political Science Association Annual Meeting, Los Angeles, September.

BURKE, T. R. (1970) "Law and development: the Chilean housing program." Lawyer of the Americas (Coral Gables, Fla.) 2 (June): 173-199.

CONNING, A. M. (1971) "Rural community differentiation and the rate of rural-urban migration in Chile." Rural Sociology 36 (September): 296-314.

–– (1969) "Origin variables affecting rural-urban outmigration: a theoretical framework and an exploratory study of seven rural Chilean communities." Ph.D. dissertation. Cornell University.

FRANKENHOFF, C. A. (1970) "Housing in Chile: the economics of stimulus-response." J. of Inter-Amer. Studies and World Affairs 12 (July): 379-391.

GUARDA, G. (1968) "La ciudad chilena del siglo XVIII." Buenos Aires. La urbanización en América Latina. Monografías de historia urbana, No. 2.

GURRIERI, A. (1968) "Consideraciones sobre los sindicatos chilenos." Aportes 9 (July): 77-114.

JOHNSON, D. L. (1968-69) "The national and progressive bourgeoisie in Chile." Studies in Comparative International Development 4, 4.

MATETIC FERNANDEZ, J. "Migration problems in Chile." Migration News 20, 1: 12-16.

MERRILL, R. N. (1971) "Toward a structural housing policy: an analysis of Chile's low income housing program." Ph.D. dissertation. Cornell University.

PETRAS, J. (1969) Political and Social Forces in Chilean Development. Berkeley and Los Angeles: Univ. of California Press.

–– (1969) "La política de integración: la burocracia chilena." Desarrollo Económico 9 (April-June): 67-94.

PORTES, A. (1970) "The Chilean urban slum: types and correlates." Presented at the Midwestern Sociological Society meeting, St. Louis.

SANDERS, T. G. "Juan Pérez buys a house: housing options for the Chilean worker." American Universities Field Staff. West Coast South America series, No. 16 (April).

Colombia

ANGULO, A., S. J. (1969) "El movimiento de la población colombiana." Bogotá: Centro de Investigaciones y Acción Social. Colección Monografías y Documentos, No. 4.

CAMACHO, A. and N. CAMACHO (1970) "Colombia: obreros marginados y participación electoral." Revista Mexicana de Sociología 32 (January-February): 35-48.

CARDONA GUTIERREZ, R. (1970) Migración y desarrollo urbano en Colombia. Bogotá: Asociación Colombiana de Facultades de Medicina.

–– (1969) "Las invasiones de terrenos urbanos: elementos para un diagnóstico." Bogotá: Colección el Dedo en la Herida, No. 33.

Centro de Investigaciones para el Desarrollo (CID) (1968) "Política urbana y alternativas de desarrollo." Bogotá: Universidad Nacional de Colombia. (mimeo)

COBOS, E. P. (1969) "Sottosviluppo, orbanizzazione e azione comunitaria in Colombia." International Rev. of Community Development 21-22 (December): 221-244.

Departamento Nacional de Planeación, Unidad de Recursos Humanos, División Socio-Demográfica (1969) "La población en Colombia: Diagnóstico y Política." Revista de Planeación y Desarrollo 1 (December): 19-81.

DUQUE YEPES, J. F. (1968) Municipios de Colombia: Granada-Antioquia, 1807-1968. Medellín.

FLINN, W. L. and J. W. CONVERSE (1970) "Eight assumptions concerning rural-urban migration in Colombia: a three-shantytown test." Land Economics 46, 4: 456-466.

FORNAGUERA, M. (1969) Colombia: Ordenación del territorio en base del epicentrismo regional. Bogotá: Universidad Nacional de Colombia, Centro de Investigaciones para el Desarrollo.

GARCIA NAVIA, C. (1968) "Movilidad ocupacional: Análisis de una encuesta en cinco ciudades colombianas." Bogotá: Universidad de Los Andes, Centro de Estudios sobre Desarrollo Económico (CEDE), Monografía No. 26.

Instituto de Crédito Territorial (1969?) Vivienda y desarrollo urbano. Bogotá.

—— (1968?) Conjunto habitacional "Paulo VI." Bogotá.

—— (1968) Plan de mejoramiento de barrios. Cartagena. Memoria al XII Congreso Panamericano de Arquitectos. Bogotá.

—— Oficina de Planeación (1970) Informe para la programación del barrio Alboraya. Bogotá.

—— (1970) Vivienda y desarrollo urbano. Informe al Señor Presidente de la República ... por el Gerente General del ICT y Director del Seminario Mundial sobre Mejoramiento de Tugurios y Asentamientos no Controlados. Bogotá.

ISAZA B., R. and F. J. ORTEGA (1969) "Encuestas urbanas de empleo y desempleo: Análisis de resultados." Bogotá: Universidad de Los Andes, Centro de Estudios sobre Desarrollo Económico (CEDE), Monografía No. 29.

LOPEZ TORO, A. (1968) "Migración y cambio social en Antioquia durante el siglo XIX." Demografía y Economía 2: 351-403. Also Bogotá: Universidad de Los Andes, 1970.

—— (1968) Análisis demográfico de los censos colombianos 1951 y 1964. Bogotá: Ediciones Universidad de Los Andes.

MAINGOT, A. P. (1969) "Social structure, social status, and civil-military conflict in urban Colombia, 1810-1858," pp. 297-355 in S. Thernstrom and R. Bennett, eds., Nineteenth Century Cities. New Haven, Conn.: Yale Univ. Press.

MORCILLO, P. P. (1968) Las condiciones para la planeación departamental y municipal en Colombia. VII Congreso Nacional de Municipalidades, Cúcuta, February.

Municipios Asociados del Valle del Aburra (1969) Compilación de disposiciones legales sobre planeación, áreas metropolitanas y asociaciones de municipios y comentarios. Medellín.

—— (1969) Proyectos de ley sobre áreas metropolitanas, planeación y desarrollo urbano. Medellín.

—— Departamento Administrativo de Planeación Nacional, Oficina de Planeación Nacional (1968) Programación de los estudios para el Plan de desarrollo integral, regional y metropolitano del Valle del Aburra. Medellín.

SANTA, E. (1969) Realidad y futuro del municipio colombiano. Bogotá: Universidad Nacional de Colombia.

VILLEGAS MORENO, L. A. (1969?) "Aspectos económicos de la política de vivencia del Instituto de Crédito Territorial." IX Congreso Nacional de Ingeniería, Pereira, December, 1968. Bogotá.

WATSON, L. C. (1968) "Guajiro personality and urbanization." University of California at Los Angeles, Latin American Studies Series, No. 10.

WEISS, A. (1968) "Tendencias de la participación electoral en Colombia, 1935-1966." Bogotá: Universidad Nacional de Colombia. Presente y Futuro de América Latina, No. 2.

Costa Rica

BAKER, C. E., R. FERNANDEZ PINTO, and S. Z. STONE (1971) "Municipal government in Costa Rica: Its characteristics and functions." San José: Associated Colleges of the Midwest Central American Field Program and School of Political Science, University of Costa Rica. AID/ACM Contract No. AID-515-198-T.

CHAVES, L. F. (1970) "Observaciones sobre el sistema de ciudades en Costa Rica." Informe Semestral (July-December): 109-117. Translated from Przeglad Geograficzny.

GIBSON, J. R. (1970) "A demographic analysis of urbanization: evolution of a system of cities in Honduras, El Salvador and Costa Rica." Ph.D. dissertation. Cornell University.

Cuba

ACOSTA, M. and J. E. HARDOY (1971) "Políticas urbanas y reforma urbana en Cuba." Buenos Aires: Centro de Estudios Urbanos y Regionales, Instituto Torcuato di Tella. Working paper. (mimeo)
— — (1971) Reforma urbana en Cuba revolucionaria. Caracas: Ediciones Síntesis Dos Mil.
HARDOY, J. E. (1970) "Urban land policies and land use control measures in Cuba." Report for the United Nations Centre for Housing, Building and Planning.
MERCADO, R. (1969) La reforma urbana. Lima: Fondo de Cultura Popular.

Dominican Republic

Estudios Sociales (Santo Domingo) (n.d.) "Análisis sociográfico de una pequeña ciudad de la República Dominicana." Cotuí. 2
SCOTT, I. A. (1971) "Regional development in the Dominican Republic: an assessment of the spatial dynamics of economic activity in the Dominican Republic in the period 1958-1968 and a review of alternative strategies for regional planning in the context of political, technical and information constraints." Durham, Eng.: University of Durham, Department of Geography.

Ecuador

Junta Nacional de Planificación y Coordinación Económica (1969) Normas sobre presupuestos por programas para los municipios. Quito.
— — (1969?) Encuesta de fecundidad levantada en las principales ciudades y en algunas parroquias rurales del país. Año 1967. Quito.

El Salvador

GIBSON, J. R. (1970) "A demographic analysis of urbanization: evolution of a system of cities in Honduras, El Salvador and Costa Rica." Ph.D. dissertation. Cornell University.
REED, M. E. (1970) "The effect of the presence of change agencies on the modernity of attitudes of individuals in El Salvadoran villages." Ph.D. dissertation. University of California.

Guatemala

AMARO VICTORIA, N. (1968) Encuesta sobre el condicionamiento socio-cultural de la fecundidad en áreas marginales, urbanas, metropolitanas, ladinorurales e indígenas-tradicionales. (Primera parte: Marco teórico y metodológico.) Guatemala: Instituto Centroamericano de Población y Familia. Ediciones ICAPF-IDESAC, Vol. 5.
DURSTON, J. W. (1970) "Institutional differentiation in Guatemalan communities." Part 1. Economic Development and Cultural Change 18 (July): 598-617.
HOY, D. R. (1970) "A review of development planning in Guatemala." J. of Inter-Amer. Studies and World Affairs 12 (April): 217-228.
JICKLING, D. (1968) "Human resources in local government: a vital factor in Guatemalan development," pp. 72-86 in F. T. Bachmura, ed., Human Resources in Latin America. Bloomington: Indiana University Business Paper 16.
MICKLIN, M. (1969) "Urbanization, technology, and traditional values in Guatemala: some consequences of a changing social structure." Social Forces 47 (June): 438-446.
TONESS, O. A., Jr. (1969) Relaciones de poder en un barrio marginal de Centroamérica. Guatemala: Editorial José de Pineda Ibarra.

280 *Latin American Urban Research*

Honduras

GIBSON, J. R. (1970) "A demographic analysis of urbanization: evolution of a system of cities in Honduras, El Salvador and Costa Rica." Ph.D. dissertation. Cornell University.
PETERSON, D. D. (1970) "A study of manpower requirements in selected Honduran communities with implications for secondary education program development." Ph.D. dissertation. University of Pittsburgh.

Mexico

ALVARADO, R. (1970) "Proyección de la población total en 1960-2000 y de la población económicamente activa 1960-1985." Revista Mexicana de Sociología 32.
BALL, J. M. (1971) Migration and the Rural Municipio in Mexico. Atlanta: Georgia State University, Bureau of Business and Economic Research.
BATAILLON, C. (1971) Ville et campagnes dans la région de Mexico. Paris: Editions Anthropos.
BUIRA, A. (1969) "Desarrollo y estabilidad de precios en México." Demografía y Economía 2: 309-327.
CARDENAS, L., Jr. (1970) "Trends and problems of urbanization in the United States–Mexico border area," pp. 39-54 in E. R. Stoddard, ed., Comparative U.S.-Mexico Border Studies. El Paso, Texas: Border State Consortium for Latin America, Occasional Paper 1.
CASTRO MORALES, E. et al. (1969) Estudios y documentos de la région de Puebla-Tlaxcala. Puebla: Universidad Autónoma de Puebla.
CORDERO, E. (1968) "La subestimación de la mortalidad infantil en México." Demografía y Economía 2: 44-62.
FOX, D. J. (1969) "Urbanization and economic development in Mexico," in Latin American Publications Fund, Cities in a Changing Latin America: Two Studies of Urban Growth in the Development of Mexico and Venezuela. London.
GIBSON, C. (1969) "Spanish-Indian institutions and colonial urbanism in New Spain," in J. E. Hardoy and R. P. Schaedel, eds., The Urbanization Process in America from its Origins to the Present Day. Buenos Aires: Editorial del Instituto Torcuato di Tella.
ISBISTER, J. (1971) "Urban employment and wages in a developing economy: the case of Mexico." Economic Development and Cultural Change 20 (October): 24-46.
LAJOUS VARGAS, A. (1968) "Aspectos regionales de la expansión de la educación superior en México, 1959-1967." Demografía y Economía 2: 404-427.
MORENO TOSCANO, A. (1970) "Economía regional y urbanización: tres ejemplos de relación entre ciudades y regiones en Nueva España a finales del siglo XVIII." Paper for Thirty-Ninth Congress of Americanists, August 2-9, Lima.
NIE, N. H., A. B. POWELL, and K. PREWITT (1969) "Social structure and political participation: developmental relations." Amer. Pol. Sci. Rev. 58, 2 (June) and 3 (September): 808-832.
PEREZ JIMENEZ, G. (1968) La institución del municipio libre: Prontuario de legislación orgánica municipal. Mexico.
PONTONES CHICO, E. (1968) "La migración interna en México." Investigación Económica (Mexico) 28 (June-December): 197-211.
RAMOS G., S. (1970) "El proceso de urbanización ecológico-demográfico en México." Revista Mexicana de Sociología 5 (September-October): 1251-1270.
REYNA, J. L. (1968) "Algunas dimensiones de la movilidad ocupacional en México: un análisis global." Demografía y Economía 2: 241-259.
ROLLWAGEN, J. R. (1971) "Region of origin and rural-urban migration in Mexico: some general comments and a case study of entrepreneurial migration from the West." International Migration Rev. 5 (Fall): 325-338.
SINGER, M. (1969) Growth, equality and the Mexican experience. University of Texas Latin American monographs 16.

STANISLAWSKI, D. (1969) The anatomy of eleven towns in Michoacán. Westport, Conn.: Greenwood Press, Inc. Reprint of 1950 edition, University of Texas Latin American monographs 10.

STOLTMAN, J. P. and J. M. BALL (1971) "Migration and the local economic factor in rural Mexico." Human Organization 30 (Spring): 47-56.

UGALDE, A. (1969) "Conflict and consensus in a Mexican city: a study of political integration." Ph.D. dissertation. Stanford University.

UNIKEL, L. (1970) "El proceso de urbanización," pp. 221-229 in El perfil de México en 1980. Mexico: Universidad Nacional Autónoma de México, Instituto de Investigaciones Sociales.

UNIKEL, L. and A. NECOCHEA (1971) "Jerarquía y sistema de ciudades en México." Demografía y Economía 5, 1: 27-39.

UNIKEL, L. and F. TORRES (1970) "La población económicamente activa en México y sus principales ciudades, 1940-1960." Demografía y Economía 4, 1: 1-42.

Universidad Nacional Autónoma de México (1969) Proyecciones de la población de México: Proyección de la población urbana, semiurbana y rural de los municipios de la República Mexicana al 1 de enero de 1968 y al 28 de enero de 1970. Mexico.

Panama

ESCALA, V. (1969) "La planificación en Panamá." Revista de la Sociedad Interamericana de Planificación 3 (March-June): 33-38.

Paraguay

RIVAROLA, D. and G. HEISECKE, eds. (1969) Población, urbanización y recursos humanos en el Paraguay. Asunción: Centro Paraguayo de Estudios Sociológicos.

Universidad Nacional de Asunción, Facultad de Arquitectura (1970) Ciudad de Puerto Presidente Stroessner. Estudio socio económico. Propuesta de desarrollo urbano. Asunción: Universidad Nacional de Asunción.

—— (1968) Censo de población y vivienda, Puerto Presidente Stroessner-Puerto Presidente Franco. Asunción: Universidad Nacional de Asunción.

Peru

Acción Comunitaria del Perú (1969) "Estudio económico familiar de Pamplona Alta." Lima, July.

ALBERTI, G. (1970) "Inter-village systems development: a study of social change in highland Peru." Ph.D. dissertation. Cornell University.

BERTOLI, F. and F. PORTOCARRERO (1968) "La modernización y la migración interna en el Perú." Lima: Instituto de Estudios Peruanos. Serie urbanización, migración y cambios, No. 2.

BOGGIO CARRILLO, K. (1969) Estudio de los rituales del ciclo vital en Pamplona Alta. Lima: Centro de Estudios y Promoción del Desarrollo.

BUESCO, M. (1968) Planificação, a experiência dos Incas. Verbum (Rio de Janeiro) 25 (March): 33-53.

CLAUX CARRIQUIRY, I. (1968) "Ayuda técnica para 'La Flor.' " M.A. thesis. Universidad Nacional de Ingeniería, Facultad de Arquitectura.

COTLER, J. (1970) "The mechanics of internal domination and social change in Peru," pp. 407-444 in I. L. Horowitz, ed., Masses in Latin America. New York.

—— (1971) "Tipología política de las ciudades peruanas." (mimeo)

DELGADO, C. (1969) "An analysis of 'arribismo' in Peru." Human Organization 28, 2: 113-39.

Dirección Nacional de Estadísticas y Censos (1969) Informe de fecundidad en el Agustino. Lima. April

FLORES BAO, F. et al., ed. (1967) Urbanismo y vivienda. Lima: Oficina Nacional de Planeamiento y Urbanismo.

GURRIERI, A. (1969) La mujer jóven y el trabajo (Un estudio en el Perú). Santiago, Chile: Instituto Latinoamericano de Planificación Económica y Social. May.

Junta Nacional de la Vivienda (1968) Información sobre la labor de la Junta Nacional de la Vivienda dada en la conferencia de prensa del 12 de enero de 1968. Lima.

LARSON, M. S. and A. E. BERGMAN (1969) Social Stratification in Peru. Berkeley, California: Institute of International Studies.

MANGIN, W. P. (1970) "Urbanization case history in Peru," pp. 47-54 in W. P. Mangin, ed., Peasants in Cities: Readings in the Anthropology of Urbanization. Boston.

Oficina Nacional de Desarrollo de Pueblos Jóvenes (ONDPJ) (1969) "Ponencia presentada por la ONDPJ al Seminario de Asentamientos Populares organizado por el A.I.D." Washington, D.C. Boletín No. 5.

–– (1969) Plan de ácción inmediata (a ejecutarse en los pueblos jóvenes de los distritos de San Martín de Porres, Independencia, Comas, Surco y Chorrillos). Lima. June.

–– (1969) "Organización y funcionamiento de las oficinas locales de desarrollo de pueblos jóvenes." Lima. Boletín No. 4.

–– (1969) "Normas generales para el establecimiento de oficinas locales." Lima. Boletín No. 3.

–– (1969) "La organización para el desarrollo de los pueblos jóvenes." Lima. Boletín No. 2.

–– (1969) "Esquema de organización y funcionamiento." Lima. Boletín No. 1.

ROEL PINEDA, V. (1968) La planificación económica en el Perú. Lima: Editorial Gráfica Labor.

ROLLAND, T. and G. PAULSTON (1969) "Educación y el cambio dirigido de la comunidad. Una bibliografía anotada con referencia especial al Perú." Cambridge, Mass.: Harvard University Center for Studies in Education and Development, Occasional Papers No. 3, April.

SCHAEDEL, R. P. (1969) "Patrones de poblamiento del Altiplano Sur-peruano: Una hipótesis sobre la urbanización subdesarrollada." Etnia 10 (July-December): 1-7.

Puerto Rico

BELCHER, J. C. and P. V. VAZQUEZ CALCERRADA (1969) "Factores que influyen en los niveles de vida en Puerto Rico." Caribbean Studies 9: 95-103.

MONTOULIEU, E. (1968) "La administración de terrenos de Puerto Rico y su programa de adquisición anticipada de terrenos." Revista de la Sociedad Interamericana de Planificación 2 (September).

Uruguay

ANDER-EGG, E. (1969) El papel del desarrollo de la comunidad en la planificación y ejecución del desarrollo nacional. Montevideo: Publicaciones del Instituto de Estudios Políticos para América Latina (I.E.P.A.L.).

AZMAREZ, C. A. and J. E. CANAS, (1969) Tupamaros. Fracaso del Ché? Un análisis objetivo de la actualidad uruguaya. Buenos Aires.

Venezuela

ALLEN, R. L. (1969) "Regional planning and development in Venezuela." Annals of Regional Sci. (December).

BAMBERGER, M. and T. A. BAUSCH (1968) "In defense of urban community development: the Venezuelan case." Rev. of Social Economy (Chicago) 26 (September): 130-144.

BARRIOS, S. and F. GONZALO (1971) "Proceso histórico del desarrollo urbano en Venezuela." Cuadernos de la Sociedad Venezolana de Planifacación 84-86 (January-March): 31-51.
CASTRO GUEVARA, J. (1968) Esquema de la evolución municipal en Venezuela. Caracas.
CHEN, C.-Y. (1968) "Migrations and occupations in Venezuela," pp. 36-48 in F. T. Bachmura, ed., Human Resources in Latin America. Bloomington: Indiana University Business Paper 16.
Corporación Venezolana de Guayana (1968) Informe anual. Caracas.
CORRALES, W. and J. GIORDINI (1971) "El desarrollo industrial en función del desarrollo urbano en Venezuela." Cuadernos de la Sociedad Venezolana de Planificación 84-86 (January-March): 53-73.
Cuadernos de la Sociedad Venezolana de Planificación (1971) "Desarrollo urbano y desarrollo nacional de Venezuela: conclusiones y recomendaciones." Volumes 84-86 (January-March): 135-142.
DINKELSPIEL, J. (1970) "Technology and tradition: regional and urban development in the Guayana." Inter-Amer. Economic Affairs 23 (Spring): 47-79.
LANDER, L. and M. J. DE RANGEL (1970) La planificación en Venezuela. Caracas: Sociedad Venezolana de Planificación.
LEVY, F. D. (1968) Economic Planning in Venezuela. New York: Praeger.
ROBINSON, D. J. (1969) "The city as centre of change in modern Venezuela," in Latin American Publications Fund, Cities in a Changing Latin America: Two Studies of Urban Growth in the Development of Mexico and Venezuela. London.
SCARPATI, R. and E. GAMUS (1969) Problemática del desarrollo de la comunidad en Venezuela. Caracas: Fondo Editorial Común S.R.L.
TRAVIESO, F. and S. BARRIOS (1971) "El sistema de ciudades en Venezuela." Cuadernos de la Sociedad Venezolana de Planificación 84-86 (January-March): 75-118.
TRAVIESO, F. and A. URDANETA (1971) "Marco de referencia del desarrollo urbano en Venezuela." Cuadernos de la Sociedad Venezolana de Planificación 84-86 (January-March): 3-30.
URDANETA, A. (1971) "Costos de urbanización en Venezuela." Cuadernos de la Sociedad Venezolana de Planificación 84-86 (January-March): 119-133.
VELAZQUEZ DE ROJAS, N. (1969) "Accidentes de tránsito en Cumaná." Ciencias Sociales (Cumaná) 5 (June): 179-206.

GENERAL LATIN AMERICA

Aportes (1970) Entire issue devoted to symposium on "Migraciones internas y desarrollo" 15.
ARRIAGA, E. E. (1970) A New Approach to the Measurements of Urbanization. Berkeley: University of California, Institute of International Studies.
BOCK, F. W. and S. IUTAKA (1969) "Rural-urban migration and social mobility. The controversy on Latin America." Rural Sociology (September): 343-355.
BORAH, W. (1971) "La influencia cultural europea en la formación del primer plan para centros urbanos que perdura hasta nuestros días." Revista de la Sociedad Interamericana de Planificación 5, 17 (March-June): 3-15. From a paper originally presented at the Thirty-Ninth International Congress of Americanists, Lima, August, 1970.
BOYCE, C. P. (n.d.) "Confronting the problem of low-income settlement in Latin America." Iowa City: Institute of Urban and Regional Research, Working Paper Series 4.
CAMINOS, H., J.F.C. TURNER and J. A. STEFFIAN (1969) "Urban dwelling environments: an elementary survey of settlements for the study of design determinants." Cambridge, Mass.: MIT Press Report 16.
CARDOSO, F. H. (1969) Sociologie du développement en Amérique Latine. Paris.

CASASCO, J. A. (1969) "The social function of the slum in Latin America: some positive aspects." Ekistics (Athens) 28 (September): 168-175. Also appears in América Latina 12 (July-September): 87-111.

CELESTIN, G. and J. M. COLOMA, (1969) La participación de la población en el desarrollo. Montevideo: Publicaciones del Instituto de Estudios Políticos para América Latina (I.E.P.A.L.).

Cuaderno Trimestral (Buenos Aires) (1969) "Misión Urbana en América Latina" (special MISUR issue on housing, squatters, slums). 4/5 (March).

DALAND, R. T. (1969) "Urbanization policy and political development in Latin America." Amer. Behavioral Scientist 12, 5: 22-33.

DIETZ, A. (1970) Housing in Latin America. Cambridge, Mass.: MIT Press.

FALS BORDA, O. (1970-1971) "Marginality and revolution in Latin America: 1809-1969." Studies in Comparative International Development. Beverly Hills, Calif.: Sage Pubns.

FLINN, W. L. and D. G. CARTANO (1970) "A comparison of the migration process to an urban barrio and to a rural community: two case studies." Inter-Amer. Economic Affairs 24 (Autumn): 37-48.

FRANK, A. G. (1970) "Urban poverty in Latin America," pp. 215-234 in I. L. Horowitz, ed., Masses in Latin America. New York: Oxford University Press.

FRIEDMANN, J. (1970) "The future of urbanization in Latin America." Studies in Comparative International Development 5: 179-202.

—— (1969) "Modelo burocrático y modelo inovador de la vida urbana." Cuadernos de Desarrollo Urbano Regional (Santiago, Chile) (March): 27-54.

GAKENHEIMER, R. A. (1970) "Administración metropolitana: Problemas y perspectivas en América Latina." Revista de la Sociedad Interamericana de Planificación 4 (March-June): 39-47.

—— (1968) "Determinantes de la estructura física de la ciudad colonial." Revista de la Sociedad Interamericana de Planificación 2 (September).

GERMANI, G. (1969-1970) "Stages of modernization in Latin America." Studies in Comparative International Development. Beverly Hills, Calif.: Sage Pubns.

GIUSTI, J. (1971) "Organizational characteristics of the Latin American urban marginal settler." International Journal of Politics 1 (Spring): 45-53.

GLASSMANN, R. M. (1969) "The limiting social and structural conditions for Latin American modernization." Social Research 36 (June): 182-205.

HARDOY, J. E. (1970) "Las formas urbanas durante los siglos XV al XVII y su utilización en América Latina." Presented to Thirty-Ninth Congress of Americanists, August 2-9, Lima.

—— (1970) "La urbanización de la población de América Latina." Historia de la cultura de América Latina II. Buenos Aires: Editorial de Instituto Torcuato di Tella.

—— (1969) "El paisaje urbano de Sudamerica." Revista de la Sociedad Interamericana de Planificación 3 (September): 27-42.

—— R. O. BASALDUA, and O. A. MORENO (1969) "La tierra urbana: políticas y mecanismos para su regulación y tenencia." Desarrollo Económico 9 (April-June): 163-194.

HARDOY, J. E. and R. P. SCHAEDEL, eds. (1969) "The urbanization process in America from its origins to the present day." Buenos Aires: Editorial del Instituto Torcuato di Tella.

HARDOY, J. E. and C. ARANOVICH (1970) "Urban scales and functions in Spanish America toward the year 1600: first conclusions." Latin American Research Rev. 5, 3: 57-91. Spanish version, "Escalas y funciones urbanas en América Hispánica hacia al año 1600: primeras conclusiones," pp. 171-208 in J. E. Hardoy and R. P. Schaedel, eds., The Urbanization Process in America from its Origins to the Present Day. Buenos Aires: Editorial del Instituto Torcuato di Tella, 1969. Amplified version, "Urbánización en América Hispánica entre 1580 y 1630." Boletín del Centro de Investigaciones Históricas y Estéticas (Caracas) 11 (1969): 9-89.

HARRIS, W. (1971) The Growth of Latin American Cities. Athens, Ohio: Ohio Univ. Press.

HERNANDEZ, P. F. (1971) "A sociologist's view of Latin American urbanism." Annals of Southeastern Conference on Latin Amer. Studies 2 (March): 73-81.

HERRERA, F. (1971) "A urbanização e o desenvolvimento econômico da América Latina." Revista de Administração Municipal 105 (March-April): 63-76. Translation of paper delivered in Santiago de Chile on October 10, 1966.

HOROWITZ, I. L., ed. (1970) Masses in Latin America. New York: Oxford Univ. Press.

HUBNER GALLO, J. I. (1968) El mito de la explosión demográfica. Buenos Aires: Joaquín Almendros Editor.

KAPLAN, M. (1968) Problemas del desarrollo y de la integración en América Latina. Caracas.

—— (1968) "Estado y urbanización en América Latina." Revista Colegio de Economistas de México, A.C. 2: 5-21.

—— (1970) "La ciudad como factor de transmisión de control socioeconómico y político externo durante el período contemporáneo." Presented to the Thirty-Ninth Congress of Americanists, August 2-9, Lima.

—— and R. O. BASALDUA (1968) Problemas estructurales de América Latina y planificación para el desarrollo. Buenos Aires.

KAUFMAN, C. (1970) "Latin American urban inquiry." Urban Affairs Q. 5 (June).

—— (1968) "Urban poverty leadership and political change in the Americas." Inter-Amer. Conference on Poverty Leadership Styles, November, Philadelphia.

KEMPER, R. V. (1970) "El estudio antropológico de la migración a las ciudades en América Latina." América Indígena 33 (July): 609-633.

LEEDS, A. (1969) "The significant variables determining the character of squatter settlements." América Latina 12 (July-September): 44-86.

LEON, P. (1969) Economies et sociétés de l'Amérique Latine. Montreal: SEDES.

MAMALAKIS, M. J. (1970) "Urbanization and sectoral transformation in Latin America, 1950-65." University of Wisconsin, Latin American Center Discussion Paper 24.

MANGALAM, J. J. (1968) Human Migration: A Guide to Migration Literature in English, 1955-1962. Lexington: Univ. of Kentucky Press.

MARGULIS, M. (1970) Aspectos ideológicos y psicosociales de la marginalidad. Aportes 15: 110-117.

MARTIN, W., ed. (1970) "Bibliography about urbanization—with emphasis on Latin America." East Lansing: Michigan State University, School of Urban Planning. (mimeo)

McDONALD, L. D. and J. S. McDONALD (1969) "Motives and objectives of migration." Ekistics 28 (November): 321-327.

MEISTER, A. (1969) "Transformazione sociale nella periferia delle grandi citta dell'America Latina: modello e prano di ricerca." International Rev. of Community Development 21-22 (December): 45-76.

MILLER, J. and R. A. GAKENHEIMER, eds. (1971) Latin American Urban Policies and the Social Sciences. Beverly Hills, Calif.: Sage Pubns.

MIN MAN-SHIK (1970) "Oriental immigrations into Latin America." Korea Observer 3 (October): 79-96.

MONTEFORTE TOLEDO, M. (1968) Bibliografía sociopolítica latinoamericana. Mexico: Universidad Nacional Autónoma de México.

MORCILLO, P. P., ed. (1971) "Política y administración en el municipio." Bogotá: Organización Interamericana de Cooperación Intermunicipal. VII Seminario Universitario sobre Asuntos Municipales, Cali, July 2-4, 1970.

MORSE, R. M. (1971) "A framework for Latin American urban history." New Haven: Center for Latin American Studies. (mimeo)

—— (1971) "Trends and issues in Latin American urban research, 1965-1970." Part I, Latin American Research Rev. 6 (Spring): 3-52; Part II, 6 (Summer): 19-75.

—— (1971) "Planning, history, politics: reflections on John Friedmann's 'the role of cities in national development,'" in J. D. Miller and R. Gakenheimer, eds., Latin American Urban Policies and the Social Sciences. Beverly Hills, Calif.: Sage Pubns.

NELSON, J. (1969) "Migrants, urban poverty and instability in developing nations." Harvard University Occasional Papers in International Affairs.

—— (1971) "The urban poor: disruption of political integration in Third World cities." World Politics 22: 393-414.

NEWTON, R. C. (1970) "On 'functional groups,' 'fragmentation' and 'pluralism' in Spanish American political society." Hispanic Amer. Historical Rev. 50, 1: 1-29.

NICHAMIN, J. (1968) "Shantytowns in Latin America: prospects for political change." Papers of the Michigan Academy of Sciences, Arts and Letters (Ann Arbor) 53: 167-175.

PEDERSON, P. O. and W. B. STOHR (1969) "Economic integration and the spatial development of South America." Amer. Behavioral Scientist 12 (May-June): 2-12.

PEDREGAL, H. (1968) "Vivienda y población." Boletín Informativo de la Dirección de Malariología y Saneamiento Ambiental de Venezuela (Caracas) 8 (February): 24-29.

PETRAS, J. F. (1969) "Class structure and its effects on political development." Social Research 36 (Summer): 206-230.

PORTES, A. (1970) "El proceso de urbanización y su impacto en la modernización de las instituciones políticas locales." Revista de la Sociedad Interamericana de Planificación 4 (March-June): 5-21.

—— (1969) "La marginalidad sorpresa." Revista del Domingo (Santiago, Chile) (October 5): 8-9.

PRESTON, D. A. (1969) "Rural emigration in Andean America." Human Organization 28 (Winter): 279-286.

RATINOFF, L. (1968-1969) "Problems in the formation and use of human capital in recent Latin American development." Studies in Comparative International Development 4, 9.

Revista de la Sociedad Interamericana de Planificación (1968) "El problema de la migración urbana en América Latina." Volume 2 (December).

ROPP, S. C. (1970) "The military and urbanization in Latin America: some implications of trends in recruitment." Inter-Amer. Economic Affairs 24 (Autumn): 27-35.

ROSON, H. (1968) "Mutaciones de la administración pública en América Latina." Economía y Ciencias Sociales 10, 2: 38-60.

SANTOS, M. (1968) "Le Rôle moteur du tertiaire primitif dans les villes du tiers monde." Civilizations 18, 2: 186-203.

SERAFINI, O. (1971) "Validación concurrente de dos tests de rendimiento utilizados en la investigación de la educación en barrios populares urbanos en Latinoamérica (CLACSO, 1970)." Revista Paraguaya de Sociología 8, 20 (January-April): 128-132.

SOLOW, A. A. (1968) "Tools and techniques for implementation of urban planning," in Urbanization in Developing Countries. The Hague: International Union of Local Authorities.

SUNKEL, O. (1968) "La tarea política y teórica del planificador en América Latina." Revista de la Sociedad Interamericana de Planificación 2 (December).

TESTA, J. C. (1970) "Las migraciones internas en el contexto del desarrollo social latinoamericano." Aportes 15: 96-109.

TURNER, J. (1968) "Uncontrolled urban settlement." International Social Development Rev. 1: 107-130.

United Nations Economic Commission for Latin America (1970) Development Problems in Latin America: An Analysis by the United Nations Economic Commission for Latin America. Austin and London: University of Texas Press.

U.S. Agency for International Development (AID) (1968) "Colonias de invasión—el problema y la oportunidad." Intercambio de Ideas y Métodos Número 63, Planeamiento Urbano 302. Washington, D.C.: Department of Housing and Urban Development.

Universidad Nacional de la Plata, Facultad de Arquitectura y Urbanismo, Biblioteca (1969) Catálogo bibliográfico. Buenos Aires. April.

URQUIDI, V. L. (1969) "El desarrollo económico y el crecimiento de la población." Demografía y Economía (Mexico) 3, 1: 94-103.

–– (1970) "Tecnología, planificación y desarrollo latinoamericano." Foro Internacional 10 (January-March): 229-236.

VALENZUELA, J. and R. POSADA (1968) Reglamento de zonificación y subdivisión de areas residenciales en América Latina. Bogotá: Organización de los Estados Americas, Centro Interamericano de Vivienda y Planeamiento.

VAN FLEET, J. A. (1969) "The popular housing sector in Latin America: its implications for urban social and economic development." Ph.D. dissertation. Syracuse University.

–– (1969) "Recursos de vivienda en comunidades marginales." Temas del Banco Interamericano de Desarrollo (U.S.) 11 (April): 18-32.

VEKEMANS, R., S. J., and J. GUISTI (1969-1970) "Marginality and ideology in Latin American development." Studies in Comparative International Development. Beverly Hills, Calif.: Sage Pubns.

VILLEGAS MORENO, L. A. (1970) Aspectos de la política social y económica de los tugurios y asentamientos no controlados. Seminario Mundial sobre Mejoramiento de Tugurios y Asentamientos no Controlados. Medellín: Instituto de Crédito Territorial. February.

VIOLICH, F. (1968) "Desarrollo comunal y planificación urbana en América Latina." Revista de la Sociedad Interamericana de Planificación 2 (December).

World Council of Churches, Secretariat for Migration (1969) Internal Migration in Latin America with Special Emphasis on Bolivia, Brazil, Peru. Geneva. Originally published in Portuguese and Spanish.

REGIONAL DEVELOPMENT AND PLANNING

BABAROVIC, I. (1967-1968) "Algunas notas sobre desarrollo regional y planificación del espacio nacional." Economía (Santiago) 26, 95-96: 17-30.

BOUDEVILLE, J. R. (1968) L'espace et les pôles de croissance. Paris: Presses Universitaires de France. Collection Bibliothèque d'Economie Contemporaine.

CASIMIR, J. (1968) "Algunas consideraciones en torno a la planificación regional en las zonas deprimidas." Revista Mexicana de Ciencia Política 14 (April-June): 273-279.

CASTILLO ROJAS, A. (1970) "Aspectos administrativos de los planes de desarrollo." Revista Mexicana de Ciencia Política 16, 60: 169-180.

CORAGGIO, J. L. (1969) "Eiementos para una discusión sobre eficiencia, equidad y conjunto entre regiones." Working paper. Buenos Aires: Centro de Estudios Urbanos y Regionales, Instituto Torcuato di Tella.

COSTA, J.M.M. DA (1968) "Planejamento regional e diversificação da economia." Revista de Administração Municipal 15 (May-June): 245-268.

DI TELLA, T. S. (1969) "El concepto de desarrollo polarizado en planeación regional: un enfoque sociológico." Revista de la Sociedad Interamericana de Planificación 3 (December): 26-31.

FRANCO NETTO, E. and L. HESS (1971) "O mobiliário urbano." Revista de Administração Municipal 18, (May-June): 23-35.

FRIEDMANN, J. (1971) "The implementation of urban-regional development policies: lessons of experience." University of California at Los Angeles, School of Architecture and Urban Planning. (mimeo)

–– (forthcoming) Urbanization, Planning and National Development. Beverly Hills, Calif.: Sage Pubns.

–– (1969) "La estrategia de los polos de crecimiento como instrumento de la política de desarrollo." Revista de la Sociedad Interamericana de Planificación 3 (March-June): 16-26.

GRAHAM, D. (1970) "Divergent and convergent regional economic growth and internal migration in Brazil, 1940-1960." Economic Development and Cultural Change 18, 3 (April): 362-82.

Instituto Panamericano de Geografía e Historia, Comité de Geografía Regional (1969) "La regionalización de las políticas de desarrollo en América Latina, conclusiones y recomendaciones." Segundo Seminario Interamericano, Santiago de Chile, September 8-12. Revista de la Sociedad Interamericana de Planificación 3 (December): 32-39.

── (1969) Documentación del Primer Seminario Interamericano sobre Regionalización. Rio de Janeiro: APEC Editóra, S.A.

KUKLINSKI, A. R. (1969) "Tendencias de la investigación del desarrollo regional integral." Desarrollo Económico (Buenos Aires) 9 (July-September): 282-300.

MACHADO, J. R., Jr. (1971) "O orçamento da Câmara de Vereadores." Revista de Administração Municipal 18 (May-June): 37-44.

── (1971) "Contrôle físico do orçamento." Revista de Administração Municipal 18 (July-August): 5-21.

── and D. L. DE MELLO, (1970) Orçamento-programa a nível municipal. Rio de Janeiro: Instituto Brasileiro de Administração Municipal.

MARTINEZ SILVA, M. (1970) "Discusiones sobre administración pública y política." Revista Mexicana de Ciencia Política 16, 60: 209-240.

MATUS ROMO, C. (1969) "El espacio físico en la política de desarrollo." Revista de la Sociedad Interamericana de Planificación 3 (December)· 17-25.

MELLO, D. L. DE (1971) "O município na organização nacional." Rio de Janeiro: Instituto Brasileiro de Administração Municipal. From a lecture given by the author at the Escola Superior de Guerra in July 1971.

MORCILLO, P. P. (1971) "Idéias para uma reforma urbana." Revista de Administração Municipal 18 (July-August): 23-38.

NEIRA ALVA, E. (1969) "La regionalización de las políticas de desarrollo en América Latina." Revista de la Sociedad Interamericana de Planificación 3 (December): 4-16.

PERLOFF, H. S. (1968) "Elementos claves de planificación regional." Revista de la Sociedad Interamericana de Planificación 2 (September).

PLANDES (Sociedad Chilena de Planificación y Desarrollo) (1968) Entire issue devoted to regional planning. Volume 26 (March-April).

POVINA, A. (1969) La integración regional y el municipio. Córdoba, Argentina: Imprenta de la Universidad Nacional de Córdoba.

ROBOCK, S. H. (1969) "Estratégias do desenvolvimento econômico." Revista Econômica (Fortaleza, Ceará) 1 (July-September): 3-17.

SARNO, B. (1971) "A habitação e os arquitetos." Revista de Administração Municipal 18 (July-August): 103-108.

STOHR, W. B. (1969) "Materials on regional development in Latin America: experience and prospects." Presented at Seminar on Social Aspects of Regional Development. Santiago, Chile, November 3-14. UN document ST/ECLA/conf. 34/L.4, Oct. 19.

── (1969) "The definition of regions in relation to national and regional development in Latin America," pp. 63-82 in Instituto Panamericano de Geografía e Historia. Comisión de Geografía. "Documentación del I Seminario sobre Regionalización." Rio de Janeiro.

United Nations (1969) "Informe final (parte tercera) del Seminario sobre Aspectos Sociales del Desarrollo Regional, Santiago de Chile, November 3-14." Revista de la Sociedad Interamericana de Planificación 3 (December): 40-52.

UTRIA, R. D. (1969) "La regionalización de la política social," p. 66 in Working Papers of the Instituto Panamericano de Geografía e Historia, Comisión de Geografía. Second Seminar on Regional Development Policy in Latin America, September 8-12, Santiago, Chile.

VELASCO IBARRA, E. et al. (1970) Administración pública y desarrollo. México: Universidad Nacional Autónoma de México, Facultad de Ciencias Políticas y Sociales.

VERA, L. (1968) "Aspectos regionales." Revista de la Sociedad Interamericana de Planificación 2 (September).

WESTEBBE, R. M. (1970) "Problemas y perspectivas de la urbanización." Finanzas y Desarrollo 7, 4 (December). Appeared simultaneously in English edition of Finance and

Development, and later in translation as "O desafio da urbanização," Revista de Administração Municipal 18 (March-April, 1971): 49-62.

GENERAL URBAN TOPICS

BALVE, B. C. and N. D'ALESSIO (1970) "Migraciones internas en el proceso productivo." Aportes 18 (October): 148-160.

Banco Hipotecario Nacional (B.A.) (1968?) Plantas de monoblock-tipo. Construídas por acción directa. Buenos Aires.

BOYCE, C. (1968) Elementos de planificación urbana. Caracas: Fundación para el Desarrollo de la Comunidad y Fomento Municipal, Departamento de Programas Municipales.

BRODE, J. (1969) The Process of Modernization: An Annotated Bibliography on the Sociocultural Aspects of Development. Cambridge, Mass.: Harvard University Center for International Affairs.

BRUNN, S. (1971) "Urbanization in developing countries: an international bibliography." Michigan State University, Latin American Studies Center Research Report 8.

BUGARIN PEREZ, I. (1969) "Las cooperativas de vivienda." Revista de Economía 32 (March): 149-154.

CASTELLS, M. (1970) "El análisis sociológico del proceso de urbanización." Santiago: Universidad Católica de Chile.

–– (1970) "Structures sociales et processus d'urbanisation: analyse comparatif intersociétale." Annales–Economies Sociétés Civilisations, 25, 4: 1155-1199.

CHUECA GOITIA, F. (1968) "Breve historia del urbanismo." Madrid: Alianza Editorial.

CINTA, R. (1969) Desarrollo económico, urbanización y radicalismo político. Boletín ELAS (Santiago de Chile) 2 (December): 31-62.

–– (1968) "Un enfoque socioeconómico de la urbanización." Demografía y Economía 2, 1: 62-80.

FLORES, E. (1968) "La gran amenaza no es el hambre, sino la desocupación." Investigación Económica (Mexico) 28 (January-June): 5-12.

FRIEDMANN, J. et al. (1970) "Urbanization and national development: a comparative analysis." University of California at Los Angeles, School of Architecture and Urban Planning. (mimeo)

GEISSE, G. (1968) "Notes on implications of a project of 'popular industries' for urban poverty leadership styles." Inter-Amer. Conference on Poverty Leadership Styles, November, Philadelphia.

GONZALEZ, N. L. (1970) "The neoteric society." Comparative Studies in Society and History 12, 1: 1-13.

GORDER, A. Z. (1968) "Programa de promoção para serviços de utilidade pública." Revista de Administração Municipal 15 (March-April): 169-180.

GRACIARENA, J. (1969) "Desarrollo, educación y ocupaciones técnicas." América Latina 12 (January-March): 17-39.

GUTIERREZ, R. C. and G. E. ALARCON (1971) "Estudio descriptivo-exploratorio sobre migración y familia." Revista Paraguaya de Sociología 8 (January-April): 115-127.

Institut International des Civilisations Différentes (1971) Les agglomérations urbaines dans les pays du Tiers Monde: Leur rôle politique, social et économique. Brussels: Editions de l'Institut de Sociologie, Université Libre de Bruxelles. Collection de l'Institut International des Civilisations Différentes.

Instituto del Cemento Portland Argentino (1968) Construcciones de hormigón para municipios. Buenos Aires.

KAHL, J. (1969) "A review of Glenn H. Beyer: the urban explosion in Latin America." Economic Development and Cultural Change 17 (April): 420-25.

LAQUIAN, A. and P. DUTTON (1971) A Selected Bibliography on Rural-Urban Migrants' Slums and Squatters in Developing Countries. Monticello, Illinois: Council of Planning Librarians.

LIMA FILHO, A. DE O. (1969) "Shopping centers como novos sistemas de operação varejista." Revista de Administração de Emprêsas 9 (June): 37-49.

MAMALAKIS, M. J. (1969) "The theory of sectoral clashes." Latin Amer. Research Rev. 4, 3: 9-46.

MANGIN, W., ed. (1970) Peasants in Cities: Readings in Urban Anthropology. Boston: Houghton Mifflin.

MARMORA, L. (1968) "Marginalidad y conciencia nacional en grupos migrantes." Aportes 7 (January): 29-46.

MARTORELLI, H. (1969) La sociedad urbana. Montevideo: Editorial Nuestra Tierra.

NORTH, G. (1970) "La remodelación urbana y la doctrina de los costos realizados." Orientación Económica 32 (February): 17-21.

PAIX, C. (1971) "L'urbanisation: statistiques et réalités." Tiers-Monde 12 (April-June): 393-411.

PEDERSON, P. O. (1970) "Innovation diffusion within and between national urban systems." Geographical Analysis 2, 3: 203-254.

PEREIRA, R. DE M. and N. FERRARI (1969) "Organização administrativa para o planejamento municipal." Rio de Janeiro: Cadernos de Administração Pública, No. 74.

PRAKASH, V. (1969) "La planificación de la inversión municipal." Revista de la Sociedad Interamericana de Planificación 3 (September).

REISSMAN, L. (1969) "Bases sociales para la acción urbana." Revista de la Sociedad Interamericana de Planificación 3 (March-June).

Revista de la Sociedad Interamericana de Planificación (1968) "La comunicación en la planificación urbana." Revista de la Sociedad Interamericana de Planificación 2 (December).

RODWIN, L. (1970) Nations and Cities: A Comparison of Strategies for Urban Growth. Boston: Houghton Mifflin.

ROFMAN, A. B. (1970) "La influencia del proceso histórico en la dependencia externa en la estructuración de las redes regionales y urbanas actuales." Presented to Thirty-Ninth Congress of Americanists, August 2-9, Lima.

—— (1969) "Obstáculos para las relaciones entre el científico del desarrollo urbano y regional, el político y el administrador." Working paper. Buenos Aires: Centro de Estudios Urbanos y Regionales, Instituto Torcuato de Tella.

SAJON, R. (1969) "Protección de la infancia en las zonas semi-urbanas." Boletín del Instituto Interamericano del Niño 43 (September): 326-383.

SANTOS, M., ed. (1971) "La ville et l'organisation de l'espace dans les pays en voie de développement." Revue Tiers-Monde 12 (January-March).

—— (1971) Le métier de géographe en pays sous développé: Un essai méthodologique. Paris: Editions OPHRYS.

—— (1970) Dix essais sur les villes des pays sous-développés. Paris: Editions OPHRYS.

—— (1969) "Mecanismos de crescimento urbano nos países em vias de desenvolvimento." América Latina 12, 4: 134-148.

SUBRAMANIAN, M. (1971) "An operational measure of urban concentration." Economic Development and Cultural Change 20 (October): 105-116.

THERNSTROM, S. and R. BENNETT, eds. (1969) Nineteenth Century Cities. New Haven, Conn.: Yale Univ. Press.

TINBERGEN, J. (1969) "Enlace de la planificación nacional con la planificación urbana y regional." Revista de la Sociedad Interamericana de Planificación 3 (March-June).

TROUT, G., Jr. (1968) "Urbanization as a social process: what cities do to migrants and what migrants do to cities." Paper for American Universities Field Staff Conference on Urbanization: Freedom and Diversity in the Modern City, University of Alabama, December 12-13.

TURNER, J. C. (1970) "Barriers and channels for housing development in modernizing countries," pp. 1-19 in W. P. Mangin, ed., Peasants in Cities: Readings in the Anthropology of Urbanization. Boston: Houghton Mifflin.

United Nations, Department of Economic and Social Affairs (1970) Urbanization in the Second U.N. Development Decade.

United Nations, Instituto de Crédito Territorial (1970) "Informe Final." Seminario Mundial sobre Mejoramiento de Tugurios y Asentamientos no Centralizados. Medellín. (mimeo)

URIBE, P., Jr. (1968) "Comparaciones interregionales de niveles de precios y de consumo real *per capita*." Demografía y Economía 2, 1: 81-108.

VAPNARSKY, C. A. (1969) "On rank-size distribution of cities: an ecological approach." Economic Development and Cultural Change 17, 4: 584-595.

VIDAL, E. and V. GAGLIOTTI (1968) La clase obrera: Empobrecimiento absoluto y relativo. Buenos Aires.

WILHEIM, J. (1969) Urbanismo no subdesenvolvimento. Rio de Janeiro: Editôra Sage.

YUJNOVSKY, O. and M. MALAJOVICH (1969) "Optimación de sistemas de equipamiento público." Working paper. Buenos Aires: Centro de Estudios Urbanos y Regionales, Instituto Torcuato di Tella.

ZICCARDI, H. (1969) "Locación de inmuebles y dividendos de acciones. Su tratamiento en el impuesto a las actividades lucrativas." Revista de Ciencias Económicas 57 (July-September): 349-355.

ABOUT THE AUTHORS AND EDITORS

MANUEL ACHURRA LARRAIN is an FAO consultant in fisheries economics in Latin America, based in Santiago, Chile, and is a former regional subdirector of the Chilean National Planning Office (ODEPLAN). He is also a director of the Inter-American Planning Society (SIAP) and of the Chilean Planning Society (PLANDES). He was educated at the School of Economics of the University of Chile in Santiago, and in recent years has served as professor of economic development at the University of Chile in Valparaíso. His publications include studies of the fisheries industry, and regional and national planning.

MARUJA ACOSTA LEON is a Venezuelan sociologist who is at present in charge of the "Sociological Aspects of the Process of Urbanization in Venezuela" research project for the Venezuelan Central Office of Coordination and National Planning (CORDIPLAN). She was educated at the Central University of Venezuela and has served that institution in a variety of capacities, including assistant professor of urban sociology. She also spent a research year at Yale University under the auspices of the Central University. Her publications include studies of urbanization in Caracas and (with Jorge E. Hardoy) *Reforma urbana en Cuba revolucionaria* (Caracas: 1971).

IVO BABAROVIC DENEGRI recently served as a UN Technical Assistance adviser to the Brazilian Institute of Economic and Social Planning (IPEA) and is now residing in Santiago, Chile. He was educated as a civil engineer at the University of Chile, and holds a Master's degree in regional planning from Harvard University. He has collaborated in research projects and teaching at the Centro Interdisciplinario de Desarrollo Urbano y Regional (CIDU) of the Catholic University of Chile. His publications include studies of economic and social development, regional development in Yugoslavia, and the planning of national space.

293

RAUL O. BASALDUA is an Argentine lawyer with degrees from the National University of La Plata and the University of Buenos Aires, who also studied urban and regional planning at Vanderbilt and Columbia universities. A researcher for the Centro de Estudios Urbanos y Regionales (CEUR) of the Instituto Torcuato di Tella in Buenos Aires, he also holds a career research appointment from the Argentine National Scientific and Technical Research Council. His publications include studies of urban land use and development planning. He is the author (with Jorge E. Hardoy and Oscar A. Moreno) of *Política de la tierra urbana y mecanismos para su regulación en América del Sur* (Buenos Aires: 1968).

CARLOS CALVIMONTES ROJAS, Director-General of Urban Development for the Bolivian Ministry of Urbanism and Housing, received his litentiate in architecture and urbanism from the Universidad Mayor de San Andrés in La Paz, and also holds a Master's degree in urban and regional planning. He has been associated with the Peruvian National Planning Institute, and with various Bolivian private and public planning and housing agencies. He has taught both at the Universidad Mayor de San Andrés and for the Organization of American States (OAS). His publications includes studies of housing and community facilities.

CUAUHTEMOC CARDENAS SOLORZANO, President of the Inter-American Planning Society (SIAP), is a Mexican civil engineer who is also subdirector-general of Siderúrgica Las Truchas, S.A. His association with the Río Balsas Commission dates from 1959, and many of his publications concern this agency and other regional-development agencies and projects. He is at present completing a study of "Economic growth and urbanization in Mexico."

JOSE LUIS CORAGGIO, adjunct professor in the Faculty of Economic Sciences of the National University of Buenos Aires and director of the Department of Economics of the Universidad Nacional del Sur, received his licentiate in economics from the University of Buenos Aires and is completing requirements for the Ph.D. in regional science at the University of Pennsylvania. He holds a Master's degree in regional science from that institution as well. In addition to his university duties, he has been associated with various Argentine economic agencies, and with the Centro de Estudios Urbanos y Regionales (CEUR) of the Instituto Torcuato di Tella in Buenos Aires and the Centro Interdisciplinario de Desarrollo Urbano y Regional (CIDU) of the Catholic University of Chile in Santiago. He is the author of the forthcoming *Diseño de normas para la elaboración de planes regionales, Argentina, 1970* (Instituto Torcuato di Tella) and is at present concentrating his research efforts on a project involving the localization of economic activity and spatial ordering.

GUILLERMO GEISSE GROVE, director of the Centro Interdisciplinario de Desarrollo Urbano y Regional (CIDU) of the Catholic University of Chile in

Santiago, received a degree in architecture from the Catholic University of Chile and a Master's degree in city planning from the University of California at Berkeley. He was in private architectural practice for more than a decade, and designed numerous public-housing projects in the greater Santiago area. He has also served as a consultant to various public agencies and ministries. Author of *Problemas del desarrollo urbano y regional de Chile* (Catholic University of Chile Press), he is at present completing *Urbanización y medio ambiente en América Latina* for the Centro Editor de América Latina in Buenos Aires.

JORGE E. HARDOY, former director of the Centro de Estudios Urbanos y Regionales (CEUR) of the Instituto Torcuato di Tella in Buenos Aires, earned an architecture degree from the University of Buenos Aires and M.A. and Ph.D. degrees in regional and urban planning from Harvard University. A former President of the Inter-American Planning Society (SIAP), he holds a career research appointment from the Argentine National Scientific and Technical Research Council. His publications include *Urban Planning in Pre-Columbian America* (New York: 1968), *Reforma urbana en Cuba revolucionaria* (Caracas: 1971; with Maruja Acosta), and a forthcoming illustrated study of colonial cartography in Latin America.

ANTONIO LABADIA CAUFRIEZ, former Director-General of Planning and Budget for the Chilean Ministry of Housing and Urbanism, is an architect trained at the Catholic University of Chile. He has been both a practicing architect and a professor of architecture. He has served as counselor to the Chilean Planning Society (PLANDES) and to the Chilean College of Architects.

ENRIQUE RUBEN MELCHIOR, a research economist with the Institute for Latin-American Integration (INTAL) in Buenos Aires and coordinator of the publication *Revista de la Integración* holds the licentiate in political economy from the National University of Buenos Aires. From 1962 to 1967, he was chief of the Regional Programming Section of the Argentine Federal Investment Council, and has also served or advised other Argentine government agencies. His publications include studies of Argentine and Patagonian regional development, national development strategies, and spatial integration.

PEDRO PABLO MORCILLO, secretary for public administration of the Colombian Presidency in Bogotá, holds a doctor's degree in law and political science from the National University of Bogotá and a Master's degree in urban and regional planning from the University of Pennsylvania. He has had an active teaching, administrative, and research career at the Universidad del Valle in Cali, and has served as an adviser or consultant in public administration and planning to Colombian government agencies and departments as well as to the governments of Panama and Peru. His publications include studies of regional and integral planning, and national and municipal planning laws and legislation.

OSCAR A. MORENO, who holds a research appointment with the Centro de Estudios Urbanos y Regionales (CEUR) of the Instituto Torcuato di Tella in Buenos Aires, received an honors law degree from the University of Buenos Aires. Formerly associated with the Institute of Political Economy and Finance of the Faculty of Law of the University of Buenos Aires, he has in recent years concentrated his research efforts in the area of land use studies and policies. He co-authored (with Jorge E. Hardoy and Raúl O. Basaldúa) *Política de la tierra urbana y mecanismos para su regulación en América del Sur* (Buenos Aires: 1968).

EDUARDO NEIRA ALVA, a consultant to the state government of Bahia for implementation of the Recôncavo Baiano project, is on leave from his post as Urban Development Consultant to the Inter-American Development Bank in Washington, D.C. A Peruvian with an architecture degree from the National University of Engineering and a degree in city planning from the University of Liverpool, he is a former head of the planning department of the Peruvian Ministry of Public Works and has taught at the Lima Planning Institute and at the School of Architecture and City Planning of the Central University of Venezuela. He is Editor of *Cuadernos de la Sociedad Venezolana de Planificación.*

EUGENIO PEREZ MONTAS, director of the program department of the Dominican Office of Community Development, holds an architecture degree from the University of Santo Domingo and has also studied at the University of Oregon, the Institute of Social Studies in The Hague, and the Central University of Madrid. He is a director of the Inter-American Planning Society (SIAP), and was a founding member of the Pedro Henríquez Ureña National University in Santo Domingo and director of its Department of Urbanism. He has had an active career as an architect and planner, and his publications are primarily devoted to urban and rural development and planning.

ROBERTO PINEDA GIRALDO, field director of the Inter-American Housing and Planning Center (CINVA) in Bogotá, headed the planning office of the Colombian Instituto de Crédito Territorial for six years. An anthropologist with a doctor's degree in social and economic sciences, he has been a Guggenheim Fellow and a professor at the National University in Bogotá. His research interests and publications include studies of native Indian communities in Colombia, countrywide studies leading to establishment of the Colombian social security system in rural areas, and analyses of the social situation in urban environments.

DIEGO ROBLES RIVAS, an official of the Oficina Nacional de Desarrollo de Pueblos Jóvenes (barriadas) in Lima, received a degree in architecture from the Faculty of Architecture of the Peruvian University of Engineering and also studied at the Lima Planning Institute and the Architectural Association School of Architecture's Department of Tropical Studies in London. His professional involvement in community and barriada development dates from 1959, and he has been active in such development as a researcher, teacher, planner, and government official. His publications are primarily devoted to studies of marginal settlements and communities, and urbanization.

GUILLERMO SANJINES ROJAS, director-general of urban development for the municipality of La Paz, received his licentiate in architecture and urbanism from the Universidad Mayor de San Andrés in La Paz. He also pursued special studies in housing and urban planning in Bogotá, and regional and urban planning in Paris. He is a former president of the Bolivian College of Architects and has also served as professor of regional and urban planning at the Universidad Mayor de San Andrés. Prior to assuming his present post, he served in various official capacities including director-general of Acción Comunal, director-general of the municipal agency in charge of expropriating urban land, and director-general of the municipal Department of Public Housing.

WALTER B. STOHR, associate professor of geography at McMaster University, Ontario, Canada, received his Doctor's degree in economic geography from the Hochschule fur Welthandel in Vienna. After a lengthy period of service as chief economist for the Austrian Institute for Urban and Regional Planning in Vienna, he served as Senior Regional Planning Adviser to the Chilean National Planning Office in Santiago, 1964-1969. He is the author of the forthcoming study, *Regional Development in Latin America.*

CARLOS TOBAR, a researcher with the Centro de Estudios Urbanos y Regionales (CEUR) of the Instituto Torcuato di Tella in Buenos Aires, also serves as an adviser to the directorate-general of the city of Buenos Aires' master plan and to the Argentine Consejo Nacional de Seguridad. Educated as a sociologist at the National University of Buenos Aires, he holds the licentiate in sociology from the Latin American Faculty of Social Sciences (FLACSO) in Santiago where he also pursued postgraduate studies. Active in urban development planning and research, he has also taught courses in sociology and regional development at various Argentine universities. He co-edited (with Jorge E. Hardoy) *El proceso de urbanización en América Latina* (Buenos Aires: 1969).

RUBEN D. UTRIA, a Colombian architect serving as an adviser to the United Nations in social aspects of regional development policy and planning, has long been interested in housing and community development. He has been a researcher with the Inter-American Housing Center (CINVA) in Bogotá, a professor at Colombian universities, and has served as Secretary-General of the Colombian Planning Society. His publications include studies of housing, urban planning, and community and regional development.

ABOUT THE SERIES EDITORS

FRANCINE F. RABINOVITZ is Associate Professor of Political Science at the University of California at Los Angeles. She is currently serving concurrently as a member of the faculty of the School of Architecture and Urban Planning. Her research interests lie in the field of comparative urban politics. She is at present completing a book, with Robert Fried, concerning comparative urban government which arises in part from work under a Social Science Research Council grant for Latin American studies of municipal performance and development in Latin America. She is the author of *City Politics and Planning* (1970), and co-author of *Urban Government for Greater Stockholm* (1968), and (with Fred Wirt, Ben Walter, and Deborah Hensler) *On the City's Rim: Politics and Policy in Suburbia* (1972).

FELICITY M. TRUEBLOOD is Assistant Professor of Comprehensive English and a member of the Latin American Faculty of the University of Florida. In September 1972, she will become Executive Secretary of the Latin American Studies Association (LASA). She is a former editor of the *Southeastern Latin Americanist,* the quarterly bulletin of the Southeastern Conference on Latin-American Studies, and previously served for five years as assistant editor of the *Journal of Inter-American Studies.* She is a consultant to various presses specializing in Latin-American publications, and has published translations of Spanish language fiction and nonfiction.

The series editors have previously collaborated in the preparation of *Latin American Political Systems in an Urban Setting: A Preliminary Bibliography* (Center for Latin-American Studies, University of Florida, 1967), with Charles J. Savio.